Introduction

From middle school fun and frolics to the big wide world of work. Recollections & memories of moving to, and growing up, on the Isle of Wight. A pastoral view of growing up in this most rural of settings. Adventures & antics from the sublime to the ridiculous, including advice & tips on how not to ride a bicycle with no brakes whilst wearing roller skates! A roller coaster ride of loves and the tragedy of loss.

Chapter 1

Moving to the Isle of Wight

My first experience of living close to the sea and being able to just walk to the water was when we lived above T. Smoth's butcher's shop in Cowes, on the Isle of Wight, opposite the Vectis Tavern in the high street.

We had come from a little village called Haslingfield, just outside Cambridge and only experiencing rivers and river banks and no beaches or the sea; it was such a change of scenery for us all. It was nineteen sixty nine and we had previously travelled down to the Island on holiday; to visit my grandparents on my Mother's side of the family, who had recently moved to Cowes from Ottershaw in Surrey. The move was my second journey on the Red Funnel ferry, and to all of us kids it was so exciting to be on such a massive ship.

My Mother and Father had purchased a very derelict shop with stables and quite a lot of land in Haslingfield. My Father had started his vegetable delivery round in the village, which later extended to a wider area around south west Cambridgeshire.

My parents rented a small cottage when they had moved from Guildford that was supposedly once owned by an earl. They eventually bought the property and as the business grew, they were able to save up for the shop. Dad was on regular trips to London with his van to collect produce from the markets and also to a lot of local farmers who sold directly from their fields. The plan was to refurbish this shop and living accommodation and open it as both a butchers shop and general stores. It took a vast amount of work and money to achieve this plan and we lived in relative squalor for many months while each room was finished and made habitable. There was no toilet inside the house at that time, with just an outhouse in the back garden. There was a very large basement under the shop which was used for the storage of vegetables because of the low temperatures and darkness and was a haven for spiders, which I hated.

After over a year of demolishing and rebuilding, the house was finished and of course the priority was the shop for income. My parents had an extension built on the back of the house, where the old stables and well were situated. Apparently the building was in fact an old coaching Inn; hence the stables and deep well for water.

I went to the local primary school in the village but I am not sure how long I stayed there from memory. I remember the first day at the school and crying most of the day because I hated it. Mum had to come and collect me in the end, I was inconsolable apparently. So school and being away from my family was definitely not going to be my ambition at that early age.

My Father on his vegetable van, Haslingfield, Cambridge. Circa 1967.

I only remember one young boy at the school called Clive and he and I had become friends, he also lived in the village as I was later informed by my Mother.

The only remarkable aspect of that school that sticks in my mind, was a bubble car parked in the car park every day. Why it has stayed in my mind is a mystery and I just cannot figure out what was so significant about it? It is strange that only certain points in history remain with you from your childhood, such as the only school trip we went on; to a silk farm and I remember the coach and the silk worms etc. That's it, just three things out of probably millions of memorable events during my short period at that school.

So from selling vegetables from the back of a little van, my parents had acquired a shop with accommodation and even had a new bungalow built, just outside the village of Haslingfield; all from the proceeds of selling vegetables. Pretty impressive I reckon and I wish I had the same ability and drive as they did back then. My Father had also bought a large lorry for his increased stock of vegetable collections from the markets in London. He told me all about the coldest winter of 1963, when he said the lorry's diesel had frozen in the tank and he had to light a small fire underneath the tank to start the engine. I also learned from my parents all about the vegetables being frozen in the ground and how Dad had gone to one of his regular supplier's fields and literally chiselled the cabbages and other veg from the ground.

Apparently the sprouts just snapped off from the ground when trying to pick the individual fruits. Dad also said that they made so much more money in that winter than at any other time because he had gone out of his way to get this stock and no one else for miles around had anything to sell; even the markets were empty of all root vegetables, so I can imagine what it was like to have the only cabbages, cauliflowers and sprouts for sale in the whole of the surrounding areas and further.

The last Christmas that we were at that house and shop was the most magical for me because I just remember looking out of the lounge window on Christmas morning and seeing everything white with snow. Because the lounge was on the top of the extension, the view was especially nice. I could see small footprints in the deep snow which my parents informed us were from a fox. The beauty of that moment lives on and whenever there is snow on the ground, I'm taken back to that time in my life.

There was the Guy Fawkes Night when Dad had slightly over ordered on the fireworks for sale in the shop and because he was left with so many boxes, we had the most amazing firework display I have ever seen.

My Dad and Uncle had lined up a row of milk bottles on the garden wall and various Catherine wheels and roman candles all over the place. The result was incredible as we watched so many rockets going off and wheels spinning on the walls of the shed in the garden.

We had a big bonfire and probably the first time I had tasted proper jacket potatoes, cooked in foil in the fire. Packets of sparklers seemed endless that night and us kids danced around drawing imaginary pictures with the sticks of fire in our hands. Of course the next day, it was time to explore the garden for burnt out rockets and other missiles that had been launched the night before. This was always a kind of ritualistic thing with us kids, collecting all the used fireworks and seeing if we could possibly find one or two that hadn't gone off ,which was so exciting.The garden shed was unfortunately destroyed by a fire which was caused by me and my cousin Jamie, playing with a box of matches one afternoon. I can only remember running down the garden to the house to find Mum and tell her the shed was alight. I don't know who actually set light to the shed exactly and what actually happened that day but my

Father blamed my cousin and subsequently fell out with my relations over it and another issue which I won't mention. So after that event, a tall wire mesh fence was erected between our adjoining gardens and we were segregated forever. It was a shame that it happened like that but I was too young to understand the reasons for my Father's actions.

It was not long after we moved from the village that my uncle died of a heart attack. I don't recall much about him at all so I cannot really make any comment on the whole sorry affair. I don't have any issues with my cousins and in fact, we got on very well during our latter years on the rare occasions that we spent time together. My cousin Joni was and is still a very special person in my world because we were once soul mates and spent a lot of time kicking about on motorcycles.

My parents bought a brand new estate car while we lived at the shop and it was a Morris 1300 in maroon red. My Mother unfortunately wrecked the engine as she drove through a very deep flood just outside the village, she stopped in the middle of the flood and the water went in the engine and that was the end of that.

On the subject of vehicles, I will never forget the day I climbed into the back of Dad's lorry and hid behind some veg crates. My uncle, mum's brother, who lived next door to us, used to take deliveries out for my parents. So he takes the lorry out with various orders in the back and sets off for wherever he had to go. I remember looking over the tailgate and seeing a duck pond with railings around it and then the brakes suddenly being applied. Uncle had seen me in the mirror and couldn't believe what he could see.

He was pretty angry with me as I remember but shared his Twix bar with me on the way home. Now why do I remember the bloody Twix bar and not anything else about my adventure? My parents were frantic back at the shop because no one could find me and they were very worried until I was returned to them in my shameful state. Now that story was the talk of the village for quite a while so my parents told me and I wasn't allowed anywhere near that lorry again.

As you may have gathered, my uncle and aunt and their two children lived next door to us. We had no fence between the gardens and as both plots were at least third of an acre, we had a massive playground to explore.

My cousin Jamie was a couple of months older than me and my cousin Joni was roughly the same age as my brother Tony, three years younger.

My Father once put a ladder up to my uncle and aunts bedroom window one night as he caught a bat in the cellar and thus decided to release it in their bedroom. The screams could be heard for miles and Dad said it was the funniest thing he ever saw or did; I don't think my aunt spoke to my Father for quite a while after that joke.

There was also the tale of my dad going off ice skating on a frozen pond down the road one afternoon and the ice breaking and him coming home, almost frozen solid. My Mother said his sheepskin coat just stood up on its own after she had prized it off him.

Tony somehow got quicklime in his eyes one day and had to be rushed off to hospital for treatment. I think it was used for the cement they were using whilst building the extension or something and he had been playing with it.

Another moment that sticks in my mind was when friends of my parents who lived in London had come to our house to visit.

Nothing spectacular about that I guess but this friend drove a brand new Jaguar and took us out for a drive in it. I can still smell the leather and see the chestnut dashboard and all the chrome switches etc. Dad's friend let me sit on his lap and steer the car as he drove around the village.

I don't know much about this friend of the family but I learned that he had a racing car in his garage back in London and his wife worked for a television company. I'm assuming they were a wealthy couple and lived rather well by their new Jaguar and a racing car and various other details that I learnt a lot later on in life but I won't bore you with it. Where or how they were connected to my family is also a mystery because no one appears to know the answers.

To cut a long story short, my parents sold the whole business and because my Mother's parents had relocated to the Isle of Wight and I guess because it was somewhere completely new, we moved to the island.

Obviously my parents had made a fair amount of money from the sale of the shop and business and this gave them a good start when we arrived. As my Father had accommodation included with the new job he had found, they could pick and choose to a certain degree where we were going to live next. Back in the early seventies, Cowes was a very busy town during the summer months, bustling with both local people and visitors who had disembarked from the Red Funnel pontoon; it never seemed to be quiet at any time of the day. We could walk down the side of the Fountain Hotel and be standing on the small slipway along side what is now the new Red Jet terminal.

We used to scrounge large marrowbones and butcher's string from my Dad in his butchers shop and spend the whole day catching the biggest bucket of crabs off the sea wall. There used to be so many attached to the large bones that it was hard to get them off the bones and hours were spent there just paddling and crabbing while Mum sat on the bench knitting and keeping an eye on us boys as we were prone to getting into mischief rather easily.

The Customs boat always seemed to be moored up against the wall and sometimes a pilot boat would be next to it and on the side of the Red Funnel pontoon, were the instantly recognisable Nelson Class boats of the Thomas Bros. They were always towing small pontoons out to the Royal Navy ships and collecting rubbish and delivering things to the ships moored off of Cowes.

When the Cowes week festivities arrived, then the town was truly magical. I can still smell the fish and chips mixed with the smell of beer that seemed to flow down the streets and together with the early evening sun keeping the streets so warm, the whole high street was sizzling with life. Sailors from every country wandered from pub to bar all dressed in their uniforms looking so smart in their appearance. I remember the French sailors walking around with their little red pom poms on their hats. I thought they looked so different from the rest of the crews.

The seafront was truly amazing in the evening and we regularly walked as a family down through the town and onto the parade, stopping at the little pub down an alley that lead to the sea front for bottles of coke and crisps for us kids.

More often than not, we went to the Doughnut shop where you could watch the machine making the doughnuts and then frying and turning them, a fascinating machine to us kids but not as nice as tasting them.

Myself, Liam and Tony on Cowes Parade in 1972.

Looking out to sea from the Parade with its stone balustrades and seeing the whole horizon filled with naval ships, the Royal Yacht and thousands of boats of all shapes and sizes, bobbing about with the ferry trying to weave its way through the floating maze and all the passengers waving as they past the sea front; there never seemed to be any room for ferry to manoeuvre past this mass of ships anchored in the bay. The big ships never seemed to rock about even when the sea was rough it was if they were fixed to the seabed like the buoys that surrounded them. Watching the cars embark and disembark from the ferry on Cowes pontoon and the amazing turntable device that they put the cars on to revolve them for easier parking.

There was that strange looking, three-wheeled contraption that flew up and down the hill from the pontoon, to the Fountain Coaches depot, towing a cage like trailer full of suitcases. The driver was always dressed smartly and wore a white captain's cap and invariably had a cigarette hanging out of his mouth.

Pleasure boat rides operated from one of the large concrete jetties, taking people around the gigantic warships and of course Britannia with her pale yellow funnel which I often mistook for Tommy Sopwith's large motor yacht that always seemed to be there for the annual power boat races. The atmosphere in Cowes harbour at the start of the Cowes to Torquay power boat event was probably equal to what a Formula One race is now. The noise from banks of outboards perched on these long thin boats, the wash and exhaust from the souped up motor cruisers was uniquely amazing.

We normally sat on the grass just past the mini cannons of the Royal yacht squadron. Those bloody cannons would always go off when we walked past them and scare the hell out of you. As a kid I was unaware of their purpose, and did they really fire cannon balls?

The visits to the little restaurant just past what is Pascall Atkey's yacht chandlers, which was an amazing shop that seemed to have everything and the smell of rope mixed with varnish, always reminds me of it when I smell either of those things. I cannot remember its name but it had small bow windows and really cosy little cubicle-type seating and the red velvet seats were gorgeous at the time.

The food served in that tiny eating house was gorgeous and I loved it when we went there on the rare occasions that Dad had some time away from his job. Mum and Dad always had Mateus Rose wine with their dinner in the restaurant and I remember the dumpy little bottle it came in; a very popular wine back in the seventies so they say.

My Father was the area manager of one of the most popular butchers shop in the town, and as such he dealt with the super rich yachtsmen and the high ranking officers of most of the British warships visiting Cowes week. He served all the posh houses with masses of steak and other expensive cuts of meat. He also produced mountains of ice which he supplied to a lot of boats and ships. He even supplied Ted Heath with meat at one time. Similarly, the power boat teams were a massive affair.
Mechanics, drivers and transport people made up a very large part of the visitors that descended on the town for a week or so. The local pubs and guest houses were all packed with visitors and music played from most of the pubs at night and I remember hearing Mott the Hoople for the first time, outside The Anchor pub.

Mum and Dad were regularly invited to parties in the wealthy households in the town and more often or not, on the boats and yachts. We have a nice photo of my Dad walking along the parade during Cowes week in 1975, as captured by the County Press newspaper.

My Mother played piano and for some extra income, she played in some of the local pubs in the evening. The only pub that I can remember hearing Mum on her piano was the Painters Arms, which was very close to Brian's newsagents if anyone reading this remembers that particular shop? I used to go in that shop on my way home from school with Tony as we were both at Denmark Road School together and if we walked through the alley way that came out near what was the Fountain Coach station, it was a really short trip home. Also I remember the sherbet shop directly opposite the school gates, which sold sherbets of all descriptions; including sherbet drinks, which I couldn't stand the taste of. They were very popular back in those days. Mrs Slocombe was the headmistress of Denmark Road school she always wore this big fur-like coat. The only really memorable moments I had were winning my first raffle prize of a Corgi Formula 1 model car and the visit to the school by Lord Mountbatten of Burma.

Sunday mornings, if the sea was not too rough and Dad had his Sunday paper, 20 No6 cigarettes and some sweets for us kids, always included a trip up the Medina to the Folly Inn from the Red Funnel pontoon in Frank's boat. Frank was a mate of Dad's and he lived very near the large freezer building at the top of Terminus Road. I always regarded Frank as a lot older than he really was and I suppose it was because he smoked a pipe and wore a flat cap. His hearing aid scared the hell out of me for some unknown reason, it always looked as though he had this clear jelly stuff coming out of his ear, but of course it was just clear plastic. Funny how everyday things scare you when you are young. We would climb aboard his clinker built dinghy and it would usually take him quite a while to start the little seagull engine as we drifted under the pontoon bridge or into the piles. His little engine would gurgle and splutter as we headed towards the floating bridge and sometimes stop at the fuel pontoon en route. There would be Frank on the helm and Dad sitting opposite him and us three boys sitting on the bow as the little boat pushed its way through the water. Reaching our destination at the Folly Inn was always an exciting event for us kids as we knew it meant a bottle of coke with a straw and a bag of crisps. Sitting outside the Inn on the picnic tables and watching all the boats going past the jetty. Dad and Frank would disappear off into the pub for a while, and we entertained ourselves.

Sometimes, Dad would borrow Frank's boat and we would go up to the Folly or round the Yacht Squadron point and out along the shoreline towards Gurnard. A few trips over to East Cowes wall or past the point towards Osborne, but we didn't like going over to the other side of the sea wall as it was always choppy out there and the boat was very small. I am sure we went out for the fireworks at the end of Cowes week in the little dinghy too. It was Frank that got my Father interested in boats because he was very knowledgeable in that field and knew all the tricks of the tides and currents around his locality.

Tony, Mum, Liam and I on the HM Customs slipway in 1972.

My Father bought various boats and one of the first ones he ever had was a Shakespear thirteen foot speed boat with a Mercury fifty horse power outboard on the back. Now I am damn sure that outboard motor was far too big for the size of boat but my God did it fly across the water. We were always out in that boat and racing across to Southampton and just flying around Cowes sea front and the parade. One Cowes week, we took the boat out for the seasonal fireworks display for the Cowes week finale and Dad moored up, just off the parade, roughly opposite where the Globe pub used to be situated.

Suddenly a large rocket, complete with its parachute, landed in the back of the boat and very close to the fuel tank and rubber fuel line. Dad quickly threw it overboard and averted a really dangerous situation from occurring. I really hated getting into that boat because the first time I went aboard, it was moored on the Groves and Gutteridge pontoon and as I looked at the transom and the water was lapping up and around the control cables and that was enough for me. "I'm not getting in that thing, it's going to sink" I said to Dad as he laughed and so did Mum as they explained it was designed like that and it will not sink. Still scared the life out of me and took my family a long time to persuade me into the boat.

Dad always managed to get hold of or get into somewhere that no one else seemed to be able to. One of these occasions took place one day during Cowes week when we were flying around the Solent in the speed boat, we were heading towards Egypt Point just off Cowes sea front and then Dad heads towards this destroyer and circles it and there we are in awe of this massive ship. There were sailors on the decks with fishing rods and some were just watching us go around it, then Dad slows right down and heads straight for the huge steps that go up the side of the vessel and stops next to the small pontoon at the bottom of the steps. As kids, we were really worried and were telling Dad "we shouldn't be stopping next to this navy ship", I remember him replying "don't worry" with a chuckle and a smile that usually meant he was up to no good. He secured the boat with a rope and said "you just wait there" as he was tying up to the pontoon a sailor walks down the gangway towards us. Dad just calmly walks up to meet the sailor half way up the stairway, but we cannot hear what they are saying and then Dad comes back down the gangway and say's " come on, we are going aboard." We don't know what he is up to and are rather hesitant to say the least and Dad reassures us and tells us the captain has invited us on board. So off we go, up the gangway and right up to the bridge to meet the captain and then he shows us all over the ship. I still have no idea to this day what strings my Father pulled to allow us three boys and him to spend the whole afternoon looking round a Royal Navy destroyer. That was Dad all over, he could get into anything and anywhere if he wanted something and that trait has been installed in my younger brother.

The only Christmas that really sticks out above the rest in my memories was in the little house we moved to in Park Road, Cowes. It was for some reason, the most exciting time that we ever had at that time of year.
All three of us boys had sneaked into Mum and Dad's bedroom and found all the presents hidden in the wardrobe. They were all wrapped so we had no idea what was contained in those colourful parcels and we didn't rip the paper or try to look along the openings either.

It was probably more memorable for me because it was the first time we were given pillow cases instead of big socks for our presents. I can still feel the weight of the pillow case stuffed with presents on my feet as I woke up.

The sound of paper creaking and rustling as my brothers woke up and started to open their presents was beautiful. I received this toy record player with these rather thick records that played a variety of nursery rhymes. Tony had a toy snake that was articulated at its joints and moved like a real snake. I think Liam had one of those toy telephones that played a tune when the dial was rotated or something similar anyhow. It was a truly magical moment that stays with me forever.

Dad sold the speed boat in the spring time and quickly acquired a 17ft Sea Sledge as they were known, flat bottomed but with chines to stop it rolling too much with the waves. We collected it from Wootton Bridge one afternoon and took it back into Cowes and to the sea wall which was where the HM Customs building is now. I cannot believe they filled in the small harbour wall because it was such a cute place to sit and watch the boats coming down the river.
That boat had a Johnson fifty five horse power outboard and was a lot quicker than the Shakespear by far and had a lot more space to move about too. Dad did not keep that one very long, mainly because he had his eye on bigger fish so to speak.

We travelled around the country looking at boats and I remember going to Ipswich on night to view this boat in a small dry dock. We did not buy that one but Dad bought his dream boat eventually, after weeks of searching for the perfect vessel. He found this boat named *Phantom* and he and his mate Mark Merchant went to get it from the Groves and Gutteridge yard in Cowes and it had been stored for a while inside one of the boat sheds. It had to have a lot of work done on the engines before it could be used at sea, so it was taken out of the water on a huge trolley thing and pulled up at the Groves and Gutteridge yard, which was at the top end of Shooters Hill next to what was Bekens chemists shop and down a steep hill to the sheds and a sea wall. We had no idea what this boat looked like as Dad kept it all secret from us, until she was completely overhauled and seaworthy once again.

It is funny what you imagine when you are a child and our imaginations were very healthy indeed. We thought that maybe the boat was similar to a pirate ship or a navy frigate even. Imagination was one of our greatest traits as a family of three young brothers and drove my Dad absolutely mad at times.

The time came for the great re launching of the Phantom as she was on Groves and Gutteridge's slipway for engine servicing and I was the lucky one who was with Dad on the boat when they let the trolley go down its tracks and into the river Medina. I looked around the boat as Dad showed me all the cabin space and the galley, the engines and the superstructure which had a massive searchlight mounted on top of it. I did not realise that this boat was an ex RAF rescue boat and was over 30ft in length and fitted with two Rolls Royce diesel engines. She was a beautiful boat and I loved being on her very much. It was such a change from the tiny speed boats that rocked around on the smallest wave, this boat hardly moved when the Red Funnel Cowes Castle went past. Dad had certainly found his perfect boat this time but it was not without a lot of expensive overhauling and refurbishing.

Such an amazing experience to behold and something I will never forget as the boat trundled down the slipway and the metal wheels rumbled as it gathered speed and the sight of the tracks as they disappeared into the water and the boat hit the river with a whoosh.

The paddle steamer The Medway Queen had just gone past the slipway too and the people on it were watching as the Phantom was back at sea. It was not long after we were afloat, that Dad fired up the two engines and we were moving off towards Cowes harbour, passing the "Red Funnel" on our way. A few laps of the harbour and we were going back up the river towards the Folly Inn and to our pole mooring and then rowing back into Groves and Gutteridge pontoon and home. Unfortunately because the boat had been dry-stored for some months and all the timbers had dried up and hence shrunk and made the boat leak like a sieve for quite a few weeks until the timbers had become moist and thus expanded.

I remember my Father being very annoyed with the boatyard one day. They had lifted the Phantom out of the water for repainting and anti-fouling but had painted her the wrong shade of blue. The intended colour was navy blue but alas she ended up sky blue for some months until she was taken back out and painted the correct colour.

We had some fantastic outings on that boat and one in particular that sticks in my mind was when we anchored off of Alum Bay and during the night the boat had drifted quite a long way with the current. Obviously the anchor had not gripped properly, but luckily the tide had taken us out rather than in to shore, which would have been pretty scary indeed. After a cooked breakfast, we made our way to this bay and it had the remains of an old fort on the cliff. I had no idea where we were but I remember the huge concrete slabs which were clearly visible through the very clear water beneath us. We were anchored in about 5ft of water and Dad carried us children on his shoulders in to shore and we stayed on that beach all day and evening.

It was such a hot day and we had been swimming and playing in the sand all day long. Mum and Dad had built a camp fire and we had a barbecue that night, before Dad had realised that the boat was in slightly deeper water now and he had to swim out to the boat and bring her in close to shore so we could all get back on board again.

It was not until the early eighties that I realised exactly what that bay was called, Brambles beach was its name and from memory it had changed so much since the early seventies, gone were the concrete slabs that you could walk on in the sea and the fort is now completely demolished. The most dramatic change to the beach is the stones that now cover three quarters of the shore now, whereas back than it was all pure sand. One day my Dad and his mate Mark were out on the water and were about to moor up on the side of Red Funnel pontoon, which the public were allowed to moor up. My Dad accidentally accelerated instead of putting the engines to full stop and bumped into the pontoon rather to fast and his mate Mark had shot off the bow holding onto the mooring line and went running across the length of the pontoon. Another memory that just stays with me forever was when we had moored the boat up the Beaulieu River on the swing moorings near Bucklers Hard. Mum had just prepared lunch in the galley and Dad had called us all together from various parts of the boat. Tony was in the wheelhouse, sitting on one of the revolving seats, just looking at all the controls in front of him.

We all sat down to lunch and Dad was calling Tony again as he had a habit of taking his time when called. There was a sudden surge forward and the starter motors began to whir as Dad ran out of the galley to the wheel house, where he found Tony in a state of panic at the wheel. He had pressed both start buttons and the engines had started and then he moved the Morse control to forward and the boat was pulling on the rear mooring rope. Dad quickly shut down the engines and everything became calm once again. Tony wasn't really at fault because the battery isolators should have been turned off to prevent accidental starting of the engines, dad should have taken more care on that occasion. Mum did tell dad off for that and poor Tony was quite nervous of the boat for the rest of the day.

I went out alone with my Father in the boat, just around Cowes and to Egypt Point and back and there was a very fierce storm blowing and the waves were substantially higher than the boat. It was my first experience of seriously rough seas and I'm sure it weaned me from being afraid of such massive waves in my latter years in boats.

One such rough day at sea, my Father was out with his mate Mark Merchant and Mark was pulling on the bow rope which was attached to the swing mooring and a huge wave came from nowhere and his fingers were between the rope and the clevis. He lost his finger that day and as the story goes, Dad had to release the bow rope and the stern line and take Mark into the Red Funnel pontoon and get someone to call an ambulance. That instance certainly made me wary of ropes and rough seas and how easy accidents can happen on boats and such like. This was only one such dangerous adventure that Dad and Mark experienced while at sea, the other is to follow….

The next boat that came our way was a small fishing boat with a little cabin and an inboard engine. Her name was Wendy and I think Dad bought her from Ryde and then brought her back to Cowes and the Medina. We went out in the smaller boat but it was not as nice as the glorious Phantom. I think Dad was falling out of love with the sea and maybe looking for an easier and less expensive pastime to get into.

Dad and Mark Merchant put to sea on a relatively routine trip to Southampton to pick up my Uncle Jack from the Red Funnel area. They left late afternoon and were expecting to collect their passenger around 1900. They only got as far as the Spitbank Buoy when the engine died and they were left drifting towards Portsmouth with the tide. Using the floorboards of the deck as oars, they managed to get the boat on to a beach not far from the Hamble river entrance. It was pitch black when they reached the shore and they had to walk quite a few miles to reach civilisation.

All aboard the tractor that Dad borrowed to clear the landat the shop in Haslingfield, Cambridge. Circa 1967.

Meanwhile Uncle Jack had been telephoning my Mother to ask where they were and he had been waiting for two hours on the dockside. My Mum called the coastguard and they found the boat on the beach but my Dad and Mark had walked to Hamble and got a taxi to Southampton Red Funnel terminal and got on the ferry – My uncle had gone back home. I am sure that the incident with the boat breaking down and scaring the hell out of Dad and his mate was the reason why he gave up on boats completely and decided to turn his attention to horses instead. Poor Mark Merchant died not very long after Dad sold the last of his boats. He died of a brain tumour and it was a great shock to all of us in the family as he was a very nice bloke and was always at our house drinking tea and talking boats with my Father...Rest in Peace Mr. Merchant.

In nineteen seventy one, the best playground in Cowes was the disused railway line and its station buildings which were situated at the top of Terminus Road, where the Coop shop is now. It was as if the railway company had just left it to us kids to play in because none of it was locked up or demolished at that time and it was a fantastic place to explore.

I remember walking along its platforms and into the waiting rooms, exploring the ticket offices and even the signal box just down the track. We built camps in the tunnels and in the inspection pits along the tracks. I found a lovely bronze railway lantern down a pit and it was stolen by our next door neighbour in Granville Road. She was the weirdest old woman I have ever seen and her name was Rita whatsit or something like that. She used to scare the hell out of myself and my friends because we really believed she was a witch and because we found lots of bird skulls in the adjoining hedge, this confirmed our suspicions. She chased my friend and me along the railway line, near to the station and we hid in one of the ticket offices and she never found us, thank god. Her house was always black and never any lights on at night. The curtains always drawn and the windows were black from dirt and mould. No one ever seemed to visit her house either and we were sure she had bodies in the house. Her reputation extended further than just our Road in Cowes because everyone at Solent middle knew of her and was terrified of her.

I remember the time when Dad had repainted all the window sills on the house in a shiny white paint and it had taken quite a long time to do all the windows of the house. He went out the front door on the Sunday morning and someone had tipped black paint all over the lounge window sill. We knew who it was and Dad reported it to the police because he had enough of this old woman causing hassle to our family. I was very glad the day we moved from that house and no more witch next door. The house in Granville Road was a lot bigger than our previous home in Park Road. It had a large cellar and a garage and workshop at the bottom of a very steep drive, which also had a very large loft room that ran the whole length of the building. Mum and Dad had new storage heaters fitted in the house and I can still remember the awful smell they made when they heated up at night. We acquired our first colour TV in this house and it was one of those rental sets with large sliding doors on it, but still had the famous indoor aerial that never really gave you a good reception unless you stood near the window with it above your head.

It was the year that Slade were number one in the charts with "Well here it is, Merry Christmas" and Mum and Dad had a party on Christmas Eve. Lots of friends from the butchers shop were there and I think even Nan and Granddad were at the party that night.

The strangest thing was that while we kids were all upstairs in our bedroom, we could hear a lot of music coming from our lounge and it was not the TV making it? We could not figure out where this noise was coming from because we did not have a record player or tape recorder like the ones that Granddad had.

The party seemed to go on for a long time through the night and because it was Christmas Eve, us little ones were very over excited and sleeping was the last thing we wanted to do. We tried to stay awake all night but it never worked, we always fell asleep before midnight.

It was not until Christmas morning when Father Christmas had delivered our pillow cases full of crunchy sounding presents on the end of our beds, which sometimes fell off the bed and woke us up. It was a magical moment when we realised Santa had been to our house, and one of us would have to get out of bed and turn the big light on so we could look inside the massive sacks of presents.

When we had all got up after falling asleep again due to the exTime excitement of the present opening and playing with our new toys, we all congregated in the lounge which was not looking as tidy as it normally did, due to the noisy party the night before.

There were these strange looking bottles of drink on the sideboard and one particular bottle that took my eye was the Babycham bottles, which was a small bottle with a reindeer similar to Bambi on the blue sparkly label. I don't know why I was attracted to them, but I was. It was not long after Mum and Dad had got up that the lounge back to its Christmas glory, with the tree twinkling in the corner of the room and vast pile of more presents under it. On the top of the sideboard was a strange looking box with a wire coming out of the bottom?

I could not see what it contained as it had a large lid on top of it, which had a label ITT on it.   The lid had grooves in it and was made of plastic and also had a catch on each side of the lid.

By the time breakfast was done and we all went
back to our bedroom to get dressed, I had forgot
all about this new addition to our lounge and it
was not until after we had opened all our
presents that Dad showed us what he had
bought Mum for Christmas as he took off the lid
and revealed a new record player. So that
Christmas was a musical one and we had lots of
those *Top Of The Pops* albums and enjoyed
playing them and I also liked looking at the
sleeves with their attractive ladies on them. It
was not until years later that I learnt that those
albums were just cover records and none of the
artists were the originals. Oh well they still gave
us hours of entertainment in our younger days.

Having this new machine opened up a
completely new world to me and it was so much
better than the radio because we could listen to
our choice in music and not what the station
dictated. One of the first records that Mum
bought was Amazing Grace played by a band of
bagpipes and *On Top Of The World* by *The
Carpenters* was a favourite of my Mother.

It was when we all went to Woolworth's in Cowes and managed to find a long player of an episode of Thunderbirds and it was bought for us boys to listen to, that gave having a record player another facet and growing up with technology, even though quite primitive. There were some other memorable songs that our record player used to bang out in that lounge in Granville Road and one of them was *Tie a Yellow Ribbon* which I think was worn out by the time we moved house.

Now my Granddad had a much better understanding of these new gadgets such as record players and tape machines and he seemed to have every machine available at that time in his house. He had one of those massive Radiograms in his lounge, which was a long sideboard type piece of furniture but with a record player and radio built in to it, with speakers at each end.

I remember Mum and Dad letting out the front rooms as bed and breakfast in Granville Road and various guests arriving in the summer months. One particular family came from Scotland and my brother and I could not understand a word that they spoke to us. I guess it was the first time I had actually met a Scottish person in the flesh, as there were none at school who spoke this very strange language.

Another thing that happened in that house was that we were infested with some strange mites that lived in the cellar. They had to be sent off to the Natural History Museum in London to be identified as they were very unusual indeed. It turned out they were some paper eating creature that had made its home in the old books in the cellar that the previous owner of the house had left there. The whole house had to be fumigated and we had to stay at granddad's house the night while it was being done.

At the bottom of the steep driveway was a garage and workshop with a loft that stretched the whole length of the building. Unfortunately there were no stairs or ladder to get up there so we used to climb up the wall and window frame and also use the outside tap to get up the last couple of feet.

One day all of us brothers wanted to get up into the loft for some reason or other and I was the first one up there because I was the tallest. I got one of my brothers up there easily and then I had to pull my youngest brother up there but I could not hold him and he slipped down the wall and hit his forehead on the tap.

That was a scary moment because the gash was rather deep and blood went everywhere. We got down as quick as we could and took him into Mum and there was sheer panic as she rushed him to the Doctors surgery and he had to have it stitched up. We never went up there again after that incident and I received a damn good telling off for attempting to pull my little brother up into the loft.

Opposite our house there was a massive house and a garden that was surrounded by a very high wall. The garden was lovely and to us, it was the biggest we had ever seen. Our bedroom looked out over that wall and we always watched the swallows and swifts darting around in the evenings and our favourite scene was the large number of local cats that were always playing with each other and chasing one another around the wall.
We watched them every night and spent hours laughing at their antics and I remember the swallows cheeping and diving in the cooler air of the summer evenings. I never did find out whose garden it was or what the name of the house was and if there is one sound I really miss, it's the swallows and perhaps house martins during their nesting times.

It was in this house that Dad played his nastiest trick on us boys one night after we all watched *The Day of the Triffids* on the television. He went into our room and tied a piece of string to a teddy and placed it on the top shelf of our cupboard in the wall, the second piece of string was tied to the door of the cupboard. So when we went to bed after being scared to death by the film, he waited until we were all in bed and crept up the stairs and waited outside our door. I will never forget that bump in the cupboard and then the door slowly opening and our faces and suddenly the bedroom door slowly opened and rubber plant started to move into the room, around the door. We all screamed and went under the covers and we could hear Dad in tears of laughter on the stairs and Mum telling him off for scaring us. Has to be the most apt and well planned scare I have ever experienced to date.

I lost my grandmother when we lived in Newport Road in Cowes. She died of complications from diabetes and heart failure and it was a great shock to all of the family as it happened so quickly. Granddad was lost without her and could not cook for himself, not out of the lack of know-how; he just could not bring himself to use the kitchen after his wife had died.

I remember Mum taking him dinners round every week day and at the weekends we would go there and she would cook a meal for all of us, except Dad of course as he and granddad did not see eye to eye. After a about six months of Mum delivering dinners to him, he finally ventured into the kitchen and cooked for himself, well that is what we thought he was doing.

It turned out that he had met a lady and she was going round there every day and cooking for him and in the end she was almost living there. This caused a lot of friction between certain other relations because they thought that she was only there to grab as much as she could if granddad died and she could inherit the lot. Small minded and bloody greedy is what it was all about, no thoughts of what granddad wanted from life or the fact that maybe he liked this lady very much. Well it seemed to be going well for him and it certainly made my Dad happier because Mum did not have to cook for him all the time. We all visited this lady's house and her family and granddad would go round there and do little diy jobs for her too.

It was not until several months after my granddad met this lady that it all seemed to be going wrong. I remember Mum arguing with Dad about it all and we also heard that this lady was not being treated very well by granddad. I don't know the ins and outs of it all but it was not long after they stopped seeing each other that granddad died. I felt that this story had to be included in this book because it was my earliest experience of how families are so down right greed orientated and think of nothing but them selves and grab at anything they can. Sad but true and it is rife among everyone.

I was around twelve years old and was given the task of baby sitting for friends of Mum and Dad one Christmas Eve. The family had a daughter and she was about five years old at the time. It was the first time I had ever done anything like this before and I was very nervous about the whole thing at first, but soon settled into the job after a few hours.

An employee of Dad's in the butchers in Cowes had leant me a whole box of single records and Mum had brought her little record player for me to listen to the singles on.

I had glass bottles of Coke and as many bags of crisps and mountains of peanuts to eat. One song that always stands out in my memory was Gonna Make You a Star by David Essex. Loved this song and I must have played a fair few times that night. I really enjoyed the whole evening very much because I could watch TV or play some records and had enough food and drink to last me several days. I only saw the little girl once all night and she came downstairs for a drink and some crisps and stayed with me for about half hour then went back to bed I watched *Dave Allen* too and even though I did not really understand all of his humour, I loved watching his shows for the silly sketches he made. I was there all alone but enjoying my little self until well after one o'clock in the morning. Mum and Dad had gone to the Christmas Do at Northwood Cricket Club as the Father of the little girl I was looking after played for the team.

My Father was a very keen footballer and had trials for The Arsenal when he lived in London but unfortunately National Service came up and he had to go off and do that for a year so he missed out on the football career. He was in the same class at school as the late Bobby Moore and had all the skills to have been a professional football player. When he was in the Royal Army Service Corps at Pirbright camp in Surrey, he played a lot of football for the regiment and also did a lot of boxing and table tennis too. He had a bad experience when he was first called up for service; he contracted Polio in the stomach and was very ill for weeks afterwards. He loved driving large vehicles and was soon driving the Scammell tank transporters and the amphibious DUKW's. He had to go to Canvey Island as part of the rescue squad in the great floods of 1953. He also drove ambulances for some time and was chucked in the glass house for splitting up the Cold Stream Guards on the Mall in London. He also drove across one of the parks in London and broke off a branch from a Royal Oak tree and got locked up for that too; he always said that if you are driving an ambulance then the priority was the passengers and not the guards marching up the middle of the Road. Shame the top brass did not see it like that.

He was a very sporty individual indeed and when he left the army and returned to Civvy Street, he did not give up on his football but gave up the boxing and table tennis though.

Tony and me in 1967, Haslingfield, Cambridge.

Dad always tried to get us boys interested in football by playing the silly game in Northwood park every weekend or up at the recreation ground in Cowes. I hated the game with a passion and would much prefer to ride my bicycle than kick a silly ball about all afternoon. He tried his best but we three lads were not interested in this game one little bit and I'm sure he was quite disappointed because we had no interest in the game. After we had settled in to our new surroundings in Cowes and Dad had made quite a few new friends through his job and going to parties at weekends, he joined a football club called Westwood, which was near the top of Park Road and it was situated just behind granddad's house in Firs Close.

He would train up there a couple of times a week and I had to go with him a few times. Oh how I loved those evenings so much, all those men shouting at each other and chasing one another around a field. He was never going to convert me to play or even watch that bloody game and even though we all had to watch match of the day on Saturday nights, I was having none of it. Dad played a few games against various Island teams and enjoyed it very much, until he damaged one of his ligaments in his leg and that was the end of football for Dad.

I always remember my Granddad telling me that there was buried treasure in the flower bed outside the front door of the bungalow. I would be out there digging away and finding so many coins, every time I went visiting this is what I would do. It wasn't until last year that Mum told me that he had buried the coins when I went home, ready for my next visit. I was gutted, all those years I thought I had discovered this treasure in his garden but in reality, it was all a game.

Berry, Tony, Liam and our friends from Granville Road, Cowes, Andy and Dawn. Circa 1972.

Chapter 2

Brand New School

We were all very excited about starting our new school named Solent Middle School in September, the school was brand new and only just going to be ready for the onslaught by us hooligan kids.

I remember arriving on the Yellow bus at the top of the small road that led to the school and we all walked down to the steps that led down to a large paved area with a very large ships anchor mounted on a plinth to the right side and the main entrance in front of us. We all congregated in the main assembly hall and were instructed into our classrooms. Then we were shown around the school in groups.

Our headmaster was Mr. Flay and my form teacher was Mr. Cenway, a jolly but firm chap with an orange Volkswagen beetle.

The school playground was completed but the fields beyond that were still in the process of being landscaped and there were these massive mounds of earth to play on, which we were told not to go on.

There was a hedge line between the small field and the larger field that led to the cliffs above Gurnard. This larger field was used for sports and the smaller, for orienteering or science classes, or in our case, camps, piggy back fights and the like. The small field backed onto the home of one of the most fearsome of teachers at the school, Mr. Barnmett was his name and both he and his wife worked at the school as teachers. Mr. Barnmett taught woodwork and Mrs. Barnmett taught home economics. If you ever messed about in Mr. Barnett's lesson you would certainly regret it, as did so many cheeky idiots who tried to get the better of him. His best weapon against noisy, misbehaving boys was the wooden blackboard rubber but in exTime cases, when he could no find the rubber he would just throw a wooden mallet at you.

He was very strict but a fair chap really, gave a damn good lesson and you learnt lots of things or you would die.

The only other feared teacher that I hated at the time was Mrs. Harmonica, a small red headed lady with a very gravely voice who would teach sewing or in fact any subject if a teacher was away.

Strict was not the right word for her and the worst part of knowing of her was she moved up from Denmark Road school with us, a real down period in my book. The school on a whole was pretty good and we had some really nice teachers and in particular, Mr. Kitten taught us English and Mr. Fussy was our religious tutor. I cannot remember an after school club or in fact any out of school activity that Mr. Fussy was not involved in, he was always doing something such as Guitar club or model railway club – one of the best teachers I ever knew and commitment beyond the call of duty for sure.

One of our favourite games was piggy back wars and its self explanatory what took place during this game. This is one of the only games that me and my mate Churchill won all the time; this was because at 12 years old, Churchill was nearly 6ft tall and a giant compared with all the other kids at school. He was always my steed, and we beat the hell out of everyone else.

The second field that was used as our sports field had the most stubbly and sharp grass that you would not want to fall on it.

I think that when they took over the field for the school, they did not bother ploughing it and sowing a good grass seed and instead they kept the old ryegrass lay and that's why it was so rough. The perimeter of the field was mostly hedgerows but at the far end it was just a muddy cliff edge that looked over Gurnard sea front. One day, Electrical Bunny, a friend, and another mate made some weed killer and sugar bombs and tried to blow up the cliffs, it didn't work and just made a cloud of dust and dirt, plus a lot of smoke.

My dearest brother Tony in his Solent Middle School photograph. Circa 1975.

Believe it or not, but it was common practice to make weed killer and sugar bombs back in those days and also bolt bombs were very popular with us boys. Electrical Bunny had got his Dad to buy the weed killer and he nicked the sugar from the kitchen and got hold of some copper pipe and that was our kit.

We made some of these lethal bloody things and went down to the old railway bridge, which was close to the Arctic Road end of the Cowes to Newport railway line. We thought if we could blow up the bridge then we could block off the track so boys from Newport could not get to us; great plan but as usual it never worked. I didn't like these bombs and much preferred the bolt bombs as they would not blow you up and definitely would not cause too much damage to your hands.

Newport subway was the only place to use these bombs because of the echo from the tunnel. We never threw them when there were other people in the subway, only when it was empty. Some of the bolts we got hold of were massive and packed with either black or red match heads, screwed up with one nut but not too tightly and then thrown in the air.

When one end hits the ground then the compression produced makes the matches explode and the bolts blow apart. Electrical Bunny had a brother in law who ran his own mobile disco and was very into rocket building and this is a true story of what happened when this chap built a massive rocket out of an old fire extinguisher and launched it from somewhere in West Cowes. It landed in the gas works in East Cowes, along the River Medina. This rocket was propelled by weed killer and sugar and even had a war head, a twelve bore cartridge and a nail to set it off. My god that must have been some sight and how bloody dangerous too, not my cup of tea at all but an interesting tale though.

Talking of serious injuries, my old friend Ant with whom I did carol singing with had a very nasty thing happen to him one day on the pontoon at Groves and Gutteridge in Cowes. He was fishing off one of the pontoons and this German boy who was on one of the yachts in the marina, aimed a spear gun at him and it went off. It went straight through poor Anthony's leg and out the other side. He was so lucky that it didn't cut the main artery in his leg.

It is very true when they say "Never point a gun at anyone". My brother was playing around with my air rifle one night and pointed it at his mate. He had no idea it was loaded with a pellet and he had pumped this rifle up and bang, the pellet went straight between the legs of his mate and dug itself into his flesh. He had to go to hospital and have it removed and my brother was interviewed by the police about it too, bad practice and he did not do that again.

The anchor and propeller greeted us when we first arrived at the school was very impressive and I remember official opening ceremony of the school when the Labour politician *Reg Prentice* came and cut the ribbon. It was a beautifully clean and tidy school with lots of modern designed rooms such as the music room, which was kind of octagonal and looked over the grass banks at the back of the school. The canteen was probably my favourite area and it was just inside the front doors and the seating doubled as seating for the library. The food was fantastic and there was always seconds or thirds if you could manage it.

Cottage pie was absolutely gorgeous and all cooked in the kitchens at the school and none of this modern rubbish here. Chocolate covered sugar puffs and mint flavoured custard was to die for and I loved it when that was on the menu and similarly coffee and a doughnut was another gorgeous treat at lunchtime. The coffee was the hot milk variety and I can still see it in its little Pyrex cup and saucer.

At Solent we always had interesting assignments to do and one of the biggest ones we undertook was visiting Wroxall on many occasions and finding out about the railway line and tunnel and Appledurcombe House, home to the Worsley family. We had tape recorders given to us and interviewed the man who was responsible for the house and its grounds. We interviewed him in the small gate keepers' lodge which was a small museum at the time. I remember the little tape deck had one of those microphones with the on/off switches so you could pause the recording from the mic.

Apart from having our own radio station in the school we also had a lovely assembly hall/sports hall. Every week there was a play which was written and performed by the different classes. I took part in lots of those plays because I enjoyed drama lessons and standing up in front of all the other people.

I was normally a very shy little lad but for some reason unknown to me, I loved acting in those plays. I remember the air sea rescue play and we converted the trolley that carried all the gym bars into a helicopter and had some kids in canoes etc. I was so impressed with the trolley conversion that we did, it looked so good and even had the blades and tail rotor. I had the job of providing the siren noise and I did this by making the sound through a small metal tube from the gym equipment. One teacher came up to me afterwards and asked how did you make that siren sound so real? Maybe I should have taken up doing sound effects with just my voice.

Another fantastic trip we had was to visit Sandown Airport and go up for a flight in a Cessna four seater plane and fly around the whole of the south of the Island. It was amazing and bumping along the grass runway and off towards the coast and seeing how the sea appeared to be made up of so many different shades of blue and seeing all the glass houses in Arreton was of particular interest to us. I will never forget that flight because it was the very first time I had flown and I adored the whole experience. I feel so privileged to have had such experiences at such a young age because not many people have been in a plane at all. It was all down to the school and how well they thought out the lessons etc.

We had some lovely teachers at Solent Middle and looking back on all the wonderful things they did for us and the way they made our education so much more fulfilling they deserve a Thank You from me and I think all the other children that attended the school with me. I do not need to mention names because they know who they are.

Mr. Taylor was our science teacher and his wife was also a science teacher but at Cowes High School. I remember whenever there was a school day trip and he was on it, he would ask if anyone would like to travel with him in his souped up mini. Everyone wanted to go in his mini and I was lucky to go in it on more than one occasion. He had long fur on the dashboard and the longest switches you have ever seen, masses of lights on the front and wide wheels too. Brilliant bloke and made the lessons so interesting that you could not do anything else but to take it all in. My brother Tony was also at Solent when I was there an it is a strange thing to be at school with another member of your family because you would think that you would spend a lot of time together during break times. In fact I hardly ever saw him at school because being in a higher year, we had different timetables and classes did not blend in with each other. I saw more of him at Denmark Road school, than I did at Solent.

I always remember walking home from school with him at Denmark Road as we only had to cross the railway bridge and walk along to the end of Granville Road. Catching the number 33 bus from Cowes to Solent Middle or even walking through Crossfield Avenue and along Baring Road. The former, being a particularly good route as there was a nice sweet shop on the way. There was a very tame Jackdaw who used to rest on the school railings next to the railway bridge at Denmark Road. He was so friendly and would crow at us for bread and take it from our hand.

Because of my episode with the bullying and other emotional nightmares, I really feel that I missed out on a hell of a lot of schooling. This was relative to both my middle school and high school education. It is not until you grow much older and look back at what your life was like and what you did, do you realise that if things had been happier then I would have not left school with not a qualification to my name and perhaps would of perhaps gained a degree or something as equal to it.

I was very friendly with a ginger haired girl who I met in the playground one lunch break. She was always with a dark haired girl and they seemed inseparable to me. I always chatted to her and we talked about music in the charts and whatever else you talk about at middle school. I really liked her and after a month or so I found out her name from someone who went on her bus. We never kissed or went out with each other but always talked and smiled at one another.

When I moved from Solent to Cowes High School I never ever saw her and wondered where she had gone. It was not until I moved to Totland and had to start using the yellow buses that our paths crossed once again. I was sitting quite nervously on the bus as it was my first week of travelling with total strangers and watching all the kids getting on the bus in the morning. I could not believe my eyes when this girl got on the bus at the tiny island in the Road, just past the bridge in Porchfield. It was the girl from the playground and she smiled and we talked again on the bus in the morning. For almost two years we chatted and smiled at each other but that was all we ever did.

Her dark haired friend's parents owned a gift shop in Cowes High Street and it was somewhere on the same side of the road as where my Dad worked at T Smoths the butchers. When I finished school in nineteen seventy eight

I did not see or hear of my ginger haired friend again and it was only until the creation of Face book that I suddenly became aware of this girl from Porchfield and who had the same surname as the girl in the playground at Solent Middle school. I added her as a friend and also sent her a message asking if she was related to my friend? I got a reply almost instantly and she was indeed related, it was her younger sister whom I had befriended. After a long conversation about how I had always talked to this girl and we smiled at each other all the time,

I found out that that poor girl died of cancer that year, I was absolutely stunned, how could she be dead? It took a long time for it to sink in and I found out that she was a nurse for years and was married with children and she died at a relatively young age too.

I hope that she is happy now and without pain. You were so beautiful and so friendly to a boy who was so lost and nervous on those first trips on the bus. Without you it would have been horrible but you made it safe for me and for that I am eternally thankful to you my sweet and caring friend. I have to write her name in my book because I think she more than deserves it. Sarah Winsor was her name………..Rest In Peace Sarah.

As a young boy, I loved watching *Dads Army* in the evenings with my family we would all be glued to our telly as the platoon of old men did the silliest of things. I also loved the colour version of *Tarzan* with the American actor Ron Ely, which I enjoyed it was so much more than the black and white versions.
Colour gave the jungle and animals more realistic tones and depth to me. Tony loved to watch Tarzan too and I remember us two sitting on the sofa sharing a packet of biscuits and staring at the TV together, such lovely times.

I also loved the school holiday TV programmes which usually consisted of *Champion the Wonder Horse, Casey Jones, Robinson Crusoe, Pogles Wood and White Horses. Trumpton, Chigley, Camberwick Green* of course was legendary and I think it was Brian Cant's voice that made those animated programmes so good, oh and the guitar playing and songs of course.

The music from *Robinson Crusoe* was lovely and I always remember those waves lapping up that sandy beach and wished I could be there on a deserted island. *Doctor Who* was another favourite programme and so was *Crackerjack* with that funny man with the glasses, *Peter Glaze.*

I disliked that totally weird series *Vision On* apart from that chap in the white coat and lines following him everywhere? *Scooby Doo* was good too but I hated anything made by Disney, I have no idea why I disliked those particular cartoons so much, but I do. I loved *Blue Peter* with John Noakes, Peter Purves and Leslie Judd. The best time to watch *Blue Peter* was the run up to Christmas and the eight candles that they mounted on the four coat hangers covered in tinsel.

Brilliant and really made my Christmas's how they should always have been. These are just a snapshot of what I loved on TV as there are too many to really talk about in depth. I will always adore *Dad's Army* because I can honestly say there will never be a comedy series that matches it. I have collected a lot of books on the subject and even the complete radio series. Just wish I had a time machine now.

In the school holidays and on some summer evenings we would nearly always be playing in Northwood Park or the surrounding area, it was a fantastic place when we were young because it had everything you needed for all sorts of games and activities.
You could ride your bike around the paths and across the grass, go putting on the public putting green and climb trees, collect bird's eggs or collect the best conkers. Endless hours were spent by my brothers and I, collecting Walnuts in the graveyard by climbing up on to the wall and reaching up into the branches.

My first date with a girl from my class took place in the trees opposite the putting green in Northwood Park. We stood under a tree in the rain and both had our hoods up to keep dry and warm and we got closer and closer and kissed just once and then we parted and went our separate ways.

She lived on Crossfield Avenue and I lived in Belle Vue Road back then and it was the only time we met out of school, no idea why that was but we were boyfriend and girlfriend for several weeks after the kiss. The amazing thing about it all was when I went to St Mary's for a blood test a few years ago, who should I see working there- the girl under the tree, amazing...

Behind Northwood House there was an area where cars parked and various council vehicles went. I was with my friend Ant and my brother Tony and we walked down there to see what went on. When we walked along the back of the house we saw a big garage with a lorry inside, the doors were open and then the lorry came out and stopped outside the doors. It was bright yellow and had this tanker on the back and with a huge hoover pipe and brush on the side. We had seen this thing going along our road and it was so noisy but a very interesting machine to us young lads.

We started talking to the driver and he was a really lovely chap and showed us all the parts of the machine and inside the cab. He would have given us a ride in the lorry but he said he was not allowed to.

We were fascinated by the fact that it had two steering wheels and we thought it had two drivers – funny what you think of when you're a kid. I cannot remember the chap's name now but he used to pick all the stones out of the treads on the wheels and we used to help him do it, we always went down to see him when we could and he was always pleased to see us. It was lovely to meet such people like him and it makes the world a better place when you did.

One day when we lived ay Granville Road in Cowes, we were all outside the front door and probably hiding behind the hedge to avoid the evil old witch next door. As were standing there, this strange row of vehicles came along the Road and they all had this strange plate on the front of them. There were hundreds of cars, vans and Lorries in the queue and it took ages for them to go past our house. I have no idea what it was all in aid of and still don't either.

Whenever there were any sort of road works nearby, I was there, I loved watching that curious machine they had for compacting the tarmac down, to me it was called a Jumping Jack as I had heard from a friend that was its name. It used to jump right up in the air and looked like a torpedo at the top.

I would watch that thing for ages and I bet the blokes fixing the Roads wondered why this kid kept following them around and just stood there staring at them working. They always had that tin shed on the back of the truck and would disappear inside it for tea breaks and lunch times. There was this very fat chap who used to always be around Cowes, fixing the roads, his trousers were like clown trousers, massive and he invariably never had a tee shirt that fitted properly, in fact it must have been 3 sizes too small for him, always reminded me of Oliver Hardy but in orange trousers.

Dad used to go up to the farm in Gurnard which was part of the firm that owned the butcher's shops that Dad managed. At Christmas he would go up there and pluck turkeys with all the other chaps from the firm and one of them I instantly recognised, it was the chap from the Road works with the big trousers and Dad knew him very well and told him that it was his son that watched the Road works- it's a small world.

I remember that we had a chap that used to come along our Road with this electric hand cart thing that had four wheels and sliding doors on each side and a long handle with the controls on it.

He used to trundle about all over the place with his flat cap and black donkey jacket. He always shouted at us for some reason and scared us with his loud voice. I don't know if he was deaf or just mad but he was a strange character indeed and feared by all of us.

I joined the scout troupe at about twelve years old and it was the first Methodist's in West Hill Road in Cowes.

Our leaders were excellent and provided us with so much fun and activities every week. I have nothing but praise for those two blokes because of the way they organised and joined in the fun and games.
Scout leaders have had a very hard time in more modern epoch's and it is a shame because not all of them were dirty old men who preyed on boys and girls under their care. I remember Mum taking me to the clothes shop on the corner of Shooters Hill and buying me my scout uniform one Saturday afternoon. I was so proud of my gear and loved the yellow sash thing and the woggle of course.

I could not wait until I got my first badge too.
Our hall was typical of all the old style
community buildings and very similar to the one
depicted in Dad's Army. We had one of those
dumb waiters and one evening a scout actually
got in it and we sent him down to the ground
floor, bloody dangerous but at the time daringly
good fun. We met every week and paid our
subs and then took part in some very interesting
activities such as building rafts, knots and
splices and my favourite one was making
pancakes and cooking them on an empty baked
bean tin, now that was clever. We cut a section
out of the can and put a candle underneath the
top of the can and added a little butter to the top
and poured the batter mix onto the tiny top –
few seconds later and you had a mini pancake.
We also did these *Y Games* at night around
Cowes, there were various points marked on a
map and you had to get to them before the other
teams and find the clues. My god, I remember
running from our hall and all the way up to
Crossfield Avenue and then onto Gurnard to
find these clues. You were certainly fit after
those games but the fun was fantastic and
especially at night. It lasted for hours and by the
time we got back to the hall, we only had time to
have a drink of squash or my fave was a cocktail
of orange and lemon, which our leader seemed
to enjoy making and find out who won the
games, before it was time to go home.

Grandad Ezzard in his garden, Firs Close, Cowes. Circa 1978.

Going home from scouts was yet another adventure and because most of the other scouts were at least two years older than me and seemed more streetwise than I did, we always went to Corries Cabin chip shop in Shooters Hill to get a portion of chips on the way back home. I can still smell those chips in the newspaper and looking in all the shop windows as we slowly made our way up past the library and down to Gordon Road where two of my mates lived.

One of the older scouts was a kind of hero of ours because he was very friendly and could do any of the tasks given to him; he lived on the corner of Mill Hill Road in a big house with a massive garden. Another older chap was a really big dude for his age and was very funny with it. Of course when you are a scout in a gang then you had to have an enemy and this turned out to be the sea scouts of Arctic Road. You learnt to hate them because they were learner sailors and fairies ha. We chased them every week after scouts and one night we met some of them in our chip shop, they looked like they were going to start some trouble and they did too. One of them said something nasty to the big lad in our group about his weight, so he turned round and kicked this Sea Scout's chips right out of his hands and then booted him in the pants and the rest of them ran off. He was a handy bloke to have on our side and kept those sea scouts at bay.

We all went to Corfe camp in Newtown for a weekend of camping and some adventures, even my Brother Tony went as he was a cub at the same time I was a scout. I loved every minute of it and the first day we were there, we had to track another troupe of scouts and also build a fire to make smoke signals.

We had the best war against the sea scouts who were across the creek from us. A new weapon came into my life and this was the *Pug Stick*. A very accurate and messy weapon and basically all it consisted of was a long stick and some nice stinky river mud. You had to grab a lump of mud and make a ball of it in your hand and then push it on the end of the stick, just enough so when you swung the stick towards the enemy, the mud ball flew off towards them, we spent hours playing this game and even our leader took part too.

For some reason, I was detailed to the camp kitchen and was either cooking or washing up. It was not just me that did all these tasks but some of my friends were doing it too, I loved the cooking part of it and cooked the bacon and eggs on Saturday morning for everyone in our troupe, which looking back was quite good for a twelve year old boy.

Mum and Dad came out to see Tony and I on the Saturday evening and talked to the leader and myself, just to see if I was enjoying it all. It was both character building and confidence building and if I could go back and do it all again, I would.

Every child should experience the scouts, guides or cubs because it gives you something that a TV or computer game cannot. It's about being part a team and being outside and getting dirty for instance, learning new skills and away from concrete jungles.

When you are so young and at middle school love is something unheard of at the time but soon creeps up on you as your body develops and your feelings start to change.

Embarrassing things start to happen to your body and thank God for parka coats and the fact they covered my school trousers nicely. It's a kind of blur when you get given a booklet by your Mum all about the facts of life and the ways to relieve yourself of such feelings.

I had strange feelings at twelve years old and one of them was amazingly when I climbed up the ropes in PE lessons. I could climb right up to the ceiling on those ropes and would get this amazing rush of feelings of love or whatever they were, go through my body from my crotch to my head.

It made me think of the girl I had a huge crush on in the school and she was to me, an angel. She had long wavy dark hair and quite tall for her age, freckles on her face and the cutest smile too. I adored this creature and would do anything to sit with her or work in her group. She was very friendly towards me too and I think that made it more frustrating in a way.

What with these strange feelings which I now understand were my first orgasms and this girl that was on my mind all the time, it was all very confusing because when you don't know what was happening to your body at that age. It is hard to deal with at that age. Many years later I met that girl in an insurance office in Cowes and could not believe it was her. She looked even prettier than she did all those years ago and it was a nice surprise to see her again after so very long.

We moved to Newport Road in approximately nineteen seventy four and very close to St Faiths Church which had the most awful sounding bell I ever heard, it sounded like someone banging a metal bucket with a hammer and we all hated it very much.

It was a nice house and had a long garden and the biggest conservatory I had ever seen, inside this glass room there were grape vines running its entire length and we were always picking the grapes and eating them, even if they didn't actually taste very sweet.

We moved houses more than times than any of my school mates and it was becoming the norm in the end. Removal Lorries were regular occurrences for us and we always had fish and chips on the first evening in our new house. We didn't stay in the house at Bellevue Road very long because my parents were in the business of buying a selling and making money, so off we went again, new neighbours and a new play area. So from nineteen sixty nine when we moved to the flat above the butchery, we moved to Park Road, Granville Road, Bellevue Road and now Newport Road by nineteen seventy four. Wondered why I felt rather nomadic at times....

Our neighbours at our new house were very friendly indeed, which was a real bonus to us kids because the last house had old grumpy and his hippy son living next to us. With their constant complaining about not being able to park his car outside his house, it was a relief all round.

One Christmas I had a chemistry set and loved mixing up different chemicals to see what they did. One day I mixed Sulphur with something and shook up the test tube with a cork in the top and was standing by the fence that divided Grumpy's garden with ours and suddenly there was this pop and the cork blew off, spewing out yellow foaming liquid straight over the fence and into Grumpy's fish pond. I was so worried he may have seen what happened that I put all the chemical set away and went out on my bicycle for the afternoon. When I came back home it was all quiet and nothing more was said, so I thought that I had got away with the chemical incident and had not harmed the fish in grumpy's pond. Some months later, my Mum had heard Grumpy complaining that all his goldfish had died. Oops...

On our left side of the house was a bungalow with rather a posh chap and his wife and three daughters. We got on very well with them and although they were exTimely snobbish in their ways, they were nice people. My brothers and I played with the daughters for hours and got on very well indeed. On the right side of us there was a builder and his Mum and he was a very nice chap as well. So at last we had nice neighbours for a change and it made a big difference within the family because no one was walking on egg shells all the time.

One day in the summer, we had just come back from the circus and the posh man next door was mowing his lawn with the very first electric hover mower we had ever seen. Unfortunately he hit a stone and it went straight through Dad's *Ford Zodiac* side window. It was a complete accident and the neighbour was so concerned when he came round to tell Dad, it was soon fixed and peace was once again restored. The chap always reminded me of Jerry from *The Good Life*, with his frightfully accent and mannerisms. I think from memory, he was a designer and worked for The British Hovercraft Corporation.

The first Christmas in that house had to have been the worst Christmas I had ever had because every one of us had the flu and it was horrendous to say the least. I remember having a temperature and coughing a lot and we must have got through more flu medicine that week or so than we did in two years. We did not have a Christmas dinner as Mum was too ill to cook and I remember Grandma came round to help out with us kids. It was terrible and the strain of flu was so strong back in those days too, it was a long time getting over that and we missed the whole Christmas celebrations completely.

It was that Christmas that my aunt set me a model submarine which had a motor and would apparently dive and surface on its own. It was a long time after the flu thing that I could actually take it to a big enough pond or lake to play with it.

We all went to Ventnor one Sunday afternoon and walked along by the paddling pool with the *Isle of Wight* shape in the middle of it and the big boating lake. Time for the submarine to go on its first mission I thought as I placed it in the boating lake and watched it go under the water and re surface and then it bobbed along the lake and then stopped right in the middle. I was so upset and because it was deep water and very muddy, Dad would not go in after it, so I had to leave it in the lake for someone else to find and I cried all the way back to the car. Dad was not in my good books that day.

Mum and Dad took in a lodger when we were living in Newport Road and he lived in a downstairs bedroom and shared the bathroom/kitchen etc. I remember he was a very skinny man of about 50 years old with round spectacles and odd looking hair and he always seemed to wear sandals with no socks, which I though quite odd at the time as every other grown up I came into contact with, wore socks.

Tony and I at Thorness Bay campsite during the two summers that our house was let out during Cowes Week 1974/5.

We hardly ever saw Harry during the daytime as he went out to work and the only time he was around the house would be weekends.
I have no idea what he did for a living or where he went when we let out our house. He never really talked to us children much but talked to my parents when he came into the lounge, but very rarely left his room. Mum said that he burnt a lot of candles in his room and read the bible a lot, so I guess he must have been a fairly religious chap. He did not cook any dinners because Mum always did his dinner along with ours and if we had a rare treat of fish and chips, then she would cook a dinner just for him.

I think he moved out before we actually moved house because although he brought extra money into the household, he was a bind if we wanted to go on a holiday, which although it was very rare at that time, were in the pipeline.

Cowes week back in the seventies was very busy with visitors and there was a lack of places for them to stay within the Cowes area. My Mum and Dad came up with this wonderful money making scheme of letting out our house to the visiting *Yachties* and going to stay at Thorness Bay Campsite near Porchfield and living in a large 3 bed roomed tent for two weeks.

I remember all our personal belongings being shifted in to one bedroom and a lock being fitted to the door. This was a complete nightmare because all of our toys had disappeared and been locked away for a while. The total upheaval of moving out of our house and into this big orange tent, which had partitions to make it seem that there were separate bedrooms and a large porch area that Mum turned into the kitchen. So the second two weeks of our summer holidays were spent at Thorness Bay and apart from the moving part, was a great place to spend your holidays back then.

They had a large swimming pool and various activities around the site and a wicked playground area too. My Brothers and I all had a thoroughly good time there and met lots of new friends, I met a young lady from Staines near London and she was a very pretty little girl and we went for long walks together in the lovely warm evenings. We spent hours together and it was a very sad day when she had to go home because I really missed her very much.

One day we were all playing by the large slide and I was with my two brothers, chatting to some other children when suddenly there was a scream from the car park, which was about 100ft away from the playground. A three wheeler was rolling down the steep grass bank towards us on the playground and there was a little boy standing right in the path of this Reliant as it got faster and closer to us. I grabbed the little boy and pushed him away from the car and luckily no one else was injured as the car hit the end of the slide and put a huge hole in the side of the Reliant. I had a lot of praise for my quick actions on that day but to me it was nothing really dangerous or heroic, because when you are so young, it does not really mean a lot to save someone from injury.

We stayed in that tent for two consecutive years and Mum and Dad made enough money in those 4 weeks to buy a large boat and a nice car, plus some decent camping holidays in both a tent and a caravan. It was worth the upheaval in the end and I think if we had stayed in Cowes, they would have bought another property and just let it out all the time.

Having a new bicycle when I was twelve was a fantastic event in my life and one that sticks with me. It was not a brand new bike, but a refurbished machine which my Mother had bought from Cowes Cycle Shop.

This shop was in Lower Denmark Road – down the hill from the railway bridge and on the left hand side corner as you went down the hill towards St Mary's Road and Gordon Road. I remember the colour of the bike was a green/blue with those full length white mudguards. In later life I realised that it was painted with Hammerite paint. It did not have any gears at all, but that did not matter to me at the time as I hated those Sturmey Archer three geared hubs with a passion.

Because I was riding my friend's Raleigh Chopper up hill and the bloody gears slipped and I landed on the cross bars with my nuts and that hurt like hell. Every damn 3 geared bike I ever rode and the gears always slipped when you put a lot of pressure on the pedals. On the rear wheel it had a built in dynamo hub which I considered more important than any gears or fancy mudguards. There were no lights fitted to the bike but I managed to rig up a front light from the dynamo, which was great until you stopped at traffic lights or a zebra crossing and the lights went out.

I went everywhere on that bike and it took some serious abuse during the off road rides we went on. It never seemed to break down and was always the only bike that was left standing after a good race through the old copse which was between of Cowes Cemetery and Milton Road. One Friday evening, Tony and I, my old pal Churchill had planned an adventure bike ride, mainly because Churchill had got hold of a map of the Island and this was a very rare thing to have back then.

My friend Churchill always claimed he was American and came from a place called Oakland – I did not know if he was telling the truth or not, I never questioned him on the subject either because I didn't want to upset him. Anyway, it was decided that we would ride to a place called *Brook* that was on the south west coast and a good 20 miles from Cowes. Now we were living in Bellevue Road at the time and Churchill lived just up the Road, at the top of Coronation Road, near *John Groves's* builder's yard. Riding to Brook was a real epic adventure at that age as none of us knew or had been to any part of the island before, especially on our own without grown ups.

We packed up a lunch and the all important penknives and other very important stuff and set off on this long ride from Cowes. I remember that we went up Newport Road and turned off at Plessey Radar towards Pallance Road and on towards Porchfield. Then we went up Elm Lane towards Calbourne and then headed for Chessell and turned up the road towards Brook Shute. The ride seemed to take forever until we reached *Brook Shute* and that was a flipping fantastic hill to go down on a bicycle, it seemed to go on forever and God knows what speed we reached.

When we had reached the bottom of the hill, we went into the small car park at Brook and sat on the grass and had lunch. I think we left about 0900 and got there around 1300 ish. It was a lovely sunny day and the ride was excellent fun, exploring another part of the world in our young eyes and seeing the sea from a different perspective was very impressive indeed.

On the ride back, we went a different way home and rode down through Shalfleet which had no traffic lights in those days and had the smallest little shop on the left hand side as you rode towards Porchfield.
I had heard rumours at school from one of the teachers that it was in fact the smallest shop in England, so we had to stop and buy some sweets from it. Back through Porchfield and eventually, back to Bellevue Road in Cowes. We had planned more rides to explore the island, but for some reason they did not materialise. I lost contact with my old pal Churchill when we moved up to high school and in fact I didn't really see a lot of my middle school friends after the move.

There was a Cycling Proficiency thing being run at Solent Middle and if you wanted to cycle to school, you had to pass this test or the school would not allow you to ride in.

As I was keen to cycle to school, I had to enroll in the course, which was held on a Saturday morning in the playground and in a classroom by a Policeman. We had to cycle around cones in the playground and read and answer questions on the Highway Code. The fact that a Policeman was running the show, made everyone quite nervous as we hardly had any contact with the constabulary at that age and daunting, was an under statement.

The policeman was very strict and he always checked our bicycles over before we started the course and would advise us on what clothing and shoes to wear on our bikes. He even setup a pair of real traffic lights in the classroom and then in the area just outside the main doors of the school, near where the Tuck-shop was. I have no idea how long the course ran, but it was very pleasing to receive my little triangular badge and the large metal disc to attach to the front of my bike to let others know I had passed the test.

It was not long after passing my test that we had planned a sponsored cycle ride at school and we were to cycle the entire circumference of the island.

When I was asked if I wanted to take part by my teacher Mr. Cenway, I automatically thought of the ride to Brook and how easy it was to do, therefore this adventure would be better and with the added attraction of camping overnight, somewhere on the Military Road. There were at least 4 of us that took part but I cannot remember all the names of the kids that took part. Tim Porteus, Michael Robots, myself and one other.

We set off from outside the school, loaded to the gunnels with enough gear to last a week and made our way across the Floating Bridge and towards East Cowes and on to Ryde. I remember cycling out past the area between Ryde and Brading and turning off towards Bembridge, then we made our way into Sandown, Shanklin and then up that bloody big hill to Ventnor.

It was about mid afternoon when we were pushing the bikes up Cowleaze hill and Mr. Cenway flew past us in his orange Beetle, beeping his horn and waving as he past us. That was probably the worst hill I ever cycled and would not want to do it again in a hurry. We went through Ventnor, which is the hilliest place on the planet according to my legs, there just didn't seem to be a flat length of Road anywhere.

Reaching Niton and then Blackgang was very exciting because although we had all been there with our parents at some point in our childhood, it was so very different going there on your own, plus it was daylight too as we had only ever been there at night to experience the illuminations of the cliff tops.

In fact everything looked completely different on a bicycle because you can see so much more than being in a car or bus. We reached our campsite in Atherfield and booked in and set up camp. It was early evening and very misty as I remember. We had done exTimely well during that first day and were working out how much sponsor money we could be collecting in our tents. We had beans for tea as some one had a gas stove and was designated Cook and provisions carrier, mainly because he had panniers on this bike. Tea was made and we all got into our sleeping bags and soon fell asleep. The next morning we headed for Freshwater bay and then Yarmouth and by the time the afternoon had arrived, we had got back to Cowes in good time. The school was so impressed by our efforts that they put a wooden bench in the small area between the classrooms with our names on it. I often wonder if it is still there, one day I may go and find out.

Being boys and being very interested in all things from Police stations to road sweepers, we got up to quite a few things during the summer holidays, but nothing really bad or illegal. One day we were searching Northwood Park for the secret tunnels that had supposed to have been built during the war and led from the large war memorial to Northwood House. We had only heard rumours of these tunnels and had planned to try and get inside them somehow but we had no idea how. We went to the war memorial and it had a large concrete drain cover on top of it and had large metal rings which were obviously there to lift the lid off, there was no way we could lift the lid up so we went to look for another entrance. We found a sort of entrance opposite the toilets in the car park at the bottom of Park Road and it looked like some sort of hole that had been filed in at some point in time. We managed to dig around inside it and came across the mass of paper files which were stamped Cowes Urban District Council. This was very exciting stuff because we were convinced that they were secret files that someone had hidden in this hole and the things that went through our heads were quite serious back then, but now we can laugh at our innocent mind. There were only three of us that had found these files and it was my brother Tony and my friend Ant and I who then decided to take the files to the police station and hand them in. We were all convinced someone would be following our every step and would be trying to get the files back, so we took the railway route from Denmark Road and through the tunnel and coming out near Arctic Road and then walked down to the police station and took them inside.

The policeman at the desk was very interested in what we had found and took our names and addresses just in case there was a reward for the item, now that sounded very exciting stuff; reward, went into our heads and made us think of how we could possibly get the chance of more rewards? This is when we came up with the brilliant plan of combing Cowes for lost property and taking it to the police station. We first of all found a dog lead and collar and it had a name tag on it so that went to the police station to the delight of the desk sergeant who had to book it all in. The next thing was a pair of gloves and various other things. In the end we were told by the police that we should not really be going looking for lost property because it was taking so much time for them to book it all in and fill out all the forms. They must have dreaded the moment when we walked in to the station every day and with a handful of things that had been lost. Looking back on that brilliant idea makes me laugh and it was so funny when we were told by the police not to go looking for things.

It was with my friend Ant, who I have to say, came from a very poor family indeed and there were times when I went around to his house that they hardly had enough food to feed themselves on, it made me feel very guilty; even at that age. He had two or three sisters and they were really nice children and his Mum and Dad were very nice to me and we got along very well. Being the son of a butcher did have it's downside because some of the poorer parents would treat me so differently and go into my Dad's shop and expect cheap meat or worse, free meat just because they had entertained me for an afternoon. It is quite unbelievable I know but it was a fact and Dad just told me not to accept gifts or anything from certain parents because it was just a ticket to come and get something free.

Ant's parents were not of this breed and were never interested what my Dad did for a living or any other personal information, they treated me as any other member of the family and I appreciated it very much at the time.

We were always coming up with money making schemes such as *Penny for the Guy* and paraded around the high street collecting money for fireworks, even though we did not even buy any fireworks, it all seemed a fun thing to do and we made a lot of money at it too.

It was Christmas holidays and we needed to make some money to buy presents for our families. Pocket money just didn't stretch enough to buy gifts for my two brothers, sister and Mum and Dad.

Ant certainly could not afford anything because his parents could not afford pocket money for the kids. I think it was his sister that came up with the excellent plan to go carol singing. We had no idea of what we were going to sing and certainly, we had no idea what the words to the songs were but luckily for us, Ant's sister wrote out all the words on two sheets of paper from a book she got from the school library, so we now had a list of songs and the words.

Ant's two sisters joined us in the carol singing scheme and with the help of both our parents, we managed to make a couple of lanterns with a candle in each of them, they looked very bland in the daylight but at night, they really looked pretty.

We started our singing rounds along Mill Hill Road and then down Newport Road until we reached the lower end of my road, Bellevue Road.

By the time we had reached the bottom of Mill Hill Road we had accumulated quite a few coins already and to be absolutely honest here, our singing was bloody good and with the two sisters and the song sheets, we must have sounded as good as the Salvation Army.

We had just started up Bellevue Road and knocked on this door and stood there waiting for the "No thanks" from the home owner, when the door opened and there stood a vicar in his black cloak and collar. We were quite nervous at this point because I guess vicars knew their carol singing and we were about to be judged for the first time that night.

Anyway, the vicar was very nice and asked us to sing our carols and when we had finished he said "May I record you on my tape recorder while you sing two more carols, because I would like to play them for the people in hospital on Christmas day?" "Yes" we replied and he went inside and came out again with his wife and the tape recorder and recorded our carols.
He gave us a vast amount of money for the songs we sang and it was the highlight of the night because we felt very pleased with ourselves and slightly famous because we were going to be played at the hospital on Christmas day.

We carried on up the Road and nearly every door we knocked upon; let us sing for them and by the end of the night I think we had taken somewhere near £5.00 or more. We shared it all out when we arrived at my house and I said goodbye to Ant and his dear sisters and I went to bed very contented indeed. I think that Ant and his sisters had a merrier Christmas that year and we helped to make someone happy in the process.

It brought tears to my eyes when I wrote this story because Ant's family was so poor and it just gave me the determination to be thankful for what I have. I hope he and his sisters prospered.

My two brothers and I attended Piano lessons once a week at this old house at the top of Park Road and the house was painted in a maroon colour on the outside and had one of those built-in extended porches that ran from the front door to the end of the first floor window. Inside this house was immaculately clean and always smelt of polish and the sounds of the piano and her scary sounding cat.

The lady who taught us was very strict and if you played the piano in an uncaring way, she would make you play the piece over and over until you paid attention. My mind was always in another place back then and my primary thoughts were going to Granddads house and watching *The Six Million Dollar Man* after the lesson.

She was called Ms Grace Malarel with countless letters after her name on the brass plaque that was on the wall by the front door. Her pet cat was the most annoying thing in that house, apart from the piano of course. The cat was a Siamese and I hated its meow very much and it sometimes scared the hell out of me when it jumped on my lap and the end of the lesson. I think it must have been the very first cat of that breed I had ever seen and from that time until now, I dislike that breed with a passion.
I remember the cupboard under the stairs in the teacher's house; it was adjacent to the chair I had to sit on when waiting for the lesson to begin. It had a key in the lock and one evening I locked it and hid the key in a flower pot in the hall.

I have no idea why I did it, just for fun and to be annoying I suppose. Later that evening there was a knock on the door of our house and it was Ms Malarel asking if I had seen the key to her cupboard as she could not get to her cat food or something like that. I got a serious telling off for that little trick by Mum, but Dad laughed and this did not go down well with my Mum at all.

I was only 6 years old when I started my visits to that house and left just after I was 12. I tried to keep up with the lessons and homework, but alas I had better things to do with my time as I grew older. I always went to my Grandparents house before the lesson on my bicycle and after the lesson I would cycle back up the hill of Firs Close which incidentally, was just opposite the piano teacher's home.

One evening I left my Grandparents house and cycled down the hill but instead of going to my lesson, I kept cycling up to the *Roundhouse* and along Place Road near to the car showroom Sparshatts or whatever it was called.
I stayed there long enough to fool my Grandparents that I had been for my lesson, and then I went to watch telly at Granddads then cycled home to our third house in Cowes, Belle Vue Road.

It was not long until Mum was on my case and interrogated me about missing the lesson and it was decided that I was not really interested enough to carry on. Hence I gave it all up.

I tried trumpet lessons at middle school but that only lasted about a month or so. It was not for me and although the teacher was a good laugh and nice bloke, I didn't carry on with it and Mum had to take the instrument back to *Teagues* in Newport as it was on hire from them.

Being bullied at middle school for a year or so had a devastating effect on me and probably pushed me into giving up piano because of the fear of being outside my home. The whole year I endured no physical violence or harm but mental torture and the worst kind of torture to a young lad - fear.

The fear of that bully seeing me in the street or at the park after school. After being taken to hospital for tests and psychologists asking me endless questions, I was diagnosed by a specialist at St Mary's hospital as being a victim of bullying. My parents had no idea of what I was going through, but thought I was ill because of my weight loss and bed wetting, which continued until I was 12 years old.

My Father knew the bully and his family as his older brother worked for my Father when he was area manager for T. Smoths Butchers in Cowes. He went straight round to the boy's house and threatened to throw him in the Solent if he went near me again.

I think my Dad scared the life out of him so much that the very next day at school, the boy brought me presents of toy soldiers and other gifts. From that day onwards we became friends for the rest of the remaining two years. When I moved up to the big high school Cowes High School, the boy who once I feared did not come with us and no one knew where he had gone either?
It wasn't until half way through the 3rd year at Cowes high school; I was given a letter by my form teacher which was from a strange named school, as it was printed on the envelope. At first I had no clue that had sent me this letter until I reached the bottom of the page and saw the name Pedro.

It was my friend who had disappeared on the move up to high school and he wrote of canoeing, rugby and other sports that were alien to me at this time of life.

I did reply to his letter and told him of how everyone wondered where he had gone and the amazing technology department we had here. I received another letter from him some months later but by this time my head was being taken over by music and girls, so I never replied to his letter and I did not hear another word about him again.

Deep down, I wanted to forget him and all the hell I experienced because of him. Although we became friends, I never forgot the hurt and the dark side of his personality. He had an amazing talent for writing stories and would not take part in any lesson that was being taught. It was as if the teacher's had given up on him and just opted for the quiet life and let him write his stories in class.

Looking back to the final years of Solent Middle School, the bully and I collaborated on a Friday afternoon radio show. Solent had its own internal radio studio named SBC or Solent Broadcasting Company, which basically transmitted to speakers in all the rooms in the school.

This included the canteen, sports hall and staff room. We were allowed to miss all lessons on Friday morning to record our show, which to me was a licence to skive.

Many years later I heard the sad news that the bully had committed suicide by jumping in front of a train whilst training as a priest somewhere in Scotland. Also his brother who once worked for my Dad in the butchers in Cowes had drowned in the Medina River.

It was sad about the way in which the bully died but I am afraid I was not sad about him dying one bit. I can't forgive very easily and he messed up my first year of middle school and caused me so much worry and pain that I was so glad he was now dead so he will never be able to bully anyone else.

A priest, now forgive me but how the hell did he become one of the cloth with his deranged mind and the often dark side of his personality? Imagine him as the Sunday school teacher, does not bear thinking about does it?

This radio studio was the brainchild of one of the most special teachers I have ever met, Mr. Janna was his name and I think he lived near Wootton Bridge. He was an ex RAF pilot, a sailor in his spare time and one of the most generous, helpful and kindest people one could ever wish to have as a teacher.

He appeared to know everything about radio, electronics and other things that only seemed to appeal to a teenage boy. He helped open up my mind to the wonders of music, radio and other related concepts which broadened new interests for me. We spent hours recording our own show which went out on Fridays, after the lunchtime news programme.

Playing in the garden of our Newport Road house
In Cowes. Circa 1975.

Many other pupils were involved with SBC and without their input it would never had succeeded. I cannot remember many of them but one particular lad named Electrical Bunny, was well known for his passion in radio and electronics. There were not many 12 year olds bringing radio signal jammers to school and in one very funny incident, he acquired a large amount of computer punch cards. These were large cards with lots of square holes in them with strange sci-fi type numbers on the sides. He raided the Cowes Urban District Council depot and found these cards in a bin. Of course these things were very special to us kids and we regarded them as almost from another world. I can laugh now but these were serious currency at the time and poor Bunny got the slipper for selling dozens of these things at school. Thinking about it, I reckon someone from the council depot was tipped off by a parent. Happy days.

Tony holding Misty in 1976.

My first ever interest in chart music came from this radio that my Granddad gave me. A rectangular box of electronics with a blue vinyl covering which could be removed if needed? Why the hell you would want a cover on a radio I will never know and it also had a socket for plugging into your car aerial too. This must have been because not all cars had radios in them; well that's what I thought anyway. The battery in the set, as Granddad called it, was very heavy and oblong in shape with blue cardboard flaps over the terminals on the top. *Ever Ready* was the make and that's the only make we ever saw in the 70's. I remember finding radio Luxembourg on the dial but every few minutes it would fade in and out so I could not hear the whole song. I investigated this problem at the age of nine years old and found if I removed the rear cover of the radio and put my fingers on this large silver thing that resembled a runner bean slicer that Granddad always used, I could get a much better sound and it would not fade out completely.

I later learnt that this was in fact the tuner of the radio and not a runner bean slicer. Every night I lay in my bed with my hand stretched out touching the radio tuner and Mum used to tell me I always fell asleep doing this.

The only name I remembered from those early radio shows was Stuart Henry; he was the DJ that seemed to be on every night when I went to bed. In those days it was *Abba* or *Showaddywaddy* on the shows plus some *Dawn* or *Simon and Garfunkel*. I didn't particularly like this music but then came *T Rex* and the other glam rock artists and I quite liked the percussion in this type of music and when some of the bands started to use double drum kits, it was a good sound to me.

Dad trying to get us to play football in Northwood Park, Cowes. Circa 1975.

The single most dangerous thing that I have ever done as a kid follows here. Looking back I have absolutely no idea why I thought this was a good plan. My brother's bike had no brakes and he was riding it around the garages opposite our house in Bellevue Road in Cowes.

I was roller skating at the time and spent many hours on those things. Anyway, I got on his bike with my roller skates still attached and rode around for a while and then headed down Fellows Road. Now that Road was quite a hill and I soon picked up a fair rate of knots and oh hang on, when I put my feet down to stop it did not have the expected effect due to the skates! What a stupid thing to do and the speed I was going at, I did not have much time to figure out that this trick was going to hurt. Hurtling down the pavement and nearly reaching the bottom of the road, I spotted a large building site in front of me and a huge pile of sand, so I hit the sand and amazingly I stayed upright on the bike and was saved from certain death. If I had not seen the sand and carried on, I would have gone straight into the steepest road in Cowes and that would have been fatal for sure. I did not attempt that trick again.

We got our first kitten from Fellows Road and called her Misty because she was a dusky black and grey colour and very placid. We had that cat all the time I was growing up and right up until I was almost sixteen years old, until she was bitten by something and died of her injuries and was buried in our garden at Totland.

It is a long time to share your life with such a beautiful little animal and you really grow so attached to them. I was very sad when we lost her and more so because my brother Tony absolutely adored her.

My little sister Sarah in the garden of Belle Vue Road. Circa 1974.

Chapter 3

Moving once again

We were moving house yet again and this time away from Cowes and to Newport. The new house was of a reasonable size but the most exciting aspect was the huge and very long garden. It must have been over 200 feet in length and about 90 feet in width, with its own little pond and a small parking space. The lounge was a lot smaller than the last house but the kitchen was bigger and large enough for a table and six chairs in the middle of it. Dad decided to enlarge the parking area and turn the lower part of the garden into a vegetable plot. He borrowed a tractor from his boss and removed a large part of the hedge and had tarmac put down so the space was large enough for more than three cars. This was before the change in hobbies from boats to horses I hasten to add.

The lounge had a large bay window with French doors leading out onto the garden path, with a small flat roof for which we made good use of in latter days. The first major addition to the place was the giant caravan that appeared one day and it took some work getting it into the driveway.

This thing was a not a normal size caravan, it was over 28 feet long and apparently was bought to do up and sell. This giant caravan only remained in the garden for a month or so, after it was cleaned and repaired and subsequently sold.

Next was a much smaller caravan that arrived and Mum and Dad spent hours cleaning and refurbishing the thing for some reason. Little did I know that we were off on one of our first family holidays to Norfolk, Northumberland and Cambridge in a few weeks time. We were loading up the car and caravan on a Friday evening and I remember Dad deciding to test the lights on the van. Nothing would work and after some of the wires were changed in the trailer plug, all the fuses blew in the *Ford Zodiac* too.

So Dad had to go across the road to Hunnyhill garage and get the mechanic over to sort the lights out, early on Saturday morning. So here we were again, a mad panic and as the ferry was booked for later that morning, we were all bundled in the car and went like hell to catch the boat to Portsmouth. That was in the days when the driver of the vehicle was given a free cup of tea, which was served on the car deck from a little hatch.

We arrived in Norfolk and camped in Cromer and then Great Yarmouth. We had recently got our first pet dog called Sally and she was the loveliest black Labrador and had the shiniest coat I had ever seen. In Great Yarmouth she ran off from the campsite and it took my parents' ages to find her. She had a good telling off that night, but she never ran off again as far as I can remember anyway.

We went pony trekking whilst we were there and I am sure that episode is what planted the seed for my Dad to suddenly want to buy horses instead of boats. I don't remember much about Northumberland, apart from it wasn't very warm when it was dry and rained a fair bit on occasions. Cambridge was a nice visit because we went to stay with my uncle and cousins for a change. We never seemed to go and visit our distant relatives very often when we were kids for some reason. We had a good time apart from when my little brother thumped my uncle in the stomach and winded him, God knows why he did it but my uncle gave him a kick up the pants for doing it. Anyway, we returned home relatively intact and unscathed and settled back into normality for a short time.

Then came the horses and the three hundred pine poles that arrived in the drive one day from the Forestry Commission at Parkhurst. Why did I remember that? So my Dad and Mack the lodger were in the garden all weekend cutting, concreting and nailing these poles all over the garden and eventually, we had what resembled a small archway such as you would find on a ranch in a western film, complete with a horseshoe on the top. Think of *Southfork* from the popular programme *Dallas*, and that was the impression it gave. The shed at the back of the garden was converted into a stable and poles were assembled in front for tying up the horses, even though we didn't actually have one. My brothers, sister and I didn't have to wait long before a pony arrived in the stable and then another and another appeared on the scene. Three horses were bought and next came riding lessons for all of us kids. Funny really, I don't remember actually showing too much interest in riding horses from memory, but that wasn't the point I guess. If Dad wanted us to learn to ride and look after horses, then so be it…

The first single record I bought whilst living in this house in Newport, was by *Hot Chocolate* and the song was called *Man to Man* The second record I bought was by *The Stylistics* but I can't remember for the life of me which song it was but I loved it very much.

The biggest event in my musical taste was the time I heard a song called *Strange Magic* by a band called *The Electric Light Orchestra*, Just the name alone was intriguing to me because I imagined that the band was powered by electricity or something like that.

The oddest thing about this new house was the address; Parkhurst Road but actually situated in Banner Lane. Never did understand that one. We had some really good times in that little house and some of them I am going to share, because they were so funny. My Father being a big practical joker and this certainly rubbed off on me as I was always up to some prank or another. Back in the seventies the local chemist shop in Cowes used to have a life-size cardboard cut out of a woman holding a camera, and it was a *Kodak* advertisement.

Dad managed to get hold of it and brought it home and put it between two fir trees that stood in front of our tiny fish pond. He then sent my brother, Tony, up to the top of the garden to fetch something from his van. Yes, my brother jumped out of his skin when he reached the pond. Dad played this trick on everyone who visited our house and it certainly got a lot of laughs.

Our new lodger moved in with us while we were living in this house and he worked for my Father in the butchers shop in Cowes. One night my brother Tony and I managed to run a speaker cable from the lounge, out of the French doors and up to our bedroom. The wire was connected to the record player's speaker and when our lodger went to bed, I touched the end of the wires onto a nine volt battery and the scratching sound must have scared the poor chap to death. He ran out of the room and called Dad downstairs to see what the hell was in the lounge. There were us three brothers in tears laughing, in our room and then Dad must have heard us and came up and asked us why were we laughing so much? We explained about the wire and he thought it was brilliant too and told the lodger what I had done.

Dad had a friend who lived in Upper Bellevue Road in Cowes and he was a really old chap who did a lot of woodwork for Dad. Anyway, for some reason this chap had two of those mannequins that the clothes shops used for displaying garments etc. Both of these things looked out of his shed window at you and scared the hell out of us when we went with Dad to see this fellow. I remember Doctor Who had some of those things that came alive and it was at that time when we saw the damn things in his shed.

I do not really know where Dad's interest in horses came from, maybe from his experience of being evacuated to Exford on Exmoor during the Second World War and being brought up on a little farm? Must have been one hell of a thing to go through when you were just five years old and being taken from your parents and shipped off to some strange place.

He was not alone though, his two sisters and three brothers went with him.
He told me lots of stories of helping out on the farm and riding on hay carts and running to the top of a hill to watch the spitfires chasing off the German planes over the Bristol Channel.
It was not all fun though; apparently the farmer's wife was an evil woman and did some very nasty things to the younger members of the family but would not touch Dad's older brothers because she was scared of them.

So this could be where his love of horses came from and like all of us at some point in our lives, we want to re-live the fun experiences of our childhood. We got into horses and our first pony was Nutmeg, a very clever and awkward old mare who knew every trick in the book to avoid doing anything she didn't particularly want to do that day. Like most women I have met!

Her character was so funny and although she was stubborn and bloody minded, she was gorgeous to ride and would go anywhere if she was in the right mood. See my above comment. She loved the beach and paddling in the surf down at Gurnard beach near Cowes.

Not long after we had bought Nutmeg, we acquired my horse Whiskee.
On one occasion he escaped from a field up near Parkhurst Forest, you can guess which direction he went - yes, straight into the forest and looking for him in that expanse of woodland would have been impossible on foot, so Dad got permission from the Forestry Commission chap to drive the car around the tracks and look for my horse.

We had a big roof rack on the car and we had our tractor inner tubes in the back as we had just been to Sandown beach for the day, so we put the inner tubes on the roof and sat on them while Dad drove around the forest. It was like a scene from *Daktari* for us kids. We spent all evening going around the forest and eventually found the horse that had gone out of the forest and into Camp Hill estate.

Mum was walking up that little road that goes from Forest Road to the estate and she grabbed him and brought him back with my little sister, while we were still searching the forest. I bet not many people have driven around that forest on top of a Ford Zodiac.

At that time we had a Welsh friend staying and the niece of my Dad's friend .This young lady was from Nottingham, and was absolutely beautiful in my eyes. Unfortunately my brother Tony felt the same way. I went riding with her every day during the school holidays and I grew fonder and fonder of her. She was the same age as me, thirteen, and had long dark hair and a lovely figure. Her accent was very curious; almost addictive at times, and similarly, were the strange words and phrases she came out with. Although we had no idea what they meant, we agreed with her every time she said one of them, so not to appear stupid.
I'm sure she caused a lot of swimmers to sink when we went to the swimming pool at Seaclose and everyone was staring at her in her bikini. She was a lovely girl and I truly fell in love with her during that summer of seventy six and then she had to go back to the North and I did not see her again after that. Tony kissed her but I didn't, because she liked him more than me, there was no friction between us over her and in fact we never had a cross word, ever.

I heard that some years later, she moved back to the island and got pregnant and married. She called me up when I lived in Totland one day and I could not believe it was her and she came over to see us on the bus from Newport, where she lived and she looked as gorgeous as ever too. No idea what happened to her after that though.

Nineteen seventy six was the hottest summer and I remember when we got our first pony, walking from Newport to Northwood and to Wyatts Lane where we kept the pony. It was Tony, Michael, my Welsh friend, and I who went into the field to try and catch Nutmeg. She could only be captured with a large amount of pony nuts in a bucket and you had to entice her slowly because she wasn't stupid.

We finally got her into the small lane that led up to the gate and she was eating her food when Michael walked behind her. WHACK! A hoof print suddenly glowed red on his thigh and he was in agony. She was the most cunning and clever horse I ever knew and it just amazed me how she could hit an object with her rear hooves whilst looking forward. Michael only had a large bruise with horseshoes imprinted in his leg, no fractures, thank God. We did learn from that day that you should never walk behind a horse or cow if it comes to that, because they hurt.

We moved our horses from various stables and livery yards like we moved house. The Alamo Ranch was the weirdest place that we used to visit and that was situated up a small lane off Fairlee Road, almost opposite the private hospital buildings.

When we first went there and saw all the buildings which resembled a real American Wild-West town and even had a saloon too. The fields were not bad in the summer months but come the winter, they were boggy and soon turned into a clay mud slide after walking the horses around a few times.

The owner was an American fellow called Irskine or something like that. He was a quiet chap who I hardly ever saw. There were a couple of other horse owners who rented stables and grazing there and one particular chap I remember was a very good horseman. He taught me to jump and look after the horses properly. He came and babysat for us kids one night and I tied his shoe laces together for a laugh. He was there with his mate and their two ladies, nice people and the girlfriends were giggling at the laces trick.

We played a lot of tricks that night and also stayed downstairs for longer than we were supposed to, which I think annoyed them because they had other things they wanted to be doing. The funniest event that occurred whilst at the ranch type buildings was when a lot of blokes used to turn up in full cowboy outfits and took part in quick draw competitions in the saloon. One of the chaps dressed up, was our delivery driver for a meat supplier in Cowes and he got a fair amount of stick when he delivered to the shop after that.

So then we left the Alamo and went to a farm in Cowes which I think was up at Pallance Road. This livery was a lot bigger than the previous one, with vast acres of good dry land and grass. They had a proper tack room and sand ménage for training and breaking the young horses in. I met two really nice girls there and often went out riding with them across the fields or on the roads. One of the girls lived not far from me and I used to stand and chat to her at the bus stop in the morning as she also went to Cowes High School.

Her name was Yvonne, if my memory is firing on all cylinders; she had a lot of freckles and long dark hair and lived up Albany Road. I obviously had a thing for long dark hair.

I would love to meet her again because we were very good friends back then and also she would remember a lot of things about Tony too, as she rode around the fields with him frequently. All these long lost people whom I met and became good friends with, it's quite a shame we have to leave them behind as we grow up and move away from each other because good friends are not the easiest ones to find.

I cannot remember about the other girl other than she too had long dark hair. We eventually moved our horses from these stables and I never saw the girls again. When I was thirteen I started working in the butcher's shop on Saturday mornings.

I got up at six am and was in the shop for six thirty ready to start putting the window displays in. I worked mainly in a small room, which was up the hill about thirty metres from the shop back door. This was known as *The Sausage House* and it was where sausages, burgers and dripping were made. I quickly learnt how to make sausages and make the dripping and pack it into those white, waxed paper packets with a picture of a cow on it in blue.

My mentor was the chap who became our lodger for many years after that. One of our favourite things to do in that room was to make a burger and cook it on the electric cooker and have it for a sort of breakfast break.

Normally, after all the sausages were made and the whole sausage house was washed down completely with hot water and occasionally, some caustic soda, it was usually coffee time in the shop and one of the best bits of Saturday mornings, the "Wimpy Bar" cheeseburger.

I can honestly say that I have never tasted anything as gorgeous as those Saturday snacks, no other cheeseburger ever tasted as good as they did and I have no idea why, they just did. I would never go into such a place because it was too damn scary for me at that age. There were too many teenagers in there, so I never actually went into that place where they made the best food ever. Luckily I didn't have to, the lads who worked for my Dad went for me. I was chronically shy at that age.

Having been paid a massive £5 for my morning's work, I would go across the road to the Red Funnel Arcade and to the paper shop to get my favourite chocolate bar, *Old Jamaica Rum and Raisin*. Dad's friend owned the paper shop so it was ok for me to get his twenty *No6* cigarettes and take them to him in the shop. I was addicted to that chocolate and bought one every Saturday after work. Whilst I was getting my chocolate, I would stop and stare in awe at the lodger's brand new *Yamaha FS1E* parked against the wall in the Arcade. It was purple and a fantastic looking bike. I wanted one from the first time I saw it and promised myself that one day I would get one the very same colour – I did too.

My mother and Liam in Northwood Park Cowes. Circa 1973.

Chapter 4

Moving to Totland Bay

The village of Totland was bustling with life. Dad had opened his butcher's shop a few weeks prior to us moving to the property, which was to become our home for the next three years or so. The house was a three storey building and was situated right next to the butcher's shop. I had only been to the West Wight once before and that was at Christmas when my uncle and cousins came to stay with us in Newport. We went out for a drive one morning and ended up on Headon Warren at the old fort which features later on in this story. The lane which branches off of the main drag into Alum Bay almost runs parallel with the main Road but is separated by a large cove or Dell and a huge drop that was thick with trees and bushes. As you go along this lane you reach a fork in the Road, one track leads down the cliffs to the chairlift base and the other goes up to the fort and cafe. The cafe track forks off the fort lane a few hundred yards from the cliff track. The lane past the cafe entrance had the deepest ruts I had ever seen, they were over a foot deep and almost a foot wide in places. My uncle took his new Triumph TC car up the lane, following my Dad.

The butchers shop had the same use for some years; this was obvious as it already had a walk in chiller in the back room. None of the fridge motors worked, so Dad had to have new motors fitted and various fridge counters put in. This must have cost a small fortune to kit it all out, but Dad had made a lot of money working as the area manager for the Cowes-based farmer T Smoth and Sons and he had worked for them since about nineteen sixty nine until nineteen seventy seven and made a lot of business contacts in the process. This gave him good grounding to start up his own shop. Dad and Mum built that business up from nothing and it was so busy in the booming years of the West Wight that they were able to convert the shop and ground floor space of *Bon Accord* into a bakery a few years later. Dad was the master of not wasting a single penny and that is how he made so much in those few short years. The butchers shop was sold in nineteen eighty three and the bakery was sold in nineteen eighty four and then we all went our separate ways, well Dad did anyway.

Christmas time was the busiest time in the butchers shop and I remember going up to Smithfield market in a hired van with Dad to get his turkeys and fresh chickens.

Arriving there at around 0400 in the morning and wandering around looking at stalls and stalls of turkeys, ducks, chickens and all other types of meat was freezing and very tiring. Dad got the best deal he could and a barrow boy, very respected so Dad said, brought everything to our van and we loaded it all up and were away by 10 ish. Bacon sandwiches in a café full of cockneys and you knew you were amongst market people and meat traders by their accents and mannerisms. There were masses of the longest lorries I had ever seen, all lit up with coloured lights and mini Christmas trees in the cabs. Magical, almost but with the smell of meat and diesel mixed in; Loved the experience and would love to visit it again one day.

Dad would be dressing the birds all night and he and our lodger would not stop until the lot were finished and that would be over 200 hundred turkeys, plus chickens and the odd goose or two. Then all the joints would have to be prepped up and doing the orders for Christmas week was a bloody nightmare with carrier bags hanging on hooks with labels pinned to them. This was the way Dad organised the meat orders. Bags with all sorts were crammed in the chiller and everywhere there was space to put them. I had to make a lot of the sausages and some of the burgers too.

Apparently, I was good at making sausages- so that was a job I was given from the word go. Dad bought an original butchers bicycle, complete with the basket on the front and it was the heaviest bloody bike I ever rode and it was very awkward to ride with all that weight on the front wheel. Why they designed such a machine that was so unbalanced I will never know. I had to ride that bloody thing right up to the old Alum Bay Road and to one of the hotels there and then back to Moons Hill, it was a killer bike and you certainly were pleased when you were given a Christmas tip after all that work.

My Mother started to make meat pies to sell in Dad's shop. At first it was only a very small operation and she would make up around two dozen a week but after a short time it grew and grew and it was not very long when we were travelling off to Cowes and Yarmouth to deliver her wares and production was in full swing. She started this business in our kitchen in the flat and then when we opened the bakery, she did all her pie making there.

We bought presses and millions of pie tins, extra mixers and various other pieces of catering equipment to make the job easier for Mum, as it was a long laborious task in the end.

Mum broke her arm in one of our big mixers as she was taking pastry out of it, before it had stopped rotating. She was not concentrating when she did it and looked so very exhausted with all the work involved.

As the bakery business grew, we were able to knock that business on the head and give Mum more of a rest for a change, as she worked every damn hour there was on that business and built it from nothing and grew it into a massive concern in the end.

I'm so glad we stopped it because it was getting to become a pain in the bum, as some of the shops would take the Mick and send stock back saying it was broken or out of date. Doing sale or return was not the way to make money in that kind of trade because it's open to abuse and certainly was in Mum's case. We all learn by our mistakes I guess.

We had a saying in the butcher's shop and it was "F the pies" which all started when Dad was moaning that there was not enough room in his chiller cabinet for his cold meats as Mum had invaded it with pies.

When Totland Pier was complete and open to the public, Tony and I used to fish off of it. We only had butchers string and a marrow bone in the beginning until we started to go on Friday evenings and got very friendly with an older chap and his nephew, who we nick named Fisherman Bill. They were very nice people and we spent all evening on that pier with them catching all sorts but the prize was the big crabs.

They had these nets that they had made from Bicycle wheels and garden netting and then a long rope to lower them down to the sea bed. Tony and I went up to our little treasure pit, which was the little dump up on the New Alum Bay Road, just past the turning on the right for Cliff Road. It was owned by the Burton family of Stoats Farm and they extracted sand from it before it became a sort of landfill site.

There was always a good selection of bike wheels up there so we got ourselves around 12 wheels and that was a good start. Then we went to Hitchmans in Freshwater to buy the garden netting and also the nylon rope.

We made up our nets which were called drop nets. So now we had our own nets and then we scrounged enough marrow bones and other bones from Dad and tied them in the bottom of the nets so the crabs could not pull them out again. This was such a move forward from the old marrow bone on a string, mainly because pulling a huge bone which was covered in crabs, up the side of a pier on string was an absolute killer on your hands and most of the time, the crabs fell off the bone. Our first night with our own nets was incredible as we caught about twenty odd big crabs and put them in a couple of big buckets, which also came from Dad's butchery.

The biggest problem we had was carrying the nets and the buckets back home from the pier. We also really needed a lantern for on the pier at night as there were no lights apart from a navigation lamp on the end of the pier. We came up with a good solution to the transport problem by using the butcher's bike and putting all the nets in the front basket. Our lantern was a road works paraffin lamp with one of the amber glasses removed, it worked very well and gave us some warmth too.

We were on the pier whatever the weather and I remember walking down the pier with Tony with ice on the wooden boards and freezing hands from the wet nets and ropes. Fisherman Bill was always there with us and that made Mum and Dad feel better about us two kids staying on that pier til at least half eleven at night.

The original butchers advert from the County Press. Circa 1977.

Sometimes we didn't take all our nets because it got too much and we didn't want to catch too many crabs either. We always brought them home and boiled them up in the kitchen of the flat, to the horror of my Mum and her big saucepan she used for stews. Dad thought it was a brilliant idea, and let us sell them in his shop fridge cabinet.

We always sold everything that we caught and never wasted a single crab, which was good because we did not take anything that we did not need. Fisherman Bill and his nephew always helped us if we had trouble getting our nets in or if there was a spider crab in them as we hated picking those things up, so we got Bill to do it for us. One night we were on the pier as usual and there was a lot of shouting and noise coming from the esplanade end of the pier.

We had no idea what was going on but it sounded and looked like a load of punk rockers from Freshwater had come up to cause trouble somewhere, as they quite often did. Anyway, we packed up all our gear and walked down to the end of the pier and our bike had gone. Someone had stolen it and we were so worried about what Dad was going to say.

Fisherman Bill and his nephew came down and looked for it but to no avail, so they gave us a lift home and we went and told Dad. He was not angry with us but he said he saw the punks over the road earlier, by the Broadway Inn. He went up to the police house the next morning to report the bike stolen. It was not long until the policeman found the bike half way up the grass bank in front of the closed up Totland Chalet Hotel and by the steps. It was damaged but repairable and we got it back and Dad fixed it up.

The queue outside the shop during the last week before Christmas was amazing. It stretched right down to the bus stop about fifty feet away. It always reminded me of a scene from the Second World War with rationing and the queues. People came from miles around to buy Dad's wares, even from places like Ryde and Sandown.

He had an excellent reputation and that was crystal clear when you saw all the customers waiting patiently to be served. Now this was a golden opportunity for a young lad to play some tricks on both the customers and his Dad.

One of the most hilarious moments in that shop was when all the turkeys were hanging on the metal rails that went all around the ceiling. They went right up to the doorway onto the street and what I did was to tie a length of string onto the last turkey's neck and run it right around the rail and to the tiny office at the back of the shop, so when it was completely queued up and right out of the door, I pulled on the string and the turkey's neck would flinch and it's head would swing outwards into the face of the customer standing next to it.

My God, it makes me cry with laughter now to think of the scream that was heard from the unsuspecting lady standing next to this turkey and then another scream from another lady standing nearby. We were in bloody tears, all of us crying with laughter and I can still see Dad with tears streaming down his face as these ladies were telling him off for scaring them to death, it was the best joke I have ever played on anyone and takes some beating.

I did a similar thing with a pig's head and lowered it down onto customers as they stood by the door. Dad could never keep a straight face when a customer standing in the doorway would scream as this head would come down in front of them.

Some would flinch and say I had an evil sense of humour and threaten me with retribution of some kind!

I definitely think that I get my joker attributes from Dad and what he did to a poor unsuspecting lady that worked in NatWest bank in Cowes. He sellotaped a row of sheep's eyes to the rear window of her car so when she looked into her rear view mirror, all she saw was all these eyes looking her. It must have been bloody scary and especially as it was pitch black when she got into her car and looked into the mirror to reverse the car out.

We had a delivery driver who was very friendly and always had a good laugh with him. We had nick named him Porky because he was a big bloke and he always delivered the pigs to the shop, pretty obvious really.

Anyway, we found out that he had been coming over to Totland to see a certain young lady that we knew quite well and this gave us a brilliant idea for a joke on him. We had heard that she was pregnant and gave him a lot of stick about what we had heard. He denied it all of course, but it didn't really matter because we had the perfect wind up for him.

What we did was to borrow a child's carry cot and an old blanket and we put a pig's head in the cot and hid it out the back. When he came in we told him that the girl, whose name was Sue incidentally, had come in and left something for him to collect and it was out the back. Dad went out there and got it and his face was a picture, fright and surprise and a sense of "Oh my God" was what his face was saying. When Dad handed it to him and he saw the head with a blanket he was in bloody tears and saying "You Bastards, you wait. I will get you all for this."

People seemed very friendly in this small village and it was not long until my brothers and I had new mates to hang about with. Of course my little sister was too young to be going out to play with us boys, but as time went on she began to join us in our adventures. Slowly we began to settle into our new home and surroundings and we kids had all been relocated to our new schools, well all but myself anyway. I stayed on at Cowes High because it would have been pointless moving as I was just about settled half way into the 3rd year.

After about 5 months, Dad, who had stayed on with the butchers in Cowes, finished there and got his own shop up and running.

It was quite weird to have Dad at home nearly all the time as previously he spent a lot of time at work and we really didn't see him that much.

It was time to start exploring this new place and look for places that boys need to make camps and to have other adventures. The first place we investigated was down on Totland beach, particularly along past the old lifeboat building, towards the rocks. While we were walking along we kept coming across tins washed up on the shoreline. These were tins of baby milk powder and hundreds of them too. I remember us opening some of them and throwing this dried milk powder over each other and they made excellent grenades if you opened the top slightly and threw them. Looked like smoke coming out of them, what fun that was and I can still see the beach covered in these cans and the occasional white rock.

We always walked that part of the beach and always found something to amuse ourselves with. We never got bored or into any trouble either. One day, we decided to try and climb up to Headon Warren from the beach but we had never encountered blue slipper clay before.

You can imagine the mess we got into trying to reach the Warren. Knee deep it was in places and looking back, we were quite lucky we didn't get into a dangerous situation as that stuff can be like quicksand when wet.

The eerie sound from the Needles lighthouse was a winter feature in Totland and something you got immune to after a time. When the thick fog rolled in from Alum Bay, across the warren and surrounded the whole village, the sound of the foghorn blasting out into dense nothingness was reminiscent of a horror film. Another sound that we were all brought up with was the chiming buoys out at sea. It always sounded as though there were at least two of these buoys ringing away when the winds or tide started to rock them on the waves.

It's a sound that is always there in the background but you just don't notice it until it's suddenly gone. I always believed these buoys had a giant brass bell inside them, similar to the ones fitted to the old ferries in Cowes in the 70's. Mainly because they sounded exactly the same as a bell and what else would make this sound? I was shocked to learn that there were no magnificent old bells inside the buoys at all and just an old piece of RSJ hanging on a length of chain and banging against the sides of the steel cage of the buoy.

Disappointed and amazed at the same time was the feeling I had as I went along side one of the buoys just off of Fort Victoria, many years later in my boat. It is strange what the mind will perceive when you hear such a sound all through your childhood and then discover it was completely different.

Headon Warren is a vast hilly place that is mostly covered in thick gorse and it lies between Totland and Alum bay and is now protected by the National Trust. Now when we first discovered this arid and strange looking place there was very little protection in place and certainly no barriers or fancy metal signs anywhere. We used to build bases in the lower areas on the coastal side where there was an old concrete building like a sort of lookout post. We managed to get some of Dad's string from the shop and made communication systems with a plastic cup each end and an aerial runway that only Action Men could travel on.

We ran these a long way down the hillside and it took ages to retrieve the things and climb all the way back up. One day we got hold of one of Dad's old filleting knives and used that to cut branches and build a roof on our shelter.

We hid the knife in a large mound, just off the main path, before what is now the Barrow or burial ground. I often wonder if it is still there and was tempted to take my metal detector up there to find it, but I don't think it would go down too well with the National Trust.

One of the most exciting finds we kids had, was, as I mentioned earlier, the small rubbish tip at the base of the Warren on the Alum Bay New Road.

The treasures we found in there were too great for us to tell anyone else of. Out of all the old cars, fridges, ovens and other household scrap we managed to cobble together three bicycles. All had wheels and tyres, although some were solid tyres. We had saddles, pedals wired onto the frame so they didn't go round and that was about it. Absolutely no brakes or mudguards were present but it really didn't matter as these were scrambler bikes as we called them.

We rode all of them home that night and Dad couldn't believe what we had made up out of rubbish. The next day after the rain had stopped, my brothers and I went up to the top of the Warren with our scrambler bikes and from the highest point we free wheeled all the way down to Cliff Road and came out by the Hermitage Hotel. It was the scariest ride I have ever had, no brakes and without mudguards, we were plastered in mud from head to foot. I do not know to this day how we survived the speed at which we travelled and because all the grassed areas were wet, how we stayed on these lethal machines?

After we had made it home and got a telling off for being so muddy we all had to have baths and clean clothes, hence Mum was not very happy with us at all.
The following day we took the bikes back to the dump on Dad's orders as he didn't want junk around the garden, so the recycled bikes gave us some thrills and some trouble but they went back to where they came from, and never to be seen again.

We spent a lot of time on the beach and on the pier too. There was a small arcade on the end of the pier. We became very friendly with the owner of the arcade and his son, who was the same age as I was. We used to help put some of the machines back together after repairs and just watch the friend's father fix the pinball machines. This was fascinating to both Tony and I. We really wanted one of these things at home, but at the time, we couldn't afford one.

The house we moved into included a disused shop with storeroom and separate kitchen and bathroom. This was before it was converted into the bakery and shop. It was very roughly turned into a ground floor flat but with no separate entrance or dividing walls. It shared the main hallway and was not separated from the rest of the building. When we first moved into this house I shared the downstairs room behind the shop with our lodger. It was quite cool having our own little place and our own shower etc. The lodger had his radio cassette player which gave us some music to listen to in the evenings. After a while the lodger moved upstairs to his own room and I took over the shop as my bedroom because my parents needed the middle room for Mum's pie business.

There was something funny about that place and the whole family noticed it from the day that we moved in. Very often, Dad would be sitting in his favourite armchair and facing the television, which was in the corner of the room next to the door. He would be sitting there watching something on telly and suddenly he would see out of the corner of his eye, a shadow go past the crack in the door and it would block out the light momentarily from the hallway. He used to get up and go and see if it was one of us children playing about, when we should have been in bed asleep. He could never actually catch whoever or whatever was going past the doorway and it always puzzled him.

The two neighbours had told us of ghostly things that had happened in their flats and often asked if we had noticed anything odd. We started to put two and two together and figured out that there was something uncanny going on in the house.

When our dog had puppies downstairs, in what is now the bakery, we kept her down there because the flat was not really big enough for the three dogs running about and especially on the masses of stairs. The dogs had their own old sofa to sleep on and were always curled up on it at night, but shivering, even on a hot summer's night.

When the downstairs rooms were so very warm, the dogs would be laying there shivering as if it was freezing cold or maybe scared of something. It was the weirdest thing and we could not understand why this was happening to the dogs, so we moved them upstairs because we thought maybe it was too cold for them down there and they stopped the night shivering and seemed much happier after that.

Solent Middle School, Class of 1975. The four teachers in the centre are: Mrs Terry, Mr Fessy, Mr Jacobs and Mr Terry.

There was the night when my brother's hamster had escaped from its cage and gone missing from the downstairs room where the dogs used to sleep. It was around one o'clock in the morning when Mum's piano started to play on its own; there was no tune but just random notes ringing out occasionally. Everyone heard the piano that night and we were all too scared to go down there until the morning. My brother and I were investigating how the piano had been played because the heavy wooden lid was down over the keys and there was no way anything could have lifted it without making some loud noises. Perhaps we had a burglar? We set about searching the place for any signs of a break in or unlocked doors. There was nothing to suggest that anyone had been in that room at night. So we gave up on that idea as the evidence suggests.

As we were looking around the piano and lifting the lid to the strings inside, the bloody thing started playing again. It made us both jump out of our wits and I think I was about to make a run for it when suddenly this semi black and cream hamster crawled out of the side of the piano, covered in dust and cobwebs. It was the funniest thing to see and it solved the mystery piano player theory.

We did not experience anymore odd things happening in the house for quite a while and I think that was mainly because it was summer time and all of us kids were out playing all day and Mum and Dad were busy with the butcher's shop.

It all kicked off again when my sister was lying in bed waiting for Mum to come up and say goodnight as she always did. As she was lying there, the door was slightly open and an old man poked his head around the door and smiled a ghastly smile at my sister. She was petrified, to say the least, and went screaming downstairs to the lounge, where Mum and Dad were sitting. They all went up to the bedroom but as usual there was nothing to be seen and eventually my sister calmed down and went to sleep.

My second bedroom in Bon Accord was a small cupboard off the main back bedroom and it was sort of triangular in shape due to the roof trusses. It had a tiny window in the roof and a small cupboard at the end, which led into a small loft area with beams and plaster.
I closed that door off because all of the spiders used to come into my room from there and I was not keen on them at the time.

I had a secret floorboard that lifted up and I could hide my treasures under it. I needed that hiding place with my Arthur Daly brother Liam around as he liked selling stuff and usually my things too.

There was not a lot of room when the bed was put in it, but it was cosy and I could close the door for some privacy if I needed it. My two brothers and my sister slept in the adjoining room and this room had an interesting little loft hatch thing above the window. It had a fire escape rope ladder built into the hatch, but we never had any reason to use the thing thank God.

I always wondered what it would have been like to have to climb down it and reach the ground because it was a three storey building. It was a long way down from the window and especially as it led down to this small oblong area, below the banks of the car park and where all the drains from the house appeared to meet.

After about three years of living in that flat, my Mum and Dad had accumulated quite a lot of money from the butchers shop and they decided to buy the house at the rear of our garden and parking area.

We had a large area of concrete and tarmac that belonged with the flat and there was originally one of those pre fabricated concrete garages in one corner but we had that demolished and my Dad had a wooden stable built there instead. We still had enough space to park at least three cars easily and it was very handy to have all the space because the actual grassed area of garden was about 25ft x 10ft and was pretty much useless as a garden. We had a small wooden shed at the very top of the lawn which I decided to convert into a special shed for my moped. I took the door off and put hinges on the bottom and a large rope to lift up the door. So the door was also my ramp into the shed and if I had designed it properly, I would have been able to close the door but as the door was so heavy, I could not lift it with the ropes. That shed was demolished later on and we did not bother to put another up in its place.

The problem with the flat and its garden was the fact that we had to drive under the archway which was next door to the butchery, to get to the rear of the property. This was fine in the summer months and in a standard size car, but when the snow and ice arrived or you had to drive a van under it, it was a nightmare job.

So many people scraped their vehicles on the walls or crashed into the large banks as they came down the steep hill on ice. The previous owner of the new house we bought was a grumpy old chap with huge sideburns and a young French house keeper that followed him around everywhere he went. We never actually worked out if she was his au pair or his mistress. His wife lived in the same house and would often go out alone, while he always went out with this French girl. The rumours were rife at the time and it was almost like a soap opera living in that village.

One winter, when the snow had poured down all day and we had all been sent home from school early, we decided it would be a good thing to build a toboggan track down the hill and under the archway. So we secretly left Dad's hose pipe, outside his stable, trickling down the hill all night.
The next morning we had a beautiful ice slide; but not a small one by any standards. This was the entire width of the road and around three inches thick and we made it even better by shovelling fresh snow on top of it, compacting it with a fertiliser bag full of straw. We just did not take into account that Old Grumpy would want to drive down the hill that morning.

Because of the amount of snow that had fallen over night, we were sure he would have not risked driving down the hill in his new Renault Fuego. Wrong. He drove his car down the hill and just before he reached the arch, he decided to apply the brakes and whoosh! Up the large bank and that was that for the rest of the day. The car was well and truly wedged between the bank and the snow drift on the opposite side and he was going nowhere until the snow had melted. It stayed for about 4 days and none of us wanted to help recovering the car anyway.

When the house at the top of the drive had come up for sale, then my family were determined to own it. Mainly because it was so close to the butchers shop and set right back away from the road. It had so many out buildings with it too, which my Dad was more than happy about. I don't think that I actually got to look around the house before we bought it because I was, by that time, working every daylight hour on the farm.

The flat, *Bon Accord,* as it was known, was adjacent to what was the front lawn of the *Hill House Hotel*. This hotel had apparently burnt down and was demolished and replaced with flats.

The original stone wall and gateway with steps stood in what is now the entrance to Totland car park. There was a wrought iron archway in the gateway with the name of the hotel set in the metal arch. As it was a kind of wasteland and no one ever went there, we often played there and built camps and put Tarzan ropes up in the trees. Many a day was spent playing on that land and it was almost an extension to our small postage stamp garden. We went through a phase of digging massive holes and covering them in sticks and grass as sort of traps to catch any unsuspecting invader. Often we would fill the traps with water and churn up the bottom into a thick wet mud, just to make the whole experience more inviting as it were. Later the following year the whole wasteland was turned into the car park for the village and I met a new friend too. The head of the construction company was staying in the village and he had brought his daughter with him. He was a friendly chap and was always in Dad's shop chatting. Anyway to cut a long story short, the daughter was somewhat bored sitting around all day with no one to talk to and nothing to do as her father was working all day, so my Dad suggested that she come to our house and hang around with me all day. This was the start of the summer holidays and she came over every day and we would go to the beach or listen to records in my room.

My Father was very good at putting me in awkward situations and embarrassing the hell out of me. I cannot remember her name but she was just a friend and no romance developed, mainly because I was too shy at fourteen and was not ready for girls just yet.

Our neighbour was a middle aged lady called Jean; she lived in a flat above the butchery with her son. He was a fair bit older than us kids but regardless, we got on reasonably well with him. Our neighbour was such a sport and put up with such antics from myself and Dad. When she used to lie out on her lawn taking in some sun, we sneaked up with a bucket of water and drenched her; she screamed and chased us all the way down the driveway and into my Dad's shop. One of the best ways of winding her up was to walk up the driveway early in the morning in the summer, because she would always have her bedroom window wide open and I used to throw bread rolls through the window and hear the scream and run for dear life. She always took the pranks in good stead and was never angry at us. If she was, she never showed it.

It was some years after, when we found out about our neighbour Jean falling into one of our traps and getting covered in mud on the wasteland. She used to sneak over the fence and collect kindling for her open fire and one evening she was wandering about looking for dry sticks and she walked over one of our traps and disappeared down this hole and up to her knees in pure mud. She never knew it was us that dug the hole and we never knew that we actually caught someone in the traps until then.

She was the only person I knew who would swim every day of the year down at Totland Bay. Rain or shine, there she was swimming in that freezing water without a care in the world. Sadly passed away a few years ago and my Mum attended the funeral. One in a million, salt of the earth and a lovely neighbour!

Opposite my Dad's butcher's shop was a traditional sweet shop which was probably the busiest little shop in the village. It had everything and anything you desired when you were a sweet toothed kid. Getting off the school coach, I often went straight into the shop to get something to munch on as I was usually starving after the coach ride from Cowes High School.

It was the owner's two sons who I first got to know in the village as they often hung around outside the shop chatting to various people. The eldest son had very long hair and very thick lenses on his glasses. He always reminded me of a cross between Ian Gillan and a Chinese man, because of his glasses. When I first got to know him, I was a bit wary of him because he looked quite scary with his denim jacket with patches all over it. However, as I got to know him, I soon realised he was a fairly quiet chap and not scary at all. I don't think he missed one single game of football because every week, on went the red and white scarf and away to the ferry to see his beloved Saints playing at the Dell or away. There didn't seem to be very many football fans around the village and that was just fine with me. The younger son was a much quieter person, a really nice chap to talk to and was always smiling. He was also a denim jacket with patches sort of dude and I'm sure, a Saint's fan too if I can remember correctly. I got on very well with him and these two lads crop up a little later in my memoirs.

How my dad became friendly with the "Elvis" family, as we knew them I don't know. All I can remember, it was to do with horses. The family were rather old fashioned in their ways and they only seemed to talk about horses or chickens. Their son was about the same age as my brother Tony and was quite a character even then. He was always trying to buy and sell things to us, plus he had false teeth at twelve. This family were always welcoming and kind towards my family. I am sure Tony learnt some tricks from the son because not long after he became friends with them, he was very soon into bottle digging and selling what he found at a local dealers shop. Tony also accompanied his other new friend little Wol on bottle digging adventures. They spent hours together in fields and other remote places, rummaging about in the soil and extracting some kind of treasure to pass on and make money. Little Wol is probably the only friend of Tony's that regularly visits Tony's grave and puts flowers on it for him. I hold that man in the highest regard for his kind and compassionate thoughts of my dear brother.

I could never understand why Jack, the school bus driver, didn't really want me to get off the bus that afternoon at the Elvis family home. I later learned that they had a slight reputation for being wheeler dealers.

On reflection I can see his way of thinking. This bus driver was one in a million as far as the care of his child passengers went. He deserves an award for his care and trust, but I doubt whether anyone would remember his efforts and enthusiasm for his job. I remember one trip. Our whole year at Solent Middle were going to Wroxall to study the disused railway and village. The teachers who were supervising the trip were telling us all about the itinerary of the day and so many children were excited about the fact we were going on the yellow buses and asking to have Jack driving them. That's a reputation, never to be repeated.

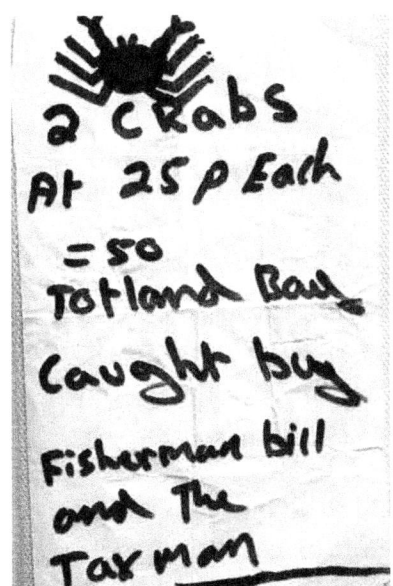

The little sign that Tony made for the sale of crabs
In Dad's butchers shop. Circa 1977.

Anyway, as the bus approached my specially requested stop, I could see my Dad's Daimler parked in the little driveway of the cottage. This car seemed so luxurious with its leather seats and so many buttons on the dashboard.. I loved the purr from the engine and its smell when it was warm inside. Tony was such a little snob when it came to being dropped off at school because if either of my parents attempted to take him to school in anything other than the Daimler he would almost refuse to be dropped outside the school. If he had no choice and Mum used our Vauxhall Viva Estate, she had to drop him away from the school gates in case anyone saw him. He was so funny in his young ways and could reduce us to tears of laughter with his impersonations of family members and people we knew. He would dress up in coats and hats and had very good observation skills for his age.

It was very warm as I stepped off the bus into the road as there were no footpaths on either side plus it was on a sharp bend too. The driver told me to cross in front of the bus as he could see the road both ways.

So I crossed and waved to the bus when I was safely through the gate of the cottage. As I walked round the car I could see the Elvis son Johnny and my younger brother Tony playing together in the garden/yard.

I went into the kitchen around the back of the cottage and there sitting in the lounge was my Dad, drinking tea and chatting about horses to this Elvis friend of his. They always sat in the lounge drinking tea and laughing and joking about some comical horsey story. Looking back, I can remember the lounge being the sacred place of that cottage and the amount of ornaments stacked on shelves and relics of the horse drawn past littering the walls and floor. There were pictures of horses and hunting and God knows how many pictures of Elvis everywhere you looked, plus horse memorabilia on the fireplace and shelves, this was without doubt the home of a family that perhaps travelled the roads by horse and cart or similar. Real traveller folk.

Their garden was a mass of chicken sheds, stables and lean-to constructions housing carriages and traps of many eras. Also there was the log area. This consisted of a large tin shed with the biggest circular saw and engine I have ever seen. I remember being there when logs were being cut and the make shift exhaust of the engine blowing smoke into the air every time the blade slowed down as a large log was pushed onto this gigantic blade and the smell of sawdust, mixed with exhaust smoke and diesel oil wafting around the bottom of the garden.

It was the first time I ever came across a chainsaw in this garden as these things were laying about in the sawdust Dad's friend went out and cleared wood for people and carted it back to the yard for cutting into logs to sell outside the front of the cottage. A roughly painted sign stood next to the wall of the house advertising logs and horse manure.

One afternoon while we were sitting in their lounge and sipping tea, the phone rang and Elvis quickly said to his wife "I'm not here OK." and she obeyed his wishes and told the person on the other end of the phone that he was not here. As Elvis sat there wondering who was on the phone, dad shouted across the lounge "turn the bloody lights off, he'll see you mate." Elvis quickly jumped up and turned the lights off without even thinking about what dad had said. So funny and Elvis didn't live that one down for a long time.

My younger brother adored this friend of my Dad's and would try and go to visit whenever Dad was going there. This friend used to have a thing about 'Elvis' and always had his hair styled like his idol with masses of Brylcream. I never ever saw him wear anything but a blue shirt which was always undone down to his naval, like his hero. His wife was a nice lady but didn't feel the need to copy anyone.

She was always busy with cooking and making endless teas for her man and his friends. Because my little brother was in awe of this fellow then it was only fitting if he had his hair in the same style. It was the funniest thing I ever saw, my brother coming back from the Elvis cottage with Dad and having tons of this Brylcream all over his hair and this new side parting on his head. He thought it was so good and even had his own tub of this greasy muck too. I guess he had been given the stuff by Elvis.

Even after the constant ribbing he got for wearing this stuff, my brother wore it to middle school and even had a school photo of him taken. Luckily he didn't wear a blue shirt or the over decorated cowboy boots that his idol wore. It was the true meaning of innocents and what being a child was like back then.

My final weeks at Cowes high were looming and my thoughts were mainly centered on the end of the long and boring coach journeys every day from Totland to Cowes and back. Originally, this journey was made on a Yellow bus, one of the vehicles provided by the council /education department on the island. Rattly, drafty things and with manually operated folding doors.

I was always fascinated by the locking system, which consisted of a motorcycle lever running a cable to a bolt and the driver used to push down to unlock the doors, very primitive by today's standards but it worked.

During winter months, these buses were bloody freezing cold and the heaters never warmed the thing up at all. It was a fantastic day when were informed by our friendly driver Jack" that the yellow buses were to be phased out and we would be travelling with Fountain Coaches of Cowes. Deepest joy.

I became very friendly with Jack and often went to the bus garage at Spinfish in Freshwater to park the bus and clean it out with him. He used to give me a lift home in his little Morris Minor pickup truck. I liked jack because he was never above you so to speak and always came down to your way of thinking. I had planned to go to Scotland with him to see the sights and visit his family. It seemed such an adventure in his truck, camping out. I was very excited about it indeed and I can see with hindsight, that people would question his motives nowadays for travelling with a fifteen year old boy. I can honestly say there was nothing sinister about Jack in any way, he was just a nice bloke who like me, enjoyed a sense of adventure.

The great Scottish adventure never materialised though because my parents would not let me go.

The Greaves bike in 1980.

The CX500C bike at The Dreens house in 1981.

Chapter 5

19th April 1977 – The saddest day of our lives

I was especially excited at today's bus trip because I had asked the driver if he would drop me off at the top of Hampstead lane in Ningwood, which he agreed to do, although he did question my reasons for getting off at this place again. The strangest thing that has always played upon my mind was when he asked me why I was ending my journey at this place, even though I had got off the bus here countless times before. The look on his face was very disapproving, even after I explained about the horse etc. Jack was never like this towards me, he was very firm with kids who messed about near the doors or who had to get off on a dangerous piece of road for instance.

My Dad had recently bought another horse from his friend and today was the day we were going to take it for a ride down a bridleway and into a meadow near Wellow. It was about a mile walk on the horse from where we kept the animals in Ningwood.

We all left the cottage and drove down to the paddock and went into the field with a bucket of pony nuts which was essential for luring the horses over to you, head collar hidden out of sight of the unsuspecting animal.

Once the horse was enticed you could just about get the collar on if you were quick, but invariably the horse would be quicker in its thinking and you would have to try other lures. We caught the new horse which was a dusky black coloured animal, fairly jumpy at first but seemed to calm after a few munches on its food.

My Dad tacked it up which was fine and my Dad, Tony, Johnny and I went on our way down the main road towards Wellow Top Road. This road lead to first the grain dryer of Harrows farm and then the entrance to the bridleway on the left side. Elvis followed in his pickup truck just to make sure the horse behaved itself on the roads.

I remember walking down the chalk bridle path which was a very rough track indeed and as we walked, my Dad rode the horse towards a very large meadow of lush grass and clover. if you walked through the meadow, you joined another small track which comes out at the entrance of Chessell Quarry.

The sun was shining and walking through this gorgeous meadow felt very lovely and as Dad trotted the horse up and down we sat on the grass just watching Dad and chatted.
After a few lengths of the meadow, Dad swapped with Johnny, Elvis's son and he rode the horse up and down a few times but decided to canter the animal and was almost at the point of galloping but seemed to stop short of this.

Johnny was a very fearless boy and was always breaking in his Dads wild horses for him. He always seemed to have a cut or graze on his arms and once he had cuts all over his face because I think the horse he was riding bucked him off into the hedge.

Tony was sitting near me on the grass and pulling stalks of grass and chewing on them like some cowboy would. It was not long when Johnny decided to swap with me. I got on this dark horse and rode it round a few times but I was not as confident as Johnny was, so I didn't race the thing up and down too much.
My jeans were irritating my legs because riding horses with jeans on is not advisable because the legs ride up and rub your skin, just below the knee and is bloody painful after an hour or so.

I had noticed Tony and Johnny chatting together on the grass as I rode back up to where the others were sitting and got off the horse and Dad said 'was it alright?' I said yes it was a bit nervous but seemed to be ok. With that my Dad asked Tony if he wanted to have a ride. He said yes and climbed aboard and rode around for a while.

Not really watching what Tony was doing as I was talking to Johnny as he was only trotting around the meadow in a gentle manner. He took the horse to the end of the grassland, towards the track and cantered back towards us. He looked very happy flying across the grass at speed until he reached the hedges at the end where he slowed up and began to turn around and head back towards us.

When I originally wrote this book, I could not bring myself to describe what actually happened the day that Tony died. It was too traumatic to relive that moment. We, the children, did not attend his funeral because Mum and Dad did not want us to suffer the pain of it all, so our lodger took us to Ventnor Pier for the afternoon and I remember asking him half way through the afternoon "do you think it's over yet?" he did not know and just said "forget about that and have fun on the machines."

I was too young to understand a funeral and it may have hurt me even more inside, or perhaps it would have given me the chance to say my goodbyes to Tony in a more positive way. I was very traumatised by the accident.

I personally always relate what I saw to what people saw in the War because it was that graphic and horrible.
However, at least during the war it was somewhat expected, whereas the accident was so unexpected that it was difficult to make any logical sense of it.

I had no counselling for that experience and my school just seemed to forget about me at the time. Since over forty years have passed, I now know I should have had some sort of help with what happened because everyone I have ever talked to about that day has said "did you have counselling?" I have tried to seek help with the memories that are still as clear now as they ever were and I saw my GP and told him all about the accident, but not in detail.

Since the original manuscript was compiled, I have for the first time been able to describe what happened. I overcame this by actually writing the whole event down one night and printing it. It wasn't as difficult to type as it would have been to describe verbally. After achieving this barrier that had stood for almost forty years in my head, I finally broke down the wall. I wanted to share this with my mother, brother and sister but they were not ready for this and so I didn't at that time. Later, whilst speaking to my mum about that day, she told me something that I had completely forgotten about in the aftermath of shock. She told me that my Father had said that I had put Tony in the recovery position by the time my Dad had reached us. This was because I had passed my first aid exam at school some weeks before the accident. What follows is the full detailed account of what happened;-

As I ran down the bumpy lane and trying not to trip over the large stones, my dad was just behind me as I watched Tony fall from the side of the horse and land on the track in front of me.
There was a lot of dust in the air as I reached my brother lying motionless on the ground. My dad arrived just as I looked down at Tony and he tried to shield me from seeing him but i just stared down at Tony laying there and pushed dad away from me.

I could see blood pouring from his nose and ears and his head was split open at the back. I couldn't believe what I was seeing; I couldn't speak as I saw his hands were grazed and bleeding. My Tony looked so still, I wanted him to wake up and open his eyes again but I knew he couldn't. He didn't move at all and I could hear his breathing but it wasn't how he normally breathed. His eyes were closed as I knelt down to talk to him and I could see his favourite black boots were scuffed all over and one was ripped to shreds on one side.

His tee shirt was torn apart and covered in dust and blood. Suddenly Tony gave out a sigh and I was trying to talk to him, but Dad and his friends, who had driven up the track, took me away from him and I was crying for my Tony. Dad was crying and I saw him hold Tony in his arms as the ambulance arrived and I heard Dad say "he's dying" to the people surrounding him.

I was taken to Dad's friend's grandfather's bungalow and given brandy as I was crying and so scared at what I had seen. I was there for more than an hour and I cannot remember who came and took me home to Totland.

Mum asked me where Tony and Dad was when I arrived home but I just couldn't speak to her, I couldn't tell her, I just couldn't. I remember being in the kitchen when Dad came home and came up the stairs and told my mum what had happened. She knew something was wrong and I remember her screaming at Dad, not believing what she was hearing as Dad told her Tony had died in his arms as the ambulance men arrived on the scene.

I ran upstairs and looked at the empty bed next to mine with Tony's little rabbit teddy bear on it. Colin came home and was told of Tony's death and he was hysterical and cried all night long. Clare was a lot younger and I don't think she really understood exactly what had happened to Tony. I wanted Tony to be with me that night because I kept looking at that empty bed all night, hoping that he would be there asleep and wake up with us, as he always did.

It was only this year when I was walking around a car boot sale and I bumped into Johnny, my brother's friend who was there that day. He said to me "I remember the last words that Tony said to me and I can't go a single day without thinking about that day." I was absolutely shocked that someone else had the same feelings as I did. I have made arrangements to go and see him soon and talk about what happened, maybe it will help us both.

My uncle came over to look after Mum and Dad and help out with the butcher's shop. It was closed for nearly a week because of it all.

First of all the police were kind and understanding to the needs of the parents but one such officer was hell bent on blaming my Dad for his son's death. Trying to put a manslaughter charge for what happened and I never knew that this happened until a very long time afterwards when Dad told me. No wonder he ran away to the mainland after all of that hassle and thanks to the stupid police officer.

I missed out on nearly six months of schooling and it destroyed all my chances of getting any qualifications before I left school which was not too long afterwards. It was hell on earth and no one should have to endure such things, but I'm afraid during that era the needs of teenagers was not high on the list of priorities.

Tony playing badminton at Totland Country Club in 1977. Tony Isaacs was his coach.

Chapter 6

The last year of high school

The final 5th year class at school was designed I think, to give us a more vocational insight into working for a living, rather than taking exams and leaving school with no idea of what was expected of you at work. 5-PA was its title and the abbreviation stood for personal achievement. We spent one week in school and the following week at a hospital or special needs institution. Our choices were:

1. St Catherine's or Whitwell ward at St Mary's.
2. Browning ward at Whitecroft.
3. Medina house.
4. Shopping for old people in Cowes.
5. School runner.
6. Haylands farm.

I did the shopping job once but never did the runner thing, because I was too shy to go into classes of pupils or teachers I did not know.
I often saw the other year's runners coming into our class and thought you would need to be a bit thick to do that job, hence another reason I never put my hand up for that one.

I spent most of my out weeks between St Catherine's ward and Browning ward at Whitecroft hospital. The latter was a scary place with the longest corridors and cell like rooms and the smallest staff canteen I ever went to. The patients were mainly there for mental or psychological reasons and some were very frightening to me. One particular lady chased me and my friend with slippers, trying to beat us. Not the nicest place to be but the staff were very nice and really involved us kids in every possible activity when they could.

Our main teachers were our form teachers in the PA group and they were reasonably strict. I remember having English with Mr. Chart and instead of concentrating on the punctuation exercise we were all doing, he wandered off the subject and we ended up hearing all about the Second World War instead. He was ex RAF and undoubtedly experienced some fighting in the war. He was a fair chap and only got angry at some of the complete idiots in our class, who often disrupted everyone else's learning. I liked Mr. Chart and his well known names for idiots, such as Fat Head, followed by the black board rubber flying towards his victim's head. Many a head he caught with that rubber thing and he was an excellent shot with it too.

Mrs. Ding was a very quiet person as far as I could tell and she always taught her lessons calmly and without too much shouting. Although you dare not get on the wrong side of her because she was very firm and would have you down to the year head's office like a shot. I often saw her in town when we were loitering with intent of something and she always said "Hello" to me, and that was before she was my form teacher. I am sure that she taught Tony at Denmark Road School at some point because she always spoke to him when she saw him out of school as well.

Our class were often looked down upon from a great height by the sixth form kids and teachers. We were known as the *thick group* who were not taking any exams before leaving school. Talk about tarring everything with the same brush.

There were some people in our class who could have taken exams and even reached university if they had the right up bringing and were guided correctly at school.
To me, it is nothing to do with exams because all they are is a memory test and no practical use in the real life that you will go through.

I learnt more at thirty five than I did at school and ended up with a HND in Managing Outdoor Environments from Portsmouth University, GNVQ Advanced Leisure and Tourism with Distinction and a (B) in English Language. This just goes to show that learning can be achieved whatever your age. Being a fifteen year old kid was not, in my view, the time to be stuck in a bloody classroom. Kids should be learning life skills at that age and finding out what is going to be lying ahead in their lifetime. Another example was one of the chaps in my class is now a manager of a supermarket and many others have achieved success in life without exams.

I was in the same class with a boy who was a complete loony, and caused so much trouble in and out of school. He could be quite violent at times too and everyone was wary of him and his mood swings. He lived in Gurnard when he first came to our class and had moved down from the mainland as his parents had bought a shop here.

I really did not like this lad one little bit because he was a thief and a liar and made up these fantastic stories about his Dad's boat and how we could borrow it at the weekend.

We had all planned a trip on this boat and were ready to meet up on the beach one Saturday morning, when someone who knew his Dad told us he had no boat and how we should not listen to this boy as he lied all the time.

After that episode, no one wanted to know him and he started hanging around with some really unsavoury characters. In the end he got into trouble with the police for shoplifting.

I went right through the fifth year after missing almost all of the fourth year due to my brother's death. The loony boy was out of our lives at long last and did not follow us into the PA group thank God. When I left school I had never seen or heard of him at all and that was fine by me, because I was too busy with my first girlfriend to be bothered by him.

I was riding my Suzuki 400 through Freshwater one evening and when I got home my brother Liam said he had met someone who knew me, and wanted some help with his silver Superdream, which was not running very well. I asked who this chap with the bike was and my brother said "a bloke called Ian". I said I don't know anyone called "Ian" and my brother said "Well he knows you from school he said."

I was still none the wiser and told my brother I would have a look at his bike for him, so when you see him you can let him know.

A week later and I was in my workshop fixing someone's Yamaha RD200's, when this Superdream turned up with this skinny looking dude aboard it. He had what looked like trousers made of bar cloths with all the beer and lager brand names on them. He looked a right mess to be honest and I wondered if that's the rider, what is the bike going to be like? He came over and took off his crash helmet and I could not believe my pigging eyes, it was that "Ian" the loony from school but with a completely different personality from back then.

We chatted all evening as I fixed up his bike and it now ran as it should. It turned out he was living in Freshwater and his parents had bought a restaurant but he did not live with them anymore.
We kicked about on the bikes for quite a while and one night I had to do a disco at a biker's party out near Shalfleet and he came along and did some of the music for me. Ian still hung about with us Dudes on bikes for quite a while.

His parents moved off the island and went up to Cambridge somewhere and it was on a trip up there on his Superdream that he died suddenly. Apparently he pulled over in a lay by and died at the side of the road from liver failure or something equally fatal. I could not believe it when I heard from one of our mates one night. He had changed like no one had changed before and I had never seen such a turn round of character in my life from a violent person to a calm personality. Rest in Peace my friend, you are missed greatly. RIP Ian Moore.

Going to back to our work experience, St Catherine's ward was for the elderly patients and compared with Whitecroft, was easy. We had some fun times here and played board games with the patients who were able to. We took them out to the duck pond in their wheelchairs and fed the ducks with bread that was saved by the nurses from dinner time.

We learnt to make beds and always helped the nurses with various tasks. There were two special nurses on this ward who I am not going to name because it could possibly cause them some trouble and in my mind, they did no wrong.

They used to tease us a lot and one of them was always making suggestive comments to me. She was a pretty nurse too which probably didn't help the situation at all. I don't remember exactly what or how it happened but the nurse asked me to help her make up a bed which had the screens around it and got me to lay on the bed and then she stroked my hair and kissed me and I responded and kissed her for quite a while. I have no regrets about what happened that day because I had a crush on her and wanted to kiss her very much. She was only 3 years older than me so what the hell if I was only fifteen.

I enjoyed what she did and it was a wonderful moment in my mind which I will never forget. You have to remember that this was the 70's and Safeguarding was a whole different ballgame- pun intended.

In the last year of school it seems music almost crept up behind me and jumped into my head without any warning. What made me suddenly take an interest in the radio or charts I don't know.

It's a strange transition from a normal fifteen year old to the punk rock loving person I became, almost overnight too.. I went from wearing home made school trousers and a pair of normal wedge shoes, to the black Dr Marten boots with safety pins with a part of the pin cut out with a pair of pliers so that it looked as if the pin was through the skin.

I coloured my hair with food colouring from Mum's food cupboard, and carried my first portable tape deck around with me. They had the tone of a radio in a metal barrel and ate batteries like there was no tomorrow, but they were all we had back then and the *Sex Pistols, Stranglers* and anything else that was slightly rebellious, sounded great at the time.

We were scorned upon at the Hospital canteen when working on the wards and people just thought we were mad wearing hundreds of safety pins and sometimes, linked up paper clips to form a chain that went from the pin in your ear to the badge on your blazer. My God it was so silly and if there is one thing I can look back on and cringe, it was the punk dress code thing.

I attended two weeks of work experience which was arranged by my school. This consisted of one week at St Mary's Hospital catering department, and a week at my Father's butchers shop.

The catering department was very interesting and I really enjoyed the company of the staff there. My tasks were varied and one of the most fascinating things I had to do was use the bread and buttering machine. I remember putting reams of bread through and wondering how much bread do the patients eat?

The manager was a nice chap and gave me a good report when I had finished my five days. Lunch time was particularly good, as being classed as a full staff member; I could choose between anything on the menu and enjoy coffee after dinner. It made me feel quite privileged and important, having lunch amongst all these professional people.

Being a fifteen year old lad, unworldly and rather shy, I was constantly teased by the female staff and particularly by one student nurse whom I knew very well, as she travelled on my school coach and was the girlfriend of our long term lodger.

I dreaded meeting her in the vast corridors of the hospital because she was always with the biggest gang of student nurse friends who giggled and turned my face into a furnace with their smiles.

She knew it embarrassed me and damn well used it for her pleasure too. You will read more about her later because she played a very important part in my life.

My next work experience appointment was with my Father in the family butchers shop and this was truly my wake up call and made me realise work was not like school in any way. The early mornings, freezing cold hands all the time and the mincing of stuff that turned my stomach, contributed towards my later decision not to pursue this occupation.

One job I truly hated was making pet food, which consisted of putting the innards of cows, sheep and pigs through a mincer. I did it but hated every minute of it. My only forte was making sausages, which I seemed to have had a natural talent in doing that job. Mind you, after the second batch of 20lb, the novelty soon wore off.

My Father worked hard and made the business a success. He really enjoyed embarrassing me in the shop in front of customers. A favourite trick of his was to stand behind the counter which faced the front window with me and whistle to some pretty girl outside and then duck down, leaving me standing there as the girl smiled at me.

My face turned to a deep beetroot colour and I used to run to the back of the shop and hit my Dad in a playful manner. One week of beef burger making, sausage and bloody pet food and I was glad to be back at school for two weeks until I left.

It was a Wednesday afternoon and early closing in Totland and Dad had closed up the shop and come indoors for a cup of tea. It had started to snow around ten o'clock and it was starting to settle on the pavement outside the shop. I was at home and so was Mum, when Dad came indoors and we all sat in the lounge window seat and watched the snow pouring down on the roundabout.

Then Dad said that he would go down to Freshwater and drive up by the middle school and see if Tony and Liam were let out early because there would not be any buses running by the time the school kicked out.

So I went with Dad in his little Bedford butcher's van and we made our way down through the village and then down to Freshwater High Street.

The snow was getting worse, with much heavier flakes landing on the little van windscreen. I remember it was bloody freezing in that van because the heater was useless and being a panel van; the thing was never warm inside and always had that butcher's smell about it too.

It was not the best vehicle in the world for snow exploration and mainly because it had the narrowest wheels and tyres that Bedford could possibly find to put on it. Glad we did not own it, it was bloody awful. It belonged to the butcher in Cowes that Dad had worked for and it was probably the last weeks of his employment with that firm. He was clever and used the van a lot to get his own shop set up first before he had to give up the thing.

We went down to Moa Place and turned up towards the school and sure enough all the kids were already running about in the snow throwing snowballs at everything that moved.

It was a very happy day for the whole school to come out early and to have deep snow all around them. We looked for Tony and Liam but they were nowhere to be found near the school so we started to drive back up through the village and up near the fire station.

There walking along together were the unmistakeable couple of likely looking lads, Tony and Liam. We put them in the back of the van and took them back to Totland. Dad couldn't get the van up the hill and under the archway as the snow was so heavy and had settled all the way up the hill, so he parked it in front of the shop and my bedroom.

Christmas dinner for Liam and Sarah in Bon Accord. Circa 1977.

Now we had a coach to travel to school on, with radio, luxury seats and heating. No more draughty yellow bus with rattling doors and hardly any heating. Taking into account that I had to be on the coach at seven fifteen am and it arrived at school at eight forty five am, it was a fairly long trip to make twice every day and was probably twice the amount of time that most other school children spent travelling.

A new bunch of drivers to get to know and a journey that was made so much more comfortable with the change in vehicles for us kids. There were a couple of very dramatic moments on our journeys to and from school and one in particular, sticks in my mind.

We were just about to go up the Thorness side of Rolls Hill, it was very icy and snowing, as we went up the hill the coach slid off the road and ended up with the rear section hanging over the hedge on the left side. The field beyond the hedge line was a hell of a lot lower than the road and it reminded me of *The Italian Job* and their coach hanging off the cliff. It was a very scary experience and we had to wait until another coach came to get us and that took over an hour so we were late for school, oh dear.

Another incident was when one of the front leaf springs on the coach snapped and came right up through the floor, right by my bloody feet too. The coach started to lean right over and there was a terrible scraping sound coming from the side where the spring had broken. Another hour long wait, and very late for school again.

Finishing my day at the hospital as part of my week there, I would have to wait for over an hour until the coach came anywhere near me, so I decided to see how far I could walk from St Mary's hospital towards Thorness Bay. I got as far as Rolls Hill on the first walk and then as far as the *Little Whitehouse* petrol station just along the road.

It was a nice walk and it was on that walk that I discovered the plaque on the side of a small cottage that claimed the original headmaster from Rugby school was born there. Funny what you see when you walk instead of riding in a car or bus. I got very wet one day but I still carried on and soon dried out on the coach and at least it was better than sitting at the boring bus stop for an hour.

There were only three of the Fountain coach drivers who I really liked. They were Dave, Barry and Timmy.

Our regular driver was Timmy, who happened to own the tea rooms at Brook known as *Hanover House*. I always remember him asking me to get him a pork pie from my parent's butchers in the morning.

I was quite often late getting up in the morning but Timmy would always wait for me or waste some time by chatting to my Dad, while I got myself together.

He was very partial to my Mum's home made pies and I often had to carry one over to him when he had dropped us off at the bus stop. Dave the driver was always driving at speeds I never knew a coach could travel at. He always had the radio turned up loud to the delight of some of us who had made the discovery of music. Dave was very strict with regard to safety and the correct procedures on the coaches.

On one occasion, a stupid boy from Bouldnor, near Yarmouth, who loved himself and was very upper class, threw a bottle out of the window while speeding along the road towards Shalfleet. It hit the verge and bounced back and hit the rear of the coach. The noise attracted the attention of Dave and he just slammed the brakes on, reversed up to where the bottle lay and ordered the idiot off the coach and told him to pick the bottle up then drove off

That idiot never got on the coach again and I think he was banned by the company from travelling on our coach. Good riddance I thought, as I disliked him because he always chatted to my girlfriend and this made me jealous, although I never showed it. A typical upper class twit, who had the common sense of a snail.

One of the funniest coach drivers we had after Timmy passed away, was Barry. He was a very comical chap and we always had a good laugh with him. He wasn't always a happy, smiley man because he got really stressed when his coach had been filled with litter after a coach trip somewhere Barry lived in Freshwater himself, so he knew most of us and where we came from.

The Yamaha YR5 350cc twin that Marcus and I were *rebuilding in 1981.*

Chapter 7

First Love

Whilst travelling from school on the yellow bus I managed to overcome my shyness and began to chat with a pretty girl who had dark hair cut quite short. S tall compared to the other girls on the bus. She had a curvy figure and to me she was perfect in every way.

I remember how she would always flick back her hair and give me a smile as she walked past me on the school bus.

This made me feel excited but not in a sexual way, but rather in a more romantic feeling. We sat together on the coach occasionally but most of the time she sat with her friends, because it just wasn't the done thing to sit with a boy for God's sake. She was quite shy too and I think that is why she hardly ever came close to me in front of her mates and other children.

We phoned each other every night and chatted for hours, to the horror of my parents and their phone bill. I was invited to her house one weekend and stayed the whole Sunday which was great because she lived on a farm and had a swimming pool in the garden.

We walked around her fields and were chatting about such things as music or the most popular thing around at this time - Star Wars.

One day I heard her talking to another girl on the bus about horses. She apparently went horse riding at weekends and because I rode my Father's horse a lot, I realised that I had something in common with my future girlfriend

Some of the following extracts are from my diary and I may have modified the entries slightly, to save any embarrassment.

Sunday the fifteenth of January nineteen seventy eight; I could not pluck up enough courage to actually ask her out myself. So I asked her friend to do it for me but I think she just mentioned that I liked her a lot and did not really ask her out for me. So I had to just get enough courage to actually ask her myself and it took me a long time to do this. Every time I managed to chat to her, I just couldn't do it. Eventually I just asked if she wanted to meet up on her horse and go riding together. She said she would have to check with her parents and arrange it all properly.

Happiness was an understatement; I was in awe of her and could not stop thinking about the coming Sunday afternoon.

Our parents would of course have to be involved because we were riding alone and my Father's horse was kept some 3 miles away from the place where we were to meet up. I think it was my Mum that called her Mum and made sure it was all ok to go ahead with this ride. I remember getting dressed up in my jodhpurs and shiny black boots. I wore a riding hat with the very fashionable chin harness too, which I thought made me look very dapper at the time.

Mum and Dad took me to the paddock that we rented from the Elvis family. We caught the horse and I tacked him up but it was not easy on my own so Dad had to help me.
I seemed to have no strength in my arms and my belly was quivering all over and this was so intense and not what I had felt ever before. It was time to make tracks and say goodbye to my family, who said "take care and have fun!"
I took the main road through the tiny village of Shalfleet and this was before traffic lights were installed. Traffic was minimal and the ride to the little lane that goes from Hebberdens Farm buildings, towards Newtown was deserted and very quiet. It was bright but cold, one of those days when you would not want to be on a horse when the sun went down.

I waited for a long time for my girl to appear, all the while worrying that she would not show up. I walked the horse up and down the small lane because he was very partial to verges and his strength was a hundred times of mine. When he wanted something he usually won the battle and munched on the long wild grasses and anything else he could reach, boredom sets in very easily when you stand in one place for long periods on a horse. So constant moving is the best solution, it keeps the animal's mind occupied.
In theory anyway.

After the tenth or so walk up and down the lane, my heart suddenly lifted as my girlfriend appeared from the bend in the road.
As she drew closer I could see she was not very happy by the look on her face. I searched my mind for a milliseconds, for anything that I may have done which would cause her to be unhappy.

My worries were wasted because as she came up to me she apologised for being late. She continued to explain that there had been some trouble with either catching her horse in the field or tacking up, I can't remember exactly what went wrong but she was cursing her mother for some reason.

Ellie's horse was called *Sovereign* and seemed pretty good on the roads but had the same obsession as my horse with verges and low trees. We had a nice ride together and it seemed we had quite a lot in common with each other and we made each other laugh, which was nice because I was so nervous all the time I was with her. Having common interests helped to break the ice and overcome the shyness that we both appeared to share. She asked me to ring her later that evening so we could talk some more.

My proper first date done and a success as far as I was concerned. We very soon realised it was time for me to leave as I had a few miles to ride back to the paddock and hopefully, my dad will be there before me.

I said goodbye and watched her ride down the main Road to her lane. I set off back to Ningwood and got there before the cold air started to fall. Dad was waiting and after taking the tack off Topaz and giving him a feed, we set off home for dinner with me walking on air!

That was the first and only time I have ever gone on a date by horseback, unusually romantic and completely innocent in every respect, meaning there was no lust or passion involved just pure excitement and young love. I will always remember with fondness that first date.

That evening I rang her to make sure she got back home safely and I think we talked for over an hour. I could feel my whole body tingling inside during the following days. I did not seem to need to eat very much and my outside interests were almost redundant as my thoughts turned to this beautiful girl. I dreamt of her and wrote her name on so many things, it was if I needed to broadcast my feelings to the world and inform everyone that I was falling in love.

My whole life changed in a matter of days as my thoughts and feelings centered upon this dark haired girl. She had the power to turn me into jelly with the flick of her hair or the glow of her smile. Young love!

Twenty ninth of January nineteen seventy eight, our First Kiss; It was some 20 days until we had our first kiss and that feeling was the most beautiful moment that I remember. It was gentle and without the physical passion of a more mature sexual encounter. Everything seemed so simple because there were no complications of sexual responsibility. She had the most beautiful skin, soft and warm on my lips. I was falling in love and my life had ignited and the feeling was like no other that I had experienced before.

Reading back over this after some forty five years, makes me realise what a soppy, romantic I was, and still am.

The diary I had for Christmas in nineteen seventy seven was just a little tiny one which had the underground map inside and a few other interesting pages. I put my school coach pass inside it along with my first aid certificate from school.

Here are some other short excerpts from the diary on various interesting subjects throughout the year: - One excerpt reads; *The Sex pistols break up Thursday the nineteenth of January nineteen seventy eight.* I loved the pistols when they were in their heyday but not so keen on them now I have matured, musically anyway.

Another memorable date for me was the *third of April the nineteenth seventy eight* because it was the day my parents bought my moped from Calbourne motorcycles. Moped was delivered on the *eighth of April nineteen seventy eight* but I was not allowed to ride on it until my birthday, the following Thursday. I have taken entries from this diary and added them to various subjects in this book. It just adds a sense of validity to when and how all of these things occurred in my young life.

Me and Topaz, the horse I rode on my first date with Ellie In 1978.

I really missed our dear little cat Misty who had past away earlier that year. I was given the chance to pick out a kitten from my new girlfriend's farm.

I chose this little black bundle of fun and brought him home to the flat. I picked him out because when Ellie was making up the powdered milk for the calves on her farm, Monty was the first kitten in the bucket lapping up so much milk I thought he may explode any moment. He was a lovely cat and had so many tricks up his paws and even Dad loved him and he was not a cat lover at all.

One day my Dad came into the kitchen from the bathroom with no shirt on and Monty thought that's a nice climbing thing and pounced from the table and straight onto Dad's bare chest. My god that made him jump as all claws went out for adhesion to his skin. Dad screamed like a little girl. So funny and one of many things that cat would get up to. He lived from the time we were in the flat in Totland, right up until around nineteen ninety, when we moved back into Newport. I loved him very much and was not there when he had to be put down as someone had shot him with an air gun and I am pretty sure that I know who that was too.

Nineteen seventy eight started with deep snow when our village got cut off from the rest of the island. Taking walks up to Tennyson downs through the deepest snow I have ever seen and seeing the whole area in peace with its white duvet.

Not a car or lorry to be seen anywhere, an eerie quiet came to us and lasted for what seemed a lifetime. Even the meat deliveries and food lorries could not get through, hence shops started to run out of things to sell. I remember the milk from dairy farms had to be dumped because tankers could not get to the farms.

I never forget Kitty's brilliant idea to go out in the snow with a full diver's wetsuit on. He said it would be warmer and drier than clothes, which was probably right but he did look bloody stupid walking through the village in this black rubber suit with the hood on and his tall skinny physique.

What a laugh me and Dad had when we saw him. I don't think we left our village for at least 10 days or so, school was cancelled to the joy of all us kids but the biggest problem for me was I could not get to see my girl.
We talked on the phone and discussed our frustration of not being able to see each other for so long, I toyed with walking to her place but it was about ten miles and in these conditions, Mum would not let me. Eventually the snow melted and life started to get back to normal, school did too, worse luck.

Horse Show in Sandown eleventh of June nineteen seventy eight; Every chance Ellie and I had to spend time together, we managed to persuade our parents that they should give us a lift to each others houses. One Sunday she came over to my house early so we could go with my family to a horse show for the day. I remember we were getting a bit bored with the show so we went for a walk around the town for a couple of hours.

Ellie stole my diary and wrote; *Went to horse show with Berry and his family. Really enjoyed myself, went down Sandown and to beach. Hurt Berry, wish I'd never done it, he must think I'm a bitch.* I think what she meant was accidentally knelt between my legs and caught the veg. The feelings between us were so innocent and so happy we got along very well and became very close indeed.

Regardless of actually getting lost walking around Lake for the first time in our lives. We came back to my house in Totland and went for a walk down to the pier and sat on the grass above the pier and kissed.

Then a group of lads that knew me walked past and shouting out some embarrassing things, I went red as a beetroot and she was laughing at my embarrassment. Typical of my luck and I thought to myself "I'm not going through that again today so we shall go back to my house instead." So off we went back to my bedroom which was now at the very back of the flat.

Ellie wrote; *really missing Berry ringing and talking to me, what have I gone and done?"* So this was not my doing this time and she wrote; *I hoped barbecue would work out. It was a good idea, house point for planning barbecue.* This was Ellie's plan to get us back together and it was due to take place at Totland beach on Saturday the thirteenth of May. Ellie wrote; *Barbecue at Totland, Berry and I back together again. Great, I love him so much.*

I remember it so well and it was a lovely night down on the beach and Ellie looked gorgeous as ever. It took us a while to actually build up the courage to talk to each other again, but it was a success and I was so happy that night.
I really loved that girl and adored her with all my heart.

On the eighth of August the diary reads; *Ellie came over and we had a great time up in the hay.* That referred to Dad's stables up at the back of Bon Accord, He had one stable as a feed store and it was full of horse feeds and straw. He built a lean-to at the back of the feed store and it was full of hay. We spent quite a lot of time sneaking up there when Ellie was over at my house.

Dad bought all three of us these Stunt kites which were supposed to be strong and good for special tricks etc. I think we used them once or twice and after that they live in the toy cupboard for years. I could never really see the attraction of the things, mainly because they just went up in the air and that was it.

One Sunday morning, myself, my brother Liam and his mate Dave went up to the playing field behind the houses in St Saviour's Road and decided to take this kite with us for some fun. So the kite was launched and the thirty odd miles of string was in a right tangle within the first few minutes of flying.

So we had to de tangle it all and finally got it back up in the air. Unfortunately, Dave had no idea how to fly the thing and as it ploughed into the electric cables of a nearby pole, there was a huge bang and a flash as molten aluminium poles dripped down on to the grass, mixed with melting plastic. Luckily the string that was used on the kite was not conductive and Dave got away with no shocks but just sustained some hot plastic on his head.

Obviously we were all laughing at Dave and his flying skills until we met up with kitty, who lived across the Road as he said that the whole Road had lost electricity and being a Sunday late morning when everyone was cooking their long awaited Sunday roasts. We got out of the area as quick as we could and saw an electricity truck flying past us as we reached our house on the boadway.

We later learned that the whole village was without power for several hours that day and no one had a roasty that day I can tell you. Even my Mother was complaining about the electricity going off, but we kept quiet and no one ever knew it was us three and the ill fated kite that did it.

There was an unfortunate incident that I wasn't directly responsible for but anyway I got the blame for. I had swapped my old moped for this motocross 125 Suzuki and it needed some doing up, well I thought it did. The side panels were plastic and needed repainting so I went down to the local garage and got myself a couple of cans of yellow spray paint and sprayed these panels in my bedroom.

Now we all know that you should not use this stuff indoors if you can help it because the fumes are lethal and you end up with coloured nostrils too. Being so naive and unaware of these facts, I just carried on until the panels were nice and shiny and they looked so much better too. Alas the hamster which my youngest brother had put in its cage in the adjoining room did not look as good. It didn't survive the paint spraying and died the next day. I just did not realise and got a good telling off for that episode and on reflection, quite rightly too.

It was a very unique bedroom with so many curtains on the front windows and quite a few extra cupboards built into the walls. A door straight onto the pavement and enough room to park a car outside the window, not that I had a car but the space was there just in case.
When my mate Kitty came round, we used to walk over to the special side door of the pub and buy some crisps or a mars bar and then play records while reading bike mags. We spent many nights drooling over pictures of bikes and models in crash helmets. Life was so easy then and as long as you had records and food, you were fine and dandy.

The lodger decided to go out one night and buy a KTM motocross bike for riding on the Warren. He went down to the phone box, next to the bus shelter and rang this bloke in Ryde about the bike. Then we had the problem of transporting it back to Totland. The lodger had a car but it would never fit in that.

I think it was my mate Kitty who came up with a plan to go and see the bloke who lived opposite his house on St Saviour's Road. The bloke had a big land rover and that would carry the bike easily. So we went up to see the chap, who lived right on the corner and had double the garden of everyone else in the street. He did a lot of tree cutting and logging and you could always hear a chainsaw going in his garden. The lodger agreed a price and we all went to Ryde that night to get the bike.

The KTM was in very nice condition and I don't think it had been used very much and especially not off road as it was spotless. We got it home and we didn't have a shed so we put it in my bedroom, which I had no complaints about. It stayed in my room for ages because basically, the lodger was scared to take it out, firstly because of the fear of getting nicked by the local Bobbie and secondly, because the bike was so powerful and he had only ridden a FS1E moped before.

I had never actually seen a motocross bike before and this thing had some unusual features, such as these weird panels on the sides with big oval plates mounted on them. I later learned that these were for the rider's number to be placed. There was also the oval plate on the front, where the head lamp would have been.

Also there was a third lever on the handlebars, which was smaller than that of the clutch and front brake levers? This lever was of course a decompression device which was used to make starting the bike easier. It had the biggest knobbly tyres I had ever seen before and the colours were very bright. The tank was red but not made of steel, but made of fibreglass - never seen such an unusual machine before but it was nice to look at and very good at making my mates jealous too.

One Sunday morning, we pushed the KTM up the footpath behind the Hermitage Hotel, on cliff Road. It was very muddy and the weight of that bike was a killer pushing it up that narrow and steep lane.

We reached the first open space and tried to start it. Now when you are fifteen years old and never tried to kick start a motocross bike, you get a pretty nasty shock if it kicks back at you because the compression is unbelievable and pushing that lever down took all my might. I was not strong or experienced enough to start it.

The lodger managed to make it fire once, but gave up after the fifteenth kick. We decided the only way forward was to push it right to the top of the Warren and he would bump start it. So after the longest push up the hill on a very damp, early Sunday morning, we reached the top and he got on the bike and started to freewheel in neutral, down the hill. He stamped on the gear lever and suddenly there were a few puffs of blue smoke and the bike fired up at last.

The noise was deafening and quite scary in a way. He rode it about for half hour til it ran out of fuel, so I didn't get a go on this beast but I really was not keen on riding it because of the noise and sheer power. So we rode it without the engine going and I sat on the back while we managed to freewheel most of the way home.

The winter was a very cold one and I remember one afternoon in particular when I was at school and Mack, the bloke who lived with us came and picked me up from the school gates.

It was *Wednesday the eleventh of January nineteen seventy eight*; It was snowing heavily when we left Cowes High and the lodger was worrying about getting all the way back to Totland. We got as far as Ningwood and then decided to turn off up towards Newbridge and then we went up towards Chessell, along this winding little lane with snow drifts building up around each side of the car.

The little Austin A40 was going well and really held onto the road considering there were almost 3 inches of snow lying on the road already. As we neared the top of the hill and where the Road starts to go downhill towards Chessell, there was a massive wall of snow right across the road. It must have been at least six feet tall and three times the depth.

Mack said, "Let's plough through it" as he dropped the car down a gear and gave the little Austin all it had and turned the windscreen wipers onto fast wipe.

We hit this wall of snow and the car almost flew over it, I say almost because the car buried itself under the drift and all I could see was snow all around us and the steam coming from the engine. Mack put the car into reverse and I don't know how he did it, but the A40 came out of the drift and backed well away from the drift and we managed to turn round and went back down the road towards Ningwood and through the Wellow Road and eventually, home.

The whole of the West Wight was cut off from the rest of the island and even helicopters were used to bring in supplies to some farms and more remote properties. For us it was a fantastic time and we made use of the snow as much as we possibly could by sledging on any available hill we could reach and having some really good snowball fights.

There was one occasion when myself my Dad and Mack were in standing in the doorway of our butchers shop and the local policeman was across the road chatting to the owner of the sweet shop. Well we couldn't let him get away without a snowball or two could we, so a few balls were launched across the road at him and instead of him ignoring us; he picked up some snow and threw it back at us.

Now there are not many policemen that would do that sort of thing is there. It was just the way the local village kind of came together and acted in times of need that sticks in my mind so much and the way people helped each other out so much.

There was a chap who had a transit breakdown truck with chains on the wheels and he was carrying milk around the village to help out the milkman, just little things that have been lost in time and don't seem to happen anymore. Dad was running out of meat and had no eggs to sell. Mum could not get to cash and carry to get supplies either so after a while most of the shops in the village were quite empty of stock and even the petrol stations were almost out of fuel too. Something we will not see again in our lifetime mainly because we just don't seem to experience such cold winters now.

It was not until late in nineteen eighty when I was watching Top of the pops one evening and this band from the island started playing. My band mates had told me they were going to be on this week's show, so I started watching them.

I could not believe my eyes when I saw the singer, one Mark King with blonde hair and a scar down one cheek. It was the bloke with the GT380 that I spent so many lunchtimes watching at school, near the sports hall changing rooms. That was unbelievable and such a coincidence and proof that it's a small island we live on.

My first ever motorcycle, an NSU Quickly which I paid £45 for in 1977.

I remember the view from the flat in Totland looking down on the roundabout was particularly good and because it was a bay window, we could the Road all the way to the crest of the hill towards Alum Bay and in the opposite direction, towards Colwell.

It was nineteen seventy eight and the reign of the mark one Ford Cortina was in full swing. Everyone who was anyone had this model and the thing that stuck in my mind the most was the green sun strips with the girls name on one side and the boys name on the other.

Many hours I spent sitting on the ledge of that window with our first ever record player, listening to ELO records on this mono ITT contraption, watching the world go by. Evenings were by far the best times because the Magic Roundabout would begin. Dad called it by this name because of the strange things that drivers of these Cortina's did as soon as the sun went down over the Needles.

A car would drive down from the Colwell end and go slowly round the roundabout and then return from where it came from.
Next would be another one, same model, different colour and with different names on the sun strip. It would do exactly the same manoeuvre and drive off to where ever it came from. Then another one would come down the road, same model, different colour and different names on the sun strip. Now this went on all bloody evening. Round and round they would go all night, and what seemed for weeks on end

This did not just apply to owners of Ford Cortina's; there were certain motorcycles that would the same circuit every night, every week all year long. It was so comical to watch and we knew every evening would be the same, unless the carnival was on or the fairground had arrived in Freshwater.

It was because of Jack the yellow bus driver that I first learnt to ride a motorcycle. His son had an off road bike and I was soon riding the thing around the old fort on Headon Warren. I was hooked and somewhat possessed by the bike and spent most of the weekends up at the fort and riding down to Headon cafe or the strange shed like building known as Isaacs cafe. Nearly every coach driver that visited Alum bay was fed and watered at this iconic café. Not surprising because the tea and cakes were lovely.

Headon cafe was a slightly strange place I remember, it was never very busy but we liked it because they had these triangular solitaire games on the tables plus a small putting green. I decided that I needed a motorcycle of my own so I asked my Mum and Dad if I could sell my racing bicycle and buy a moped or whatever was available.

My bicycle sold very quickly and I really can't remember how I heard of it, but a small moped was for sale in Freshwater for exactly the same price as what I got for my bicycle. I purchased my first motorcycle, an NSU Quickly from one Scooby Parnell of Freshwater Bay. Whoever came up with the name was a liar, this machine was in no way quick and had the most awful gear change system ever made.

The gears were similar to a scooter, where by you twisted the left hand grip whilst pulling in the clutch on the same side. The bike constantly jumped out of gear and was a nightmare to change gear on the move. My Dad used to shove it into the boot of our Vauxhall Viva estate and trundle off to the lane at Alum bay that lead to the Warren.

It was the best six weeks holidays I ever had, every possible opportunity was spent riding around all day until Dad would come and collect me and the bike in the evening, when he had shut the shop. My obsession with motorcycles was born and remained with me for years, but that's another story.

In around the middle of March, my parents took me out one Sunday to a motorcycle shop, which was quite close to where my girlfriend lived, in Calbourne. We looked at lots of mopeds and I chose a 50cc Yamaha trail bike. It looked so gorgeous, a sort of miniature of a big bike but with no less of its looks or styling. I fell in love with this machine and my parents bought it on HP for me and I had to pay for it out of my wages, when I started earning.

They had it delivered to our house and I put it down the little alley, behind the house where the dustbins lived. Because my birthday fell in April of course I was sixteen, well before the official leaving period in July. My Father had requested the school let me leave earlier so I could start work in the butchers and because I had a job to go straight into, they agreed that I could leave school at the end of April. That was a lucky escape and who didn't enjoy leaving school?

The first album I bought was by ELO and it was one of their early albums, which was Face the Music. Now this was the album that contained the track Fire on High which apparently if played backwards, would produce the voice of the devil.

Not having any knowledge of such things at the time, I didn't actually play it backwards until the 80's and even then. Nothing amazing happened when I did play it backwards, just a voice saying *"Time is reversible, turn back"*, very disappointing indeed. Anyway, this was my very first album and I liked every song very much indeed. It was an odd sort of sound compared with all the other music being produced.

The orchestral string sound mixed with guitars and drums was in my eyes, fantastic and totally unique. The most attractive part of this kind of music was the use of these strange synthesizer machines. The sounds that came out of these instruments were amazing. My love of the synthesizer was kindled and it never left me from that time onwards. Richard Tandy was the keyboard man and made my addiction to this sound grow and grow. I was just fourteen when ELO released the most amazing album Out of the Blue. A double album which took the synthesizer to deeper reaches of sound and some of the best sounds I had ever heard. The best track or tracks, in my view was *A Concerto for a rainy day.*

Moving on from the amazing ELO and the great singles they released from Out of the Blue, I started to listen to *The Stranglers* and this was the very beginnings of the punk era in mid seventy eight. I had bought the album *No more Heroes* and loved the title track with its twangy bass line and great synth sounds too. I bought all their albums up to around nineteen eighty four, by which time I had made countless discoveries of varying music types, but mostly synth based.

One of my all time favourite albums was *Jean Michel Jarre's Equinoxe* which I heard at a party in Porchfield. I had never heard an album quite like it before. There were no divisions between tracks, one continuous piece that merged cleverly into the next track. This piece of electronic wizardry was to me, the type of music I wanted to hear and was mesmerised by the sounds that were being produced by this artist. Headphones were another discovery I had made and to me, essential for listening to Mr. Jarre.

I moved further down the dark road of punk and borrowed *Never mind the Bollocks* by the *Sex Pistols*. Now this album was not really what I was searching for but I liked the anarchic lyrics and some of the guitar chords used.

We all had this album on tape and a few of us had those mono tape players with the built in microphone. They were the only way you could listen to your music on the move and god knows how many batteries we got through during that last year of school.

Taping an album was not as easy as it is today because there were no easy connectors between the record player and the tape deck to a recording tape machine. You had to have access to a music centre. This was a large machine with a record player, tape deck and stereo radio all built into one. They usually have smoked Perspex lids to keep the dust off the record deck. They were able to record to cassette tapes directly from the record player or radio.

This was the beginning of the true taped album or for most people, the best way to record the Top Forty radio show on Radio One on a Sunday eve. I think before these machines came along, we all tried to tape this radio show using the microphone on the portable tape decks. It was always a noisy recording and most people had their family members talking in the background or a baby crying.

I had the cat to contend with, who always wanted to play sniff the mic or purring into it. It was a kind of ritual to listen to the top forty and tape it so you could play it at school on your portable tape deck. Did you ever experience recording the Top Forty?

I had managed to save up fourteen pounds in my post office savings book and had visited that most spectacular toy shop in Newport high street, known as *Birds*. It must have been the longest shop that was ever built. You would walk through the different sections of stationery, toys and finally the modelling department, which was right at the back.

In a glass case with the till mounted on top, sat a variety of model aeroplane engines all in their little boxes and they looked so beautiful to me. It was a dream to own one of these motors for a very long time and for what purpose I really have no idea.

It was while I was doing one of my week long stints at St Mary's hospital and we had all met up and walked down to town at lunchtime to go to this shop. I first went to the post office to withdraw twelve of my fourteen pounds and bought my little engine, complete with some fuel and a propeller.

It was sheer bliss when I opened up the box on my way home on the coach that afternoon and looked at this tiny piece of engineering excellence. I had no planes or any other model to actually use it in so I had to come up with a plan for the engine. As soon as the coach arrived outside *Mary Martin's* sweet shop and we all got off, I was straight into Dad's shop, showing him what I had bought with my money from the post office.

He was not too impressed with it at all and thought it a waste of money. Regardless of his views, I took into my room and stared at the tiny thing for ages. Then I came up with mounting it on a piece of wood, so I could start it up. I got some tiny bolts from my mate Kitty's brother and put it on this plank of wood. The only thing I knew about this motor was the propeller. There was a small spring that you attached to the base of the prop and turned it against the spring. When released, the propeller would spin in the opposite direction with a whir and the sound of compression in its tiny cylinder. I had a small metal fuel tank and hose that Kitty's brother had given me and that was mounted on the wooden board too.

I tried so many times to start it but due to my lack of understanding and experience of such things, I never managed to start my new toy.

I came up with a new application for the motor and this was a roller skate and the board nailed to the skate and I had a plan to send it down the *Turf Walk* one Sunday morning It would go like a rocket I thought – if I could actually start it.

It was a Saturday afternoon and we were all in the lounge watching a video movie and I had taken my roller skate plane thing into the lounge to show Mum's friend. I remember playing with the propeller and clipping the spring onto the prop and turning it against the spring and whoosh the bloody thing started. It scared the life out of me as it pulled against me as it revved and poured fumes out of its tiny exhaust. The whole room filled with smoke and then it just stopped again.

All that time I had tried to get the thing going and it decides to start up in the lounge. Dad was not impressed and told me to take it back to my room or go outside with the smelly bloody thing. I never did use it on the roller skate because the engine had frightened the life out of me. I dismantled it all and put the engine back into its box and eventually sold it to Kitty's brother.

Yet again Kitty, that skinny and fearless friend of mine, made me laugh with another of his mental adventures. He had been down to Alum Bay with his brother big Jimmy to do some more beachcombing and they had discovered a large amount of ammunition on the beach, under the chalk cliffs. This stuff consisted of shells and probably mortar rounds and which could have easily been live rounds in the state they were in.

So off he goes up to the shed with these things and starts firstly rubbing the rust and dirt off with a wire brush, now if that was not dangerous enough he starts hitting them with a bloody hammer to get them apart. Crazy bloke and damn lucky they did not go off in his shed. Another time, down by the pier in Totland Bay,

Kitty finds another suspicious looking shell on the sand. Because he hated one of the blokes that went into the amusements at the end of the pier, he decided to throw this shell against the piles of the pier. He was a complete loony and had no idea of danger. The best and most dangerous thing this lad attempted was to dive down a well near Spinfish in Freshwater with his diving gear on. Would you dive down a well?

Chapter 8

The Lodger's Girl

I have already mentioned Cally while I worked at St Mary's hospital while at school. She was the student nurse, who always managed to embarrass me with her friends. I first met her on the school bus to Cowes High school. She always sat on the back seats with all her mates, but I didn't talk to her as I would dare go to the back of the bus, it was too scary.

It was such a surprise when she started to go out with our lodger and was always in our house in the evenings and at weekends. I couldn't believe she was actually in our house and I got to see her almost every evening. She was so much friendlier than she was on the school bus too; I guess it was the situation that was completely different.

We always sat in the kitchen in *Bon Accord* as it seemed to be the warmest room in the house and we had this breakfast bar thing which you could almost sit in a circle around the table. Many evenings we spent in our kitchen, Cally and Mack would be just chatting around the table and occasionally Mum or Dad would be there too.

If I had the chance to join in the conversation, I would stay there with them and chat about school or whatever I could think of. Yes I had a crush on her but no one knew my feelings towards Cally.

She started bringing LP's round for me to listen to and I would go off to my shop room and listen to them. It was one Sunday evening, we were all sitting in the kitchen chatting. The top forty was playing in the background and Cally asked "would I like to come over to her house one afternoon as she was on day off from college and listen to the top forty?" Now trying to get the courage to actually go to her house on my own was a big problem for me. I said "yes" and remember counting the days leading up to the day with sheer excitement.

The day arrived and Mum gave me a lift up to Cally's house, which was down a windy lane and backed onto some fields that her family owned. I knocked on the door and Cally's mum let me in and I met her little sister as I went inside the house. Their lounge, dining room and kitchen was on the first floor and the bathrooms and bedrooms were downstairs.

I followed her very nervously as she walked downstairs and showed me her room. It was a very large room and very tidy. She put the latest tape of the top forty on and then she made coffees and we chatted all afternoon. She showed me some of her treasured things and her singles collection and talked about her student friends quite a lot. She mentioned that I went completely red when her friends came up to me at the hospital. I didn't say much in reply as I was twice as nervous as I was when Cally and her friends embarrassed me. She knew I was shy and was teasing me that afternoon, not nastily, just in a friendly way.

Looking back at this special occasion, I am surprised a relationship did not develop from our friendship; we got along so well and had a very similar taste in music too. She was two years older than me and so much more grown up than I ever came close to at her age. I fell in love that afternoon but alas, I never got a chance to tell her my feelings. I don't know why she liked me enough to spend time alone with me and share her world with me, because she had lots of friends her own age to do that with; maybe she felt sorry for me.

Cally was very slim with long dark hair and had the most beautiful figure. She was about five foot two but made up for it with those high platform boots, which were so fashionable in the seventies. This made her as tall as I was at the time and I was around five foot nine then. To some people she appeared to be quite a hard nut because she was one of the kids that smoked and her school tie was always wrapped up into the biggest knot possible. Why I didn't seize the moment alone with her, I adored her, dreamt of her but never even kissed her.

I didn't see her for more than thirty odd years. She suffered a period of extreme health problems in the late 1990's and had to undergo chemotherapy in Southampton hospital. I read about her in the local paper and actually managed to contact her by email, through the school reunion site *Friends Reunited.* It was so nice to hear from her after so long.

Cally recovered well from her illnesses and became a well respected chef. I finally met her in person when I got a part time job in a small bakery. I could not believe it when I learned that she was the lady that came in to bake cakes, one day a week.

I worked with her a few times and got on very well with her. She had not changed much at all, still the same bubbly personality and she still loved to chat too. She started to pop round to my chalet down at Brambles Chine for tea in the afternoon and we got on really well.

My five year old sister Sarah on my Yamaha TY50P in 1978.

My best friend and the first person I became friends with in Totland was the lad named Kitty, who lived in St Saviour's Road.

His house was at the bottom of the road, opposite a small grassy area in front of other houses set further back off the road. He lived there with his Mum and Dad and his older brother big Jimmy who was as his nickname suggests a big chap and very strong too. Jimmy had a small bass boat with a cabin, which he kept on a mooring, just off of Totland bay.

I first met Kitty when I was off school with some rash all over my body and I had just been to the stationer's shop and was on my way to Frank Rolf's garage to get a spark plug for my moped. Kitty was walking into the garage and buying some oil and I said the customary "Alright" and he replied with the same words. I don't know exactly how we got chatting, but we did and it was moped talk and it brought us together as friends for many years after that day. It was not til I had been to the doctors that I later discovered I had German measles and was therefore confined to the house for a week or so.

Kitty was very much into motorcycles like I was and we both dreamt of owning one in the not so distant future. Luckily for us both, Kitty's brother was also into bikes and had just bought a brand new Honda 250 Dream.

We spent hours with Jimmy in his shed, just watching him clean and look after his pride and joy. I did not know many people of my age who owned a bike at that time, so Kitty's house was the place to be when Jimmy was not out fishing in his boat. Now the boat was another love of mine and that is mentioned in a later chapter.

When I had finally got off the school coach from Cowes High school and had my tea, then it was time to call up Kitty and see if he was coming round to listen to the record player or maybe go down to the beach, as we often did. We would always walk over to the Broadway Inn and go in the side door and buy a mars bar and a can of shandy and then we would make our way down to the beach and pier and see if Kitty's brother was around.

Often, Jimmy would be there with his boat, fixing it up in some way or painting it. His boat was usually on a mooring out in the bay which he made himself out of a 45 gallon barrel, filled with concrete.

Sometimes though, Jimmy would have winched the boat up onto wooden skids and up onto the shingle bank. It was a hell of a job to winch that boat up the beach, but Jimmy was like a giant and had the strength of no one I had seen before.

He could drag that boat up the beach on his own and carry the massive outboard engine on his shoulder, without a grimace. The engine weighed a ton and I remember myself and Kitty trying to lift it off the ground, no chance, we could not get it an inch off the floor, let alone on a shoulder.

If Jimmy was not down on the beach, then we would go and play on the machines in the tiny amusements on the end of the pier. There were not many things in the amusements at all, but it wasn't just the machines that attracted us, it was the crowds of local ladies that congregated around the pier and sea wall in the evenings. We spent hours just hanging around watching the pretty girls coming and going. Most of them I did not know because most of the kids of my age in Totland went to a different high school than I did.

When the beach had become boring and the pier had lost its fun factor, we went back to my bedroom and listened to Jean Michel Jarre's Equinoxe LP. It was our favourite album at the time. We would play some singles too and one of the most played songs was *Into the Valley* by *The Skids*, which was on white vinyl. A classic song which to this day, I could not understand the lyrics sung by Richard Jobson and I bet most people just pretended to understand the words.

One night I decided to rig up a light switch onto a lamp I had mounted on the wall, above my bed. Unfortunately I had forgotten how to wire it up and blew the bloody thing off the wall. Kitty found that one very amusing, especially when it made me jump out of my skin when it went bang. He always referred to any work that I did as an *Ezzard Bodge* for some reason?

I always looked for the cheapest and easiest way to make of fix something and although that "Yes" I had made a few bodges in my time; I also found some good ways of getting by on the cheap.

One of my mad inventions was to take the head off an electric strimmer and get Kitty's brother Jimmy to weld a small circular saw blade on to it. I did this because I was tired of loading strimmer line into it when I was tending to the garden and it was always my job to strim. The first time I used this lethal piece of kit, it nearly cut my leg off. I tried to cut off some rather thick branches and as the blade cut into the wood, it shot backwards and skimmed my jeans at the top of my leg. Kitty was watching and nearly fell over laughing at me, so I decided not to pursue this modified strimmer idea and threw it in the bin.

I will always remember was when we anchored about one hundred metres from the beach below Tennyson cliffs in Jimmy's boat. Big Jimmy and his brother Kitty had a small aluminium dinghy, which we used for beaching on little coves and inlets on our adventures.

We all got in the dinghy and Jimmy rowed us in close to the giant rocks that line the whole of that part of the coast. It was very scary and rather eerie as we got closer to the rocks. Below us, through the clear water you could see masses of seaweed and rocks so big that it would be instant disaster if we hit one of them. There was a gentle swell as we came in and we glided over the top of this large flat boulder and with a shout from Jimmy, we both leapt onto a rock and onto the shingle beach. Jimmy rowed along the beach a bit further and found a nice flat rock that was only semi submerged and we managed to haul the dinghy up and out of the water.

We had to make sure that waves could not move it before we could go exploring properly. Jimmy had told us that there was always things washed up on the part of the coastline and because the only way to reach it was by boat, no one ever came to search this beach.

He was absolutely right too; we found countless buoys which were the very large type and lobster pots were washed up there. I found a strange thing embedded into the cliff face, a large perfectly round rock like thing but it looked partly metallic. I'm sure in was a meteorite that had hit the cliff and embedded itself into the chalk. I kept that rock for years but someone stole it when we moved house.

We spent most of the day on that shore, searching the little caves and rocks for whatever treasures the sea had carried in. Jimmy fished from his boat because the swell was getting stronger, so he rowed back out to the boat. Getting back into the dinghy was exciting stuff and although the tide had dropped a fair bit, there were no easier places to board. On the way back to Totland bay we went past the needles rocks and read the plaque on the side of the lighthouse, relating to the wreck of the *Varvassi*.

I remember one morning we all met up on the sea wall near to where the dinghy lay on the shingle. It was a hot summer's day and it was getting very busy on the beach.

We just went for a short trip in the dinghy around the bay while Jimmy was doing something to his boat. We had got back in and hauled the tiny boat up the sandy beach and just sat on the wall watching the world go by. Suddenly there was this scream and a big splash in the water and we could see this young lad picking himself up out of the surf.

What had happened was a mystery until we heard this woman shouting at Jimmy on the beach and Jimmy was telling her to "buck off" and they both looked really angry. As I have said, Jimmy was a very strong chap and this young lad had apparently been throwing stones at Jimmy's boat and after Jimmy had said to the lad "don't throw stones at my boat", the kid carried on. Bad move. Jimmy went over to him and picked him up and threw him out to sea. This kid flew out at least fifteen feet and the mother went absolutely mad at Jimmy.

It was Christmas Eve when Jimmy went to the local pub and got very drunk and instead of walking up the Road, he decided to walk through a series of gardens, which lead to his house, but without climbing any fences, he just literally walked through them.

One day Kitty and I had been down to help
Jimmy with his boat and walked up from the
beach back to Totland.   On passing the pub on
the corner we encountered some very drunk
greasy looking people. There were three blokes
and this girl who was shouting obscenities at
one of the chaps walking out of the pub. We had
not said a thing but one of these drunken blokes
started to have a go at us and so did this very
mouthy girl too. We just ignored them as they
were telling us to go away in a nasty manner.

So we went back to s house and Jimmy arrived
on his bike and we told him about these idiots
outside the pub. He said we would all go back
there and sort them out.   Well I was pretty
nervous about Jimmy's plan. I was not a fighter
at all and had never hit anyone, Kitty was scared
too. So we all walked down to the pub and as
we rounded the corner, they were still there,
even more drunk and mouthing off to everyone
who walked past them.

I will never forget the look on the drunken
idiot's faces when they saw big Jimmy with us;
they looked petrified of him and rightly too. He
told them to clear out and not to come back
again and they soon disappeared and we never
saw those people again. One advantage of
knowing a giant when you are fifteen.

A storm blew up from nowhere one night in November 79 and I was woken up by Kitty banging on my bedroom door the next morning and he wanted some help to pull a boat in or something? I got up and made a drink and had to be at work at seven thirty am and it was only six am.

I went down the beach with him and there was Jimmy and some other chaps pointing out to sea and shouting at each other. The wind had died down a little but the sea had quite a swell going on and the waves were crashing on the shingle and sand with a thunderous noise. Jimmy's boat had sunk and god knows how, but he had swum out to the boat and secured a rope onto it and then swam back in with the rope. I said he was strong but this dude was something else.

Swimming out in a force 8 wind with waves as big as a bus and pulling a large rope with him. Unreal. We all heaved on the rope until Jimmy could reach out to the bow of the boat and fix the hand winch cable to it. The cuddy had been ripped off his boat and so was his twenty five horse power outboard, gone forever because Jimmy and Kitty dived the surrounding area many times just after the storm but could not locate it anywhere in the bay.

We got the boat off the shore and onto the shingle and that was all we could do that morning. I remember riding to work and feeling like I had done a days work already after heaving on that rope in the wind and rain.

Kitty was on one of his beachcombing missions one morning during the winter and it was just after a really bad storm, which was the best time to go. He came across a lovely aluminium dinghy washed up in the rocks in Totland bay, way past the lifeboat house at the end of the sea wall. It was a bit dented from crashing into the rocks but otherwise it was perfectly seaworthy and we used it for years after he found it.

On the subject of storms, the heavy metal gang from the roundabout and myself decided it would be really good fun to drive to Compton Bay in a force eight storm to do some dinghy surfing. We bought a kids dinghy from the shop in Totland and then went off to the beach. When we arrived there were lots of people parked in the car park, just watching the violent sea crashing against the cliffs and beaches. There were no other surfers there that day for some reason but this did not deter us from our new found sport.

We walked along the beach and went to the right of the car park, just past the old wreck that is visible on low tides and set out in the dinghy for the first breaker. The waves were over three metres in height and trying to paddle out past the first one was nigh impossible. We made it though after being thrown back into the beach a couple of times and managed to surf this thing right up to the base of the cliffs.

My God, it was a stupid thing to do but incredibly exciting at the time. I remember one of the rides in on the dinghy and we all fell out of it and went into this massive hollow in the sea bed, now that was bloody scary because I don't think anyone actually touched the bottom of it. I had heard that there was a hole out there but did not realise how close to shore it was.

When we were completely exhausted from that game, we walked back to our friend's car and had towels to dry off and get warmed up. As we sat in the car, Little Wol noticed the mast of a yacht about half a mile out and bouncing around all over the place.

We watched as it got closer and there was then the excited chat about salvage rights and how we could claim it if it did not touch the beach, we really did not have bloody clue what we were talking about but watched as it headed towards Brook beach.

We drove down to the car park at Brook and walked down onto the beach and saw the yacht actually around fifty feet off the beach. We were not the only people who had seen it and a huge crowd of people gathered around it as it washed up. The owners who were rescued from it somewhere off the Needles rock were there too.

It was so lucky that the boat stayed upright and was left sat on its twin keels on the sand by the retreating tide. There was little damage to it but apparently someone had stolen the outboard and a few bits of electronic equipment from it, when it was initially abandoned by its owners.

Jimmy was well known for chasing the odd stupid car driver who cut him up on his bike and would usually give their door a swift boot from his heavy motorcycle boots.
Another instance of Big Jimmy and his slight lack of patience was when we were trying to pull up the anchor on his boat. There were four of us in the boat that afternoon, little Wol, Jimmy, Kitty and myself.

The anchor buoy was not doing what we wanted it to do and that was to use it's buoyancy to literally pull the anchor off the seabed but at the opposite angle to how it was buried. It's quite a complex manoeuvre and rather scary if you don't know what you are doing. So there we are, all standing up and leaning over the side of the boat, trying to get hold of this buoy so Jimmy Can haul it up and attach it to the tying point so he can reverse the boat and eventually pull up this anchor.

Jimmy was getting very stressed and little Wol was just wandering about the cabin area and suddenly this massive 1lb fishing weight flew across the deck and Jimmy shouting " Sit down you idiot". Well he soon sat down and Jimmy got the anchor free and that was the end of another exciting boat trip.

It was because of Big Jimmy and his Honda Dream that we all started buying *Motorcycle News* and the one and only monthly *Motorcycle Mechanics*, which was a fantastic magazine. The funniest articles I have ever read, were known as *Down at the dealers*. Stories about people buying motorcycles and not knowing a rear light from a front tyre.

One particular story in the column was this rather short bloke had bought a Honda 250 Super Dream, which as any biker knows, are very heavy bikes indeed. If you were rather short or small, you would have some difficulty touching the ground and certainly putting it on the centre stand would be virtually impossible.

So this bloke had noticed that some bikes had a small ram like linkage going from the frame to the front forks and was curious to understand the reason for this. He went down to his local bike shop and asked the mechanics if this contraption was in fact power steering for larger bikes, which would make his Super Dream easier to handle at low speeds? The guys in the shop must have fallen over laughing when he had left the shop.

Me with Yvonne and her friend, ComfortsFarm, Cowes in 1975.

Chapter 9

Lorries, Bikes and Agriculture

My Dad's friend who was a builder and part-time DJ was selling his lorry and because I had helped him out a few times and often travelled to jobs in this vehicle, I grew very fond of the little BMC truck. It had those small windows down by your feet and had a front end that had real character and almost smiled at you. I persuaded him to sell it to me, at the expense of ridicule from my friends. I did not get the flat bed as he needed that for his new one but it did not matter to me as I wanted to paint it and put a chrome exhaust up the side of the cab. Oh dear such a dreamer of a seventeen year old I was. My lorry was started up every few months and ran beautifully, apart from the clutch that had seized up due to lack of use. I tried to free it up but did not have the know-how. After a year or so, I sold the old thing and for a lot more than I paid for it too. I must have been the only young lad that owned a lorry at that age and everyone thought I was completely mental. I like it and enjoyed it so that's all that mattered to me.

Being employed in my Father's butchers shop was as far as I'm aware just a natural thing that son's did when they left school and started work. It was probably my least favourite of jobs that I have ever had to do and because I was a very shy person. Facing customers didn't help much at all and I always tried to avoid serving them. The only thing going for me was my aptitude for repairing mechanical things and taking things to bits to find out how they work.

I had repaired a few things for Dad in the shop and later, the Bakery business. I had no ambitions in life at that time. I was in a place that I didn't want to move away from. Safe and secure with a nice home and lots of friends to be with, why would I want to leave this all behind?

On reflection, I should have received lessons at home and try and carry on with lessons; not dumped and left to my own devices. Leaving school was kind of a weird experience really; leaving all those people behind after spending nearly five years in their company and suddenly you probably wont ever see them again.

Kitty started work at sixteen and worked for this turfing and gardening company in Brook. He had to be mobile pretty quick and desperately needed his own transport. His Dad took him for the first few weeks and it was a bit unfair on his father to have to take him to and from work everyday.

I kept a lookout for a moped for him and I had heard from a customer in the butchers, that a lad who lived in the coastguard cottages, down near Totland beach had a moped for sale. It turned out that this chap was the very same bloke who bought my racing pushbike off me a few years before.

Kitty and I went down to view the bike and it was the strangest looking thing I had ever seen. The way the engine protruded from the bike at the front and the tank was so skinny when you sat on it and felt like a pushbike. Anyway, Kitty bought it and rode it home that evening. Kitty now had his own bike and it was a Honda SS50, the only one in the village and probably on the island as far as we knew.

It wasn't known for its acceleration or top speed but could run on 50p's worth of petrol all week long. One day while cleaning our bikes in s front garden we always cleaned them in the garden because of the masses of girls that walked past on their way to the youth hostel at the top of the Road. Kitty decided that he could not put up with his squeaky front disc brake anymore so he sprayed it with WD40. The result was amazing, no squeaky brake and no front brake at all - Silly boy.

There are times when you wish you had not offered to do something for someone and this was one of those times when I had volunteered to go on my bike to get something, thinking it would be a nice little trip and easy. Our sausage machine had packed up and we had a massive amount of orders to fulfil that week.

We had no other option than to go to cash and carry and buy a load of frozen sausages and unpack them. So off I went on my bike with a large rucksack and went to collect the goods from Cowes. I did not realise how bloody heavy they would be and I am sure there were at least fifty packs to bring back on the bike.

Jesus, I could hardly lift the rucksack off the ground and when I got it onto the seat of the bike, I nearly fell over in the car park. The trip back was hell on my shoulders as the bag dug into my arms and pulled me backwards on the seat. Never volunteer to collect sausages from anywhere on a moped.

My Yamaha TY50M exhaust was totally blocked up and slowly the little power I did have, had gone completely. I tried the usual decoke methods and took out the baffles, put them on a bonfire and shoved caustic soda down the exhaust. Still there was hardly any pressure coming out of the end of the exhaust.

One day I took the bike into the garage down the road and was chatting to the mechanic there. I explained to him what was happening to the bike and he took it in the workshop. The exhaust came up from the engine and went high up, along the side of the frame under your left leg and the white metal grille stopped you burning the top of your leg. This section was the expansion part and was very flat shaped and this was the problem as I soon found out. The chap in the garage suggested cutting this section out and putting a straight piece of pipe in its place.

So half hour later, he had cut the flat piece out and welded a piece of two inch water pipe in it's place and also managed to tack weld the grille back on through the screw holes. We started the bike and the result was amazing. Smoke blew out of the exhaust for the first time since I had it.

I gave the mechanic five pounds for his time and thanked him, then Kitty and I rode up to alum bay and for the first time ever, I had full power and it was like someone had put a new engine in the bike and although it was slightly noisier, it wouldn't attract the presence of the village copper I hoped. I could actually go off road on the bike and enjoy going up hills without the engine dying on me. The best fiver I ever spent.

Big Jimmy once went to Newport on his bike and unbelievably he came back with a Suffolk Punch lawn mower on the back. He had a rope going around the handles and round his shoulders. He was completely mad and I had never seen anyone do anything like it.

Having the Youth Hostel in Totland meant that in the summer there were a lot of young ladies staying there and very often they would come into one of the pubs or come and chat to us when we congregated near the roundabout.

There was one of those totally spontaneous moments, which made my mate Kitty very jealous indeed. We were sitting in his front garden on St Saviour's Road cleaning out motorcycles as usual and just chatting away, when two girls walked past his gate and they both smiled as we exchanged "hellos". As they walked on up the road I gave them a whistle and shouted "where is my kiss goodnight?"

One of them said "come here then." and I ran up to her and just snogged her there and then. She didn't know me and I didn't know her but it was a lovely kiss. Poor Kitty.

My work in my Fathers butchers shop was not destined to last very long because I was not very well suited to being stuck indoors all day and certainly not really very good at butchery at all.

I tried my best at all the tasks given to me and really the only job I was good at was making sausages, which is hardly a great career prospect. The whole butchery environment was not for me and especially the cold, wet hands all day.

Your skin certainly suffers from the environment and my hands would suffer cracks in my skin which were so painful. The early mornings were not really a problem to me at all but working Saturdays didn't give much pleasure, as all my mates had that day off. So I guess that Dad realised that I was not enjoying my work much and probably decided that I should find something else to do at the same time I was thinking it.

Dad took me to see a careers adviser down at the Job Centre in Freshwater one afternoon. We looked at jobs that I could do or at least try to do, but the problem was that I left school with not a qualification to my name. The careers bloke had not come across my lack of skills before and was quite stumped. He did suggest a *Youth Training Scheme* or *YTS* and because I had a slight idea of what I wanted to do, quite a few of these schemes were available on different farms around the island.

I only had my FS1E moped at that time so I did not really want to be travelling right across the island every day and especially during the winter months. I did not have the clothing or gloves for that kind of travel at the time. So we narrowed the training schemes down to the closest farm which was in Ningwood, near Yarmouth.

Not too far away and quite familiar to me as it was just around the corner from the Elvis family's grand parents house, where we kept the horses a few years ago. The adviser called the farmer there and then and arranged an interview that week at the farm.

So I came out of the job centre with some excitement, a new job and totally new faces and environment to get used to. I was looking forward to the interview too, which was quite unusual for me as I normally hated them. I went straight round to Kitty's place and told him the good news that evening.

The days leading up to the interview were dragging and I was still in the butchers shop waiting for a release. The last days of any job always seem to go so slowly. The day arrived and Dad took me out to the farm and the careers chap was there too.

The farmer was one Tim Fenweis and I had heard this surname before, but could not remember where. He was a tall chap and had a jolly face and wore a green boiler suit. He asked me some questions and I asked a few too. The most important thing to him was did I have my own transport and am I used to hard work? Also had I driven a tractor before, which stumped me as never been near one.

All in all, the interview went well and it was agreed that I started in two weeks time. So I was at last going to leave the shop and start my new career on a farm. I was attracted to working on a farm because there didn't appear to be customers there. I had no real connections to agriculture whatsoever and I guess its just fate that directed my younger working life.

The weeks leading up to starting on the farm were not too bad and I had a week's holiday before I started because there would not be any time off in the next six months. I remember the Saturday night before the day I started I went to this disco at a scout hall in Gurnard, Cowes on my moped. It was a good party and we all got on the dance floor and did the Pogo to the sound of the *Sex Pistols* and *Sham 69*.

Unfortunately, when you attempt this bloody stupid dance move, make sure the people near you are of the same height otherwise you will end up banging heads and getting a nice black eye, similar to the one I got. On the Sunday morning my eye had puffed up nicely and a real shiner ensued.

So the Monday morning I set off to start my new job and arrived in good time on my moped. It was late October and it was quite dry and not too cold either. Now the farmer thought me a bit of a hooligan at first because of my black eye and he asked if I had been fighting? I told him about this silly dance at the disco and he just laughed.

My first day was spent meeting the rest of the staff and looking around the place. I did some clearing of a couple of calf pens, but nothing too taxing. The place was quite untidy and there was mud all over the place. The workshop was interesting to me as it had lots of big machines in it that I had never seen before. The farm was split into three areas; the main farm with milking parlour, cow yards and a large barn full of straw and hay.

There were other buildings which contained the milling machine and grain storage on one side, the workshop and empty calf pens on the other. Then there was a small yard down the road that leads to the back of Shalfleet. Two large cow yards and a dung heap. Then there were the old horse's home buildings, down the road towards Shalfleet school.

Large yards with a hay barn at one end. Some of the buildings still had plaques on them as most of them were donated to the ex horses home. One building had the plaque which read "donated by The Daily Mail newspaper".

The whole place had nice concrete roads and no mud, unlike the two other parts of the farm. The first person I met on the farm was a chap called Ivan the cowman. A nice bloke but he was always moaning about the boss, and he had been at the farm for a long time.

The second person I came to know was a cousin of the Elvis family whom my Dad was friends with, who lived opposite the Granddad's house on a small redundant farm known as Green Farm in Ningwood. He was a good laugh to work with and I got on well with him, sadly, he left about half way through my term there and was replaced by this chap from Yorkshire who resided in this dirty old caravan behind the workshop.

I went in the caravan once during lunch break with Kevin and what a mess it was, there was hardly any daylight because the windows were close to the barn walls and a tree grew over the outside windows.

Dark, damp and horrible, but this lad took up residence, although he was not in it that much because I think he was in love with the farmer's daughter and everywhere she went, so did he.

The fact that he was out every night until the early hours, showed in his work during the times that I saw him on the farm. He managed to lift the whole of the tin roof off one building with the front loader of a tractor. He had parked close to the building with a trailer and forgot that he had lowered the loader to miss the tin roof.

When he started it up, the lever for putting the loader up was engaged and as he maneuvered the trailer and not looking forward, the loader caught the tin roof and up went the whole section. The worst thing was the loader had a forked bucket on it and the tin was impaled by the fork tines. It took a lot of freeing up and the roof was never the same and now leaked when it rained.

There were various other things that this lad managed to destroy or get stuck in the mud, because he was never fully awake during the day and he burnt the candle at both ends too much. It was not long until he disappeared too.

When the bloke from Yorkshire had gone, he was not replaced. I was rolling all the grassland, collecting straw from a farm down the road towards Wellow. I was in charge of scraping out all the cow yards and loading the muck spreader. Life got better and I was just about to turn seventeen which was a major turning point in my teenage life.

I did many tasks on the farm, in fact there were only a few things that I could not do without supervision, one of them was milking and the other was taking straw and hay over to our sister farm, over at Chillerton. A remote little farm, which I think, was rented. It only had around 100 acres and mainly put down to grass. The principle business was beef cattle and a few fields for wheat or barley, no dairy unit because it was too small for that kind of farming. I always wanted to take a load of feed over to this farm mainly because I had not gained any experience of towing a trailer more than a mile or so and I felt that I needed the knowledge.

I kept on at the cowman every time the feed got low over at Rill Farm, but he never gave in to my pleads but it was fun trying to persuade him to let me go. Lovely chap Ivan was and I think he is still driving cattle lorries for John Shirlaw in Porchfield.

I spent a week over in Chillerton and did some chain harrowing, grass rolling and one ploughed field with Cambridge rolls, which was a nightmare because of the old Fordson Power Major I had to use. The steering was as loose as hell and it kept catching the furrows and spinning the wheel so fast, good job my fingers were not between the bars on the wheel.

Very powerful little machine but basic and no cab or even a decent seat and I'm glad I only had to use that tractor once. When I harrowed all the pastureland, I had a Massey Ferguson 165, which had one of the original cabs with canvas windows and rear flap. It was around November when I was up on the hillside and it was bloody cold that week and especially in a canvas cab. I remember we unloaded a lorry load of steel tubing for new cattle pens and the main yard. The pipes were bloody freezing cold and had frost all over them.

It was on the Friday that Mr Fenweis had asked me to go over to Rill Farm on the following Monday on my moped and carry on rolling a field.

It was the coldest morning and the frost was the heaviest I had ever seen. A freezing cold mist lay in the air as I set off from home, sliding all over the place and with no gloves on. I got as far as Chessell and had to turn back because even though I had a pair of socks over my hands, I could not feel them; I was frozen and felt quite sick when I got home. Mum rang my boss and explained what happened and he told me to not to worry and stay home and warm up. I never ever rode a bike without gloves again after that episode.

When there wasn't much to do at work, I was often put on machine painting and pretty much painted every implement on the farm, except the two tractors of course. It was while I was painting a bale elevator that I discovered a new type of music. I had the farm radio on, which I usually pinched from the workshop and changed the station from radio four to radio one, much to the annoyance of the boss.

I remember him coming into the workshop in the morning, ready to do some welding or drill some holes and him turning on the radio – blasting out some punk song or something and him swearing "Bloody Nipper." I used to laugh and although he appeared annoyed, he always smiled when he said it.

He wasn't a bad chap really and if I saw him for a whole day, it was the rarest event in my working week. He was always working on his boat which he had been working on for years.

The radio was turned up and I heard this new song by a band called *Tubeway Army* and I was mesmerised by this brilliant new noise. I loved this song and it was being played all the time on the radio. I memorised the name of the band and went straight to *Hitchmans* record shop on the Saturday and bought the single. I played that song so many times that my family knew every note. It was of course *Are Friend's Electric* and it was the confirmation I needed for synthesisers in my life. To me, it was the first decent song that mixed synthesizers and guitars perfectly. The hero's as it were, that I had waited for, my love of the synth and the real lack of music that was not repetitive like *Tubular Bells* or *Oxygene*.

I found the album *Replicas* in *Hitchmans* and bought that too. Here was an album of pure genius to me. Perfect sounds and the most dark and mysterious lyrics I had ever heard. The lead singer on *Top of the pops* was completely weird and almost robotic in his actions. I watched and listened in complete awe and never looked back from that day on.

This little tale is really down to not having any knowledge of motorcycles at all and inexperienced mechanical know-how.

What happened to my moped's rear brake was a mystery to me but whenever there was wet weather it would lock up at the slightest touch and cause the bike to slide all over the place. After about a week of this happening, it started to get slowly worse and the rear brake would be binding all the time and I would lose all my power as the engine was at war with the brakes. I loosened off the bolt and spring on the back of the cam on the hub but it made little difference at all. There was a party at my girlfriend's house in Porchfield and because we had recently split up over a silly misunderstanding, I really wanted to be back with her because I missed her very much.

It was a so-called mate of mine that kept the party quiet from me and I later found out that he was phoning my girl and trying to get off with her, so our friendship was doomed from that day onwards. I never told him I knew about the party and him ringing her regularly. She saw through it and never gave him the time of day thank God.

On the way to the party my brakes locked completely going along the road towards Corfe Camp, just past the turn off by Shalfleet garage and would not release however many times I stamped on the foot pedal. There was only one thing for it, take the wheel off and have a look, so I parked up in a gateway to a field and took the wheel off completely and lucky I still had the full Yamaha tool kit with the bike or I would have been stuffed.

The brake shoes were worn out completely and down to the metal in places and there was only one thing I could do now and that was to remove the shoes and ride with one brake. I would not even think of doing that now but at the time, it really did not seem that stupid in my naivety. So I set off slowly at first and used the front brakes to test how well it stopped without my rear brake, it seemed fine and I made my way around the twisty bends to Porchfield and to the party.
I went into the house but could not find my ex anywhere and it was only until I asked one of her friends where she was that I saw something I really did not need to see. There she was with bloke in the spare bedroom upstairs. They had no idea I was there and the other bloke did not see me standing in the doorway of the spare

bedroom but she saw me and she looked a little shocked and broke off her kiss with him. I stared with disbelief and said absolutely nothing to either of them. I was out of that door and on my bike within seconds and down her lane and out on to the main road, I just went as fast as I possibly could and turned left out of her driveway towards Porchfield village.

Over the bridge and around the bend by the little Island and on towards the sharp right hand bend by the old schoolhouse. I was flying along and as I came up to the bend I put my foot on the brake pedal and forgot there was no braking there and how I didn't hit the stone wall in front of the schoolhouse I will never know. I went over the grass verge and stayed on the bike all the way along its length. I was quite shaken by the incident and had to stop along the road to gather my thoughts. I was exTimely upset and did not know what to do, so I decided to turn around and go home.

Carefully this time and try and console myself in my bedroom. I got home ok and Mum said that your girlfriend rang about half hour ago, she wondered if you were OK? Hearing this news made me feel a little better inside, because it showed she still had caring thoughts for me. I just got out my diary and read all the things that she had written in it when she stole it from me one day and cried. Ellie and I were finished for good this time as she had found this new chap from Cowes to hang around with and although I still had a lot of feelings for Ellie, I had to move on in life and find someone new. It wasn't an easy thing to do by any measure and I knew I was in love with her from the first time we met, but I couldn't change how she felt and there was nothing I could do to repair it now.

If there was one thing that I did not miss about visiting Ellie, it was the long journeys on my moped to Porchfield and back at least four times a week. In all weathers I would battle my way through strong winds on my little fizzy, thrashing the sheer guts out of her all the way and I am amazed that little bike kept going with all the abuse I gave it. Everything was held together with baler twine because I had not ventured into mechanics at that time and it was always a stop gap fix to get me home but it stayed like that until I sold it.

In the New Year I was busy clearing out one of the cow yards with my trusty Fergie T20 petrol/TVO *Tractor Vapourising Oil or commonly known as Paraffin* tractor with my new Twose scraper on the back. As I turned into the dung heap the tractor started to lean over one side and the front seemed to fall a little, as if I had gone down a manhole. What happened was the front wheel had rusted through and literally broke away from the rim and fell off. That was one of the strangest things that ever happened to me and we managed to find another front wheel to replace the rusted one.

This little T20 did not have a very good battery and was a sod to start on cold mornings. Luckily though, we had the starting handle for it and always used it during cold weather.

One particular day when it was necessary to start her with the dreaded handle, Mr Fenweis sat on the tractor, ready to give the thing some throttle as I turned the engine over. Unfortunately he had the tractor in gear and as it fired up it pinned me against the workshop wall. That was the last time I started it with a wall behind me and it was only the quick reactions of my boss to knock it out of gear quickly enough that saved a bad accident from happening.

The other factor was the clutch did not work at all when the engine oil was cold, so pushing the clutch down would have been pointless and would have not saved me from being a lot thinner. I suffered no damage from the accident and it certainly shocked Mr Fenweis quite a bit and he was very concerned for my safety. All he kept saying is "are you alright nipper, you sure you're ok nipper?" I often wondered if he would actually use my name on at least one occasion.

Tim Fenweis was a comical chap in a lot of ways, because he appeared rather upper class when he spoke to other people except us farm workers but in reality he was a typical dairy farmer, messy farm, machines rusting away and never bought anything new when it could be repaired or more than often, bodged. Like I mentioned earlier, some days he would disappear for hours and other times I did not see him for days at a time.
I was not aware of his greatest passion in the beginning of my new career but Ivan soon informed me that sailing and his beloved yacht came before anything else. Apparently he was planning some epic voyage in his yacht and this had been his ambition for a long time.

When I knew him, he was in the final stages of the adventure and I suppose he was trying to sort out the farm so he could go away and leave it in the capable hands of someone. This became reality, because during the last month of my YTS, he employed a manager to run the farms for him. I met the new man when he came to look around the place, and I think his name was Roger and came from the midlands somewhere. So the plan was coming together for the boss and it was only a matter of time and he would be sailing off somewhere.

This suited me fine because I was fine working on my own and knew what to do. My days always started with scraping down and feeding and bedding the yards, checking the cows for any signs of illness or injuries. Milling enough barley for the weeks feed supply and sometimes enough for the other farm too. Then there was the grass to roll and fertilise in early April and Fences to check and maintain.

The day Mr Fenweis actually appeared for a few hours one morning, he asked me to take the Dexter and link box to the workshop and he loaded two big chainsaws in the box, fuel and some tools, plus some materials to start a bonfire.

Now I was under the impression that he was going or we were going to fell some trees or clear out some woodland. Wrong. I was going off on my own to saw up some trees that had blown down in one of the fields, behind the little yard on the Shalfleet road. I drove down to the field that had the fallen trees in and started the chainsaw and cut up as much as I could. I had never ever been anywhere near such a machine and I had no idea how to use it properly or safely.

The chainsaw was not your modern, light version either, it was a Homelite and weighed about 10kg I would think and killed my arm muscles after about ten minutes. I eventually cut up most of one of the trees and loaded it all into the link box and carted it all back to the farm. Mr. Fenweis asked me if I had got on OK with cutting up the tree and I told him it was not easy work but I managed to cut up one of the trees and he seemed quite happy with my answer.

Now if that had happened today, the farmer would have been in a lot of trouble if an accident had occurred. It was one of many amazing days at work where I was just left to get on with a task, whether I knew what I was doing or not.

My new career was going fine and started getting on well with Mr Fenweis and he used to let me use the little Ford Dexter 2000 tractor to go to the shop in Shalfleet at lunchtime. One Friday afternoon, I took the tractor all the way back to Totland because I asked if I could borrow it to help clear the brambles from the horse field that Dad used. The field did not actually belong to Dad's mate the DJ, but he was in charge of it. I don't know the exact arrangement between the owners and Dad's mate, but no one ever cut the hedges back or did any maintenance whatsoever, hence why the field was so overgrown and neglected. So I borrowed the Dexter with a very large buck rake on the back so I could push the brambles into large heaps and burn it.

On the way home I decided to go through Norton Green, a tiny village just outside Freshwater. As I drove up the hill, the tractor exhaust started throwing out masses of sparks and bellowing out smoke and I really panicked because it was not my tractor and I didn't want anything to happen to it.

I stopped and as I had gloves on, pulled the exhaust pipe off and threw it into a water logged ditch. That did the trick and the fire was out. I think that because the tractor did not ever get used much and certainly never went flat out on the roads, the exhaust had oiled up and because I was giving it a good run, it heated up the pipe and it ignited. It was a very nice feeling driving my tractor home and parking it on the bay outside our house. I later took it under the archway, up to our parking area next to our garage. It was safer up there, away from prying eyes.

It was Saturday and we all went down to the horse's field and I started clearing the bushes out into the middle of the field. It did not take long with the tractor and buck rake to clear the whole field of brambles. A good job done and Dad and his mate were pleased with the result too. I later went for a drive up to Kitty's house and he laughed as I turned up on my Dexter outside his house. Kitty worked with agricultural machines too so we had a common interest in tractors.

I have to mention the lunch that Mum used to make for me every day, because I had never said or indicated that I like a certain variety of cheese. I always had these massive bread rolls with Double Gloucester cheese inside and they were like concrete slabs. I hated that cheese so much after about two months of the same thing, hence why I used to borrow my tractor and nip down to the little shop in Shalfleet.

The shop appeared to be a room on the side of a bungalow on the corner and was full of my favourite snack – biscuits. I was so grateful for that shop, because I just couldn't face another week of those bloody rolls. No disrespect to Mum of course, she was always busy making pies for the shops but I just cannot figure out what made her give me that concrete cheese.

On wet, cold afternoons in winter I always had the daunting task of getting my Fizzy going and getting home without it stopping on me. I usually finished at four o'clock and the dark evenings were drawing in quickly. Whenever it was raining I had to push start that damn thing down the road past the farm entrance and sweating under my one piece waterproof suit and my Nammet bag swinging round and getting in the way all the time.

I pushed that Fizzy bloody miles to get it going and all because Yamaha in their wisdom, fitted a metal covered spark plug cap. Metal and rain mixed with electricity just don't mix very well. Eventually, I think I put a piece of bicycle inner tube over the cap and it stopped it arcing across to the cylinder head and stopping.

Another Fizzy adventure was when I was stopped by the police for having my rear rack held on with baler twine as the bolts had fallen out going to work one day. I knew baler twine was nice and strong so that's what I used. The police officer was not so impressed with it though and I was told to get it fixed and had to take my documents to the police station too. No idea these Police officers! I thought as I went on my way.

When I used to travel to my girlfriend's farm, which was some ten miles away. I came home quite late at night at about eleven pm, and in those days there were not too many people about at that time of night, on mopeds anyway. I always came through Yarmouth and up Hallets Shute and one night it was raining and my coat had a nice big hood on it so I came up with a cunning plan and put my hood right over the top of my crash helmet so the rain didn't run down my face and neck.

It worked a treat and I was merrily flying along in the rain and over the bridge and suddenly I saw the Blue light treatment lighting up the road around me. I stopped and saw the white Escort van pull up behind me and the policeman called me over.

Luckily it was our local village policeman and his mate and when he saw that I had a crash helmet under the hood, they both laughed and said goodnight and drove off. From that night onwards, every time that van went past me the blue light would go on as if to say "evening" as they knew my Fizzy well and never bothered stopping me again after that night.

It was the beginning of April nineteen seventy nine and my YTS was coming towards the end of its term and I was pretty hopeful that I would have been given a full time job on the farm. Alas I was completely wrong and Mr. Fenweis informed me that my time was nearly over and I would be leaving soon.

I was pretty gutted and thought I was in with a good chance of work as I got on reasonably well there and didn't wreck any machinery unlike other students who had been there. I went home that night and told my parents what I was told and went out to see my mate Kitty to tell him that I was not going to be working on the farm anymore.

It was my last week on the farm and I was out rolling grassland most of the week and the occasional barley milling stint, when we had run out of rolled grain. I remember the weather was pretty warm that week and I was enjoying being out in the fields on my own just trundling up and down the long grass on the Massey 135. I preferred the Ford Dexter as it did not have annoying doors on it and in fact no cab at all. I found cabs were ok if it was wet but in general when you need to constantly get off the tractor and check machinery, cab doors were useless.

The last day on the farm was looming. It was a Friday too and I decided that I was leaving at lunchtime because my attitude was if I had no job then I'm not staying the whole day. So I got my bag sorted and just jumped on my bike and left the farm in the reflection in my mirrors and never to return again.

Little did I know that my Dad had gone out to see the farmer and give him a good talking to about me not having a job at the end of my YTS because the farmer had promised my Dad that there would be a place there for me. Apparently Dad put the farmer up against the wall by the scruff of his neck and threatened him with whatever Dad had in store for him. He did not have work for me on his farm but agreed with my Dad that he would find me a place on a farm in the locality within a week. Three days later my Dad had a phone call from Mr Fenweis to say I had an interview on a big farm in Yarmouth this week. I could not believe it and was so excited at the thought of going back to the work and do the job that I grew to love and not having to visit that depressing dole office in the village of Freshwater. I went with my Dad to Thorley Manor Farm at the end of April for my interview.

Rear view of The Dreens house in Totland. Circa 1980.

Chapter 10

A New Age

Seventeen, what an age to be, it was more significant than being eighteen by far and brought so much more fun into my world. I had waited for months for the opportunity to move on from my trusty Fizzy to something with more power and a bike that looked like a real motorcycle instead of a bicycle with an engine bolted to it.

Like I mentioned earlier, I had foolishly swapped my Yamaha TY50m for the very first bike I ever rode, the Suzuki TS125 scrambler. I don't know what possessed me at the time to do such a thing. I was still working with Dad at the time and really did not need transport to work and most of my spare time was spent up at the sandpit with Kitty and his brother Jimmy. Of course if I had known that I was going to end up needing transport for my new job, I would have kept the moped. For a short time I had to get a lift to work with our lodger who was running our new butcher's shop in Newport, which was situated right at the bottom of town, almost next door to the police station.

The shop had hardly any space in the back rooms and you couldn't park anywhere near the shop either, so bringing in supplies was a complete nightmare. Why Dad decided to open that shop in the first place I will never know. It never made much money and was just a burden on the family business in my view. Maybe he was trying to give Mack his chance to run a shop or something, but the lodger was a useless manager of the shop and couldn't run a bath let alone his own shop.

I worked there for a while as I was in between jobs and I hated the place. Dead was an understatement and we might as well have opened a shop in the car park across the road as there would have been more customers there. Dad and Mum lost a lot of money on the place from start to finish.

It was very early April and my Fizzy had broke down and I needed to get to Ningwood for my job on the dairy farm so I went every morning in this massive Vauxhall Victor car which had the weirdest speedometer I had ever seen, a sort of coloured bar that went across a scale of numbers.

I remember we had to roll off the front pavement in front of the flat and bump the car in frosty conditions. That winter was bloody freezing and the frosts were horrendous and lasted right through April, almost until May. I had only just reached the age of seventeen and it didn't matter if the Fizzy was dead as I had plans to sell it and buy a 250.

This girl also got a lift with us as she worked on a farm in Porchfield and she was a friend of the family who rode horses. Lyn was her name and she was a real tomboy most of the time but she had a good sense of humour and wild personality to say the least. The strangest coincidence of it all was that she worked on my first girlfriend's farm and even more strange was that the bloke she worked with was a friend of mine who travelled on the school coach to Cowes High school.

After a while I grew quite attached to this Lyn girl and started seeing her in the evenings. I would go round to her house which was just around the corner in Elliston Road. She had a very big house and the biggest garden in the whole street. She lived there with her Mother, two sisters and one brother.

Her Father worked overseas and I never actually met him in all the time we lived in the village. In the garden there was a stable and hay shed and one night I went round there and was helping her with the straw for the horse and she said "I need to get some hay out of that shed and it's a tight squeeze to get in there, you coming?" I followed her through this gap in the bales, which was about the width of a bale wide and that's all.

Once inside she grabbed me and started snogging me and slowly undressing me. It was not long until we were both completely naked and laying on the soft hay kissing and exploring each others bodies. Her kiss was gorgeous and somehow mesmerised me as we kissed and kissed and I moved down to her chest and tasted the delights of her body. She was leading me into temptation without a doubt and this was my first time naked with a girl. I had never gone any further than kissing with Ellie and although certain feelings were starting to show in me, I had not experienced anything like I was feeling that night in her hay shed.

She asked me, while she was moving down my belly and holding me tightly "this is your first time isn't it." I shyly said "Yes" and she kissed me again and the feelings I was experiencing were so intense that I thought she was going to make me explode there and then.

She stopped and lay next to me and then pulled me on top of her as she took hold of me and put me inside her. That most amazing feeling of being so close for the very first time, with the moonlight shining through the little shed window and illuminating her body. I followed her guiding words and I could feel her excitement levels rise and her body arched and he guided me up and down. As I reached the point of explosion, I needed to feel her kiss again and we kissed like it was our last kiss as I came.

I do not know if she came as I was not experienced enough to know the signs if it happened, but she was smiling at me and kissing me constantly and saying that I was very good.

I am so glad that my first experience was with someone who knew what she was doing and showed me what to do. I was totally inexperienced and it would have been so embarrassing for me. I think it made it perfect and it was how it should have been and not a rushed and fumbled grope and kiss in the hay.

I saw her for a while after that until some rumours were going around that my Dad was having an affair with her and someone had seen him kissing her at the back of the flat which later became the bakery. I often wondered if there had been some collusion between her and my father to make sure I had lost my virginity. Sickening really and it would not surprise me if that is what took place either, because back in those days, if you hadn't had sex by eighteen years old then you were scorned upon by friends and family and even branded a woofter or similar terminology.

So even though my first sexual encounter was wonderful at the time, I don't regard it in a very good light now.

I had heard from my Dad's friend Roy who owned a hotel up church hill in Totland, that he knew of a 250 motorcycle for sale and it was quite cheap and only a mile away, in freshwater. I was very excited about this, couldn't wait to go and look at it. Roy was the builder and part time DJ friend of Dad's and who was a very placid sort of chap. Very inoffensive in his character and also very unaware of a lot of life's changes and even though I was just seventeen, I reckoned I was more street wise than he was.

He did not seem to move very far outside his West Wight circle and although he was reasonably wealthy, didn't use it to enhance his outlook at all. I got on quite well with him and he always came to our house for coffee and a chat with Mum and Dad. He built the breakfast bar in our kitchen and it was a good job he made of it too.

Dad was useless with anything mechanical or DIY based and would rather pay someone else to do the job. Now this is a very odd thing to me, because both my brother Liam, my Sister Sarah and I are all reasonably adept at mechanical things and DIY. I often wonder where we get those traits from, certainly not from my Father.

Roy had this mobile disco outfit and had a regular job at the only nightclub in the west Wight, *Barneys Roadhouse* a sort of diner crossed with a disco affair, situated on the Military Road, near Brighstone. The only reason I can think of for putting it there, was because of the noise or something, being so remote, not many people would have been disturbed by cars, drunken youngsters and loud music running into the early hours.

Because of his connection with the nightclub, we gained some business from him; we supplied the beef burgers every weekend for the internal takeaway, inside the disco. I think we also supplied meat to the restaurant at the rear of the nightclub too. I never visited that restaurant but my family went there once for a birthday outing.

I arranged through Dad's mate Roy, to go and look at this 250cc bike for sale and my mate Kitty came with me too. It was down at a little cottage at a place called *Spinfish,* in Freshwater. I knew the bike was British but I didn't realise it had no lights except a brake light of course. It was a Greaves frame with a Villiers 2T engine and it had a fibreglass tank and the most unusual front forks I had ever seen. They were known as Banana forks and worked in much the same way as the classic 'Honda C90/70' series because when you applied the front brake, the bike kind of surged forward a bit and then came to a sharp stop.

The rear wheel was buckled and did get slightly worse after a while but I could not afford a new wheel and I doubted whether I would find another anyway. Obviously I had not had any experience of riding British bikes as all that was available were Japanese mopeds or the odd French or Italian scooter, but nothing British.

Looking back on this saga, I don't know how that bike got through its MOT test, the tank was illegal in those days and the rear wheel would never pass in that state, the brake light was similar to a glow worm in a jar and if you could see it, you had superman's vision. The horn was one of those bicycle devices with the rubber ball and the speedo was just spinning about for the sake of it.

This was my dream come true, my long awaited seventeenth year when you were able to get off your moped for the last time, sell it and buy a real bike. Go everywhere and anywhere you liked at a descent speed, and no pedals. I bought this weird machine because it was all I could afford at the time because *YTS* didn't keep you in gold. I only paid £225 for the bike but had to get it MOT'd, taxed and insured, which I got fixed in record time and I was very soon on the road. Mind you, I had to get on the road pretty quickly because of my travelling to work every day and what would I have done in the evenings?

The Greaves was not very fast at all and very heavy around bends at slow speed but the brakes were surprisingly good and this gave me some confidence whilst riding it. For about four months I rode the Greaves all over the place, including lots of off road stuff up on the Warren fort car park. Megan's rubbish tip on the old Alum Bay Road which was only open to people who knew old Mr. Megan and because he was a good customer of Dad's, I got permission to go up there with Kitty. It was originally a sand extraction quarry and after the extraction, they used it as a landfill site.

The place was excellent and the mounds of sand and earth were brilliant for scrambling. Mr. Megan's grandson used it for Motocross practice as he raced all the time and he always had a gorgeous Maico 440 bike. There were a few other people who went up there but not many, which was good. I rode the bike all over the place but there was one governing factor that prevented me be out all evening, I had no lights on the bike, so could only ride it during daylight hours.

I got some strange looks from people when they saw the bike going past, or parked up outside the *Braemar Cafe* in Totland. Older chaps used to talk to me about the bike and especially if we went down to Yarmouth and sat outside the ferry terminal. We often sat there just watching the traffic coming off the ferry and there was the *Harbour Lights Cafe*, a favourite haunt of us young bikers.

One day I was riding the old beast home from work and I usually came along the road from Ningwood to Thorley and then up through *Wilmingham* and onto Afton Road. I had just turned onto Afton Road and suddenly my bike started to stutter and hiss and sort of started to surge and slow. Suddenly there was this massive whoosh through the exhaust and the bike suddenly burst into life, like it had never done.

What happened was the number two cylinder started to fire up and the bike sounded and went like a rocket from that day on. I always thought it was running on both cylinders and being so naive and so new to more than one cylinder on an engine, I had ridden it for over five months on one pot. How I did not damage the thing I don't know. What a shock I had and I was straight round to my mate Kitty's house to show him the difference in power and the sound of the engine.

The only negative effect was the fuel consumption went mad and I was always down the garage getting fifty pence worth of petrol from the vending machine. I came so close to running out of fuel coming home from work, but never actually broke down.

Meanwhile, Kitty's brother big Jimmy had traded his Honda 250 Dream for a brand new Honda XL250s trail bike. Now amongst all the trail bikes that came out in the very late 70's, this was one of the robust and fun machines I ever rode. It had a massive front wheel and rubber indicators and this was only some of the great features of the bike.

It had plenty of power and was brilliant off road. Not a machine you could pull wheelies on but if you wanted to almost trials ride, it handled very well just pottering about. The only pitfall was the early Bridgestone tyres were notorious for not being very good in wet weather, being made of a very shiny, almost plastic composition. They would have you sliding about on shiny parts of the road, lethal on manhole covers or pelican crossings.

Big Jimmy was in awe of this bike and looked after it as if it was his baby. I remember every Sunday afternoon, after we had been up the chalk pit at the bottom of the downs track, just up the road from the *Highdown Inn*. He would remove the chain and clean it with petrol then boil it in this large tin of grey, graphite grease and let it cool and set. This was supposed to lubricate every part of the chain and especially where normal chain oil could not reach. This was a Sunday afternoon ritual that rubbed off onto young Kitty too, *LinkLyfe* was our new saviour.

My sister Sarah pony trekking in Norfolk. Circa 1975.

Because big Jimmy had his XL and Kitty only had the SS50 it was time Kitty moved up the ladder too and it was quite predictable that he too bought a brand new XL250s. So there were now two new Honda's to compete with up on the chalk downs or the Warren. Obviously my old Greaves could not keep up with these two because it was so heavy and was completely geared wrong for off road. After all, the engine was really a road bike engine and designed similarly to the Yamaha Twin two stroke motors.

I stuck with the Greaves until early 79 and then she had to go because I had another bike in my dreams. On one particular day that I will never forget, because it was the funniest thing I ever heard regarding a Honda SS50 and a tall, lanky lad on board. One of Kitty's mad experiments was to put high octane, model aeroplane fuel in his tank just to see how much faster he could get up the big hill from Compton bay, towards Freshwater bay. Well he must have put tons of this Ether based stuff in his fuel and set off from work and a very rapid rate of knots. He said that as he came up the hill doing about 55 mph, the engine started juddering and strange noises and suddenly there was no power at all and a loud bang from the engine casing as the flywheel flew off and overtook him.

I can still picture it happening because later he disclosed that the reason the flywheel came off was because he cross threaded the nut that retained it and he'd used super glue to hold it on.

I was a nervous wreck when Dad and I drove into the main entrance to the farm because it did not look like a farm. There was none of the usual mud, machinery rusting in the yard and no baler twine holding all the doors and gates shut.

I was met by the Manager of the farm and taken with Dad to the office, which was an annex on the side of the manor house. It was a room that was quite warm and had a large map on the wall with all the field names upon it. A large desk and filing cabinet in the corner and the biggest radiator I had seen since my schooldays. The manager had a distinct northern accent and explained what the farm did and what was grown. He asked me if I was familiar with tractors and did I have a license. He explained that it would be long hours during haymaking and harvest and similarly during the cultivation periods. He also told me that the farm was over one thousand acres in total and my imagination began to wander. I was quite nervous but somehow quite confident at the same time because the manager was very open and seemed, understanding.

He asked if I had transport and I told him I had a motorcycle, so that was a plus point for me.

After the interview in the office he showed us around the farm and inside the massive grain plant, which I could not believe the size of it all and the tractors were nothing like the machines I was used to at all. I was told that I had a job if I wanted it there and then and when that happens, you kind of freeze up and can't think of what to say. I wanted this job more than anything and said "yes" I wanted the job. So it was agreed that I would start at the end of May because if I can remember correctly, a previous student was leaving at the beginning of May and the vacancy would be available.

I left the farm so excited and full of life and the thought of all those acres to work on and the machines I would be operating. I couldn't wait to start there and work on a decent farm at last. The next problem I encountered was what am I going to do for six weeks until I started at Thorley Manor. I had another appointment with the same careers adviser as I had seen before I started at the dairy farm and he knew what I had been doing for the past year and what I was used to. The only short term YTS available was on a fruit farm on the outskirts of Freshwater and he arranged for me to go there and meet the owners. I went for the interview and it was agreed that I could start there on the following Monday and stay for a six week period.

So I started at the fruit farm and got into the way they worked, well almost. I hated every minute I spent there because it was the most boring job I had ever had to do. While I was there, Dad and I went to Southampton to look at a new Honda Super Dream 250 at Rye's at West Quay Road, Southampton. I had saved some money and I really wanted a new bike as all I had was the Greaves, which would have been useless if I was working late because it had no lights.

So we looked at the bike and got all the details sorted and I bought one on HP for £749.00. I cannot remember what the monthly payments were but they were just about affordable at the time. I could not get the bike for a week as the finance had to be agreed and the bike had to be ready for collecting.

It was a daunting prospect of going over to Southampton on my own to collect the bike and worst still, riding the thing back on roads I had never been on. I went over to collect the bike on a Saturday morning and came back on the Red Funnel to East Cowes because there was no way I was riding it to Lymington as I did not know the way.

It was scary riding a brand new bike and getting used to the weight of the machine was very difficult at times because it weighed a lot more than my previous bike. Putting it on the side stand was interesting on the ferry as it was the first time I had taken a bike on the ferry too. I did not attempt to put it on the centre stand for quite a while because there was a knack to it and if you got it wrong, you would be flattened.

I lost my balance once in Kitty's garden and went to put the side stand down but missed and I was instantly trapped underneath the bike and there was no way I could get it off of me either.

The power of this new bike was fantastic and the whining sound it made going down through the gears was gorgeous. I loved the bike to bits and went all over the island on it and to places I had never been to before. There was nothing I did not like about the machine and cleaned it every weekend and kept it looking like new for most of the time I had it. I had to take it back over to Rye's for its first service and that was pretty easy as I knew the way by then and came back on the Lymington ferry instead.

I rode it to the fruit farm but thank god it was the last week there because the lane was constantly muddy or dusty and I hated my new machine getting dirty all the time, vain I know but cleaning it properly took a whole day to do. My tasks at the fruit farm were so demanding and making peat blocks was not my idea of fun and even worse was picking off the dead stems off the tomato plants in the greenhouses. The owners did not like me very much because I was always too slow in doing the tasks and constantly moaning about the job. They knew I hated the place and I think they hated me too. I prayed for my last day to come and very soon I was riding out of that place for the last time and looking forward to a week off before I started at Thorley.

One evening the so called mate who tried to get off with my girlfriend Ellie, came over to Totland from Cowes on his brand new Suzuki 250 and the only reason he came to our neck of the woods was to show off his bike and chase the girls in our group of friends. That was what he was like and I put up with it for a while, until I actually sussed out what he was up to. Unknown to him, I pre warned all the people in the café what he was really like and he didn't pull a muscle in our group. By the way, this was the dude that rang up my Ellie and was planning to take her from me behind my back at the party. I did not hate people who rode scooters because to me they are just bikers but on something completely different that's all. Just because they wear different clothes from the usual bike enthusiast did not mean they were any different from us.

For some reason this bloke liked to chase them and wanted to chase this dude through Totland and up towards the Primary School and wherever he ran to next. Because I knew the roads so well and he didn't, I followed this bloke on his scooter and he was quicker than this mate was and I turned down St Saviour's Road and the scooter went straight on down Summers Lane. I turned so quickly and then a car was coming up the road *before it was a one way street* so I braked so fast that this mate was not looking at me, but looking which way the scooter had gone and he braked so quickly that his front wheel slipped out from under him and bang – he was laying in the road with the bike on top of him.

I looked round and saw this mess on the road and laughed so much as I pulled over and was just about to ask him if he was OK and he shouted "what did you do that for you idiot?" "Oh so it was my fault was it" I replied "you were behind me so you should have been watching what is in front of you."

As he picked himself off the ground and lifted the bike up and inspected the damage, which was minimal really. He did not say much after that and I just said "You want to learn how to ride that thing before you chase people" and I swore at him and told him in no uncertain terms to "Fuck off and don't bother coming out here again." He didn't ever come back thank God and in fact I have never seen him since.
Did you ever have a shallow friend like that too?

My first day at Thorley was very interesting. As I rode my trusty Super dream into the yard and looked for somewhere to park it. I met the head tractor driver, who was waiting outside the workshop building doors, then the fitter arrived and opened the workshop doors and we all went inside. A few minutes later another chap arrived in his car and then another. I was not aware there were so many people working there and it was quite scary at first as I did not know anyone. Soon the manager arrived in his little Honda pickup truck and he walked into the workshop and said "good morning" and introduced me to all my fellow workers and they all said "hello".

The manager then told me that I needed to carry a diary with a pencil and a penknife and maybe a watch as these were essential items to have on you.

I had the watch and a penknife but not the diary so I made sure I had some paper in my boiler suit pockets. I was put with a young chap called Len, who the manager introduced to me and said that he came from Freshwater. We were to go and clear up the drier barn. Also we had to clean out the elevator pits because they have a tendency of filling up with water and mixed with grain, it was quite a mess. My new friend took me up the ladder that led up to the catwalk which went on top of the hundred ton grain bins.

He explained what the elevators and conveyors did and how you could transfer grain from one bin to another, one you had set all the slides and conveyor direction properly. It was a very complex system and took a lot of time to learn its ways. The massive array of switches on the wall near the doors was daunting to say the least. Len showed me the metal tunnel that ran parallel with the catwalk and this was where the main slides were that emptied the giant bins, this tunnel had a secondary purpose and that it was where the big fan blew air into the bins through a series of ducts that ran almost the whole length of the bins.

The grain dust covered everything in its wake and I had never seen anything like it before. We had to wear dust masks when working inside the bins or on the catwalk because if you didn't, you would know about it later. There was a small table on the left of the doors and this is where the moisture meter lived and the book that contained the records of every crop harvested. The grain pit was big too and had a large barrier in front of it to stop people falling in. Behind the top of the pit wall was this strange looking contraption that resembled two digger buckets joined together and mounted on a pivot, it also had a counter attached to it.

At first I had no idea what it was but as soon as I actually saw the drier in action I learnt that it was the machine that weighed the grain as it came from the Dresser. This machine sat to the right of the weighing machine and rose up level with the catwalk. It was in a creamy grey colour and had pipes protruding from it and these bag holders which were similar to rubbish bins that clamp the bag around the top. All very strange to me and again I had no idea what this thing did.

We cleaned up all the chaff and dust from the catwalk and the manager warned us about using fertiliser bags on the steel catwalk as some of the stuff inside the bags fell out onto the floor and quickly caused the steel to corrode in places. So we had to make sure we shook the remaining oxidising agent from the empty bags before we took them up on the catwalk. One of my first jobs after clearing up was to take a large container of Jenolite rust killer up onto the catwalk and apply it to the corroded areas of steel flooring panels. Once Len and I had finished the first drier barn then we went through the farm yard towards the back of the farm, past the large hay barn on the left and the cow yard on the right to the *Mill house*.

It had a small silo and strange looking black tanks outside the steel door. We then walked onwards to the *old drier barn* which sat parallel to the road at the rear of the farm. Going through the small green door it was very dark and dismal looking so we walked around the large drier and opened the large sliding doors. There was a large grain pit which was partly covered in railway sleepers and a couple of metal plates.

At the front of the barn, between the small and large doors sat three giant fans, these were the exhaust from the drier and caused the chaff to be sucked out of the grain as it passed through the drier. Underneath the fans was a large amount of chaff that had collected during the drier's operation.

Behind the drier was a small silo and on the door side of the drier there was this huge what looked like a jet engine thing. This was the drier's source of heat and scared the hell out of me when I first started it up, it fired a massive flame of atomised diesel into a cowling and made such a roar as it burnt. Quite often the flame would go out at first, so you would have to re start it.

There was another large array of switches on the wall opposite the burner and the main electric meters too. Just inside the small doorway there was a table and cupboard which had parts of the drier inside. On the wall, under the switches there was this very ancient looking set of scales. Walking past both the silo and drier, there was a large open barn area with wheat piled up on one side and a large auger, mounted on wheels with cables and a winch attached to it.

Another weighing machine which was mounted in a metal frame and was moveable and underneath there was a large fan thing which I guessed blew the grain into the open barn. The elevator was between the drier and silo and the pit contained a lot more water than the new drier. We emptied the water and mouldy grain, which had began to take root in the pit.

Most of the one hundred ton bins were empty and there were some strange looking things going on in the bottom of them too. Lots of Hessian and wire cages, which looked like tunnels made of mesh. I had no idea what was going on at first but very soon learned what these things were for. The bins already had a series of ducts in them and they were designed to blow the corn towards to conveyor hatches but this particular bin was having extra ducts being constructed from this mesh and yards of Hessian? The extra ducts being assembled were for rye grass seed as I later found out. Because of the size of the grass seeds and the moisture content of it being relatively high for its size and the fact that the seeds had to be very dry for storage, extra ducts were needed to achieve this. When I started on the farm it was about a month before hay making and grass cutting in general so I saw all the preparations being made for this big event in the life of the farm.

I am sure it was the second or third day that I was at Thorley and I was sent off with Mark the fitter, one Ford 5000 with a McConnell rear digger attached and a load of clay drainage pipes. We were to lay a series of trenches across the top of the *Bouldnor Block*, near the main entrance to
the fields which was down a short track next to a very large thatched house with so many fruit

trees in the gardens. We dug quite a few
trenches across the fields and had to lay the clay
pipes in the trenches with a certain amount of
fall to ensure the water was carried in the right
direction.

While we were digging and laying these
drainage pipes, the lady in the thatched cottage
gave us so many fresh plums and other fruits
from the trees, they were lovely too and I think
we ate far too many over the couple of days we
were working there. One of the trenches went
relatively close to a large block wall and we
realised by the amount of old rubbish we found,
that it was more than likely some sort of
Victorian dump.

We found lots of old smoking pipes and bottles
in that particular part of the field, but we kept it
quiet as we didn't want hoards of scavengers in
the field after dark, digging up the field. I really
enjoyed those few days doing the drainage pipes
and working with Mark because he was such a
character and always making jokes which made
the week a very nice one indeed.

I did not get to work with the other staff on the
farm until at least the end of April as hay
making began. They were out doing jobs in the
fields that were too specialised for a new comer

to the farm. I worked with Len quite a lot and had some damn good laughs too. He was a rebel when it came to overtime and was always just downing tools and going home, to the dismay of the manager who expected everyone to work on when it was needed, plus in our contract it read *Overtime to be worked when required*. He just hated working in the evenings and would rather be going out with the girls than stacking hay or straw every night. He used to go on and on about not working "tonight" and sometimes it got on some of the other peoples nerves and they would just say "if you want to go, then just bugger off and stop moaning about it!". He would go very quiet for half hour then just jump in his tractor and go back to the farm and more often than not, screech the tyres of his cut down mini as he flew up the road.

I started to go over to Cowes every Friday evenings to meet up with some of my old class mates on their bikes and we used to go down to the sea front and just hang around the Gloucester Hotel on the parade. Then to show off to the girls emerging from the discos and such like. Then we would go to the youth club which was down Arctic Road and have some laughs. It was one night on these trips that I met a Dutch girl at the youth club disco and ended up walking with her to Place Road and sitting on a bench chatting, well trying to, and grabbing few kisses for good measure. Oh those days were the best. Free and single and without a care in the world and just riding about on my bike, posing in front of whoever was around.

However, it was not all good fun as I found out, as I rode off to Cowes one night and I was going too fast around the second bend on the Afton Road. I went around the left hand bend so fast that I could not get round it on my side of the road and drifted right on the white line and my bike boot rubbed against a car coming in the other direction. That scared the life out of me and I had to stop and stop shaking before I carried on my journey. It taught me not to take bends so fast and made me slow down a lot after that.

We had a chap who would deliver some of the foodstuffs for the butchers shop and he drove one of those vans with the massive windscreen and all you could see was the tiny bald headed bloke sat in one corner, driving it. Those vans always made me laugh and were usually *BRS* or *British Road Services* vans. This chap would turn up with the rusk or flavourings for various things and try and sell us all sorts of items from the back of his van.

Chainsaws, mowers, fridges toys and you name it, he had it. Every week he would have something for sale and must have done a good trade with these things. But where did they come from, was the question in our minds, hence we never bought a thing from him but we knew plenty of people who would have done.

This went on for at least two years and every Friday the chap turned with his goodies, as we named them until one week he did not drop by. We did not see him again and wondered what had happened to him. He was a likeable fellow and we always had a good laugh with him, even though we would not buy from him, I think he liked coming to the shop because he always got a welcome and a cup of tea waiting. It was at least five weeks until we heard what had happened to him and we were pretty shocked too.

He had been arrested along with a large number of other *BRS* employees for stealing and selling items belonging to customers who had ordered them from their catalogues. They had stolen thousands of pounds worth of stuff and I am pretty sure the chap who came to us was put in prison for his crimes.

Hay making was one of my favourite times it latter years on the farm, because it meant I was back at work and earning a nice sum. The hours were never too much to make you bored with always being at work, unlike harvest or cultivation. You were able to have evenings to yourself and even the odd Saturday off, if the weather was bad. The only hay making equipment we regularly used was a Lely Acrobat, a wheeled version of the Acrobat and a Lely Golden Pheasant Tedder. Now the Acrobat was basic in any farming application and although past its sell by date, was a simple and very effective piece of kit.

I wish I could say the same for the wheeled version. It was horrendous to use because of the way the wheels were suspended on springs and pieces of old rusty wire where the springs had snapped off in the past. It would hit a deep rut in the grass and one of the wheels would just spin on its castor and almost turn the thing over.

Lely's Golden Pheasant Tedder however was a brilliant piece of kit and I was always assigned this job for some reason. Maybe it was because I liked using it or maybe some sort of punishment – who knows. It's only real failings were the wheels and the manufacturers attempt to prevent grass or whatever it was you were tedding from building up in the wheel bearings. It would always wrap itself around the bearings of the wheels and because they had welded these semi circular metal plates over the hubs, the grass would wrap itself so tightly between this plate and the hub. Often the only way to clear the wheel was to remove it, this was not easy to do because you had to carry a jack with you in the cab. A good knife was essential as was a grease gun because if the manager came out to see how the job was going and he noticed the wheel bearings were dry; prepare yourself for a good bollocking and a small lecture on greasing bearings.

Putting it in transport position was quite simple to do as long as you had sufficient room to maneuver and had plenty of air in the tyres. The operator was able to change the direction of the rotor by way of a small lever on top of the machine's gearbox. You were also able to adjust the height of the tines by winding the wheels up or down. There were a set of yellow painted doors that fitted on the rear of the machine and these allowed the tedded grass or straw to be rowed up for baling, without having to use a rake or turner.

If you managed to get a puncture while towing the Tedder down the road then you were in for a very dangerous experience as I found out one afternoon. I had just finished fluffing up the hay in a small field that we rented along Bouldnor Road, directly opposite the field which we called *Forestry*. I had just got out of the gate way and off the verge when there was this almighty bang and suddenly the machine veered off across the road, luckily there was nothing coming down the road because the Tedder would have side swiped it and caused one hell of an accident; I was always very wary towing it from that day onwards.

Once the hay had been spread out and was drying nicely, we started to rake it back into neat rows ready for baling. It was nearly lunchtime and after going back to the farm and getting a jack to remove the Tedder wheel, my mate was raking up the hay.

We stopped for lunch and sat on the grass, leaning against the wheels of the tractors when suddenly the wind started to get up and from absolutely nowhere. There was not a breath of wind when we had sat down, when this gust started to spiral in the corner of the field and it got larger and larger as it spun and picking up the hay from the freshly rowed grass. This mass of hay and the whirlwind then moved higher in the air and managed to deposit an entire row of hay onto the main road. Cars slowed down as it began to rain hay all over them. It was amazing to see and it was not the only time it happened in that field either, as I saw a lot of whirlwinds in that corner of the field for some reason.

The self propelled sprayer that was built by Malcolm and Mark. Circa 1979.

There was a chap who rode his bicycle past the farm almost every day and I noticed that one side of his face so badly disfigured and always wondered what had happened to him. I later found out from Hayward that he had gone through a very bad relationship with this wife and she was in bed with another bloke when he came in from work one day. Apparently, he was so affected by the break up that he took his shotgun and tried to commit suicide by shooting himself in the face. Unfortunately the kick from the gun going off made him miss the whole of his face and it only damaged on side. How bloody unlucky can you get and the worst bit is he is still alive and having to put up with this permanent disfiguration. It is quite weird how many farm workers and farmers try to kill themselves through either debt or from break up with a partner, as I remember a chap who worked for Kings Manor Farm and who was a good friend of our lodger, back in the late seventies. He hung himself over a divorce and money worries in his house in Freshwater. Poor chap and such a wasted life because he was a very nice bloke who would help anyone.

One of the girls that were in our bike group in Totland at that time was a Canadian girl with short brown hair and fairly tall for her age. I went out with her for quite a while back then and we had some interesting times together. She was the very first person to go on the back of my Suzuki GS400 and we went off to Alum Bay on it and took photos of it all. She was a nice girl and we always had a good laugh with her in the café or in the Broadway Inn, she would hang around with us on the bench and listen to the boys and their ghetto blaster in the evenings and laugh at PC Chizzy going around the roundabout on his CB200 police bike.

We had some very emotional times that I remember and it was because her sister still lived in Canada and she missed her dearly and I was still emotional over Tony and we would cry together some nights and comfort each other. I lost track of her when we moved to Freshwater and never saw her again after that.

It was in two thousand and sixteen, when I was looking at who my brother Liam was friends with on Facebook. I couldn't believe he was friends with her on there, so I sent a message and friend request and she accepted my request and we chatted and I found out what had happened to her since the good old days of the eighties.

Tragedy had dealt its hand to her family, as her older sister had died suddenly of a brain tumour. This must have been truly devastating for her. Having to endure the move from Canada and leaving her sister behind was bad enough and knowing how much she missed her sister and longed to be with her all the time while we were together.

It was a typical summer morning at seven thirty am, on the farm and we had all dragged ourselves out of bed to begin another dusty day in harvest time. A congregation of somewhat tired and still half asleep farm workers stood waiting in the workshop for our leader to come and give us direction for the day and perhaps a little quip to enchant our lives once more. Well there were not many smiling faces that morning because we were informed of our work mate Len's unfortunate accident the following evening in his Mini. He had turned his car over on the Afton Road. He had hurt his hand in the accident and was therefore unable to work. No one really knew what had happened to our friend that night and plenty of untruths began to flow in conversation amongst other work mates and passing visitors to the farm that day.
It wasn't until the lad's Father called into the farm to speak to the manager that we found out exactly what happened and how he was. He apparently, hit the bank and turned over but the

worst thing was he had his window open and his arm was resting on the window as it crashed. This caused his fingers to be pushed into the palm of his hand and meant that he would not be back at work for a very long time.

In fact we never saw him return to work after that day and when I met up with him one day, he seemed to be very different and not the chap I once knew. The accident had changed his whole personality and made him somewhat subdued and sad in his facial expressions.

Not everyone could see the change in him, but I was very aware of the changes to his personality and it really did not seem that I knew this chap anymore. It took many years for him to return to his old self, which he did thank God. I am still best friends with him to this day and we still exchange stories of our beloved Thorley days. Shame he left the farm at that time and I know he hated working all hours but he made the place exciting because no one else on the farm would be meeting gangs of girls in the manor gardens and instead of working, chatting to them for hours on end. He was a right little Romeo on the quiet and all the local girls would be inviting him to parties or turning up at the farm when Malcolm was out on the combine at lunch times.

My Mother had inherited one of those very fashionable electronic organs made by Farfisa. I'm pretty sure it came from my granddad's house, why my granddad had an organ was beyond me as he couldn't play anything musical. It had a double keyboard and foot pedals and complete with a very tinny drum machine, when it arrived in our flat everyone wanted to play it but after a few weeks the new toy was soon discarded and left to myself and my sister to play.

After a week or so, Mum said we should have organ lessons and she had somehow learnt of this chap in Totland that taught the subject. We had lessons every week and it was pretty good fun and one of the best lessons I had was when I produced a book of *Deep Purple* songs and managed to persuade the teacher to play a few songs from it. He could play anything in front of him and he played it brilliantly too and I think *Jon Lord* would have applauded. If there was any player of the organ that I really admired, it was *Jon Lord*.

The lessons went on for about six months or so and then we moved to the new place and I took the organ to my band practice shed and used it for the band. My sister had some strange experiences while having her lessons.

She said that someone was always behind her but when she turned around to see who it was, there was no one there. She said that it made her very nervous and almost physically sick once or twice and one of the reasons she gave it up. One of the first ghostly experiences recorded in that flat.

At the same time we were enduring the organ lessons, Mum employed a lady to clean the flat once a week and she was always there on Saturdays. This lady had the thinnest legs I have ever seen and it was not long until we had all named her various nick names, such as snap legs or lucky. Unfortunately, as my Sister was very young and had the savvy of radar for collecting all the words we said and reproducing them exactly. She only went and told the cleaner that we all call her snap legs and talk about embarrassing, my God I wished the sofa would have opened up and taken me away. I don't think she worked for us for much longer after that incident.

I was becoming bored with my two fifty bike as everyone else was taking their test and moving up to larger machines. I hadn't got around to taking my bike test and even if I had, it would have been so difficult to get the time off work to take it. There was a lovely lady who used to come into dads shop and her husband was doing up motorcycles and selling them from his house near the cliffs above Totland pier. So I badgered my dad to come with me and have a look at what bikes he had for sale and possibly swap my Superdream for something bigger. I was pretty amazed how many bikes this chap had in his garage and I was in awe of this big Suzuki GS400 sitting there in the corner. I asked if I could sit on it and possibly start it up, which I did and I fell in love with the machine there and then. The chap was more than willing to swap the four hundred for my two fifty. This was very helpful because I had no money to pay out for a bigger bike at the time.

I rode the machine straight to Freshwater and got it insured and then I was out all night on her. After a while, I was thinking of having the tank repainted as it wasn't an immaculate paint job as the original paint had faded badly. Hence why the bike was changed from blue to black and various other changes were made to it.

One day my friend Marcus and I decided it would be a rather good idea to go camping for a week in Wales on the bikes. So we got hold of a couple of road maps and one in particular, had campsites marked on it, which was very helpful indeed.

It was around the first week in September when we had loaded up the bikes and they were parked outside the butchers. I gathered my essential equipment and final checks before the ride to the ferry at Yarmouth. Marcus was on his Yamaha XS250 and I was on my Suzuki GS400, which had just been resprayed by little Wol's dad at his works. He had stove enamelled the tank black for me and helped fit a pair of clip-on handlebars, *drops for those unaware of the terminology,* and I have to say, the paint job was amazing but my choice on handlebars was the not my best move. Loaded to the gunnels and Marcus with his trusty top box mounted on his rack and me with a giant rucksack hanging off my back. We made our way to Yarmouth for the ferry and escape from the island.

I was just about to inherit some money from my granddad and I had been to the bank in Freshwater to arrange an overdraft on the promise that this money was being transferred any day now. I made sure that I had no shortage of pennies for this epic journey. We reached the Severn Bridge and it started to rain very heavily and as it was absolutely hammering it down, we stopped at a café to don our waterproofs and get some coffee inside us for the rest of the trip. After a couple of fags and a few coffees, we headed off across the bridge on our way to our planned first campsite in

Carmarthen. As we literally battled our way through the rain and spray coming off the lorries and having the old fashioned visors on our crash helmets, which fogged up as soon as they were lowered. I managed to stay in the slow lane and avoid too much water spray from the faster vehicles in the middle lane and outer one. Suddenly I see this XS250 fly past me in the mist and I could hear the bike quite clearly as it went ahead.

Now normally Marcus's bike was very quiet as it had bog standard exhaust pipes and no mods at all. Apart from the rack and top box of course. His bike was sounding like a flipping Triumph going past me and I could hear it very clearly amongst the cars and lorries. As I stayed behind him for about a mile or so and being more concerned with wiping my visor and clearing the mist and rain so I could see a bit better. I didn't notice the first piece of exhaust pipe fly past me, until suddenly this lump of gun gum mixed with a rusty piece of metal, flew past my wheels.

I was now putting two and two together and laughing to myself as the pieces of exhaust repair were going all over the place. He was totally unaware of the mess he was making behind him, well until the final lump shot off and the bike was even louder.

We stopped in a garage forecourt and I was just laughing and telling my mate how many pieces of gun gum flew past me and asking how much exhaust was actually still intact? He was laughing too as he got off the bike and inspected the damaged exhaust and luckily it was only the very end of the silencer that was missing and not the down pipe section, or *manifold*.

Marcus with the bikes as Morfa Bychan campsite, in Wales. Circa 1980.

By this time it was getting late and we were getting a bit concerned about the campsite still being open. We rode on through the evening and went from dry weather to horrendous downpours until we finally reached Carmarthen and around half eight. We had no idea where the campsites were and as it was now dark, we had no hope to able to find one open at this hour. Cold, hungry and fairly fatigued from being sat on that bike all those miles, I was ready for bed. We rode around the town and couldn't see anything open at all and it started to rain again when I saw a b and b sign outside this large house with a very wide pavement in front of it. I hooted at my mate and indicated to stop outside the guest house and we agreed that this was probably our only option in the circumstances.

So we went inside and were greeted by a lovely lady at the reception and she told us the price and we opted for a twin room and paid for the stay. Unloaded all the soaking wet luggage and carried it to the room that was at the back of the house and then we set about getting our gear off and having a shower. That was one of the most welcoming showers I have ever had and to have a nice warm room and cosy bed too.

Next morning most of the bike gear was reasonably dry, except for my leather jacket that appeared to be made of the same stuff they make sponges from. We went up to reception to thank our host for the lovely warm room and she was quite surprised that we were leaving so soon? She said "You can't leave without having your breakfast." and we looked at each other and wondered what she was talking about as we had never stayed in this type of accommodation before. She said "its bed and breakfast you paid for, so you should have a good meal before you travel onwards." So we were led into the small dining area and sat down to the loveliest breakfast and a pot of fresh tea I have ever had. Just shows our naivety really and I'm so glad we stopped there the night because putting a tent up and being very damp, would have be absolutely awful.

We made our way up the coast to Harlech Castle and various other tiny little fishing villages on the way. Crossing over the Brecon Beacons was amazing, with its winding mountain roads and complete isolation from any form of civilisation. We past little farms all on their own and literally miles from any other buildings and finally we reached Morfa Bychan and a little campsite with a small clubhouse. We set up camp and made a small porch from building membrane plastic between our tents.

I had a lamp that I connected to the bike battery which we hung inside the porch. We cooked our dinner and afterwards walked to the clubhouse and had a couple of pints of bitter shandy before returning to our tents. It was that evening when I had made us both a coffee and my mate was just about to take a swig of it, when he saw this massive crane fly staring up at him from his cup. We were in tears laughing as Marcus impersonated what the insect looked like as it looked up at him from the coffee.

That night there were no dramas and no bloody rain either, which was the biggest relief. Oh we took two hundred Marlboro smokes with us as Mum had purchased them from cash and carry for us. For our sins, they didn't last the whole seven days.

Next morning we decided to move on towards Caernarfon for the day and perhaps Bangor that evening. So we reached Caernarfon Castle and went around the beautiful old building and looked over the Menai straits etc from the ramparts. Then we found this lovely campsite just outside Bangor, which consisted of two large grassy fields, two sinks in a hedge and that's it. We set up camp at the top of the hill in the second field and went into the town for some food and then back to cook dinner.

Unfortunately, we forgot to buy some washing up liquid and by the way, we didn't take our tooth brushes with us either because we wanted to be real bikers that week. Have you ever not cleaned your teeth for a whole week? Never again! Washing up in the cold water sink was interesting at the best of times, but with no detergent, we had white grease over every utensil and my teeth felt as though they had grown in thickness.

That night we decided to go into the town and look around the place and we ended up in this tiny cinema watching *Bo Derek* in *Tarzan the Ape man*; well that was an exciting film but it had its points. After the excitement of that night out, we rode back to the camp and turned in.

In the morning I woke very early for some reason and as I unzipped the tent and peered out through semi closed eyes, there was my mate already up and dressed and had the stove on for tea. He asked if I had noticed the mist lying over the field next door, so I got up and had a look and sure enough there was this beautiful mist hovering about the grass in this field and it looked quite eerie. We thought we could see mushrooms growing in this field so off we went over the fence and there were some lovely specimens growing in that place. We picked up quite a load and went back to camp and cooked a lovely breakfast with fresh mushrooms as a bonus. We went for a long ride out that day and this when I encountered a rather drastic problem with my new bank card and a cash machine in Bangor. Put the card in and it refused to give me any money and I desperately needed fuel as I had gone on reserve the night previous. This was the first machine I had ever used other than the one in Freshwater and now I was in a fix.

I knew I had money available and the bank were aware of my money being transferred too, so I had to go into the branch and tell them the situation and ask them to call the Freshwater branch and sort it out. After all that, I tried my card and it gave me some money thank God and did I give them hell in that branch when I got home, incompetent idiots.

We rode off to Holyhead on Anglesey and saw our first heavy metal mobile disco van with Motorhead and Saxon logos painted all over it. We went into a little tearoom and had some lunch before riding back over the Menai Bridge and back to camp. Our next destination was to be Betws-y-Coed, Ffestiniog and any camps we could find within Snowdonia National Park. The miles were clicking away as it got to early evening before we stumbled upon a sign on a small hill, hanging on a tree *Free camping* and we thought this was excellent stuff and opened the small gate and rode into the tiny field. There was a little stream running through the bottom of the field and we decided that this was the most idyllic spot to make camp, so up went the tents and bikes were unladen once again. That evening, we rode up to a tiny village and went into the local pub and I have to say it was not the friendliest pub by any measure. No one spoke English and as soon as we could guzzle our bitter shandy's down, we were out of there. So back to camp but with a couple of bags of crisps from the pub and coffee was on and it was a really nice spot. I had put all the breakfast food down the side of my tent so it stayed dry and cool at the same time. Coffee done, bedtime.

I was awoken by Marcus laughing and kind of shouting my name at the same time as I lit up my gas lamp and found the zip and pulled it along the base of the tent. I couldn't see too much at that point and had to kneel on the edge of my bed to see what the hell Marcus was going on about. As I hung the lantern outside the tent door, I could see water lapping just below my tent. My mate had put his tent up below mine and right next to the stream and it was raining hard and as he unzipped his door, I could see he had less that a foot of dry floor to kneel upon as the river was lapping inside his tent. I was in bloody hysterics with laughter as I looked at the water. We managed to move both tents up the bank about six feet in relatively dark and rainy conditions and finally got to sleep about two in the morning. I had my gas stove alight inside my tent as it worked really well as a heater and dried out the sides as the rain poured down. Probably bloody dangerous but anyhow, these were canvas ridge tents and not the plastic bags they make now and therefore, they breathed.

The late morning start and breakfast was on our minds after the horrendous night of rain and flooding, so I set up the stoves and put the kettle on. I put the frying pan on the grass and went to get the new pack of bacon from the side of the tent and it wasn't there? We searched everywhere for it and it was only by chance when Marcus looked up at the oak tree nearby that he saw the packet of bacon hanging from a branch. "How the buck did that get up there?" I said as I was laughing my head off. We never knew how the hell it got up in the tree and the only explanation we came up with was a squirrel may have taken it up there because it would not have been a badger or fox, not at that height. We retrieved the bacon with a large stick by throwing it up at the branch and cooked it up in the drizzling rain.

We then made our way to a place called Welshpool and on the way we found a real greasy truckers café that did a really cooked sausage, egg and chips. It was bloody pouring down most of the day and by the time we arrived at the campsite, we were absolutely drowned. We got the tents up and then headed for a launderette we had seen on the way through the town.

I stripped right down to just my pants and sat there while my leather jacket, jeans and all my other clothes dried in a tumble dryer. We had another dryer going with the sleeping bags in it, oh and one for Marcus's clothes of course. Luckily, no one else came into that shop to see me sitting there in just my pants. I just didn't care because I was soaked to the skin and very cold, it had to be done and the sooner the better.

The campsite was nice and we stayed there two nights and I remember watching the logging going on in the forest at the top of a large hill in front of us. On one of our excursions during the day, which was always wet, we went to that mountain that had been carved out and had hydroelectric turbines built into the bottom of it. I don't know the name but it was incredible the sheer size of the thing. Oh and we tried to go and look around a nuclear power station somewhere but they wouldn't let us in as we were not with an organised party. Probably took one look at us two scruffy individuals and thought "no way."

Then it was back through the Brecon Beacons and back down through Bath and then home in one day. I was glad to be home after that trip and I couldn't wait to see my bed and have a bath, oh and clean my bloody teeth too. There were too many places to list that we went through or stopped at on the way, but I have listed the most memorable of them I think. How I rode that bike with drop handlebars all that way is absolutely amazing now, there is no way I would even attempt to do it now. The XS exhaust was fixed again and lasted over a year until the bike was finally sold on. The GS was my bike for at least another six months and in all that time I rode her, she never once broke down and I came to the conclusion that those engines were one of the best twins available at that time.

It was Easter weekend and I had my first week's holiday from Thorley and the gang from the Braemar had decided to go over to the World Championship Motocross event at Hammer Warren in Ringwood.

So the morning arrived and we were all going to meet outside the café and make our way to the ferry at Yarmouth. I was waiting with my mate on his XS and another mate arrived on his Superdream and also a chap on a Triumph Bonneville and his mate. We were now waiting for Big Wol on his Triumph and his mate on his US Special when we saw this cloud of blue smoke coming through the village. It was big Wol and he had borrowed an RD250 from a chap in Freshwater for the trip as his bike had broke down the night before.

So everyone was there and we went off to the ferry terminal and waited for the ferry to turn up etc. It was so funny when Big Wol rode onto the ferry, the smoke literally blacked out the whole car deck and people were coughing and moaning as he gave it one big rev before turning it off.

It was brilliant and a sight that you had to see to believe. The Motocross was brilliant and Brad Lackey was the world champion at that time and no one could catch him. A great day out and a lot of laughs were had by all.

Working in the butchers shop gave us our fair share of strange characters but only one is worth a mention. By far the strangest, weirdest character that frequented our shop and who I named Chicken Man. Every Friday morning this rather posh car would park across the road and out of it would come the whitest, palest woman I had ever seen and always dressed to the nines with flowing scarves and airy fairy kind of things.

Her husband was tall, thin and had the face like an old cock bird and as they walked over the road from their car towards the shop, my Father, Mack and I would hide out the back laughing and all trying to avoid serving this couple. If I was lucky, I would get out of the front door and pretend to be taking rubbish to the bins and leave Dad or Mack to the mercy of Chicken Man.

His words every damn Friday of every damned week for however many years we served him, were exactly the same. He could have just recorded the words and played it back to us, because they never differed in any way.
The almost chicken type voice that screeched at you over the counter as he lent forward in a chicken type move with his neck were "three pound fresh chicken please", that's all he ever said and all he wanted. His wife would sometimes remark on how warm/cold the

weather was but usually stood their like a porcelain doll waiting for their god damn chicken to be sealed in a bag. We really believed that he must have turned into a chicken because that's all he ever ate. I even remember having to deliver a fresh chicken to them when it was snowing heavily in nineteen seventy eight. They lived off of Moons Hill, up a small track which sat almost under the Downs in a somewhat remote location. When I think of those moments it still makes me laugh so much as does my Father when I remind him of Chicken Man.

Another of Dad's customers who was the spitting image of the actor Richard Widmark and every time I said "Here comes Richard Widmark, Dad", he used to laugh so much and try and disappear out the back to avoid the customer seeing him laughing. There were other customers who had nick names too but none as apt as the two I have mentioned in this book.

It was not long after I had fallen off the bike and broke my rear indicator glass, that I was stopped by the most feared policeman on the island, PC Gird, or Girdy as he was affectionately known. I got the blue light treatment on my way to the garage to get fuel at Freddy Rolf's garage.

He was coming through the village on his BMW police bike and he saw me just going into the forecourt to fill up with petrol. He told me to get the light fixed as soon as I could and take it easy on that bike. In all honesty, he wasn't as bad as everyone had described him and he just told me off really and did not nick me. The only other occasion that I came across this copper, was on my way to Porchfield to meet a girl I was seeing. He went past me going towards Yarmouth and I was just turning off at Shalfleet garage towards Porchfield and as I looked in my mirrors, his brake light went on and I just thought this was it, he was going to turn round and come after me. He didn't, and I was relieved. I never had the pleasure of meeting him again, although I met a few of his work mates over the years.

The first concert I had ever been to was Gary Numan plus Nash the Slash in support, at the Gaumont, Southampton, which is now *The Mayflower*. I travelled over to Lymington with my friend and we met up with my Cousin Jim and his Sister Isobel and got on the train to Southampton. We arrived at the theatre and stood around outside until the doors opened. It was so exciting and so many people had dressed up in similar clothes to Numan and everyone had make-up on, which was an eye opener for sure. Going into my first ever concert has to be one of the most exciting events of my life, the masses of fans and the sounds and strange smells all mixed with darkness and the unexpected. I remember sitting down and we were in the upper circle seats and settled down while we searched the stage area and the crowds of people sitting in anticipation of what was about to happen.

It was about eight thirty pm, and the background music started to fade out and there was visible activity behind the curtains on the stage, the house lights began to fade out and the whole theatre was plunged into darkness. There was a strange hissing sound coming from the stage and there were UV lights going on behind the curtains as the crowd started to cheer and whistles rang out amongst the screams from girls in the front rows. Suddenly the curtains swished to one side and the whole stage lit up in so many beautiful colours as this weird chap in top hat and tails, but with bandages on his hands and face like a Mummy from Egyptian times. He almost drifted out of the dry ice fog as he played his electric violin with vigour and speed like you have never seen anyone play a violin before. He was brilliant and the sounds he was producing from the violin and the various effects racks were amazing. He played a good set and even though I had never heard on of his songs before, he caught my attention both visually and audibly.

There was quite a pause between the support act and Numan coming on so we had time to go to the bar and get a coke and something to eat. We got back to our seats just as the lights dimmed for the second time and the dry ice poured over the edge of the stage like it was a waterfall of mist and the strange intro music began. There was a semi circular gantry above the front of the stage which was panelled in white Perspex type stuff and various spotlights pointing out into the crowd.

As the music got louder and the fog got thicker, the white panels above the stage began to chase in various bright colours and the whole gantry began to get lower and stopped about 12ft off the stage, then two red illuminated seats shot down to the stage and a man got into each of the seats as they shot back up to the main gantry. The semi circle began to rise up and when it had reached the top, bang, a burst of bright white light came from these strange towers on the stage. They also chased in bright colours up and down the length of the towers and you could see that these structures were not in fact solid, but contained the synthesiser players.

The two men, who got into the red seats, were the spotlight operators and stayed up there all through the gig. It was a truly magical night and with lighting and sound like I had never heard. I was dumb struck at all of it and was in my true element for sure. So much so, that we had all forgot the time and the fact that the train from Southampton did not meet up with the train to the ferry terminal in Lymington and we had missed the last ferry. I was panicking by this time because I had to be at work for 0730 the next morning and there was no way I was going to even get back to the island by that time, let alone get to work.

The Suzuki GS400 parked at the fort on Headon Warren. Circa 1980.

I had to stay at my cousin's house in Lymington for the night and we got a lift to the ferry in the morning by my auntie. As we got on the ferry I wondered how I was going to explain this episode to Malcolm the manager and what he was going to say to me in reply. I had left my bike at Yarmouth terminal and rode back home and got my lunch together as fast as I could and explained to Mum and Dad about the train times as I dashed out and onto the Superdream for a good fast ride to work.

I could not find anyone at the farm when I arrived and I thought that was just my luck. So I walked over to the manager's house across the footpath past the manor garden and luckily he was there sorting out some wood for his fire. I apologised for being so late and the fact that I had got stuck on the mainland by the trains and he sort of grumpily replied "OK, well you best be getting on with milling" or something similar as far as I can remember. I never did that again because I had not long started on the farm and doing something like that was not a good move at all.

On another occasion I got a warning from Malcolm and it was because I was off to clear out some ditches on the Roffords field and in one hand I had a rip hook and the other my big stereo tape player. He had a real go at me about carrying this stereo with me and told me that I had not been there long and should concentrate more on my work instead of carrying tape decks about. At the time I was so resilient and could not care one little bit about what he thought about what I took with me to work. I was too much of a rebel and would act before actually thinking about what I had said or done. I suppose it is part of growing up and not seeing or understanding the reasons why things are done a certain way and trying to re-invent the wheel with everything I did.

That was the beginning of the end of my first twelve months on the farm because I was immature and careless and would find conflict in everything I was told to do. I must have been incredibly hard work in that first year and now I can read the code as it were, it was such a waste of Malcolm's time and mine. That is how it was meant to be and nothing could have changed my mind after I gave my notice in. I hated working for him and could not get along at all, but then I did not really try. I just wanted out of that place and as soon as I could.

We adopted this small holiday park called The Mountfield as somewhere to go on the bikes and we had some great nights there. I think we found out about the place through one of my biker mate's girlfriend who used to work there.

There must have been about at least a dozen of us that used to go up there on a Friday and Saturday night and the owner who was a very quietly spoken chap, welcomed us with almost open arms. That was pretty unusual for a bunch of seventeen year olds on motorcycles back then. We never caused any trouble or made a nuisance of ourselves in any way possible. I guess that is why were always welcome to use the club house and bar. I loved going there and meeting up with my friends and playing pool or darts. It was a really pleasant little place and because it was tucked up a small lane, none of the idiots that seemed to frequent pubs in Totland and Freshwater knew of its existence. This where Lana and I first kissed and although such a cheesy chat up line as "There's something in my eye, can you see it?" was used, it brought us together and the beginning of a beautiful relationship.

I first visited the Sun Inn at Hulverstone, when I first got my new Honda Superdream and went there with my mates on their bikes one Saturday night. We were coming back from Newport and decided to go through Brighstone, instead of Calbourne for a change. We stopped off there and walked in to the friendliest and cosiest little pub I have ever been in. There was a big log fire burning at one end, a tiny little bar area with a dart board in one alcove near the window. The landlord and landlady were the jolliest people you could wish to meet and the landlord always reminded me so much of Arthur Askey who did the bumble bee song. We ended up going there for well over two years and every Sunday night we went there to play darts with a couple of bearded chaps from Ryde, who drove this really old car.

At Christmas, we always went to that pub and one New Year's Eve we went to a party in the pub and it was a lock in and we slept in front of the fire and rode home later the next morning. Not many pubs encouraged you could take your own records as they had a record player on the bar for anyone to play music. We had some great nights and afternoons there too and it was the only pub I actually like going to as I was not really a pub person at all. We rode out there one evening and it had been snowing hard all day long and the roads were lethal but we wanted to have a usual game of darts so we set off in the snow.

I remember coming down the hill towards Compton s bends and thinking "I'm not going to make this bend." Ice and snow, my feet down and trying to slow the bike without applying too much braking and making either wheel lock up. Scary stuff indeed but we got there and back without any accidents.

Some of the gang from the Braemar Café. L/R: Jayne, Tony Me, Marcus, Merril and Rodney. Circa 1979.

Kev and Len behind the gate of Thorley Manor Farm in 1979.

It was just after I had been to see Gary Numan in Southampton and my cousin had come over to stay with us but I have no idea who invited her over. She arrived and was a complete nightmare from the start. I had a bit of a thing with her one night and I thought I was the only one, until she informed me that my best mate had been with her a few hours earlier. Bloody hell, I was literally disgusted and felt physically sick and went and had a shower to rid myself of her.

I had never met such a person like her and it turned out that she was basically a nymphomaniac and went through nearly every one of my mates who had bikes; *she would not go with anyone who didn't have anything to give her, by the way.* Hell, it was a very difficult time for me because she was once my little sweetheart back in the days of when I lived in Newport. We all went to visit them in Cambridge and I fell for her then and we wrote to each other every week. I am glad that I found out what she was really like and didn't fall into her trap, like so many others did.

I remember it was at least two weeks later when she was seeing another bloke from the bike group up at the café. He was not on my friend's list so it did not matter to me so much but it was the way she lived at our place during the day and buggered off at night time and would come back at all hours. Mum and Dad were as fed up with her as we all were, it was not long until something was said to her.

I remember the night that she and this bloke went camping in his front garden in Totland, right next to Weston Lane. My other mate who had just been dumped by this girl, went up there after midnight and super glued that tent zip shut, end result was that they could not get out of the tent and had to get someone to cut the tent open in the morning - so funny.

Mum had some jewellery that went missing and we had money that disappeared too and we knew who was the culprit and sent her packing forever. I never saw her again to this day, and never want to either.

Marcus, Rodney and I planned a trip up to my Cousins house in Haslingfield, Cambridge. I had not seen my cousins for quite a while and because they had grown up, they didn't tend to accompany my Aunt to visit Granddad in Cowes anymore. Rodney was another friend from the Braemar café who also had a Honda 250N Superdream but with a full fairing.

He was the son of the copper that stopped me on my brothers RD250LC when I did the wheelie past the bus station in Newport, as I was going to band practice above the Beavis's shop in Newport.

Me and my Superdream in Haslingfield, Cambridge. Marcus's XS250 and Rodney's Superdream nearby. Circa 1979.

So we embarked on the so exciting ferry journey, up through the New Forest to Cadnam and onwards to the M3 and up to join the North circular and then on to the A1 to Cambridge. Well that was the plan anyway but alas my sense of direction is absolutely useless and I was responsible for getting us completely lost in Potters Bar and Hatfield. After various u turns and stopping to ask various pedestrians the bally way, we finally got the right Road which led us straight onto our chosen destination. It was so strange riding through the village because I was sure I would remember the place and more importantly, where my cousins actually lived. Well it was mainly because we came in from the wrong end of the village and I just couldn't remember where their house was, that was until I saw my cousin Jamie in the front garden next to his Yamaha RD250LC.

We had a lovely few days there and luckily I was on a week's holiday from the farm and I think Marcus and Rodney were also on holiday too.

We went into Cambridge and visited the biggest fairground I have ever seen and had a great time riding on the machines etc. My cousin's two mates accompanied us to the city and they were Hollis and Gandy on a Yamaha DT175 and another Yamaha RD250LC, very popular machines at the time.

My cousin Joni had a bike as well, she had a Yamaha YB100, a nippy little two stroke machine. I think bikes seemed to run in the family because all my cousins had one; on my Mother's side anyway.

All seven of us went to the air museum at Duxford and that was a very worthwhile trip from a personal point of view. Seeing the inside of a Concorde and other incredible flying machines was a real treat for me. After that we just rode around the country lanes and had a fantastic day. We didn't get lost once on the way back to the island and I think it was because Marcus was leading our group for a change.

I could never understand why more people of our age, didn't get on the ferry and go and explore other parts of the country. They seemed to just stay in their villages and never went anywhere further than Newport on a Saturday. I went up to Cambridge a further three times and once more with Marcus. The other trips were on my own and on larger machines. When you are a seventeen year old and working a lot of hours and having little time to enjoy all the money you were earning, there seemed to be things that were often just simple and ordinary events that seemed more special to me at the time.

This was particularly true of the times I had the fortune of leaving work at a normal hour and getting to go out with my mates as I did before I started work at Thorley Manor Farm.

Time was rare and it was cherished. The period after cultivation and before Christmas was probably the slackest time on the farm, apart from January to March of course but the weather was not usually very good then, so it didn't really give me much advantage of getting out and about. I used to meet up with my friends and we would go up top the Highdown Inn near Tennyson Downs and we got this strange idea of playing British Bulldog in the pub beer garden. It was such a good laugh and quite a crowd of us would make our way up there for some shandy and a game or two, even some of the locals in the pub would come out and have a game with us.

Unlike the strange new game we invented known as Hedge Jumping. Now for this little gem of a game, you had to be slightly drunk or a complete idiot because it was very reasonable to expect some injuries from blackthorn or at least brambles and nettles. The idea of the game was simple, you chose your hedge and then took a running jump at it and hoped that you would clear the thing and not land on anything nasty on the other side. There were some classic moments when people just landed on the top of a prickly hedge or rolled off the other side into some nice fresh stinging nettles.

There was a fair few people who would follow us and watch as the persons would launch themselves over a hedge and disappear over the other side.

I jumped over the low hedge near the Catholic Church in Totland and although it was easy to get over it, the landing was not so much fun because there were a row of large stones on the lawn edge and bloody hurt when you hit them at speed. A truly crazy game but like most of our games, it was relatively harmful fun.

When I began working on the farm, I would park my bike under the lean-to shed and right opposite was the water tanker and a strange insect-looking machine. This intriguing machine had a large cab sticking out over the front wheels with winch cables running down the front of the cab and these were attached to a framework that had large aluminium tubes attached to it, which I later learnt were called *booms*.

It had a large plastic tank sitting behind the cab. Mark who had designed and built this machine along with Malcolm the manager, told me that it was previously a David Brown 880 tractor that had been modified so the cab could be mounted as far forward of the front wheels as possible to counterbalance the weight of the water tank.

It was a magical feat of engineering to look at and way ahead of it's time, there were no other machines around of its type back in the 80's. It was apparently featured in Farmers Weekly at the time it was built but I have not been able to locate the article at this time.

However, I have a photo of it which I took with my Kodak instant camera, in it you can see Hayward the head tractor driver in his spray suit waving at me and note the original David Brown headlamps mounted on the front of the cab. Although the machine was excellent and did all the spraying on the farm right up to the early nineties, it had a tendency to get bogged down in muddy terrains very easily and was often being towed out by the County or TW's.

It was one of the coldest mornings and heaviest frosts I had seen during my time at Thorley Manor Farm. I knew the roads were going to be tricky on the bike. I made my way down through Colwell with only white patches in the centre of the road and the bike did not slip on them thank God. I hated the feeling when the back wheel slipped out on a drain cover or frost and ice. Going up the hill past *Millways* factory at Golden Hill and around the left hand bend, there was some nasty frost patches and I had to slow right down.

Down went the biker's built in stabilisers - my feet and I cautiously made it around that bend without too much problem. My thoughts now were on the steep hill of Hallets Shute as it had a real camber on that bit of road which tended to push you into the bloody wall.

As I approached the top of the hill and rounded the slight left hander I could see the white glistening tarmac going all the way down the hill, some of it was melting away from the car tracks. Feet down and down to second gear for this one I thought as my boots touched the road surface occasionally, as I crept down the hill and keeping my hand well away from the front brake. There was a cold mist coming off the fields on the left at the top of the hill and this added to my face almost freezing inside the helmet and this was no time to have my visor down as it only steamed up as soon as I took the first breath.

I made it down the hill and only once did the back wheel lose grip and that was on the stupid drain cover half way down. I got past the turning to Fort Victoria and the road seemed better thanks to the large trees that shaded most of the road from the frost.

I remember Hayward in his red Ford Escort going past me and beeping his horn at me and I saw him disappear around the up and coming right hand bend in the distance.

I was just going around the corner by Warner's holiday camp and all I remember was a slow motion crash and I was sliding on the road surface with the bike still revving and on my leg. Luckily, I had leather jeans and jacket on and gloves of course so not a scratch from the impact, but my foot was hurting a lot as the footpeg was pressing on the side of my bike boot.

I managed to turn the engine off by reaching the emergency stop switch as the handle bars had swung around to the right. Then I heard voices coming along the edge of the road and it was Hayward and a couple of other chaps and they asked if I was ok as they struggled to get the bike up off the ice and it took them at least three attempts and with the help of a fourth person. The relief on my foot as the weight was lifted off it and amazingly, that was the only spot that the weight of that bike was pressing on. I got up and surveyed the damaged rear indicator plastic lens that had smashed and that was the only thing that happened to the bike, thanks to my foot holding it all off the road.

It took a while to start the bike as all the petrol had gone from the left hand float bowl and luckily missed my leg.

After thanking the chaps for their help and adjusting my mirrors back into view of the rear of the bike and not the side, I was back on the machine and going towards Yarmouth Bridge. "Oh deep joy" I said to myself as I reached the bridge because wooden planks and frost are so grippy on bike tyres – not. Boots down and sliding about all over the show, went my back wheel on the shiny wet wood. No bloody grit either and it was the same as I went around the right hander opposite the ferry terminal.

Hayward was driving just about ten car lengths in front of me and I guess he thought he better keep me in sight, just in case. I arrived at work and Hayward had already parked his car and was telling Mark and Malcolm I fell off on the ice. They all asked if I was OK and was the bike damaged at all. I said it was all fine apart from the indicator lens and even my foot was back to normal now, mainly because I could not feel it very well, as it was almost frozen. I changed the boots for my wellies and they soon warmed up.

It was a cold and damp February morning when I got up and dressed with certain kind of nervousness that I had not experienced before.

It was the day of my bike test and I was using my mates Yamaha XS250 because I had a broken indicator on the rear of my bike and was awaiting the new cover to be posted to me from Rye's.

So I donned my leather and bike boots, complete with those useless Sea Boot Hose socks that we all wore with the bike boots. They were never warm and made you feel as though you were wearing diver's boots. Off I went to Newport and to the test centre, which was half way up Mount Pleasant Road.

I walked into the bland looking waiting room and sat down with a couple of other poor victims of nerves sat there reading posters a hundred times. Then the examiner came out and asked me to confirm my name and address to verify that I was the person that was on the forms. The first thing I had to do was to read a number plate of a parked car up the hill and a few questions on the bike. Next it was riding around town while the examiner pretended to be a spy, hiding in the doorways of shops and alleys, observing my riding.

Unfortunately for me, the XS indicators decided to stop flashing and thus I failed the test. I was gutted and very annoyed with my mate and his useless bike electrics.

I rode back home to Totland and told everyone the bad news and how the indicators stopped working etc. As soon as I calmed down and got myself together, I went up the post office for another test application form and filled it in and sent it off with a cheque. It only took around two weeks until I got my new test date and it was in May nineteen seventy nine.

My second test was on my Superdream with working electrics and a fixed rear indicator glass. Another cold and very windy day it was, but I wasn't bothered by the weather, I just wanted to pass. It went like a breeze and I passed with only one small fault.

I was out of my mind with joy and rode to the car park in Carisbrooke, next to Stevens's fish and chip shop and ripped off my L plates and put them in the bin. No more of them and now it was time to wind up the local police by carrying a passenger and getting stopped and showing them my license and feeling smug, as the policeman would look gutted that I had a full license. Had to be done!

Mark in the Claas Combine on Gouldings Marsh Circa 1979.

Thorley Manor in 1979.

Rolling the Big Ham on the day of my 18ᵗʰ party in 1980.

The old Allmet drier with our Thames Trader lorry. Circa 1980.

Chapter 11

Illness and none the wiser

One of our regular tasks was to empty the rubbish trailer which sat in a lean to next to the new drier barn. It had to be taken to a place called *Wilmingham*, where the large straw barn was situated. Len got a Ford 5000 tractor out of the muddy yard and hitched up to this rubbish trailer. We both went off to *Wilmingham* to empty it. We drove passed another small collection of barns and sheds known as *Barnsfield* and Len pointed out that the fitter lived in one of the two farm bungalows which were next to a large black, corrugated tin shed that housed the Claas Combine. As we reached the large barn at *Wilmingham* we turned up a stony track next to the barn and drove past the barn and up the track until we reached a junction and turned right which seemed to disappear into a wild patch of weeds and some small trees.

We got to the *Pond* as it was called and tipped the trailer load of chaff and rubbish onto a previous load that was still smouldering away. There was a lot of chaff in this pond and it slowly burnt away over time and needed the odd boost from some paper or whatever you had to burn.

Turning round in the tight confines of the pond was interesting too as there were some deep ruts and very big puddles which needed to be avoided if you didn't want to get stuck in.

The worst experience I had in the pond was taking a load of chaff and rubbish up to the pond in the infamous *Grey trailer* which was reputed to be an ex dustcart chassis that had been converted, complete with full leaf suspension and a three stage ram for tipping. It was all steel in construction and had low metal sides and wheel arches too. I took the trailer over the ruts and into the pond and managed to turn it round after a few attempts and reversed it up to the chaff heap.

I started to tip the trailer and stood at the rear ready to climb up and dislodge the rubbish that caught behind the wheel arches. As the trailer ram lifted up and into its third section there was a loud bang as the ram top exploded and the trailer body came hurtling down to earth on its chassis. It made me jump out of my skin and I was glad I was not climbing up it when it went bang. The ram had literally shot out of the top and blown oil everywhere, hence it was never a tipper again.

Outside the large green, sliding doors the mud was everywhere as this was the only part of the farm that was not concreted and was a nightmare when wet because the chaff had mixed with the mud and formed this strange and very sticky type of muddy gloop. I remember trying to hitch up one of the small wooden sided trailers and the jack being perched on top of a small rock and when I reversed up to it and the drawbar of the tractor nudged it and it falling off the rock and having to get a jack to lift up the trailer again in the mud.

The ground was so uneven that hitching up to trailers was quite a skill at the best of times. There was the tree on the Yarmouth side of the gateway with huge gouge marks in its trunk, as a result of being hit by the front loader bucket by Len trying to take the corner flat out in the old Ford 6600.

We had a chap who worked with us on the farm who enjoyed going out in the evenings for a pint or ten of beer. Now I have no problem with people drinking, just as long as it does not affect their ability to perform their tasks and does not hinder others in the process. Now this chap would come into work after one of his nights out and for some reason would always be given the job of stacking the hay or straw right up the roof space of the barns. The hottest place to be and there was little air in the summer months and I remember looking at him as he was sweating so much I thought he would collapse any moment through dehydration. He looked so unwell at work and he was not the type to carry a bottle of squash with him either so he looked more drained as the day went on.

He would carry on drinking during week day evenings and never seemed to learn from his mistakes, how he survived bale cart on the farm I will never know. You had to be almost one hundred percent fit and have your wits about you if you wanted to last the season. We always said to him "you must be sweating pure alcohol mate"; he just laughed and carried on. I only ever came to work with a hangover once and that was the most horrible experience I ever had at work.

I suffered very badly with my throat from the age of thirteen to twenty two and when I say I suffered, I meant it was the most horrible illness I had ever had. My glands would swell up so much in my throat that I could not swallow properly or even open my mouth more than about five centimetres at the most, meaning I could not eat solid food or sometimes even swallow saliva it was that bad.

It all started when I contracted glandular fever in about nineteen seventy six and I was off school for at least six weeks with this throat thing. My brother Liam hid behind a door in the dining room in the house at Parkhurst Road and jumped out on me, making me jump and the pain through my jaw and ears was excruciating. Normally this would have been fine but it felt almost as if my mouth was ripped open and I screamed in agony and tears. Liam got a good smack for that afterwards.

This horrible affliction stayed with me right up until I was in my twenties and it came back with the same ferocious manner as it did when I initially started to suffer with it. It disappeared as quickly as it arrived and then I suddenly a started to suffer from hay fever and migraines, which I had never ever had before.

The hay fever lasted for around seven years and then I got Eczema for a further seven years and then the hay fever came back and the Eczema went away. Completely weird seven year cycles and thankfully, the throat affliction never came back. I still get the occasional bout of hay fever but nothing like when I was working on the farm. Imagine working the grain dryers all day long and drying barley and wheat with all that dust and chaff flying around.

I went through sheer hell for a few years with my eyes streaming and so sore, with the accompanying bouts of constant sneezing.

I constantly had my head under the outside tap, next to our builder's yard on the farm during the summer months to help relieve the itching and soreness of my eyes. I really do feel sorry for anyone who gets bad bouts of hay fever because it makes a miserable time of your life. I am just glad I did not get it when I was a child because I would perhaps not been able to relieve it quite so well.

One day, I was drying wheat in the new dryer barn and was about to move the cross conveyor over to an empty bin when I started to get this awful migraine. It was affecting my vision as I walked along the cat walk and down the short ladder to the dresser area. I could hardly see anything and my head was thumping so hard I thought I may have got Meningitis or something. I have never had anything like that before or since and I had to shut down the dryer and go home on my bike. That was not a nice experience at all and when I finally got home, Mum and my girlfriend put me to bed and later they both said I was delirious and talking absolute Mumbo jumbo. I had to have the following day off work because of that migraine.

Another co worker who I spent a lot of time working with was Ned who came from somewhere in Newport and he was one of the more intelligent people who came and went through the years on the farm. He moved into one of the bungalows at *Barnsfield*, next door to Mark the fitter.

He was married to a very beautiful girl indeed and certainly turned some heads when she was around. I remember going to what was the Ryde Pavilion to watch her and Ned in an amateur dramatics production of a pantomime and she made the audience take notice, dressed as Robin Hood or some such outfit. It was probably the first time that a group of us from the farm actually went out together for an evening's entertainment, there were more than four of us who went that night and it was a good night out for a change.

Ned sang and did some acting and it was so unusual to see him in a completely different light and not in dirty jeans and driving his tractor. I got on well with him and we had some very funny moments during one particular hay making season when the farm had bought three or four fields of hay from a farm in Newport. Dodnor Farm was the destination and we had to get every piece of machinery over there to turn, bale and cart this grass.

I took the Matbro handler over with my new flat ten grab on the front and eventually we moved all the gear we needed to the farm and started baling the hay.

Malcolm had been clever with this large amount of hay, as he sold a large amount of it to various horse stables and small holdings across the island. So all we had to do was to load up the trailers and cart it off to these customers, instead of moving it all back to Thorley and the thirteen mile journey. I had the loading job so I just loaded up the trailers and the other chaps took them out and delivered them and came back for re loading.

While they were delivering, I went around the fields and made sure the bales were in their respective blocks of tens and moved a few so they were all together ready for the trailers to come back and this eased loading and reduced the running around of the handler in the fields.

We had finished one of the fields which were right down next to that old metal bridge that crosses over the marshes, down on the old railway line that ran from Newport to Cowes. The views were a complete change from the usual ones we had during hay making and it made a nice change to see the river Medina and people walking along he track.

In the late afternoon, we loaded all the trailers up and I parked up and locked the handler and travelled back to Yarmouth with Ned, in one of our two recently purchased Ford TW15's. Hayward the head tractor driver drove the other TW and Taylor took his super slow Deutz and Graham came back with his Ford 6610 with the horrible column shift gears. That way, we had all the trailers full and took them back and unloaded two of them and did the rest in the morning.

We hoped to clear the rest of the hay on the second day and after unloading the trailers and putting the huge Lister fan on to make sure the hay did not heat up and possibly catch fire; we all went off to Newport to get the rest of the bales carted. On the way over to the other farm we stopped at the little shop at the roundabout at St Mary's for some bottles of drink and food.

The day had started with a very warm misty look to it and I knew it was going to be a very hot day as I had seen the signs before. It was lunch time and I thought one of the trailers would have come back by now, but it didn't and I had to have lunch with Malcolm under an oak tree in the corner of the field. He had iced tea in a flask and said "it was the best thing to quench your thirst". Obviously I did not believe his words at that time, until a few years later when I tried the beverage and had to eat humble pie with it. It was so bloody hot that day and even the shade of the oak did not give us much cool air to breathe. I had never known such a humid day as this one and everyone was feeling it. Even Malcolm had to take his boiler suit off and that was a rare thing indeed. It just got hotter and hotter and in the end Malcolm had enough and said "we are going back to Yarmouth and that's it for the day." When Malcolm said those words, the relief was more than welcome; we had enough, and wanted to go home. So we had all the trailers loaded and went back to Yarmouth once again and parked up all the trailers and went home.

The next morning was definitely cooler and we did not suffer as much, unloading the trailers in the barn next to my drier. Well some of us did not suffer but in fact Graham the man who liked his beer was sweating more than ever on this morning and Ned was laughing at him because he was bright red in the face a he stacked the bales. He looked a bloody mess that day and he was starting to slow down very quickly in the heat of the barn. Off we went on the third day of carting the hay from Dodnor Farm and it was a great relief when we loaded the last trailer and all made our way back home to Yarmouth.

I had to take the Matbro and I stopped in Isle of Wight Radio's offices with the handler, grab and all. I nipped in there to put a request on for my girlfriend and then carried on my way home to Thorley. We heard the request as we were unloading the last of the hay but my girlfriend didn't hear it, I thought afterwards, that was a waste of time. Yet again it was Graham up in the roof of the barn, stacking bales and looking like he was going to spontaneously combust any minute. Red faced as usual and pouring sweat like it was raining on his feet and no one else were sweating at all.

Luckily for us, Malcolm had buggered off on a delivery in that awful Fiat pickup he used for delivering larger amounts than the Honda truck could carry. So we had quite a laugh and joke that morning and I think we jumped on Taylor at one point and tried to tie him up because he was being cheeky. One thing we learnt about Taylor was never try and hold him down and tie him up if he had a knife on him because he bloody well chased us around the yards with it and got quite nasty.

I was fert spinning up on the Bouldnor block one day and I had my artic trailer full of fert and had backed up to it so I could load the spinner up. We had all our fert in 25kg bags in those days and none of this modern dumpy bag technology as they all seem to use today. I heard this motorbike coming across the field and it was Ned on his Honda CB100n twin and he just came up for a visit as it was lunchtime, so I had my lunch with him and I had my camera with me and took some photos of him on his bike. I still have the photos and they will hopefully be in the book somewhere.

That Fiat pickup that I mentioned earlier was the biggest pain in the bum to start. It would never go and even with the battery charged up fully, it refused to fire up so we always ended up towing the bloody thing around the yard. When it did finally start, it sounded rough as hell and popped and banged on two or three cylinders and finally the fourth came alive. Weird bloody thing it was; and I often wondered who chose that vehicle out of all the decent trucks they could have bought and they bought that heap of scrap. Malcolm always used it for delivering down to a small stable yard, down at Brook and I always had the pleasure of accompanying Malcolm on this delivery.

We always had a nice glass of beer from the lady who owned the stables afterwards and Malcolm always made a joke about me not falling asleep in the tractor this afternoon. His little jokes were always subtle and never totally derogatory to your character.

I remember delivering some straw with Graham to a small holding down in Cranmore and it was a bloody nightmare putting the straw in the shed because it was behind another building and there was hardly any room to get in there with the trailers. About two days later, the chap who we had delivered the straw to, came into the farm yard and wanted to see Malcolm the manager. We went and found him in his office for the customer and left them alone. The funniest thing was that the chap who had the straw delivered, gave Malcolm five pounds for me and Graham and he gave it us later that day. We just did not expect any tip for the straw delivery, even though it was hard work getting it in there.

It was a Saturday night about tea time and Marcus called round to see what we were doing that night as we were both bored and I had the weekend off for a change. So after riding about on the back of his Honda CB900F for half hour we stopped at the Braemar and decided we should go off to the BMF rally in Peterborough.

So I went home and got some gear together and Marcus went home to do the same and we agreed to meet back at the Braemar in an hour. So I get my leathers on and take a few essential items and go back to the café and wait.

I didn't have to wait long and very soon we were on the ferry and then on our way up country. It didn't take us very long to get up there because we arrived at the rally site at one in the morning. We weren't allowed into the site until the morning so we had to find somewhere to sleep until morning. So we rode around the whole perimeter of the site and happened to see a group of bikers on an industrial estate, complete with campfire and all.

So we parked up and chatted to these dudes who were all from Norfolk and got on really well with them. Spent most of the early hours chatting and then went to sleep by their fire. Woke up feeling very dry and stiff but it didn't matter as the site was just opening up, so we rode in and parked amongst millions of bikes and made a bee line for the nearest food and drink outlet.

We spent the day watching different displays of old bikes and ogling at girls in bikinis on bikes and avoiding really mean looking biker dudes.

By the time three o'clock had arrived, we were both feeling bloody shagged out and especially as it was a very hot day. We decided to bugger off home and made our way down to north London. As I mentioned, I was absolutely knackered and I managed to fall asleep on the back of that 900 all the way from Peterborough to London. How I held on and didn't fall off, I will never know.

Not long after I had started working at Thorley Manor Farm, we were all invited to the head tractor driver's wedding party up at the Savoy holiday camp one Saturday in the autumn. It was the first wedding I had ever been to and I had to come home from feeding the cattle with one of the chaps I worked with called Kevin. He was a very fit chap who did gymnastics and javelin throwing for the county. He was the only bloke I knew who could run up to a five bar gate and bounce over it with his hands and land on his feet on the other side. He came back with me to my house to get changed and we went in his purple Morris Marina to the wedding reception at the Savoy in Yarmouth.

Everyone was there from the farm and from other farms in the area because Hayward's Father was a cowman at Newclose Farm in Thorley, so they knew a lot of people from the farming community.

Mark was making jokes about everyone and was trying to work out what *UHT* meant on his small pot of cream with his coffee. He said he thought it must mean *Union of hairy tits*, silly sod.

Mark held the world record for being able to say the most swear words in five seconds. If something was not going right in the workshop, everyone knew if he was in there when you heard the swear words floating through the air. I had another Sherry which incidentally, is the only alcohol I drink at Christmas and I think that is because my family always had it in the drinks cupboard at Christmas and I used to sneak the odd tot. Malcolm came up to our table and said "I hope you are going to feed the right end of the cows this afternoon Berry?"

This made everyone laugh and I went red in the face because Kevin and I had to feed the cattle later on that afternoon. It was a good party and made a change from the usual Saturday afternoon at the Braemar café on the bike. We had to fix Hayward's red Escort car with some rice and other annoying things. Kevin and a couple of others went outside with Hayward's part time fireman friend and did some nasty things to his car for the journey off on their honeymoon.

We thought we had got away with it as no one knew we were out in the car park. We told them we were going to feed the cattle. It was a few weeks after the wedding when Hayward said "I know who did my car at the party, because someone took some photos." He showed us the photos with me and Kevin standing next to Hayward's car looking very pleased with ourselves. I didn't see the manager of the Savoy taking the photos either, so we were caught red handed, good and proper.

Growing as many crops as Thorley grew during the seventies and eighties, we had quite a variety of techniques in clearing up the fields after harvest. We had only the basic machinery to carry out these tasks, compared to the farms I have worked on since those days. We had the best equipment for grain handling that was currently available but in the implement department, we probably had some of the oldest machines around for miles. Saying that, I have used exactly the same machinery in the past year as I used 30 years ago at Thorley and it seems that some machines will go on forever and ever, because of their simplistic nature which keeps running costs down.

One of the oldest and simple machines I ever used was the old fashioned rakes. These were once horse-drawn but had been fitted with a drawbar and ropes for the activation of the machine. A series of curved cast iron spikes, mounted on a bar which would use the wheel hubs as a lifting mechanism by engaging a pawl into a cog and would latch when they had reached the limit of their travel.

These machines were notorious for either not lifting when you pulled on the rope or not dropping in time. We would start at one end of the field and basically rake all the straw or whatever was in rows into larger rows, ready to be set alight or loaded onto trailers. They were horrendous things to tow across the tramlines and I am sure this caused them to unlatch at the wrong time and ruin the row you were attempting to form. We usually used them for getting rid of pea and bean straw because it was very difficult to bale and shift.

The thing that usually happened was they would fall off the antiquated jacks when you were putting them into transport position. You had to jack up one axle and remove the iron wheel and place it on the back axle, while the thing was attached to the tractor. Then you jacked up the second axle and put the other wheel in position and this is when the second jack would fall off and the whole machine laid on its side with the axle buried in the soil. What a job it was to get it back on the level; I hated the rakes with a passion and dreaded having to work with them. Len and I still reminisce about those bloody rakes.

The Rolling Stones were playing at Wembley Stadium on a Friday night and Marcus had a ticket to the gig and wanted to go, but didn't want to leave his Honda CB900F parked up there. So I came up with a plan so I could drop him off at the gig and I would ride down to my cousin's house in Ottershaw, Surrey.

So off we went on a Friday afternoon as I was on a day off and Marcus was having a week off from work. We arrived in London at possibly the worst time for travelling on the roads. The traffic was just backed up for miles to Wembley, and in the end, because the bike was getting too hot, and we were fed up starting and stopping for miles. We got on the pavement and rode over five miles past all the traffic to the stadium. Luckily, we didn't see one police car, which was probably a good thing considering. I dropped Marcus off at the top of a hill that looks over the stadium and we parked up and had a smoke before I set off back through the hell on the roads to Surrey.

For some weird reason, I didn't encounter any bloody traffic jams on my way towards Heathrow Airport. Considering what we had just gone through to reach the damned place, I was expecting at least a few jams on the way. So I reached the M25 and headed for Woking and onwards to Ottershaw which is close to Woking. I stayed with my uncle, Aunt and cousins that evening and had a nice time.

I left them at about half eleven and reached the little hill above the stadium at about ten past twelve and Marcus was there waiting for me. I did give the old bike some welly on the way back. We had a rather quick ride back down the M3 and did our regular stop at Fleet Services for a coffee and a smoke before rejoining the motorway and reaching Portsmouth at half three ish. We had to go back on the Portsmouth ferry because the Yarmouth one didn't run after ten at night.

It was the end of July and basically, we were waiting for the wheat and barley to ripen and to start cutting. This was always the way it went, just after haymaking and before harvest. There were many other tasks such as hedge cutting, grass cutting or ditch clearing, and other things that were important to stop cultivated land reverting back to woodland. When the barns and silos were cleaned and ready for the New Year's crops then our time was spent doing the aforementioned tasks around the 900 or so acres.

On this particular day, we were sent off for the *home field* on the border of the marshes to cut down some over hanging branches and clear some brambles from the hedgerow. The branches were rather large and we needed the front loader and chainsaw to trim them back, plus a fire was to be built to get rid of the debris. A firebreak was cultivated around the area of the fire and this was done using a *Ripvator* cultivator to tear up the soil and stop the fire from spreading into the barley which surrounded the area we were working on. Incidentally, the Ripvator implements were manufactured at Spence's farm at Calbourne. Before we even lit the fire I remember talking to my workmate Hayward about the risk of having a bonfire in the same field as a barley crop, but he assured me it would be fine with a good firebreak around it. It was lunchtime and we had removed all the branches and cut them up small enough to go on the fire.

We sat away from the fire because it was too warm to be near it and the smoke was annoying when you were having lunch. I had my trusty tape deck with me and listened to *Night Owl* album by *Gerry Rafferty* as I munched on my sandwiches and drank my coffee. We watched the fire burning away and everything seemed to be fine, until – a branch cracked and spat out lots of red hot ashes from the base of the fire and the next minute the barley was crackling towards the corner of the field.

We both jumped up and grabbed a prong each and tried to beat out the fire. As we did, Malcolm appeared on the track just above us and ran over with a couple of beaters. I'm pretty sure it was a Friday, because Malcolm always delivered our brown wage packets at lunchtime, or very close to that time. We beat out the fire after a good twenty minutes of the flames taking out a fair amount of the barley in the corner of the field.

That was a very close thing because if the wind had turned around and blown the flames up the field, we would have lost the whole thirty acres and I think we would have been in some danger of getting burnt too. Until you have experienced the way a crop or even stubble can travel when alight, then it is difficult to explain the panic and speed at which fire will engulf the entire field in seconds.

Unless you have your wits about you, there is a high risk of being caught by the flames and injured. That barley was gone in minutes and that was probably half an acre by the time it was beaten. Scared the hell out of us all and we decided to put a wider cultivation around the fire this time, so that ashes and sparks would not jump the gap.

I mentioned the tree at the rear of the farm with the trunk gouged out. This was due to a crash involving a Ford 6600 tractor with a front loader and the tree. A certain young driver called Len, thought he could turn in off the road at full speed and still get round the bend into the rear entrance of the farm. Wrong. The tractor slid and the front loader hit a tree in the corner of the yard and pushed the loader into the bonnet and cab. I'm sure he thought he was driving his Mini and could drive this tractor in the same manner. I didn't see the actual damage to the tractor but I did see the tree with the massive gouge out of the trunk. The accident book contained the following: Extensive damage to front loader of tractor and bonnet. The tractor returned to the farm with a new loader and repaired bonnet and cab eventually, unlike its driver.

After a very wet and windy winter, the old building that was the spray store and the nammet room, was in need of extensive repairs to the roof because it was damaged and leaking into the chemical store. Also, there was another store for the storage of seed and fertiliser. We had the job of going up on the roof and taking all the old tiles off and putting them on the upper floor of the spray store and having the timbers repaired.

It was a dirty dusty old job and not my most tenable place to be, up high on a roof as I hated heights and especially with ladders. Kevin opened the doors of his car, which was parked just below us in front of the office building and turned his car radio up loud so we had some music; he had to turn it off when Malcolm came up there to see how far we had got with the tiles. It was just an example of the wide ranging jobs that we had to do on the farm and I guess most people think you sit in a tractor all day long. How wrong they are.

I remember when we acquired a Stihl planking saw which you put on the top of a tree trunk and it would cut the tree into planks. This thing had one engine at each end of a frame, and it vibrated so much that your hands would be numb in seconds. With two people, trying to hold it nice and straight was a feat in itself, because it always wandered off line. Hated the bloody thing and so did everyone who had to operate it. After the first winter's use, it was destined to be stored at the back of the workshop to collect dust. I never saw it come out again.

We had phases of new machinery or ideas of making more money on the farm and on this occasion, Thorley Manor bought an eight wheeled buggy thing called an Argocat. This was an amphibious vehicle that would go apparently go over any terrain and came complete with a transom on the back for an outboard motor. It was chain driven and had two disk brakes under the bonnet, which allowed you to brake one side, independently of the other side of the machine. Very similar to a tracked vehicle in principle but suffered badly, through lack of testing over long periods of use. The chains always needed adjusting and the disk brake pads wore out very quickly, because of the amount of use they had from steering.

A fertiliser spinner was purchased for the machine and it was mounted on a two wheeled trailer, with its own Honda engine to power the *PTO* or *Power Take Off* shaft on the spinner.

We converted a four-wheeler trailer and Mark made a set of ramps for the buggy to drive up onto the bed of the trailer.

Hayward went out all over the island with it, doing low ground pressure fertiliser spinning as a contractor for other farmers. It only lasted for one spring season and then it was sold on. Great idea, but the machine spent more time being fixed than actually earning its keep. I guess they must have improved the design of the machine by now and I would like to have a go in one across a lake or pond because we never got the opportunity to add an outboard motor when we had our one.

I was seventeen and enjoying the work on the farm very much, plus having a nice motorbike to explore other parts of the island was fantastic. I had been almost everywhere on the bike and spent many hours just cleaning and modifying it as best I could with my limited skills. Money was not a problem at all, as I was clearing £125.00 on a flat week with no overtime.

During harvest and cultivation, I was taking home in excess of £350-£400.00 per week. This was a vast amount of money for a young lad to handle and handle it I did. Well, I spent it and frittered it away on God knows what. I was encouraged to work overtime every day, including, Saturdays and Sundays and bank holidays. I remember Christmas nineteen seventy nine very well because I spent a lot of money on my family and it was a joy to be able to actually buy expensive presents for them. Instead of the usual cheap and pointless gifts that most people give or receive. I went to cash and carry in Cowes with my Mum and bought my brother Liam a Car racing set. I bought a nice doll for my sister Sarah. It was a nice feeling and made me feel happy to give instead of receiving all the time.

A view across the Hayles fields from Wilmingham track. Circa 1985.

Chapter 12

Eighteen Years

The hours we spent in the *Braemar café*, just drinking tea and coffee, chatting and having a nice time. I met most of the friends that I spent my teenage years with there. The owner was a chap called Norman or *Norm* as we called him. He was very much into his powerboats and all things marine and also a rather big dreamer as we gradually discovered. On the whole he was a nice bloke and put up with a lot, during my time visiting his café.

The café had a kind of bar/counter on the left of the doorway and there were steps going up to more tables and the infamous back room. Now in the back room there was a dart board which was mounted on the wall near a big upright freezer. This room was only open to a select few of us who went there every night. We often played against *Norm*, who was pretty good at darts, but not as good as my mate Marcus, who beat him a fair few times.

The Braemar became the most popular place to go for most people my age in Totland and Freshwater because it was a friendly café, with decent food and nice and warm in the winter months.

The bikes parked across the road from the café increased from two or three to at least fifteen, on a good night. I'm sure it was the sight of this row of bikes parked across the road that attracted other bikers to stop and come into the café. Sometimes there were not many seats left in the place and business must have doubled as a result of our little gang spending so much time there.

One particular night we were all in the café as usual, and apart from all of us youngsters, there was this older chap with a wheelchair and crutches. Now he was always up there during the daytime. This dude was sitting in his usual seat against the left wall with his partner and these two blokes walked into the café wearing suits. They said something to *Norm* and then marched over to this dude with the wheelchair, picked him up and took him outside to an awaiting car! Everyone was dead quiet and we just sat there gob smacked as he was removed and not a word was exchanged between these suited dudes and the chap. It all came out a few days later, when we were all up at the café and *Norm* enlightened us on the facts. Apparently, the chap in the wheelchair could walk perfectly normally and he had been scamming the DSS for years and they had caught up with him and arrested him for fraud.

It was a misty Saturday morning out on the Ham fields and I was rolling the field with Cambridge rolls. This was to make sure all the stones were pushed into the soil to make combining the crop easier, also to make sure the soil is compacted around the seeds properly. As explained to me one day by Malcolm the manager. This was the day of my 18th birthday party and trying to concentrate on the job in hand was a might difficult, considering what was going through my mind that day.

I had just brought the rolls all the way from the *Bouldnor Block* of fields and as I was coming along the road, just past *Roffords House* and there was a bungalow on the left with a small rockery on the very edge of the road. When towing rollers that were not in their gang position, they tended to snake along the road, depending on your speed. I noticed they were starting to get a snake on, and started to move all over the road, I had to slow down very quickly because it was becoming dangerous. As I reached this house with the rockery, the last roller smashed into a row of rocks and sent plants and soil flying all over the road. Luckily it seemed no one was in, so I stopped, pushed all the stones and soil back off the road and carried on as fast as I could.

I had a similar experience with a Ripvator cultivator on the back of my Ford 5000 one day. I was just going up the hill from the farm towards *Barnsfield* and suddenly the hydraulics just failed and the implement went straight down on the road and gouged out a series of large lines in the tarmac. It was so visible on the road that I would never get away with no one seeing it. I had to tell Malcolm about it. He wasn't too bothered and just shrugged it off.

My cousin Al had come down for the party on the Friday afternoon from Surrey and staying at granddad's house in Cowes. He had come down on his Suzuki GS550E. Everyone at home was preparing the village hall for the party and my friends were excited about the night to come. I only had to work until lunch time, so when it was time to drop the rollers off at *Barnsfield* yard. I was out of that field like a bullet and home to meet everyone and enjoy the afternoon's fun. When I got home to the flat and parked the bike outside on the pavement, my cousin Al had turned up on his bike and came indoors with me.

In the weeks leading up to this party, my friend Marcus and I, had been working on some disco lights in the old shop front that used to be my bedroom. We made these red lights out of liver containers from Dad's shop and made a giant *V* shaped frame with just ordinary white light bulbs mounted on it. We really needed some kind of controller to flip between the two red lights and this frame of white lights. As my friend worked for Plessey Radar, he got one of his mates to make up a circuit for us, which was powered by a nine volt battery to operate the relay and looked fairly dodgy to me.

I already had the disco decks and the amp and speakers as Dad's friend Roy had recently upgraded his disco equipment. He gave me his old gear for my birthday along with two albums. *The Age of Plastic*, by *The Buggles* and *The Specials* by *The Specials* album. The plan was that we would just play a few songs to get the party going and then Dad's mate Roy would take over as the DJ for the night. He would provide his own lighting too, which was good as ours were a bit limited to say the least. The two red lamps were working fine when we tested them. We couldn't test the *V* frame properly because we didn't have enough bulbs until we went down to Hitchmans later to get them, by the time we did that, there was no time to switch it on.

The evening arrived and we all made our way up to the village hall and my God it was fantastic to see all my friends and family there. Even *PC Chizzy* came in and joined in the celebration. Very handy, when there were some gate crashers from Freshwater hanging about outside. They didn't have a chance with Chizzy on the door and some very big friends of Dad's there.

It started really well and we fired up the decks and my friend played a few songs and then we turned on the lights. Wow. The big *V* nearly blinded everyone as it flashed on for a few seconds and with twelve, sixty watt bulbs in it, the flash was like lightening. I remember everyone half blinded by the thing; we had to turn it off eventually because the flip flop device got too hot due to the slightly over wattage draw that we put through the relay device. It was so funny because we just had no bloody idea how bright an array of twelve, sixty watt bulbs were going to be.

Dads mate Roy the DJ and played nearly every song in the current charts. One memorable moment was when *the metal gang from the bench* came in with their single to play and the DJ played it for them. I remember the smile on their faces as *Rainbow's, I Surrender,* from the *Difficult to Cure* album blared out at them. So everyone was happy, well almost, as I looked over at one of the girls from our gang, Annie, who was sat there on her own while her boyfriend, the very drunk big Wol was chatting to someone else. She smiled and I longed to just carry her away with me on my bike there and then. I had always liked her and we got on really well together. I was currently going out with her best friend, so I wasn't in a position to do anything about my feelings for her. I really didn't think she liked me that much anyway, so I didn't pursue it.

I was very surprised when my new workmate Mark came to the hall with a present for me, a Swiss army knife. I thought it was bloody good of him and his wife to come along, seeing as I hardly knew them socially. You know who your true loyal friends in your life when something like that happens and I have total respect for those people because they made that night very special.

The next day I didn't have to work so I lay in for quite a while before we had to go up to the hall and clean it all up. It was not a complete mess, and nothing got broken either. I wanted to go over and see my cousin in Cowes but he had to get an early ferry as he had work on the Monday. I went up to the Braemar in the evening at met up with the lads and to see if Annie was there. Everyone who went to the party enjoyed the night and it was nice that we did not have anyone too drunk to start any trouble. Thanks to my Mum and Dad for such a memorable evening and to Dad's mate the DJ for a brilliant job on the music. All my family members who put everything into that party and made it such a special occasion.

Annie turned up in my life a very long time after that party and in fact it was 2006 when we met again. She was working in a motorcycle shop in Newport, you can work that out for yourselves. I had wanted to buy a brand new bike and went up to the shop and browsed the various models and went up to the counter to ask about a certain model. I could not believe it as she came out of the office and to the counter. We chatted for ages and she gave me her mobile number. We text each other for a while and the one thing she said that really hit home, was "I really fancied you when you had your Superdream." What can I say, I fancied her and she fancied me but it just never happened.

As I mentioned earlier, there was this group of dudes that would hang around the roundabout in Totland at night. They had a massive ghetto blaster playing mostly *Rainbow*, *Deep Purple*, very loudly opposite the Broadway Inn. I referred to them as the *metal gang from the bench* because they could always be found on the wooden bench on the green by Totland roundabout.

They were a good bunch of dudes and they started to frequent the Broadway Inn as they came of age. So now my group of friends seemed to be growing even larger. Life seemed to be falling into place at long last, social life, money and places to be, meant I was rarely at home at night during the winter months of 79. Work had slowed down in about October and I was finishing at around five o'clock and only worked Saturday mornings. We had feeding to do every other weekend, but it was not too hard work, except when it was raining or the cows decided it was time to look round the locality. It took roughly two hours to feed and bed the cows in the three yards, and there were always two of us doing it.

It was getting close to December seventy nine, and the dreaded lure of the pub had enticed us to savour the delights of bitter shandy, girls and darts. The first pub I ever went to legally was the Broadway Inn at Totland, which not far from where I lived and not a bad place really. The landlady was shrewd because all the songs in the jukebox were heavy metal songs and for some reason, there was a vast amount of *Rainbow* records on it. The influence of the *metal gang from the bench,* I think. So from the café we started moving on to the pub for darts and of course, the jukebox.

The Braemar café was becoming full of punk rockers and people we didn't want to be around, so the move was inevitable really. We never really returned to the café after that period and it wasn't long after that the whole building was sold and turned into the first food outlet. Solely set up to sell burgers, plus a nice restaurant on one side. *Charlie Brown's* as it was called and probably the first burger restaurant on the island. Their burgers were absolutely lovely and I spent my fair share of wages on those delights.

One Sunday morning, I went on the back of little Wol's Honda CB550f which was a lovely sounding bike and had a lot of character to it. I had my big ghetto blaster on my lap and we had Black Sabbath blasting out as we went through Freshwater Bay and up the hill, then down towards Compton. Going down the other side of the hill, the sun was blazing down and the sea glistened as I looked around. The beaches were full of bathers and sun seekers and we cold see cars starting to be parked on the verges as they always did in the summer months. As we got to the Compton bends, approaching the entrance to the car park and Compton farm.

A car started to pull out of the car park, I thought it was going to stop, alas it didn't. Little Wol tried to swerve out to the right and miss the car, but there was not enough time. Bang. My knee went into the front wing of the car and we both took off into the air and landed on the road, ten feet from the car. I landed on top of my mate and the ghetto blaster went flying up the road with its batteries spread everywhere.

I lay there on the road and just didn't dare move, I was not in much pain, but little Wol was hurt and half way up the verge on the far side of the road. I was on the near side verge, opposite him and as we both lay there as cars started to stack up and people were running up to us and asking us "are you OK?" Luckily one of the ladies was a nurse and she got us both off the road and onto the verges. I remember her turning me onto my back and saying "you have an injury to your knee" and as I looked down at my ripped jeans, there was the result of the car wing impact, a two inch gash just below the knee and it was so deep that I could see the bone inside .It was at this point, the pain started and I wished I had not seen the cut.

It was not long until the ambulance arrived and my mate was the first one in, because he had sustained a serious injury to his shoulder and arm. As they wheeled me into the ambulance, they didn't apply the brakes to the trolley and it started to roll towards the door. My mate was laughing and in pain at the same time as they applied the bloody brakes to the trolley and off we went to Ryde casualty department to get sewn up and fixed. My Dad arrived with my girlfriend *Lana*, to take me home. I did not see my mate after that because he was taken off for x-rays, but I was assured he was not in any danger before I was taken home. When I got home and had a cup of tea, I hobbled off up the stairs to bed. Suddenly as I reached the last flight of stairs I felt sick and very dizzy and wanted to be alone, Lana helped me up the stairs and into my bed. Shock had set in and it was an awful feeling as I remember.

Little Wol's bike was a write off but only because the front forks were bent and the clocks had been smashed. He managed to buy the bike back from the insurance company for around £100 and he rebuilt her and still owns it to this day. He named the bike *Mabel* for some strange reason and he also had the name painted on the tank.

We both received a tidy sum from the insurance and while we were recovering from our injuries, we spent most of our days watching videos in the lounge of Bon Accord. One particular film was *It's Your Move* with *Tommy Cooper, Eric Sykes and Jimmy Edwards*. It was so funny and I remember little Wol trying not to laugh because of the pain from his broken collar bone.

The funniest thing happened when I went to the video shop to get another film. I picked up this video from the rows of films and it looked quite good by the picture on the cover. I rented the film from *Halls Radio Vision* of Freshwater, which was originally the only video rental shop in the West Wight. We put it on and as the film progressed it turned into the most hard core porn film I have ever seen. We did laugh when we took the film back and asked for a replacement. The lady behind the counter didn't say much and looked quite embarrassed by what I told her about the film.

We eventually had two video hire shops in Freshwater, one being *Halls* and the other was at the bottom of the village near *Swann Wights*. I think it later became *Clothesline*.

I had driving lessons from a guy from Freshwater Bay and hated every minute of it because I had no interest in cars or driving at that time. The instructor used to nip off to the betting shop or shopping during a lesson, which I thought was a bit odd. I should have stopped after the first lesson really because I was not interested in it at all. I only did it because Mum and Dad wanted me to drive the van and so I could get on at work etc. I took the test and failed miserably and was not bothered or surprised at failing the test one little bit. I finally took my test in Southampton on roads that I had never seen, let alone driven on. I passed with a totally clean slate. Quite a feat as my examiner told me and he could not believe I had never driven on the roads I drove on, during my test. The test examiner did not take me on the practiced route that my instructor had shown me. That was in 1995 so that just goes to prove how much I longed for my car license.

My brother Liam aboard the new Honda Superdream. Circa 1979.

It was a dry day and it must have been about the end of October nineteen seventy nine, and I was feeding the cows in the main yard. I was asked to go and fuel up my tractor by Malcolm the manager because the university, mature student was going to hitch up the hedge trimmer and start on the ninety five acre field hedge line. I was so angry that this bloke, who never seemed to do any dirty jobs, was going to use my tractor for hedges and I had to re fuel it. Why he couldn't fuel it up, I thought? Chasing me around the yard towards the workshop and I was shouting "If he wants to use my tractor then he can re fuel it, he never does any dirty jobs or feeds animals, always sat on his arse in a tractor!"

I just lost it that day; it had been building up inside me for a long time and I wasn't the only one who had this opinion either. All of us full timers felt under privileged at that time. It makes me smile now, because as Malcolm finally caught up with me he said "I think we should go to the office and talk". I reluctantly agreed and we went to the office and he asked me exactly what the problem was and why was I upset. I told him that I was fed up with doing all the menial tasks and never got to learn anything new, such as hedge cutting etc.

After I had calmed down and went back to the feeding, I remember that whoever was in the workshop went completely silent as I was shouting and screaming through the farm yard. No one said a thing until lunch time, when they asked what had happened. I told them all about it and how unfair things were here. They all agreed about the university chap, all of them hated the way this bloke got out of every dirty job on the farm. You dare not tell him anything as he would grass you up to the boss.

We found out later, that he was not even a university student, as he told us. He was at an agricultural college somewhere in Devon and because he was unemployed, he worked on the farm during harvest time. He rented one of the farm bungalows at *Barnsfield*, next door to Mark the fitter.

The amazing thing was that the very next day, I was told to take my tractor with the hedge cutter up to the ninety five acre field and to meet Malcolm there for some lessons in how to cut the hedges safely. So my tantrum achieved its goal and I was learning another job on the farm at last. I will never forget that bloody hedge cutter as it was a huge disc with blades attached to it. It could take out a telegraph pole with no problem and I did manage to chip out a bit of one on my first solo adventure.

I don't remember how many watches I broke at work and got fed up with the straps always snapping off my cheap Casio digital bracelets. So I told Mum and Dad about what the other lads did on the farm and I got a pocket watch for Christmas that year.

What they did was to get a small round pipe tobacco tin and fill it with cotton wool and put the pocket watch inside. I did this with my watch and it lasted almost a year until I lost the tin and watch all at the same time in one of the yards while bedding up the cattle. I expect someone will find it one day amongst the crops in the fields.

In the end, the best watches for working on a farm were the Casio digital ones with the rubber strap. I had one for years and it must have lasted at least four years until the strap gave up but the actual watch is still going strong to this day. Yes I still have it, sad but it's nostalgia I guess. Boiler suits were another essential piece of kit the farm worker went through every season or two if you were lucky. I had various types but never wore the ones with tractor logos on them as I thought it a bit too over the top and posy.

I went with Taylor to Newport one Saturday in the winter and we bought ourselves these West German tank suits from the army surplus store. They were double lined and had a built in leather sheath for your knife. They were very heavy indeed, but very long lasting and as warm as toast in the middle of winter. I loved that suit because it was very good on the bike for my journeys to and from work.

Not good when it got wet though as it took ages to dry out. I also bought a pair of British Army camouflaged trousers with double lining. Now they were the best trousers for work that I ever bought and so damn warm in the cold weather that we seemed to have in the 80's. I had ex fire service waterproof trousers with the braces and they took some beating too. I made a jacket out of fert bags once and stitched the arms on with our bag stitcher, looked bloody ridiculous but kept out the rain most of the time and cheered up the lads on the farm when they saw it.

My first experience of working out in the fields was probably during the final weeks of harvest. When fire breaks had to be cultivated and the remainder of the straw would have to be raked off the fields and either baled or just used as a point of ignition to help the stubble burn. We never used old tyres or waste oil to set the stubble on fire because we had the system of raking the residue onto one side of the field and burning that first. Raking was a fairly big job when you had over 900 acres of stubble fields to get round and only two implements to do the job properly.

The old fashioned rakes were only really used on the pea and bean straw, as I mentioned earlier. However, if there was a lot of wet straw that we were unable to bale or rake with the acrobat machine, then the old faithful rakes came out. They did a good job in those situations but not very good when there was very little straw lying on the ground to move.

The Lely Acrobat was the best implement for the job; I must have used that machine more than any other implement on the farm. It was simple in design and use and was very hard wearing indeed, with the only maintenance required was checking and replacing some of the tines that sometimes snapped off. The bearings in the wheels required constant greasing or they would wear badly. This tended to make the wheels rotate on an eccentric axis, thus not raking properly.

A fully loaded grease gun was essential and if I had not put the thing in the back of the tractor before I went out in the field, you could bet your life that Malcolm would arrive on the headland and start walking towards you. Then he would check the wheels and tines and see if the grease nipples had been touched recently. A real bollocking would be given if you had not touched the machine and back to the farm for your grease gun too.

So when I was proficient enough to be let loose with the Acrobat on my own, I would be sent off to start raking up the fields and then move onto the next field and so on. "Press on", would be Malcolm's exact words as he left you to get as much done as you could. Darkness was irrelevant on this job. I did not have any rear *working or plough lights* as they were known as. There were none fitted to the back of the Ford 5000 when I was given it. I set about trying to find some decent lamps to fit on the back of it so I could at least see what the implement was doing at night time.

I remember looking through the bits and pieces we had in the workshop but not finding much at all. The only light I found was this ancient looking thing that had a standard indicator type 12v bulb in it. I gave up looking around the farm; none of my workmates had any spare lights either.

A trip to Newport one Saturday afternoon on the bike with my mates was on the cards. We went to the only place that sold accessories for cars and bikes, *MOACCS* in Node Hill. It was an excellent shop that sold all sorts of goodies for us young bikers and drivers. They had a set of rectangular 12v halogen spotlights and for just over £20, were a bargain. When I got home and unpacked them, I found this small black square box with terminals sticking out of it. I had no idea what this thing was for, so I discarded it and took the rest of the contents to work with me on Monday.

I raided the workshop for same wire and at lunch time I managed to get these lamps on the back of the 5000. Luckily it had been raining for two days previous, so I had to stay at the farm and do some milling I think. This meant I had the tools and equipment in the workshop, to allow me to get these lamps fitted and working.

On the rear of the 5000's there was a small rubber covered 12v output socket, which came alive when you turned the lights on. It only had two holes in at and I never managed to find the male end that fitted the thing so I just poked the wires inside the socket with a screwdriver and they seemed to stay in there.

So the first night back out raking, when the rain had moved off and the fields had dried sufficiently. It started getting dark as I was travelling around the headland of *Wilmingham*, left hand thirty acres. There is something strangely cosy and pleasing about being out in a tractor at night. It didn't matter if it was in a Ford 5000 with barely a cab and no rear window, or a tractor with a full cab.

Going around the headland and suddenly you see a fox or a badger nipping along, doing whatever they do at night and then some rabbits darting into the hedges. Owls were my favourite, as they flew past and just caught by the lights of the tractor. A very lovely feeling and the field looks so different during darkness. I don't know how to explain how it feels cosy, but it did. I loved working at night time.

Turned on the lights and wow, the whole Acrobat lit up and I could see the wheels turning and the dust coming up as the tines scraped at the surface of the soil. These lights were fantastic and everywhere I had been was illuminated for yards behind me. Shame the headlamps were so dismal and gave you light exactly where you didn't need it. Full beam was excellent if you wanted to spot pheasants roosting in trees because the aims were far too high for ground level. I tried to move the headlamps down by removing the plastic grille and pushing them. After I had done that and got back in the tractor, the low beam now lit up two feet in front of the nose and high beam was slightly better, but generally useless.

Why did tractors have the worst lights ever fitted? I always wondered if the people who designed and built them, actually tried to work at night with the lights on. They didn't appear to have any idea how much work was done during the hours of darkness, where decent lights were in fact a necessity. After about fifteen minutes of raking and completing roughly three turns of the headland. Instant darkness, as everything went out, headlamps, side lights, dashboard the lot. Now I had a big problem on my hands because not only was it pitch black and I had no torch but I could not see to put the Acrobat into transport position so I could try and get back to the farm. I was about a mile away or so, this was going to be a bit dodgy with no lights. This bloody implement, with its spiky metal wheels sticking out of the rear of the tractor. If I hit anything with those wheels, then the other vehicle would look like a teabag. I edged out of the field and slowly drove down the road from *Wilmingham* towards the farm. Nothing came behind me or the other direction until I got to the top of

Barnsfield hill, and I had to quickly reverse up into the bridleway entrance without hitting the sign at the same time in the bloody dark. I got the rake off the road and most of the tractor also, then carried on down to the farm and in through the front entrance. It was pitch dark in there too and I nearly whacked the Ford 6600 parked near the old drier barn. I managed to park up as best I could and then got my jacket and helmet on and buggered off home on the bike.

Got up a bit earlier the next morning, I was slightly worried because I had to get to the 5000 before anyone else did, to investigate why all my lights had blown and see if I could fix it. It was a warmer morning and not a chance of rain on this day. Parking the bike in the small machine shed, next to the McConnell digger that sat there most of the summer leaning on its bucket and surrounded by a pile of dried mud.

I went round to the tractor shed and opened the door of the 5000 and tried the light switch, just in case it had mysteriously repaired itself during the night, not a hope. Not a thing, as I turned the switch, so I shut the right hand door and walked around the front and opened the left door and peered in at the two small fuse holders mounted on the side of the dashboard.

One looked rather different from the other because it looked as though it had got rather hot and melted. Now I was worried that I had destroyed the electrics and Malcolm would have me hanging from the drier barn roof for this. So I thought best tell the fitter first and maybe he can sort it out before the dreaded boss got to see it. I tried to unscrew the bloody fuse holder but it was melted so badly that it had probably welded itself together.

So I shut the door and then walked around the yard and up to the workshop doors to see if they had been unlocked. No one had arrived yet so I sat on the seed drill in the shed and waited for the rest of the crew to arrive. Finally, after about 20 minutes Malcolm drove in the front gate and went round towards the office. I thought he was going to stop at the workshop and open up, but as luck would have it, Mark the fitter rode in on his bike and dinged his bell at me as he parked up under the shed.

Malcolm must have seen him coming down the road behind him and went off to the office instead. He would have asked me about last night and how I got on with the raking I wanted to try and avoid the question until I came up with a good reason why I had to finish so early first. Mark opened up the doors and I walked in after him and took my place, standing at the end of the workbench, leaning against the shelving.

It was not long and the rest of the chaps had arrived in their cars and walked into the workshop for the daily meeting with Malcolm. Then the sound of that famous whistle came trundling around the yard and Malcolm walked into the workshop and said "morning Mark" as he always did and everyone stopped with the jokes and suddenly became more serious.

Now for some reason he asked me first how I had got on last night and what I had left to do, typical of my luck. I explained that I had finished one field and moved across the track to the field next to the railway line and then I had a problem with my lights not working. I had to explain the driving back in the dark and trying to avoid cars. I was expecting some sarcastic remark but nothing? He just asked Mark to have a look at my lights first thing, as I was obviously going to be on the same job all day again.

I was relieved and thought I may have just got away with this one, until Mark stripped out the whole dashboard and showed me the melted fuse holders. "Oh" I said, "what would have caused that then Mark?" "Those bloody lights you put on the back I think." I was sussed and could not get out of this one and admitted to Mark I had fitted the lights on the back and just plugged them in the small socket on the back. He said "you didn't use a relay then?" "Ah that's what that black thing was" I replied as I thought to myself about the small black plastic box with terminals on the bottom that came with the light set. Oh dear now I'm for it I thought to myself as I walked around the tractor, watching Mark repair the fuses.

After an hour or so the tractor was back in working order with lights too. I asked Mark if I could have the new lights working and he said he would try and find a relay for them and if not, I had to find the one that come with the lights and we can get them working and without blowing the 5000 up again. So I brought the relay in to work the next morning and Mark connected it up for me. Now I had working lights at long last and was ready to get out in the field and continue raking, guess what, it poured down and that was the end of that job for a couple of days.

After the fuse thing and blowing my lights, I did learn how to fit relays to further accessories that I bolted onto the tractor or any other machine. I did not want to taken to the dreaded office for a chat with Malcolm.

You would have thought that I would have learnt my lesson with electrics by now, and not attempted to blow the electrics up on my new bike. I decided it would be a good idea to fit some air horns on the bike, so I thought a set of air horns. What could possibly go wrong with these? It did go drastically wrong as I was riding home from work one evening and I was just passing a bunch of mates who had just turned up at *Norm's*. I thought, give them a blast of the new horns and make them jump. As I approached the crest of the hill by the café, I pressed the horn button and the next thing I saw smoke pouring out of the switch block on the handlebars and more smoke coming out of the side panel. Shit! I did not bother to stop, I just carried on and turned up the hill, under the archway and parked next to Dads stable. On closer inspection, I had melted the complete horn switch assembly and the smoke from the side panel was from the fuses. I had done it all over again, no bloody relay, and I was not best pleased with myself at all.

Even the spring on the horn button had got so hot and melted completely, along with one fuse holder and surrounding plastic. I found another plastic button and used a pen spring to replace the melted one. Oh the joys of being young and inexperienced in electrics.

Back out on the raking job and I literally couldn't wait until it got dark so the new lights could go on. Funny how such simple things excite us. I was back up on the *Bouldnor Block* and in a field we called *Roffords*, which incidentally, went around the back of a large house called *Roffords House*. It was about ten acres and it had an old well in one corner of it, which was fenced off with barbed wire. I had got in this field quite late in the afternoon and started raking the straw up by going anti-clockwise around the headland.

By the time I had got about ten turns into the field, the sun was almost gone. Lights on and carry on until I had enough of raking or I had finished the field. The lights on the back were fantastic and lit up the whole damn field. When I turned the corner around the small copse at the top of the field, a beam illuminated almost the whole field for a minute or two. I carried on until about nine o'clock that night and finished the whole field.

The people who lived in these houses on the main Yarmouth road had an annoying habit of dumping there garden rubbish into our field and the rake had quite a job moving the masses of grass cuttings and other compost that they just threw over their fences. It damn well annoyed me the way these people just took it for granted that they could just dump their stuff in a farmers field and think that we would not notice it. So on more than one occasion we managed to catch the owners actually throwing stuff over the fence and their sheepish body language and faces were a picture as they went back to their sheds or indoors. I also chucked a load of it back over the fence with a pitch fork, when I was clearing out of the copse one week in early April nineteen seventy nine.

After all the raking had been done and the hedges and verges had been cut and cleared, then cultivation could commence. One of my least favourite jobs was collecting up the grass and hedge trimmings around the headlands with a pitch fork or a four grain prong. With the help of a tractor and small wooden trailer, we would stack all the cuttings on the trailer and cart it off to the pond. We were not allowed to work together on this job, or in fact any job that meant two or more people were walking around a field together. We had to start in one place and work in opposite directions around the field and when we met up and all the stuff was hopefully, in neat piles around the field. It was always the youngest member of our group who had the job of taking the grass and hedge cuttings up to *Wilmingham*.

To ensure the task of grass collecting didn't bore us completely stupid, we devised a sort of game when loading up the trailer. The object was to see how high we could stack up the cuttings, without the load falling over.

We made one stack so high that it must have been about fifteen feet high from the ground to the top. We had to have one person sitting on top with a fork, just in case it started moving. We had quite a way to cart it all, and mostly across bumpy fields.. We actually made it to the pond with that enormous load and a few pound coins changed hands that Saturday morning, to those of us who betted.

The plough was unleashed in the fields and started turning over the land as it sliced its way across the fields. We had a very nice four furrow plough in the eighties and this was pulled first by a Ford 6600 and then a Ford County, as the workload increased. Hayward, the head tractor driver was the man on the plough and he certainly knew his stuff too. He could handle that big four wheeled beast with great ease and skill and kept that machine in immaculate condition throughout. The county performed well out in the field and although cumbersome around the yard, would pull almost anything.

It was the worst tractor for reversing four wheel trailers into barns and yards. Invariably, we would swap the tractor and put a little 5000 on the trailer for such difficult manoeuvres.

From the first cultivation period that I was involved with, I was always given the disc coulters on the back of my 5000. I enjoyed using them, after I had learnt how easily they could destroy themselves from lack of maintenance. Grease went by the bucket load when you were towing this machine around the fields. One thing that this implement gave me, was hours of work at night. I would work on until I had run out of coffee and the hunger started to make me think of what dinner awaited me when I finally got home from work.

Usually my Mother had left my dinner in the oven and it would have been a little dried up by the time I had got to it at half ten. I was hooked on this night time stuff and what with my special stereo tape deck and the large headphones; I could lose myself in music and watch all the night time activity of wildlife and the things that not everyone had the chance to see. I miss that aspect of farming to this day and would really love to just have another go at it.

One day I was working in the *Home field* which was directly opposite the farm and I was quite close to the massive bomb crater that lies up in the middle of that field. The implement I had on this occasion was a *Para plough*. This was my first time using this machine and basically, it resembled a plough, but with flat blades that went into the sub soil. It was used to reduce the compression of the soil on the tramlines, by breaking it up and lifting the compacted soil.

I had just stopped the tractor near the crater for lunch, poured a coffee from my flask and suddenly there was this horrendous noise and straw and chaff blowing all over the place. Then I saw this Chinook helicopter land about sixty feet away from me. The rear doors opened and out came a dozen or so soldiers with guns. Amazing to see as it was so close to me, I had absolutely no idea it going to land there, as I did not see it fly in across Mill Copse.

A few hours later and the whole farm was surrounded by soldiers and they had permission to use the farm for their manoeuvres. There were vehicles everywhere in the West Wight and I saw a couple of armoured cars over near Shalfleet as I was going home from work that evening. I always enjoyed seeing some military exercises with all the machinery and troops. It's a man thing I guess, machines, guns etc.

Later that evening I lost the wheel from the *Para plough* and could I find it. Not a bloody chance as it must have buried itself in the subsoil and was never seen again. Malcolm wasn't too happy about the wheel either and I lost the *Para plough* job after that.

It was on a Saturday morning and I was in the same field with the bomb crater, that I experienced another odd occurrence. I was raking the headland of straw and I suddenly heard lots of metallic objects hitting my roof and windows of the tractor. I stopped the tractor for lunch and was just sitting there and I heard pitter patter on the windows again and on the tractor mudguards. I still had no bloody idea what this stuff was as it was not cloudy, so it could not be rain or hail. So I carried on with my lunch and then I heard a loud bang of a shotgun in the distance and then this strange noise on the windows etc. It was the lead shot from the shotgun cartridges that were hitting the tractor.

One of the easiest jobs on the farm was carting the grain from the combine to the drier barn. Well, it wasn't easy when I first did it because I was very nervous when I first attempted to drive along side the combine whilst it was cutting, because I was not used to the speed or gears of the tractor and the sudden increase in weight of the trailer as it was being filled. It was so easy to stall the tractor if I had it in the wrong gear or lifted the clutch too quickly. Bearing in mind, this was a little Ford 5000 towing a three ton trailer, and not a giant tractor. Most embarrassing, when you have tons of grain pouring over your cab because you have let the machine stall and the combine overtakes you while still unloading its tank. Mark was laughing when it happened and stopped the combine, opened the door and laughed again. Luckily, he could see the comical side of my inexperience.

The tractor and the trailer full of grain certainly felt heavy when getting out of the huge hole in the ground as I went down the sides of the bomb crater, and up the other side. The best part of that job was being able to climb aboard the massive Claas combine and seeing what Mark was actually doing when driving it around the fields. It all looks very easy when you see it going round the field, but when you actually see the workings and what the driver has to look for while driving the combine. It is not easy at all, plus a lot of responsibility of a machine that cost in excess of £70,000 back then. A very mesmerising thing to stand up in the cab and watch.

There was an engagement party being held at my cousins house in Ottershaw and we had all been invited, so a small group of us arranged to go up on Saturday afternoon and arrive at their house late afternoon. The group this time was made up of Marcus and my brother Liam riding pillion, Rodney on his bike and I was on my new Honda CX500C with little Wol on the back.

We had a brilliant ride up to Fleet Services and it turned into a bit of a race at times although no one had a chance against Marcus on his newly acquired bike, a Honda CB900F.

The party was a good laugh and we all got very drunk. There were lots of people who we did not know, but they were all very friendly. We met a couple of Mates of my cousin Al who were Nail and his sister Tammy who both had bikes and we had a really good evening chatting to them. Most people went home after the party except the boys from the Island, We were shacked up in the marquee for the night with our sleeping bags and loaned pillows. It was around half two in the morning, and the barbecue was still hot. As we were all starving, we started cooking the remainder of the burgers and sausages. A midnight feast was had and my Uncle was laughing at us in the morning because we had been cooking in the early hours. I was very drunk that night and was accosted by my cousin at some point during the night and well, things happen. We had a lovely weekend and rode back down to Lymington around lunchtime and came home safely.

When I first started on the farm, we used an old Thames Trader lorry for grain carting and she was a real classic old truck. Painted grey and usually covered in dust because it was always parked near the output blower of the new drier. It chucked out tons of chaff and dust all over the yard, and covered anything parked nearby. Everything worked on the lorry, apart from one of the windows would never shut properly. It had a large engine cover in the cab that always got nice and warm in the summer months, very handy indeed.

The worst thing about that lorry was the smoke it made when starting and warming up. Even when Mark had refitted a new head gasket and had the head skimmed, it still smoked like hell and you would avoid starting her up inside a building, if you could. I loved to drive the lorry and would always take it around the road instead of through the farmyard, just to get an extra few minutes in it. It never had a very good battery fitted and it always had the farm battery charger connected up to it, ready for some grain carting.

It was not long until we acquired bigger lorry for grain cart. This was an ex *Gould, Hibbard and Randall* Leyland soft drinks lorry which was modified and given higher sides to hold a larger load of grain. It still had it's illuminated company name unit above the cab, which was given the name IW Farms by one of my workmates Ned. He spent more time in that lorry than anyone else on the farm. I remember his portable radio, which he had on the passenger seat and was always blaring out cricket match commentary.

Every time he would reverse up to the pit of the new drier, I opened the tailgate and ran over towards the workshop. This was because of the dust and chaff that bounced off the back of the pit and went straight up in the air. This would cover you in seconds if you remained in the drier barn. Oats and Barley were the worst crops for dust and gave me more hay fever attacks than any other dust. Peas, tick beans and linseed were relatively dust free and apart from the noisy beans in the elevators, they were a pleasure to put through the drier and dresser.

My job was as varied as it possibly could be when I first started on the farm. On one occasion, we all went off to Yarmouth with tractors and trailers to the badminton club to help clear some trees to make way for a bigger car park and a Portakabin. There was a chap there with a JCB digger and he was clearing all the trees and undergrowth and loading it all into our trailers and we took it all up to the pond for burning at a later date. We had to help clear all the roots and debris so the rotavator could come down and prepare the ground for grassing over.

On the same subject, more or less anyway, Malcolm told us a funny story about when he was busy burning stubble in one of the fields one afternoon. Because he was in such a rush to go to Badminton, he put his white shorts on under his boiler suit so he could go to the club and take off the boiler suit and play. Well it might have worked if he was not burning stubble because all the blacks as we called them, which are the ashes of the stubble, went up his boiler suit legs. He said when he took the boiler suit off; his legs were as black as the ace of spades. I bet looked a sight down at the badminton club that night.

A very good way to create gossip around the local area was to borrow a for sale sign from a house up the *Wilmingham* lane and re position it outside the low wall at the back of Thorley Manor Farm. How many people called in to find out how much it was for sale for and people ringing about to view it. The news spread to all our neighboring farms and gossip spread so quickly, before it was taken away by Malcolm that is. So funny, and I wonder who was responsible for that one?

PIC

Tony and I on Sandown beach. Circa 1975.

Having two bulls out in the fields is relatively fine, just as long as they are not in adjacent fields or separated by a river. Our two bulls were out on the marshes behind Yarmouth Common. They seemed quite safe and happy out there at first and didn't appear bothered by each other. One was a Hereford and the other Charolais and the Hereford, although the friendliest and placid bull I have ever known, he was a completely different character when he could see his counter part in the field on the other side of the river.

Now that river looks relatively shallow and not very wide but when the Hereford decided he was going to swim the river and get that pesky Charolais bull. We had a big problem on our hands because that river was deep and also had at least three feet of mud on the bottom too. It was about sixty feet in width, which required some careful planning. Luckily for the other bull, the Hereford could not climb the steep banks of the river and was basically stuck fast in the deep mud.

We all rushed down to the marshes in the back of the Honda truck and found a small rowing boat in the rushes and rowed out to the bull and got a rope around him. Meanwhile someone had brought the Matbro down on to the river bank and attached the rope to the forks on the front and began lifting and pulling the bull up the bank. It took ages to do it because the bull didn't want to go back to the other side of the river for some strange reason. Finally, with the help of the Matbro and us lot shouting at him, the bull climbed out of the river to his own side of the river.

We had to drive him back to the farm and hose him down and check if he had sustained any injuries in the pulling out process. He was fine and cleaned up ok afterwards then he was kept in the bull pens until the other bull was moved further around the marshes.

At near enough the same place on the marsh, where the bull and gone swimming, we lost one of our cows. Somewhere between the railway track and the marsh that curved around Mill Copse. We had no idea where she had gone and it was not until we all jumped into the back of Malcolm's pickup truck that we were told that someone had rung up saying this cow was heading for the ferry terminal in Yarmouth. As we drove along the railway line and almost reached the old station, in front of us there was a really old chap with a stick, hobbling along the path. He must have been slightly deaf as he did not hear us roll up behind him. Malcolm drove very slowly along side this bloke in a flat cap and asked him "Have you seen a cow and a policeman along here?" The chap just laughed at him and walked off. It was one of those moments when you could not stop laughing at the bloke's reaction.

Mark was sat next to Malcolm and his laugh was more than infectious and everyone was laughing. The old bloke obviously thought Malcolm was telling him a joke or something. So bloody funny, I will always remember the look on that old chap's face.

One day a pheasant flew into the cow yard at lunchtime, after the barley in the troughs no doubt. Taylor and I saw it in the yard and went over to the Nammet room to tell our completely mad workmate James that a pheasant was in the yard. He went out to his car and pulled out a bloody shotgun and calmly walked over to the yard. Unfortunately as we got inside the yard, Malcolm drove in the front entrance and to his office. We had to climb out the back of the yard and into the graveyard and hide there for ages until he went home for his lunch. When we made our way back to the cow yard, the pheasant had flown off. No Pheasant for us that night.

I always enjoyed going out to the fields on my bike with Taylor on his bike and turning the gas gun bird scarers off on the way home from work. We would take the longest possible route on our trail bikes and have a jolly good off road race back to the main road again. We used to go up the track at *Wilmingham* and across the footpath and onto the railway line, and then slowly ride up to the causeway and home. We were not supposed to be riding on the footpaths but it did not matter as it went right through one of our 30 acre fields. It was only the railway track that we could have been told off for. One day in the workshop I turned a gas gun on and then went out to the drier barn and hid in there. It wasn't long until it went off and frightened the hell out of who ever it was in there.

I was up on the Ham field one day and I was just sitting down against a tree for lunch and I did not see the bloody gas gun hidden in the long grass behind me. Bang! As I jumped in the air and there goes my coffee all over my legs. I told Taylor and he laughed and said "That'll learn you, shouldn't set them off in the bloody workshop should you."

We had this friend who lived somewhere on a farm in Cranmore and he was a very skinny lad who was always into military and anything relating to war. He used to come out on the backs of our bikes and we would go to his farm and just mess about on the bikes or fire his airgun. One day we went out there to see him and pulled up on the bikes on his drive. We had to wait at the end of the drive as there was a taxi parked in front of the house waiting to take his Mum off shopping.

Well the taxi driver looked as though he was getting a bit tired of waiting in his car and got out of the taxi and walked about a bit. If by magic, Gerald the nasty Goose came around the corner and spotted the taxi driver on the drive. He went straight up to this bloke and whack, straight in the nuts went its beak and the bloke dropped to the floor like a bag of spuds. Never seen anything so bloody funny and we were crying with laughter as we watched the poor bloke pick himself up and get back in the taxi.

The trusty old discs were, as I mentioned earlier, one of my favourite implements. In the beginning, I was always receiving a good telling off from Malcolm the manager for not greasing them often enough and going around the field with the discs squeaking like hell. Believe me; you could hear the things squealing for miles, so there was no escape from Malcolm. I saw the Honda truck appear out of the corner of my eye and knew what was coming. The second cock up I made was when the bearings fell apart and the whole rows of discs were hanging on a single mounting. Trying to re assemble them in the field was very difficult indeed.

Our sets were a pain in the bum when they broke, or the bolts just undid themselves and fell apart. The ends of the shafts that held the discs had a very large and mostly worn away nut on the end and trying to get a spanner to fit the worn away edges of the nut was bloody impossible. The only thing that I ever found to either undo or tighten them was a good pair of Stilsons. These could grip the worn out nut and turn it, but I always had to use a bit of old water pipe as an extra long handle on the Stilsons.

My favourite moment on the discs was when I was about two lengths in front of the seed drill. We had a Massey Ferguson standard drill which had the old fashioned metal framed, spiked harrows being towed behind it. Malcolm would regularly ride on the rear footplate of the drill to check that all the coulters were working and that there were no blockages in the seed compartment. The soil was very heavy with clay and it was just below the pond at *Wilmingham* where I managed to reach fifth gear. I had the engine almost flat out as the discs were digging very deeply into the clay and cutting it up nicely. It was important that I stayed well ahead, so the drill didn't have to stop and wait. It was quite a rush to keep as far as I could in front of the seeding and this was because the drill was twice the width of my discs and I needed to cover twice as much ground as the drill did. I was getting further ahead of the drilling and had reached about half way from the pond track to the *Wilmingham* barn when the soil changed from heavy clay to a softer and more workable sandy tilth. I had changed up to sixth gear as the discs were not as bogged down as before. They appeared to be doing an equally sufficient job, but the engine was really working hard and the plume of smoke from the exhaust was looking fairly impressive. The cab, although semi open was starting to get very warm and I could actually feel the heat from the gearbox starting to warm up my feet.

The drill had stopped at the headland on the main track to refill with seed, so I had some leeway for a short time. Then the soil changed back to its clay consistency and the discs were once again bogging down and starting to almost skip over some of the larger lumps of clay. So I had to change back down to a lower gear and lower the discs a bit further on the hydraulics to achieve the required soil condition. As the drill got closer to my lines and Malcolm was on the back, watching me as I was powering past him with the plume of smoke, jetting out of the engine and I noticed that the silencer was starting to glow a little, I carried on regardless.

The light of the afternoon was starting to fade out, as it was getting on for six o'clock and hunger was setting in. It was almost tea time and I was watching to see if Malcolm would dismount from the drill and get in his truck and go home for his tea, as he always did at this time

in the evening. Another run up the field and he
stopped the drill and then waved at me to stop.
I stopped and got out of the 5000 and walked
over to the drill and he said "Have your bit of
tea, then keep going and get ahead as we can
finish this field tonight." So I said "OK" and
went back to the tractor as Malcolm walked to
his truck and went off home for tea.

Kevin was doing the drilling that day and he
wandered over when the coast was clear and we
had a chat about the plume of smoke I was
generating and how I bet he loved it with the
boss riding on the back. I ate the last of my
sandwiches and emptied the almost black, mud
like coffee from a ten hour flask and then started
up and moved off up the field.

I had covered about two runs and then the
dreaded squealing started coming from the disks
and also I had just noticed how low my fuel
gauge had gone all of a sudden. I jumped out
and took the grease gun to the nipples and
pumped them full of grease and as I did,
Malcolm arrived back in the field and was
walking over towards me. "Problems Berry?" he
said and I replied "No problems Malcolm, just
some grease needed in the bearings." He looked
over the implement and seemed to be looking
for something wrong; luckily I had kept them all
intact and well lubricated so I was safe from any

bollockings for a change. I got back up into the cab and moved off without the awful squealing and powered those discs really deep as I went down and back up past Malcolm. He seemed to be satisfied with the job I was doing and he walked back up to the drill and flagged Kevin down to a stop and climbed aboard the drill again. Now it was really getting dark and on went the lights and I was kind of proud of my illuminated implement and it certainly caught Malcolm's eye as I went past him. The engine was really warmed up again after the stop for tea, the heat was building up again too, which I was glad of because it was getting a bit chilly now the sun had gone down.

The discs were working a treat and my tractor was almost glowing as I flew past the drill again on another run of the field. The drill had caught up with me by now and was only about two or three widths of the discs away now, so I had to speed up a bit somehow. So I shifted back up to sixth gear and had the throttle as far back as it would go without bending the lever on the dash. Now the 5000 was working at her best and the exhaust was starting to get hotter and hotter, a glow started to appear on the rusty side of the silencer and then a flame appeared just above the end of the exhaust pipe. I was amazed by this and had never seen anything like it before. The flame grew out of the pipe and the silencer was glowing like a log on a fire and the heat in the cab was very cosy against the chilly air of the night. I was flat out by now and everything was working perfectly and as it should.

Hayward had finished ploughing and had parked up on the track and joined Malcolm on the drill, as I had just turned at the headland and was heading back up hill, towards them. I will never forget their faces as they stared in awe at the exhaust of my 5000 with its flame reaching up into the dark sky and the silencer glowing cherry red as I past them. I remember them both smiling as I went past the drill and it must have looked excellent as I reached the bottom of the field and came back up. I never ever had that experience quite the same again, although I did manage to get the flame going on a set of spring tines once.

I did not know it was physically possible to generate a flame from a tractor exhaust, but now I knew differently. I made it to the end of that field and back to the farm with my very low fuel gauge too. The following morning in the workshop, the talk of the day was my exhaust and the flames. Malcolm made a joke about it too, though I cannot remember what was said exactly, but it was a good feeling to be the talk of the farm.

It was like a pre programmed thing that happened in our village and the surrounding villages every Saturday. Everyone appeared to go off to Newport on a Saturday shopping or whatever else people did there. I was one of them and I always ended up going to the town in search of new Hitec trainers, or a pair of new jeans for the coming weekend. Of course it was the day that a lot of local youngsters, visited that iconic nightclub, Barneys Roadhouse. It was so funny to see all the trendy young lads who had been into Fosters or Burtons for there new tee shirts or jeans. You could tell the Fosters blokes a mile off as they all had the same gear on at the night club on a Saturday night.

Come on, admit it. You bought Hitec trainers once, back then.

I would go to Borough Hall Motorcycles and drool in the window, over a brand new Suzuki TS 125 that always seemed to be the centre piece in the window. Rumbling Tum for your cheese burger and that was Saturday's entertainment almost done.

Chapter 13

Joining a band and the Broadway bakery

The first band I ever joined was in late early nineteen eighty two. It was a spontaneous decision that I only had about ten minutes to decide upon. I didn't know any musicians at all at the time, although our lodger was talking to a group of chaps up the Highdown Inn recently. It must have him that had mentioned that I played the synth and had my own gear.

It was one Saturday morning and there was a knock on the door of the flat. I came downstairs and answered the door to this middle aged fellow, who I had never met before. He explained that his son was in a band that practiced up at Stoats Farm and they were looking for a keyboard player. He was so persuasive with his manner and said that the band were so desperate for this member. He asked if I was already in a band, which I said I was not and had never been. He just said "well there you go, what have you got to lose. Go up and give it a try and if you don't like it, no one's going to say anything". He gave me less than ten minutes to decide and I had no option but to say yes. I had no excuses to use and am I so glad he was so persuasive that day.

I arranged with Mack the lodger, to go up to the band practice shed and take my gear up and meet the dudes. We actually went into the Highdown to meet them, because when we went to the shed, there was no one there. Mack knew where they could always be found. So I met them and got on very well with all of them. We eventually went over to the shed and they went through a couple of songs, while I listened. I liked the sound and decided it was for me, there and then.

After at least four or five months of solid rehearsal, we agreed that we were ready to be unleashed on the public. All the songs were cover versions and most of them, I enjoyed playing. We wrote just one song of our own in all the time I was with the band, alas, we didn't play it at the one and only gig. There were a few clashes of character in the band, but on the whole, we got through our differences and gelled well.

Our first gig was coming up quickly and we were practising more than three times a week so that it went as best as we could get it. I was still nervous as hell and it's not surprising really because it's a big thing to be on a stage for the first time. The day of the gig was hectic as hell, mainly because we had to get all the gear to the clubhouse and set it all up. This was made more stressful by the club not opening until late in the morning, this gave us even less time to do a sound check and make sure everything was perfect.

We all went home at about three pm and I went back to meet up with Lana at my parent's house up the hill. I was shaking with fright and smoked too many fags that afternoon than I would usually have done. Luckily I was being picked up by Brian, the father of the guitarist. I made sure some large Captain Morgan's were consumed for some Dutch courage but I was not drunk by any standard, just a bit happy really and less nervous too.

Equinoxe from 1983, L/R Tim Haddock, Rob lyon, Terry Saunders and Nigel Green.

As we drove up to the Football Club, my stomach was buzzing and so were my fingers, perhaps in anticipation of banging those keyboards. The main doors had loads of people going through them and I recognised a lot of the faces going in, not all were ones I liked. It didn't really matter because I didn't care about who was there or what they thought of me, that night. It was my first gig and I was going to enjoy it. We all met up at the bar and got a drink to settle our nerves.

I looked over at the stage and all the gear and thought "that's our gear, we are the gods tonight and we will command all these people tonight". I was so proud of it all. We put it all together and put a lot of effort into this gig. It's a beautiful feeling when you are in that situation and it is a once in a lifetime feeling too.

As the club was filling up and various people came over and said "hello" to myself and the other band members, I noticed a chap that lived across the road from me in Totland, it was the youngest son who lived at the sweet shop. Lovely bloke he was, very placid and unassuming really and so into heavy metal too. I waved at him and he came over and we chatted about the band and how he never knew I played in a band and are going to be playing any metal? I nodded "yes there will be some songs for you", he smiled like a Cheshire cat and wandered over to his 'metal mates' in the corner. The time had come for us to rejoin our gear on the stage and because I was so damn scared and nervous, I had borrowed my mother's Farfisa organ and we mounted it on a small coffee table so I had something to hide behind. What a chicken I was! On top of the organ I had my band member's Korg synth and on another table I had my Yamaha synth, both being mono and very basic indeed. I had a foot pedal flanger which I put my Yamaha through and a lead went from that into the PA amp. I didn't own an amp then and always used the PA instead.

The gig started off well and seeing all those faces staring at me was daunting as hell, especially the ladies for some reason. I guess it was because I was so shy and having girls staring at you and having nowhere to really hide, was worse than just blokes ogling you.

When the first half of the set was done and we stopped for a break, the nerves had faded away and I felt so much better about myself. Walking up to the bar was a fantastic feeling as everyone smiled and said how good we were and sounded excellent. There were members of rival bands in the audience and even some of them commented on how damn well we played. This gave all of us a boost of confidence. I'm sure made the second half of the set sound even better. We all had a nice drink at the bar, which were free, as people just insisted on buying the drinks. I imagined this was what real rock stars felt.

The disco that was playing while we had our break was keeping the atmosphere alive and kicking, although it was the moment that the DJ started to play one of the songs we were about to cover and we had kept it back for the second set because it was one of our best covers in the set. I remember the guitarist looking over at me and the bass player at the bar and shrugging his shoulders. It didn't matter what he played, he was not going to steal our thunder that night.

Time was ticking away and before we came off, I had noticed two girls sitting at a table on the right of the stage and one kept smiling at me. I smiled back as best I could, without hitting too many bum notes. I smiled again as I walked up to the bar, as I got to the crowd of people waiting to be served, I saw that she had followed me and stood next to me at the bar. She smiled and said "the music is brilliant." I was shy but I got up the courage to thank her and said "would you like a drink?"' She said "yes please", I said "would your friend like one too"? She smiled and said "she would", so I bought them their drinks and she asked if I lived in

Freshwater and she said they were both from Southampton but visiting relatives, I told her I lived in Totland, she smiled with excitement and replied "we are staying in Totland, with my grandparents", I smiled and said "that's good because we are having a party afterwards, maybe you would like to come along?" She drank some her drink and smiled "maybe I would like to come, but I don't know your name." I laughed and apologised and told her my name and she said my name is "Suzanne and my friend is Linda". OK, well I have to go back on stage in a minute so hopefully I will see you later Suzanne.

I followed the drummer back to the stage, and as we walked back the people standing nearest the gear all clapped and cheered us on. Wow what a beautiful moment, could this be what dreams are made of? The songs we played were all number ones in the charts and one song that we kept for the second set was *Down Under* by *Men at Work* and that was still number one in the charts. It takes some guts to attempt to play a song that is still at number one because the audience will remember exactly how it is supposed to sound and one tiny wrong note or bad timing will put you under forever.
Well it went beautifully and we had nearly the whole football club dancing and singing six feet from us on the dance floor. We could not have

wished for a better outcome, everything was sounding fantastic and the audience loved it. When we had stopped playing one of the *Thin Lizzy* songs I saw the chap from the sweet shop in the front of the crowd and he was shouting Whitesnake and his mates joined in too. We were laughing and we told him we didn't know any of their songs, his face was a picture because the next song on the set list was in fact *Whitesnake's, don't break my heart again.* I watched him and his band of mates as I started playing the organ intro and after a few seconds it clicked and he was bouncing around all over the floor and that made his day.

Every time I looked over at Suzanne, she was smiling and waving at me. I was in heaven, totally in my ideal. The music rocking that club house and that pretty girl waving and smiling, I needed nothing more from life. As I played the final song and the thoughts were flying through my mind, what would happen at the party, what about Lana? I didn't want to think about her and that was because she refused to come to the gig. I really wanted to share this moment with her, but this time I had been taken by another and I didn't care about anything else now. I didn't ever find out the real reason why Lana refused to come to the gig, it was very odd at the time and still is. I often wondered if there was someone there she didn't want to meet up with because perhaps she had been shagging them too. It would not surprise me at all because when it came to being faithful, it was a word that she didn't understand at all.

I don't blame her for her ways, because she just loved the excitement and thrill of sex with someone new or it was the thrill of the chase that powered her passion. She certainly had some fun and if she could, then so was I.

After about the fifth encore, the audience was determined never to stop dancing that night. We finally stopped playing and that was only because the club steward insisted we finished because of the terms of the club's license meant they had to stop all music by midnight or something to that effect. To be honest, I could have gone on for another hour or so and so could the rest of the band.

The crowd finally had to give up their quest and slowly leave the club. There were a few people who stayed behind to chat with us and help us with the gear. The most important person was Suzanne, and she stayed with me and her friend until we had unplugged all the equipment and packed away what we could.

We were allowed to leave all the gear there until the following morning, which was the best idea in the circumstances. We all left the club and made our way to the bass player's house and had a party to celebrate the success of the gig.

Everyone was there and it was a really great gathering because we were all on a high and just chatting about the highs and lows of the gig. There were plenty of extra bedrooms in the house so after a while, some of the band went to bed and only myself, a guitarist, Suzanne and her friend were left downstairs and we were just chatting and drinking. Suzanne got closer to me and rested her head on my lap and I just lent over and kissed her and kissed her. It seemed to last for ages and we were entangled in passion. Her kiss was gorgeous and she just looked absolutely beautiful. I couldn't put her down and yes I did think momentarily of Lana but that could not stop the feelings I had for Suzanne at that moment. The guitarist tried and I mean tried to pull Suzanne's friend, but she was having none of it. She just seemed happier watching us two snogging each other to death on the floor. Before he had a chance to say anything else, Suzanne's friend said "that's OK; I will share with Suzanne and Berry." I didn't really click at what she said as I was too engrossed but if looks could kill!

So I had to share my bed with two pretty girls and it was beautiful, passionate and totally unplanned and being totally drunk on rum, I had no perception of guilt. I never dreamed of this and to be honest had never even thought about this fantasy because of my shy and somewhat, naive personality. To find myself in such a situation was pretty daunting and I think that made it all the more special. It wasn't lust that took me to that bed; it was the new experience and the draw of the unknown that made me do it. I guess everyone who knew would have expected me to have made love to both of them that night and to get what I could and disappear the next day.

I know it sounds somewhat unbelievable and untrue, but I didn't make love to either of them and just kissed and had a beautiful experience with both of them. I felt so guilty all the next morning when the effects of the alcohol had gone and I had come to my senses. Hung over and feeling very bad for being with someone else all night and not Lana. I kept telling myself that it wasn't that bad and anyway, she cheated on me first; *See the Haunted Bakery chapter*) and at least I didn't make love to anyone else. Justification I guess you would call it and trying to make myself feel better for what had happened.

The next day we all went our separate ways and I had to go to the club house and collect the gear and tidy up the stage. I went to collect my bike that was parked up at the band shed. I came home and told my parents all about the gig and was just sitting in the lounge having tea when there was a knock on the door. It was one of my mates and he had just come over from the Broadway Inn, across the road. He said there is someone called Suzanne asking where you were and she wants to meet up with you.

I had totally forgotten that I had arranged to meet her in the pub in the afternoon as I rushed over there and saw her sitting at the bar with Linda. I cautiously went over to her and she gave me the biggest smile and put her arms out and I went closer and kissed her once again. We all went from the bar to a corner of the lounge to a little table and chatted. Suzanne gave me a piece of paper with her grandparent's address on it and said she would be coming over to the island again soon and if I wanted to meet up, we could go out somewhere. Suzanne and her friend were both nurses from Southampton hospital and came over to visit Suzanne's grandparents on a regular basis. I was by this time feeling beyond the realms of guilt, my thoughts returned to Lana. I said goodbye to Suzanne and we kissed and cuddled for a while outside the pub, then I waited for her to go back inside to get her friend and I went back up the hill to my parent's house.

It was about six o'clock when Lana arrived at *Dreens* on her bike and we made a drink and disappeared off to my bedroom for the evening as we usually did. We chatted about the gig and how much I thought she would have enjoyed it, plus I told her about the chap from the sweet shop being there and how much into music he was. As I was talking to her and she was asking questions about the gig, I was feeling even guiltier than I was earlier and I just could not get rid of the thoughts. I tried the justification method once again and compared in my mind, how much she hurt me by sleeping with Marcus and decided there was no real comparison, there was no sex involved and I didn't think what I did was half as bad as what Lana had done. Of course I was thinking physically and not mentally, which are completely different and have deeper effects, which I didn't really think of at the time. That's the trouble with being so young and not understanding the upset and trauma you can cause by your actions.

So I finally got up the courage to tell her about Suzanne and her friend Linda and the party afterwards. It was not easy to tell her and I knew she would be very upset about it all, but I couldn't keep it from her any longer.

Lana was upset but didn't get too angry about what happened, although she did get up and dressed and said "I've got to go home now" and went downstairs, said "bye" to Mum and Dad then went down to get on her bike I remember her revving the hell out of that bike as she sped off down the driveway. It was a good couple of days til she came back to see me after work one evening, but when she did, she was calm and had forgiven me for my unfaithfulness at the gig and we were back to our passionate ways within hours.

Her strength of character was amazing and the way she forgave me without a moment of hesitation was something I have rarely experienced in any other person. I suppose if it had been anyone else that I had done such a thing too, they would have been off, right there and then. She looked forward and disregarded what the past had held for us, she loved me and I loved her and it was going to take a bigger thing to destroy what we had built together. We tried so many times' to find a place of our own to be together, every time it was a disappointing quest, mainly because we didn't earn enough between us to rent anything local.

Maybe it was not meant to be; perhaps we just were not destined to live together at such a young age that certainly seemed to be the case when I look back at everything we tried. Landlords were obviously a bit wary of two teenagers renting their properties and especially ones with black leather biker jackets and who rode motorcycles.

I decided to leave the farm job in around October of nineteen eighty one because I just couldn't get on the Malcolm the manager at that time. I was young and rebellious and it just was the wrong time for me, so I handed in my notice and because the bakery plan was coming together and it could be up and running in six months time. I had planned to rely on that business as my source of income. Alas, it didn't open for at least twelve months and I was in a dire position and needed some work ASAP. I was very lucky because my girlfriend Lana knew of a possible job at a holiday camp doing maintenance work and it grabbed my attention instantly when she mentioned the job. She said she knew the owners and would speak to them for me and eventually I was off to the *Totland Country Club* in for an interview. So I was back in the loop and earning again and also had some very interesting work too. My parents did not really want me to leave Thorley Manor because it was a good job and very hard to come by, even in those days. I was just too young at the time and wanted more of what my mates had, evenings out with girls and doing all those things that they enjoyed while I was working every day and evening right through the summer and autumn. The money was incredible for my age and I had wage packets that I never even opened in my secret store under the floorboards of my bedroom. I could buy anything I wanted at the end of the summer but there was no way I could buy time and that is what I longed for. It's the old saying "loads of time and no money or loads of money and no time". It took me a long time to realise where I had gone wrong and for me to get my life in order and aim for something specific in life. I'm still working on that plan but have not quite finished it….

I met some really nice people while working there and one of them is still a very good mate to this day. He was quite a chunky chap; he'd kill me if he reads this. He was into Rockabilly music in a big way. His mate was into the same music too but there was something odd about that other dude that I couldn't put my finger on exactly, I never could take to him at all. After a few weeks of working there I was offered a caravan to stay in, because they wanted to have someone on site all the time in case of an emergency.

So I moved into this caravan and it was really nice not having to go home after working all day. Now this new mate had a talent of impersonating the characters from *Rainbow* the children's TV series. He was brilliant as *Zippy* and *George* and had us in tears on many occasions. I was till band practicing and he was one of our loyal fans and came with us to rehearsals and gigs.

We had some great parties in that caravan and I met so many lovely people at these parties. I remember meeting the group of girls who had rented two chalets and they came from Somerset. We had some fantastic nights in each others abodes and one of these girls was a trainee policewoman and she was hell bent on stealing my leather jeans.

Later on in the summer, I was given a chalet to share with this manager bloke. He was the slimiest, creepiest bloke you could ever meet and I could not stand him and neither could any of the staff. He had this annoying habit of closing his eyes when he talked to you and always had a massive bunch of keys clipped to his belt loop. One of those people who had mobile phones on their belt, the type you avoided at all costs. He was seeing the boss's daughter and had a nice little number just poncing about with not a bloody clue what he was talking about. He would try and join in and be "best mates" with us in the bar in the evenings, so we made sure we didn't go in there when he was around. I don't dislike many people but that bloke was detestable.

My old pal Zippy outside the Totland Bay Country Club. Circa 1983.

The owner decided to have a swimming pool dug and I helped out with some of the work on it and was put in charge of the heating and cleaning of it when it first opened. Then they opened a Greek restaurant and we had these two Cypriot chaps living on site and running the place. The chef was a lovely bloke and I got on really well with him but the manager or whatever he was, was a typical "medallion man" and went on about that he had run this in London and did this somewhere else. I'm sure that was supposed to impress us, unfortunately it didn't and we just said "Yes" to all his stories.

The chef always had fresh Moussaka waiting for me every time I came in on my bike at night time. It was gorgeous, the first time I had ever tasted such a lovely food. They had these Greek Nights in the restaurant and plate smashing events. I helped my mate clean up the place one day and what a mess it was too. We ended up having a butter portion fight with my mate hiding behind the bar and myself and his mate hiding under the tables, oh such young fun.

I left the place after the end of the summer because our Bakery was due to open very soon and I was needed in there. It was roughly six months after I finished working at the Country club and I had been talking to the owner about a possible gig there for our band.

The new band came about from becoming good friends with the rhythm guitarist from the first band. He wasn't working and we spent vast amounts of time together, playing and messing about with lights. In fact we built some of the lights for the football club gig in the flat. He had been playing with a bunch of musicians based in Shalfleet.

They were playing a gig in the church hall where my eighteenth party was held. My mate had asked if I would like to come and do the lights for the gig, so I did. There were not many people at the gig but regardless, it was a good laugh and I got on well with them.

They had been toying with the idea of having a keyboard player, so he arranged for me to go and meet them. The difference between this band and the original one was that they played no cover versions. All their own songs were written by the three of them and I loved the sound they had, and the songs were so different from everything else. So I joined them. The interesting thing was that they too had played with the bass player from Equinox and did a gig at the Country Club, some months previous to our meeting.

It was early in nineteen eighty two, when Mum and Dad embarked on a conversion of the downstairs flat and shop into a bakery. It took a lot of work and expense to change the look of the flat and kit it out with machinery and work surfaces in the back rooms and a three deck electric oven was installed in the room directly behind the shop space. The most expensive part of the conversion was undoubtedly the three phase electric supply that was put in, plus the cabling inside the bakery. Dad's builder mate Roy did most of the building work and we had an electrician to do all the electrics. The so called mate of Dad's ripped him off with a lot of the materials and Dad found it all out from the electrician, who was more honest than his counterpart by miles. There always seems to be someone who has to be that little bit greedy and rip you off, but they always get caught out in the end.

As the bakery had no equipment whatsoever, which meant my parents had to fork out a vast amount of money for all the mixers, ovens, tins, ingredients and other stuff that you require for such a business venture. It did have a big effect on the budget of the household at the time because it drained the coffers immensely and took a lot of serious planning to get us through this massive outlay. Dad knew of a baker who had worked for Yarmouth bakery and for an American guy who owned it and he was going to come and work for us and live in the flat above with his family. This worked out really well in the beginning and the bakery took off with a flying start. Custom increased twenty fold and we had managed to pick up a lot of wholesale orders from some of the local shops. We now had a successful bakery and butcher's shop and all we now needed was the candlestick makers.

It was a hit and miss venture right from the word go, but as there was no real competition around the West Wight, it turned out well. After about six or so months, things started to fall apart in so much as my Father and the baker fell out over money. I'm not sure of what actually happened as I was not told anything about the problems. Dad had enough of it and sacked the baker and got him to move out of the flat. So now we had no baker and the empty flat above to deal with.

There was another problem we had in the butchers shop and this was petty theft of meat from the chiller, but Dad caught the culprit, thumped him and never saw him again. Also there was this chap who worked for the council and he always came into our butcher's and sat in the office next to the till and drank tea. I call it a till but in fact it was an old cash drawer that we used. Dad always told me to keep an eye on this bloke when he sat in the office because he suspected that he may be stealing money from the drawer.
We never actually caught him stealing but some years after we sold the butchery to a chap from Birmingham.

caught this bloke stealing cash from the same drawer. Dad was right about him and I bet he stole a lot of money from our shop. If I had the chance I would like to cut that bloke's hands off. You just don't know who the real honest people are because sometimes it takes years of watching and learning who the honest ones are. Dad was a very good judge of characters and I think he learnt that skill from his National Service and being in the army. He always said that you meet and work with so many different types of people in the army that you soon know how to judge a character and their traits to find out how honest they are. I guess he was right, because you would not have the chance to meet so many different characters in one particular job as he did in the services.

Not all of my parent's acquaintances or employees in the businesses were thieving scum bags by a long shot. Some were very helpful and good honest people and always remained loyal to the end.

Because we had no baker or other staff at the time meant I had to leave my holiday camp job and come and help out in the bakery. I knew nothing about baking at all and in fact, neither did any other members of the family. We had to pick up the pieces and learn how to bake bread and make cakes and other confectionery from scratch. Dad had learnt a lot from helping the original baker and had it all stored in his head. I have to say that my Father could turn his hand to anything in the catering trade and very soon learned how to do most of the bread making tasks and with help from myself and my brother Liam of course.

He did a very clever thing when he had to sack and kick out the baker, he hid all the bread recipes and no one could find them. There was a girl who worked during the day doing confectionery. She was a very loyal friend of the baker who was kicked out and obviously resented him leaving. We later found out that she was instructed by the baker to take the recipe book home with her and he would collect it later on. Dad was already one step ahead of these conniving people and made sure that girl was kicked out shortly after the baker was and never got hold of the most important item in any bakery.

We all worked together on the night shift and usually started work at about half ten in the evening, except for Friday nights when we would have to start at nine o'clock as it much busier over the weekend. It was a good job and I liked it very much and it was such a complete change of environment for me. We had some memorable nights in that place and always had a visit from the local police in the night, on their patrol around Totland. They would have a coffee with us and we gave them a loaf or two. It was all so different in that era and much friendlier and open than it seems to be now. My mates would always call in during the late evening and have a chat and a smoke out at the front of the shop and sometimes Liam's mates would come and visit too. A very sociable evening it was and it made the job so much more interesting and the night go quicker.

My brother was a little cheeky chap when he was younger and always up to no good in the bakery at night. He threw a load of flour at Dad one night and Dad didn't find it very amusing and chased the little bugger out of the shop. One night we were making hot cross buns and used this very stinky bun spice flavouring in the dough. It was so strong and overpowering when it was squirted into the mixer that we decided it would be a good idea to see who could sniff the bottle the most times before your nose fell off. It almost blew your head off after one sniff and I am sure it burnt the inside of my nose. Another silly competition we had been to see how many swigs you could take out of a four pint bottle of double cream, not for customer use I hasten to add. My god you felt so sick after a couple of gulps of that stuff.

Mum did all the work during the day and especially the cleaning up of the shop and bakery, until she employed some ladies to help her out. Everyone mucked in and helped out with that bakery and made it work, even without a professional baker. Amazing what you can achieve if you put your mind to it or when you have no other choice in the matter. The bakery worked well and we employed two girls in the shop during the day so it gave my mother a rest from it all.

One night my brother Liam had been out with his mates and it was getting quite late and he had not come home. Dad was quite strict with us on our time keeping and especially if we were not back home on time at night and we would get a good smacking if we were late home. Liam was always out with his mates and on this occasion, he thought he would get away with not coming home on time by ringing Mum from a phone box to inform her he was going to be late.

Dad was like radar and knew every trick in the book when it came to my brother and his night time activities. So when Mum answered the phone and Dad heard what she was saying to my brother and he picked up the phone upstairs. When Mum had said "that will be OK." Dad butted in and said to him "you get home right now." Liam thought he had got away with it. Dad was waiting for him on the drive and gave him a good hiding and sent him to his room.

Liam didn't try that ploy again and was never late home after that. I got a good smacking one evening after school because I had gone down to the beach with my new school shoes on and they were covered in sand and salt water. Dad caught me in the kitchen as I walked in and I thought he had gone out. He whacked me and I fell into the airing cupboard, amongst all the sheets, I did not dare go to the beach with my school shoes on again.

Kate, the girl who stole my leather jeans with Zippy in the Bar of the Country Club. Circa 1983.

Being from the east end of London and growing up through very hard times indeed, made Dad what he was and he was a fighter if he wanted to be.

The man I only knew as granddad on my father's side was not my father's father at all. I only found this out in recent times and it's amazing what you believe to be true, when you know no different. He told me that when he was very young, before he was evacuated to Exmoor during the war. A man used to always come round to his house and he was one of the only people he knew who had a motor car, so he was probably quite a wealthy man. He used to take my father out for drives in the car and spent a lot of time with him. Dad said that the sister of the man we thought was his Father, told Dad before she died, that this other man with the car was his father.

So this changes the way I think of whom my Granddad really was and also what relationship do we have with this man with the car. Obviously he is not likely to be alive now but I really want to trace this chap and see what happened to him. Luckily I have the full name of this mysterious chap and he lived in the east end of London, so it should not be too hard to find him.

My Dad's mother was a nasty evil woman. I remember going to see her in the house that my parents had bought them in York Street, Cowes. I hated going to visit her after my assumed granddad had passed away because she was never nice to us kids and he was. Dad's auntie lived with her in that house and was physically abused by Dad's mum on many occasions. Dad told me she used to beat her all the time and in the end she was almost a slave in that house. I have no idea what happened to his aunt when his mum moved up to Cambridge and eventually died. Dad did not attend her funeral because he detested the woman and after all the stories he told me about her, I wouldn't blame him for not attending her funeral.

When my Father and his two brothers and two Sisters were evacuated to Exmoor in Somerset, his mother who was working in the NAAFI in Yeovil; never bothered to come and visit her children on a regular basis. Dad said he only saw her once or twice in five years and always on the back of some soldier's army motorcycle. I think that the evacuation came at a perfect time for her as she could be rid of the kids and enjoy her life chasing men.

The small farmhouse that Dad was evacuated to with his two brothers was almost a case of jumping out of the frying pan and into the fire.

The old woman, who they lived with, didn't feed them properly and they were kicked out of the house all day long, whatever the weather. All the parcels that were sent from his parents, they did not see because the old lady gave all the food and sweets to her daughter who lived in the village. Dad's sisters were housed in the same village but in a different house to Dad and his brothers and my father said that he hardly ever saw them for the first two years. After the cruel treatment of the children in that old farmhouse, they were moved to Yeovil and it was better for them at last. The Sisters went back to London when Dad was moved and that meant he never saw them for a long time. What a life to have at the age of five years old, must have been hell for those kids.

Our village policeman and probably one of the funniest characters I ever knew and this was because he always seemed to be somewhat clumsy with his motorcycle. I forget how many times he attempted to go round the roundabout with his stand still down and was forever pulling away from the stationers shop with the stand down, with a shower of sparks following him. There was the time when we had gone down to the village recreation ground and just sat on our bikes, by the entrance. Suddenly a headlight started flashing up the muddy lane that led to what was Lanes End. We sat there in amazement as he came up the track, sliding all over the place and smiled at us as he rode past. God knows why he rode his bike up that boggy track because he didn't seem to be chasing anyone.

One of the funniest moments in the village that I can remember so vividly, was the time of the dustcart strike and all the rubbish was put in the car park next to our bakery. There was a mountain of it in there, not just bin bags either. Sofas, chairs and other stuff had been dumped there too. *The metal gang from the bench*, who always met in either the bus shelter or on the benches by the roundabout, were sitting opposite the Broadway Inn on this particular evening. It was a very warm evening and the gang were just relaxing and listening to some Rainbow on their stereo. I was with little Wol and the gang that night and it was suddenly decided that the old benches were not comfortable anymore, we could do better.

Next thing, we were carrying this massive sofa from the car park and moved the bench to the hedge and put this thing in its place. It was a picture and a moment that will not be repeated. All six of us sitting on this sofa, placed on the grass by the roundabout which was later to be named Cokes Green. Everyone that went past was laughing at us and then came the ultimate, in comical moments. PC Chizzy came down the hill towards us and he nearly fell off his bike laughing at us. He stopped to tell us we were loonies and asked if we were we going to "leave that thing on the grass?" We said we would take it back to the dump in the car park when we went home, which we did. We put it back there on most evenings until the rubbish strike was finished. So funny and unique in every way possible I should think.

Then there was the chap from Freshwater who decided his seat on his CZ motorcycle was not comfortable and welded a car seat on the bike and rode it around for ages like that. Until he got stopped by the dreaded Police Volvo and was told he had to remove it.

Another classic moment involving PC Chizzy was the night we went trail riding up on Tennyson Down. Although not allowed now, thanks to the National Trust exclusion. There were at least ten of us on trail bikes and a few other chaps on road bikes just flying up and down the downs with no headlights on and following the moonlight. Suddenly someone spots a headlamp coming up from the Freshwater Bay end of the downs and we had no idea who it was.

We all thought it might me another one of our mates coming up the path and it was mentioned that the path from the bay is dangerously close to the cliff edge in places and very slippery with mud and chalk. Regardless of the lack of traction and the almost 300 feet drop only about six feet from the track, PC Chizzy was coming up that track on his Honda CB200 road bike, complete with fairing and all. He was determined to say the least and soon as we heard the distinctive sound of that bike and the occasion sound of his radio bleeping, we were off down the track towards the small chalk pit and then towards the Highdown Inn and off to wherever we could hide.

He did not catch us but when he found our bikes parked outside the Braemar café, he knew it was us lot, but he never came in to say anything.

Winding up the local police was a damned good sport back in the day. The Police van from Freshwater was always going along the main road through Colwell at night. So we came up with a plan as it approached about seven of us. We all ran across the common. Sure enough, the van turned around and chased after us.
As we reached the road that leads to Colwell beach and we could see it was PC Chizzy and his counterpart from Freshwater. They stopped the van and asked "what are you lot up to?" We

replied "oh just having a run to keep fit". The look on those two policemen's faces was a picture, we just walked off laughing. We were a harmless gang of young bikers and metal freaks, who just enjoyed a good laugh. It was a fantastic time and growing up in our little world made us what we are now. We did not get into trouble, unlike some kids seemed to in the surrounding villages. I would love to go back and do it all again.

Me posing in the band shed at Stoats Farm in Totland. Circa 1982. My posters were the Gary Numan ones!

It was a Saturday afternoon and Dad had come in from the shop as it was only a half day opening. Mum was cooking lunch and our lodger and I were sitting in the best seat in the house, the bay window overlooking the roundabout and the lower part of the village. People watching is a great pastime and we did it all the time from that window.

The things we saw from up there could have made a brilliant weekly magazine. After seeing the usual cars and bikes go around the circuit as they did every Saturday, it was unusually quiet that afternoon. After about half hour, Mum dished up lunch and we all sat down in the kitchen and filled our hungry mouths. Afterwards it was time for a nice cup of tea and back to the grandstand seat for a while. Suddenly there was a strange noise coming down Church Hill, towards the roundabout. It sounded like things being dragged along the road and it was getting louder all the time. Then we could just see a couple of people coming down the hill on toy cars and bikes, then another and another came into view. It was some of the skinhead lads from Freshwater on these toys and the horrendous noise was from the plastic wheels on the tarmac.

They all parked their machines outside the café opposite and went inside. We were in tears of laughter at the sight of these lads parking toys outside the café and there was this huge row of them sat there. It was the funniest thing to see and apparently they rode them all the way from Alum Bay to Totland Bay.

One of the same group of lads attracted quite a crowd one day on Totland pier. He was taking money from people to watch him ride his bicycle off the end of the pier and was making a tidy sum in the process. He had this load of rope and he tied it to the pier and the bike, so he did not lose the machine when he hit the water. It was a brilliant bit of showmanship and it was excellent fun to watch him hit the water. Such characters we had in our villages and it made growing up all the more exciting.

One evening outside the Braemar café, we were all sitting on the bikes wondering what the hell we were going to spend the evening doing and one of my friends said "Hey look up at the monument on Tennyson downs, its all lit up, wonder what that's about?" That was it; everyone was starting their bikes and flying off to the chalk pit near the Highdown Inn. We all parked our bikes in the chalk pit and made our way up the long chalky lane to the base of the downs. By the time we got up there it was nearly dark and quite difficult seeing your way, until we got up in the lights. We could see lots of people and lorries up at the top of the hill and the whole area was illuminated. On closer inspection, there was a very large truck with a Hiab on the back and it had these massive lights attached to it and lifted way up above Tennyson's monument. The monument itself had been cleaned too and it looked so bright when you looked at it. We walked around the big BBC generator lorries and went over to where the filming was taking place.

Right near the edge of the cliffs, were a actor and actress dressed in what looked like Victorian costume and she had an umbrella to shade her face from the lights and he wore a striped suit and with a straw boater. I did not have a clue who these people were at the time but knew they must have been reasonably famous because it was a BBC filming unit.

Months later I was talking to a friend of mine's mother and she mentioned that there was a series on TV tonight and it was filmed on the island. So I watched the programme and there it was the exact scene we had all watched that night on the downs except the scene was filmed at night but with all the lights, it was depicted as a beautiful sunny day. Oh and the actor was Alan Bates but I cannot remember the actress's name now.

I bought a Honda CB200 bike very cheaply and my friend Dilly also knew of one that had sat outside this guys house for months and they were going to have clear out and dump it. So he managed to get it for about a tenner and we were planning to use it for spares for the one that I already had. We got both of them running and after a while, all the lights working on mine but his one had no lights at all. It was a cold frosty night and it was snowing quite heavily and we decided to take the CB's out for a spin up the Warren as it was snowing and there wouldn't be many people about. We went down the drive and waited under the archway just in case old Chizzy was about and when the coast was clear, we rode down to the turf walk and then up Cliff Road and up the bridleway to the Warren. The snow was still hammering it down and when we reached the Alum Bay end of the hills, we were bloody frozen. I had lights and Dilly was in the dark as we raced across the sandy hills and slid in the snow. The only light we had was my poor headlight and the moonlight reflecting off the snow. My bike was great in the snow and didn't slip too many times until I hit a big drift and it almost covered the bike in snow. It was a great evening's entertainment and we got home easily as all the roads were now covered in a lovely layer of snow, so no cops were about.

There comes a point in time when you play in a band that you have to make a decision whether you want to concentrate more on the band or try and earn money in the normal mundane manner of things. It was at this point when money was becoming a problem and without it I could not even get to the shed where we practiced, let alone make any money from playing. The bass player and I were both in the same situation and our fruitless visits to the job centre, which we did every week by bus. We always had a band meeting in a café in lower St James Street and would chat and plan our next assault on the music scene and browse the music gear in the little music shops that were left, such as *The Music Cave* and sometimes even went in *Teagues* if we were feeling exceptionally rich that day.

It was on one of these trips to Newport Job Centre that we were accosted by this rather posh speaking chap as we were looking at the various kitchen staff, waitresses and care home vacancies on those typed cards on stands. He asked us if we were looking for work. "No, we always came here to check the spelling on the cards" I remember thinking. He told us he was organising this *Community Task Force* thing and needed unemployed people for his project. The work paid more than being unemployed and you got clothing too. The only one problem with this scheme for me was it was based in Station Road, Wootton Bridge which was half way across the island for me to travel by bus. Similarly, it was a long distance for the bass player to travel, although it turned out to be a doddle to get there from his house in Shanklin in the end.

That is when we came up with the idea that I move in with the bass player and his family for the 12 weeks of this scheme. So I moved in and we had some great times, playing pool all evening as they had a mini table and we put bets on who would win. The lead guitarist lived not far from us but was not interested in the *Task Force* or any other task at the time.

The job we were embarking on was to clear the old railway lines from Wootton to Ryde, which I think, was around six miles of overgrown track. I mean overgrown too, because some parts of the lines you could not even see the stones on the ground between the sleepers. There were brambles by the million, trees growing out of the drainage and inspection pits at the side of the tracks and so many stumps to remove from the banks. This was a major operation and would be hard work too.

Pondy and I went to the first meeting at this brand new wooden hut on Station Road in Wootton. We walked in and sat amongst a variety of characters, waiting for their turn to be signed up. There were some pretty dodgy looking people in that hut and we were glad to be out of there after we were added to the list of participants. It was a few weeks after e started on the track clearing, that we chatting to one of the charge hands. He said he thought we looked such hard nuts and was afraid to even look at us in the hut that first day. We were totally amazed, we didn't think of ourselves as hard nuts by any measure.

We met some interesting and not so interesting people on that job. There were a few people that you wouldn't even make eye contact with, let alone talk to. But in general, it was fun and gave us some well needed cash at the time.

I did not have a motorcycle at the time I worked on the track job, but managed to get a very cheap and immaculate Yamaha RD200 bike from a chap in Arreton who worked on the track job with us. It was so good to be back on two wheels again and have transport once again. I could go back home to Totland whenever I wanted and it was not long after I got the bike that I had a message from Malcolm to come and see him, which you will read about later, when his daughter gave me the message and was laughing at my scared and nervous position. I started back on the farm at the end of April and it was great to be back there again. All my old workmates were still there too and welcomed me back to the farm. They were a good team and they would give you the shirt off their backs if you needed it. So now I had wheels and my money making job back and also back in Totland again.

Chapter 14

The Haunting

It was the last six months of nineteen eighty two, that changed the whole direction my family's lives for the following year. It all came from nowhere and started in the front bedroom at the very top of the building called Bon Accord. One night while I was in bed with my girlfriend Lana and some strange noises began on the stairs. As I mentioned earlier, the house above what was eventually our bakery business was definitely occupied by more than our family. From the very first months we lived there, we noticed odd happenings which were confined mainly to the second floor and the ground floor middle room, which ultimately became the oven room. From shadows going past the gap in the lounge door to the dogs sleeping on an old sofa in the ground floor room and always seemed to be shivering with cold. Although my bedroom was the old shop front and right next to the cold room, I had never experienced anything odd in that room at all. The house was now empty and my parents agreed that I could live in it and perhaps a friend could rent a room later on.

My family and I had moved into *The Dreens* and this house was situated in front of the new flats that were built on the site of the *Hill House Hotel*. I had heard rumours that the hotel had burnt down and the land had just remained desolate for many years after. I remember when the engineers came to start building the car park and flattened the old hotel garden and tarmac went down instead of trees.

It was at this time when work began on the large development of flats beyond the chestnut fencing that segregated the land. I still think that the hotel had something to do with the paranormal activity in that area. There was talk of ghosts and odd things happening in the new flats and as far up the road as Charlie Browns takeaway and restaurant, which was incidentally formerly the Braemar café.

We had no idea what my parent's plans were with the house above the bakery, because they didn't put it on the market when we moved out. I would have thought would have been the obvious next move and it would have given them extra capital for whatever plans they had for the future. The house stood empty for many months after the baker and his family moved out. I moved into the house on my own, well nearly on my own because my girlfriend spent a lot of time with me there and would stay there on Fridays and Saturday nights. We had some fun in that house and would buy a bottle of Captain Morgan's rum and get very drunk and spend all night making love until either the sun came up or we were totally exhausted.

Lana was sixteen and I was eighteen, the daughter of a farmer in Totland and was very mature for her age. Not childish or living in a dream world, ambitious and knew exactly what she wanted. Lana was gorgeous with her long dark hair and big eyes. The body of a goddess, which would turn me into a wreck in seconds' and. her sex drive, was unprecedented. There were times when I had to resist her teasing or I would be dead from sheer lack of sleep. It was not always so easy to say no. There were times when she could just get what she wanted and it didn't matter where we were either. She was very loving and caring and thoughtful when we were truly together, but she just couldn't resist temptation.

We got engaged because we thought it was the true meaning of love. So young and naive, it didn't really dawn on us that it was supposed to be a engagement to be married. We just did it anyway and had a lovely party at Lana's parent's house in Freshwater. I had to ask her

Father's permission to become engaged and that was scarier than any interview
or standing on a stage in front of an audience for the first time. I dreaded it for weeks and it played on my mind so much that I just did it one weekend when we were having tea at her place.

Her Father was not the most approachable person if you didn't know him well, very similar to my own father in many ways. He had one of those characters that could scare off anyone I took home for the first time, because no one knew how to take him. When you got to know Lana's dad, he was as down to earth as anyone could be, very into the country ways of life and like me, worked on a farm for many years and I guess that having a mutual interest, helped a lot.

The permission was granted and the plans for the party were in the making. We didn't have too many guests coming but just enough to have a good night. Unfortunately I got too drunk and made an absolute idiot of myself. I could not even walk properly and fell over several times in their garden. The most embarrassing thing was Lana's father had to take me home to the flat and I remember him and someone called Terry helping me up the stairs to the kitchen. I never lived that one down and to this day, I just don't know why I got so paralytic at my own engagement party?

Lana was not upset at my stupid antics that night and neither were her parents, so I got off lightly really. If there were any ghosts in the flat when I finally got to my bed after the party, there was no way I would have known. Lana came round in the morning and woke me up with a coffee and her naked body wrapped around me. She gave me lots of stick about the party and asked me if I remembered what I had said to various people. I hadn't a damned clue what I said. I fell asleep with her and woke up feeling slightly better.

We went everywhere together and had some amazing and beautiful times, and if ever I wanted to die of exhaustion, then I wanted to die making love with her. My world was now perfect and after all the troubles that I had experienced in my younger days, someone had shone a light on me and given me some happiness at last.

We planned lots of rides out on the bike and visited a fair few places on the mainland together. Everything seemed to be going so well and the band was arranging to do its first gig. Practice was taking up a lot of my time and I adored every damn minute of it too. We practiced in an old shed on a farm near the Highdown Inn and although it could be bloody freezing in that shed and very damp, we did our best and made some good music. Our intentions to write our own stuff was somewhat overshadowed by the need to play covers for the general public because it's all they really understood and playing at a football club and producing music that no one knew would have been suicide for us all. Sunday afternoons and I think Wednesday evening was our practice times and it worked very well indeed. Looking back on the people in the band, they were all totally committed to the task in hand and unlike other bands that I joined in later years, they gave it their absolute all. I remember on Sunday we would just pop over the road for a drink or three and then go back to practice in a somewhat tipsy state.

I'm not going to talk about the individual members of the band because it would be unfair to compare each member or differentiate their individual talents in this book, I want the band to remain a fond memory of a group of dedicated people who enjoyed each others company and musical abilities and were able to make some lovely music and emulate a lot of tunes that were obviously a product of hours in a studio time and reproduce something that did not differ much, from the real thing.

Parties came and went and even a holiday on my motorcycle to Bude in Cornwall and we stayed in a hotel. I had just inherited some money from my Granddad and with that money we decided a holiday was in order and sod the camping, we shall have some luxury for a change. We travelled down to Cornwall on my trusty Honda CX500 Custom and had a lovely time. We ventured out during the day and visited a few well known places such as Tintagel, Launceston Castle and this museum which I could not remember the name of for years until I visited that area, years later. It was called Dingles Fairground Museum. The evenings were spent in the hotel bar and I remember us being extremely drunk on several occasions.

One night we went for a walk in the pouring rain, down to the canal and got absolutely saturated when we reached the canal banks. I remember that we just sat on a bench and kissed passionately as the rain poured down and the raindrops flowed down our faces; so romantic and a beautiful memory that I shall never forget. I think we got a little lost on the way home to the island.

We went on another memorable journey up to a place called Cookham in Berkshire to visit Lana's auntie and also visit the site where there had been a big altercation between rival bike gangs a few weeks previous. I think we came back down to the new forest and camped for a few nights after making our way back down south that afternoon.

It was strange how I would spend most evenings in the very top bedroom of that house all alone and usually playing my synthesiser or messing about with some lights with one of my new friends, the rhythm guitarist from the band called Tim. We were building this wooden framework to mount lights on for the gig in a few weeks time. We had not noticed anything untoward in that house until Lana started to stay there at weekends and to be honest, most nights I would pick her up and bring her back to my bedroom. One night we were in bed and just laying there in recovery mode, suddenly she said "there is someone outside the bedroom door." I knew it could not have been anyone from the street as the front door was locked and only my family had spare keys. Lana started to cry for no reason and said "they are outside the door and very upset", she explained to me that they were spirits and were lost. Now by this time I was pretty scared and we could actually here footsteps outside the bedroom door. Lana was scared too and I got up and opened the door to see if there was someone there, but nothing was there and it was all quite normal after I closed the door again.

After that occasion, there was only one other time that something weird happened and that was one morning at about half past five when I had finished the night shift in the bakery and had come up to bed. I heard a violin playing and it seemed to be coming from the bedroom directly opposite my room. I lay there listening and falling asleep when something hit me on the head. I have no idea what it was because I searched the room and found nothing. It felt like something quite light and not heavy and it did not hit me hard, but gently. After that incident I did not experience any other strange happenings on my own in the house, but lots more when Lana was there. She seemed to either attract them or be able to communicate with whatever haunted the place.

There was an incident when yet again we were in bed together, we didn't spend much time out of bed. There were the footsteps outside the door again and this time something was walking up and down the second flight of stairs too. There was a sudden thump on the stairs and more banging sounds coming from the back bedroom. Lana was really scared this time and so was I, so we got dressed as quick as we could and ran down the stairs and out of the front door and went up to see my parents at the top of the driveway. We explained what we heard and Mum and Dad came down with us to check out the house. Nothing was out of the ordinary and the house was silent. We talked about getting a medium to look over the place but it never happened at that time, not for a good three years anyway.

The bakery business was expanding and the workload increased so much that eventually there were three of us working every night to fulfil the orders. Especially during the summer months and Christmas time. One of our little tricks at Easter time was to throw some bun spice in the extractor fan which blew out onto the car park, this enhanced the smell of fresh hot cross buns and really did draw people into the shop. I remember when I took a ghetto blaster into the oven room and we always had *Dire Straits* playing nice and loud at night. We had to employ staff to work in the shop as it was too much for Mum to cover the till and make pies and pasties during the day. Mum started her pie business when we first had the butchers shop and it went crazy very quickly and she supplied shops in Cowes as well as our butchers shop and this meant a lot of work had to be done in our kitchen at home.

She couldn't use the butcher's premises because of the raw meat factor. So our oven at home took some battering and was always baking something. Mum worked very hard at her pie business as did Dad in his butchers shop. They were both very hard working parents and rightly enjoyed the benefits of the hard work too.

Lana worked in our shop for a while and she was good at the customer relation part but moreover, brilliant at baking and cooking too. She had more jobs than anyone else I knew at seventeen. She could adapt her cooking skills to suit any situation and she earnt more money than I did at one time and to me, that was a bloody achievement for a teenage girl. When I woke up at around one o'clock in the afternoon and would get washed and dressed and wander downstairs to the bakery to see Lana in the shop and have coffee with her in the oven room. The large table that sat opposite the bank of ovens saw more than bread tins, miss sex drive was a bloody nightmare and loved the excitement of perhaps getting caught in unorthodox places. I will say no more......happy days.

My best friend apart from Lana was a lad called Marcus. He had a bike and was part of the gang of friends that congregated at the Braemar cafe. He was very slim and about the same height as me. We did a lot of stuff together and went all over the country on bikes and had some really memorable times together too. It was not long until Marcus found himself a lady and I guess he needed to get away from his parents and find himself somewhere to live. He decided to rent the back room of the house and we would share the amenities and bills. Marcus told his parents that he was moving out, which went down like a lead balloon and caused some bad feeling between myself and his parents because they blamed me for taking him away from them. Never understood their reasoning and thought it was a bit old fashioned to try and blame me for his actions.

What about his older girlfriend and her kids, didn't she take him away from them? I went with him to get some of his stuff in my Dad's bakery van and that was not a nice experience at all because his Mum was very upset and his Dad was very off with me and the atmosphere was thick that night. We got his stuff to the house and he had done it, moved in and was settling in well.

After a few weeks things seemed to be ticking along nicely and we had some good laughs and cooked some nice dinners between us. Most of the time he was out at work or round at his girlfriend's place in Freshwater so I was still quite alone in the house during the day. I was alone at night too. It was really strange how nothing really bothered me when I was all alone in the place and I was not frightened staying there at night either. Even though I had experienced the footsteps and banging down the stairs previously, with Lana. I really don't know how I did it, I would not do it now.

Every time Lana came over and we slept together, there would be the same old noises in the hallway and on the stairs, we became immune to it and carried on regardless. It was definitely not the wisest policy, because whatever was watching over us, had a total hate for us making love and sleeping together in that front bedroom. Marcus did not experience anything in his room and he stayed there very late at night for a week or so as his decorated the whole room. It brightened the room completely and looked really good too. It was several months later, that things started to become scary and very noisy.

I am sure it was because of one particular incident that triggered the ghost or spirits to unleash total mayhem in the house. Who they were trying to get to or get rid of, I'm not entirely sure, but I have a feeling it was one of two people or both of them.

It all started one Friday night when I was working with Dad in the bakery and Lana was staying in the house, waiting for me to finish work. Marcus was out at his girlfriend's place until after midnight and I remember him calling into see us before he went up to bed. It was a relatively easy night and we had all the bread and rolls out of the oven early plus the other confectionery was nearly ready by five o'clock in the morning. So I could go off to bed earlier than Lana was aware, because she thought I would be up at about six thirty in the morning. I went up and made a drink in the kitchen and when I was drinking my coffee, I heard someone open a door and walk over the hallway and another door closing. I thought for a moment that our ghost was up to its tricks. It did give me Goosebumps and a shiver up my back as I went upstairs slowly and turned on all the lights as I went past the lounge doorway. It was not cold and there were no mysterious noises and Lana was in bed and seemed to be sound asleep as I went into the bedroom and got undressed and climbed in.

Tim Haddock and Simon Pond of Neptune Icecap at the Country Club gig In 1984.

As I cuddled up to Lana, she was so warm that I thought perhaps she had a temperature or something. It was so hot in the bed I had to uncover myself for a while to cool down. She was not asleep and turned over and kissed me and passion took hold of us and things were getting warmer than they already were. I moved down her body with kisses and with my tongue exploring her beautiful breasts and as I went past her chest and onto her belly she said "I would not go there if I was you". I didn't think twice and stopped in my tracks by her words and asked her why? She started to cry and turned away from me and just said "I can't say why", "but why are you crying Lana?" She said nothing for a while and just continued crying, "Please tell me what is wrong!" I replied, she said "I did something very bad and you don't deserve it", I could not work out what she meant at all and turned on the bedside lamp.

I will go and make us a drink and then we can talk OK? She agreed and said "I want to come with you OK?" "Fine, come on then" I replied. So we went down into the kitchen and made some coffee and had a fag or two while we sat there and talked. I put the gas fire on and shut the door to keep it warm in there. After a while we went back up to bed with our drinks and had a smoke in bed as we cuddled up, she had calmed down by this time and was more comfortable. I still did not know what she had done that was so bad and I promised her I will be calm and not do anything stupid if she told me. She said "Marcus was in bed with me and that's why I stopped you from going down there, he fucked me and I'm so sorry." I was astounded, total horror came into my mind and I was so angry and so hurt that my best mate would do that with my girlfriend while staying in my house while I was at work downstairs. "So that is why the bed was so bloody hot when I got in", she nodded with shame and started to cry again. Although I was so angry at them both and I wanted to go into his bedroom and beat the hell out of him, I cuddled Lana and we fell asleep together.

The next day was awful and I just wanted to get on my bike and ride away forever. How could she sleep with him, why would she do such a thing to me? I didn't understand any of it and just made sure Marcus was booted out of the house and ever since that night I never trusted him again and in fact, Lana lost my trust in her, for what she did. It was not the end of our relationship, just a chink in the armour and it just made me very wary of her and who she was friendly with. About a month later when I was at a party with her, I noticed her flirting with one of our band members and wondered if she was planning to shag him in the background. I watched her like a hawk and made sure she never got the chance that night. I wasn't so jealous as I was after that incident and it made me wary, to say the least.

There was one particular night in the empty house that really did make Lana and I think twice about staying there in the evening. We were in bed and we had a half bottle of rum and some coke and got very drunk and played out some sexy fantasies. I tied her to the bed, blindfolded her and teased her all over with my tongue and mouth. I turned her over the end of the bed and made love to her from behind and it was gorgeous, but too bloody quick, but amazing. Lana tied me down afterwards and teased me all over by kissing my skin all over.

After we had made a coffee and had a fag or three, we just laid there chatting and cuddling up close when suddenly there was a really loud bump on the floor outside the door of the bedroom. We both cuddled up closer and pulled the duvet right up in a way that you would when you were a child. We waited and listened intensely for something further to happen and as we waited, there was another thump sound but this time on the stairs, then another and another. It sounded like someone with heavy boots on walking up the stairs and we really did feel frightened and the duvet went over our heads as the sound stopped again and every tiny noise was being listened to, as we lay there petrified. Suddenly the thumping got faster and sounded as if it was running up the stairs and seemed to be going into the back bedroom and then back down the stairs again. By this time I said to Lana "if it stops, I think we should get out of here and go up to the house." She said that she could not feel anything coming from whatever was out there and we should put the lights on and get dressed and go as soon as possible.

That spirit or ghost was getting seriously angry at something we had done or were doing and there was nothing we could do about it. "Bang", the noise vibrated right through the floor and it ran down the stairs and seemed to be running along the long hall, past the kitchen and towards the small bedroom at the end of the hall. I don't know if it was slamming doors on the way, but it was making a lot of noise as it travelled along the hall and back up the stairs again.
suddenly it all went silent and we got up and dressed and about to collect up our stuff, when there was a massive bang on the bedroom door. That was it for me, Lana was scared stiff too and we opened the door in terror and went down the stairs. It was very cold outside the bedroom, even though it was not very cold outside. We really didn't care how cold it was; we just

wanted to get out of that place alive. We opened the front door and went outside and stood by the front door for a while to listen and see if anything happened. Not a sound, the house was quiet once more so we closed the front door and walked up to *Dreens* and looked for a way in, as it was early morning and no one was up.

Luckily the back door was open, so I opened it slowly to prevent the dogs from attacking me, saying their names and they all came to the door wagging their tails.
I let them out so they knew who it was outside and that way they wouldn't start barking and wake everyone up. I let the dogs back in their little room and we made a coffee and then crept up to my room and went to sleep.

We didn't wake up until around ten and went downstairs to the smell of Sunday cooked breakfast and Mum buzzing around the kitchen as she did when it was cooked breakfast day. She said "what are you two doing here then?" I explained what had happened in the flat and then Dad came down from the bathroom and we told him the story too. He didn't really believe in ghostly stuff very much and just laughed it off. Mum had been going to these spiritual meetings in Freshwater Bay for a while and sort of knew a bit more about it than Dad did and also believed what I told her.

We had a lovely breakfast and all chatted about the flat and its weird happenings. Mum suggested that I move back into the house from now on. She said it was not very healthy to be staying in that place on my own and seeing as Marcus had gone, we should get the place rented out. So Lana and I went back to the flat with both Mum and Dad to get my things from the room I was sleeping in and to see if anything strange had gone on. Everything appeared normal in the flat and I suppose it would have been in the day light and with so many people in the flat at once. We turned off the gas and left the flat to its own devices and brought all my belongings up to the house. Dad turned off the power too because we didn't need it to be on until we cleaned the place up for letting it out.

So that's how the flat was left, empty and apart from going in there during the day to clean it for prospective lettings, the place remained without residents for a fair few months.

I was always going out with Kitty and his brother in their boats and being influenced by them, I wanted one for myself to play about in. I bought this plywood speed boat from a chap in Colwell and it did not come with a trailer, so that made moving it a pain. I had to borrow a tractor and trailer from Dad's mate Roy. I had taken it back to our house using the tractor and parked it on blocks next to the stables and workshop so I could do some work on it. The boat needed the steering sorting out because it was one of those cable affairs with a screw system on the back of the steering wheel. I also needed some sort of dashboard as it was just bare plywood. So I went to the scrap yard and got all the switch gear and the clock out of a Jaguar car and fitted it in.

My Mother with the baker and my Sister Sarah in the bakery. Circa 1982.

Now I needed an engine but at the time I could not afford anything very large as I was on one of my winter breaks from the farm. I had some work from Roy the builder and drove his tractors on the small holding he had bought in Cranmore. He had a small Massey 135 and a beast of a Belarus four wheel drive. I liked the Belarus very much because it was very comfortable with its incredibly large cab and two man seat. Another feature which was relatively unique to the Russian machine was it had a battery isolator under the seat. Very handy and you could guarantee it would never have a flat battery whatever the temperature. Obviously it was designed for Russian winters.

I had to go and get straw and hay for the store cattle that he and Dad had bought and one weekend I had to go over to Brook for some hay and it was at the time of the Foot and Mouth outbreak. It all started on a pig farm down at Hampstead and soon the restrictions were everywhere. Disinfectant covered straw in every gateway to all the farms on the way and I remember them spraying all the cars down at the ferry terminal in East Cowes. A terrible event and disastrous, to a lot of farmers on the island. Dad's friend asked me to go and get some straw from Thorley Manor too and as he did not have a proper trailer, he sent me off with this giant boat trailer. Imagine trying to stack straw bales on a boat trailer, very interesting indeed.

On the way back from collecting the straw one of the bales had pushed down on one of the rubber mudguards and it was rubbing on the wheel, not long until smoke was pouring out of it and I had to stop and re-stack it all.

I took a load of scrap and rubbish over to the sand pit dump on the old Alum Bay Road with the Massey and small tipper trailer for Roy. We were trying to clear all the old scrap machinery and rubbish from the smallholding. Unfortunately while I was tipping the bloody thing a hydraulic pipe burst on the side of the loader and covered me in oil. So I had to park the tractor and trailer in the car park in Totland and go and get changed and I could not really use the tractor as it lost so much oil. It was in the car park for about two weeks until Roy could be bothered to get it repaired.

There were two blokes who rented a shed out at the small holding and they were doing logs and stuff. Another bloke had a spray painting business in the largest shed and Dad had his orange Ford Capri resprayed black there. It was a good spray job and looked so much better in black.

One of the chaps that did the logs I recognised as I had seen him many times in his car. It turned out that he lived in the cottages, just past the fruit farm along *Wilmingham* lane and his nickname was Dollar. This was because he had one of those cowboy moustaches and really looked the part. One day I was chatting to them both as they were working away in the shed and suddenly I noticed a big outboard motor sitting in the corner. It was an Evinrude fifty five horse power with this Selectric gearbox thing written on it, so I asked them is it for sale. They said it was and they wanted £250 for it. I really did not have that sort of money and thought of ways I could get hold of the money for the motor. I told Lana all about it and she said that she could buy it for me in two weeks time as she got her bonus from the hotel that she worked in and I could pay her back when I went back to the farm in April or May. I was so happy and could not wait to get the engine and bolt it on the back of my boat.

The boat was coming on well and I had everything ready for the motor. I had been up to Morgan's tip and got the rear seat from the Jaguar car and mounted it on the back of the boat.

I had got hold of a car battery and mounted it under the seat and also a fuel tank. We were just about to lift the boat on the trailer and bang, one of the struts that should have had a roller on it went straight through the plywood and now I had a sinking boat.

I had asked our next door neighbour who lived in the first floor flat above the butcher's shop to fix the hole, as he was a boat builder. I bought some plywood and the boat builder had some Cascamite glue and fixed the hole perfectly. So I arranged to get a few more people to help lift the boat on the trailer this time to ensure nothing went wrong. Once it was sat on the trailer I could mount the motor on the transom and connect the steering cables. Everything seemed fine and big Jimmy came round and we got the engine started using his water muffs, connected to the hose pipe. It ran beautifully and I was so excited and itching to get it in the water for a spin around Totland Bay.

I borrowed the Belarus tractor again from Roy and we towed the boat down to the beach at Totland. There was only one place to launch the boat and that was the old lifeboat slipway. Reversing the tractor down a sea weed covered old slipway was not fun at all. The last fifteen feet had absolutely no grip and the tractor and boat just slid all the way down and onto the sand. Scary but luckily the whole rig stayed in a straight line and did not jack knife.

Could have been a bloody disaster looking back and how bloody inexperienced and stupid I was then. So I reversed the boat out into the water and Kitty, little Wol and big Jimmy launched it and all seemed fine. I took the tractor back up the beach and we tried to start the motor, alas the battery had lost its charge and would not start. I had to take the tractor down to the boat and we jumped the engine with the leads in the tractor. It started and then I took the tractor and trailer back up the dangerous slipway and onto the sea wall and parked it up along the promenade.

Then myself, little Wol, kitty and big Jimmy all went off in the boat and headed towards the pier and did a few laps around the bay to get used to the engine and steering etc. We then went off towards Alum Bay and rounded Headon point. It was fantastic being in my own boat and that engine went like a rocket across the water.
The motor was far too big for the boat really but it did not matter as gave us more power to play with. As we turned around in the bay, there was a burning smell coming from the rear of the boat and the seat had caught alight. The metal on the bottom of the seat had gone across the battery terminals and set the foam

alight. Black smoke was pouring out and what was next to the battery, the fuel tank. Mad panic ensued and Big Jimmy said "head straight for the shore flat out." So I opened up the throttle and headed for the rocky beach of Alum Bay. Kitty and Jimmy and little Wol had ripped the seat out and threw it overboard and that was the danger gone for now. We were all laughing afterwards and they had to sit on the floor on the way back to Totland.

Bloody hell that was the closest I had ever been to disaster and we were so lucky that day. The sea is a very dangerous place and people really don't understand how quickly things can go wrong. I certainly didn't until that day!

Now we had another problem. The tide had come right up the beach and there was now way I could recover the boat on the slipway. So big Jimmy had the plan to go and get his boat from Yarmouth. He would meet us by the pier and then take the boat around to Yarmouth and down the river Yar to the causeway and recover it there. We needed someone to drive the tractor down to the causeway in Freshwater and we needed two people in the boat to go round to Yarmouth.

Luckily little Wol came along with me in the boat and Kitty took the tractor and trailer to Freshwater, so we could meet him there. It was a good hour until Jimmy came around the corner from Colwell. Little Wol and I, followed him towards Colwell and Brambles Bay. The steering cable had jammed up somewhere behind the wheel and now we had hardly any bloody steering. We got past the reef at Colwell OK and then we were just going past Fort Albert and the engine started to miss fire and ran on one cylinder. Oh my god, what next I thought as I looked at little Wol. He looked so bloody scared as the engine jumped from one cylinder to two.

The crossing from Fort Albert to Fort Victoria is notorious for being rough; it never seems to be calm even on the quietest of days. On this day, it was very rough indeed. Water was coming in over the side and the engine would not fire back on two cylinders, it was a complete nightmare. At the time, I wish I had never attempted it. In the end we had to fasten a rope from Jimmy's boat and he had to tow us the rest of the way, not because we had no power but we could not steer the damn thing anymore.

We reached Yarmouth harbour and Jimmy towed us under the bridge and just up the river to his mooring on the right side of the river. He moored his boat up and came aboard my tub and we had the best high speed dash to the Causeway.

Flat out and leaning the boat around the corners, it was brilliant. As we reached the end of the river, we could see Kitty and the tractor sat on the bridge watching us. We just aimed for a flat looking bit of mud and lifted the engine as we ran out of water and slid straight up the mud bank and close to the wall. Little did we know that there was a massive metal pipe sticking out of the mud and it ripped a hole right through the bottom of the boat. I did not care I wanted to be off that thing and forget it ever happened. Kitty and Jimmy helped to release the engine and we all lifted it onto the wall and then on the tractor rear arms and tied it there.

I left the boat where it was and we all went home on the tractor, which was interesting to say the least. At least we were safe and on dry land again and glad that nightmare had ended without casualty. I later heard that some kids had managed to float the boat and were messing about with it down the river, good luck to them.

One of the oddest nights in the bakery was when I stood in front of the ovens and all three banks were pouring out the heat, I would get a shiver up my back. Dad felt how cold it was too and could not work out what was happening. We did not have any bangs on the ceiling or thumping noises on the stairs above the doorway to the shop. The only strange happening was the bucket we had hanging on a balance scale to weigh off the flour for each batch of dough, started to swing from side to side by itself.

No doors were open and nobody had walked near the bucket either. It didn't just happen once, there were several occasions that night when that bucket was swinging to and fro. Dad saw it too and we just laughed it off and carried on with the baking.

The next night was slightly different and there were very strange things going on indeed. There were footsteps directly above us and that meant it was in the long hallway that ran from the stairs to the small bedroom at the very rear of the flat. Not really heavy steps but enough for us to hear them between running a mixer or our bread moulder. Then we had a freezing cold feeling that would go right up our backs and into the bottom of our necks.

This kept happening in the middle room, where the mixers and flour scale was. It was a very strong feeling that eventually gave me a terrible headache and seemed to drain all my energy from me. Dad had the same feeling and by the time we had finished in the morning, we were both exhausted. That was not how we normally felt at the end of the night.

After a good eight hour sleep and even that was unusual for me, I got up and still had the damn headache right from the bottom of my neck to the very front of my head. I felt so bloody tired that I went back to sleep for a few more hours. I even missed band practice because I felt so drained and I remember one of the band members coming round to see me and he couldn't believe what I told him and why I couldn't practice for a while.

During that following day, my Mum had been in touch with her friend's husband about coming to have a look at the flat and see what he could find. He was an amateur medium or spiritualist for anyone who is not familiar with the term. Before the medium had a chance to go into the building, Mum had put a crucifix up in the oven room just to help and keep whatever it was at bay. Ken was the medium and he came down that afternoon and went up into the flat with myself, Lana, Mum and Dad. He went from room to room as Ken tried to get in contact with the spirit or ghost that was causing so much hassle in the building. In the back bedroom upstairs, he managed to find out who this ghost was and why it was so angry or annoyed with us mortal beings. He said that the ghost that lived in the house was an old spinster and she taught violin, a strict Catholic and who had an absolute hate for anyone who drank alcohol.

Apparently her brother lived with her and he was an alcoholic and he hid his alcohol all over the flat so his sister would not find it and throw it away.

Now this new information shed light certain happenings and why this ghost became so troublesome to us. Because Lana and I slept together, had sex, drank rum and generally did everything that this spirit detested. Also the strange violin noise I heard one morning when I had just finished work and got into bed, which came from the back bedroom. So now we knew what was what and decided to stay out of the flat for a while, apart from showing the odd prospective tenants around. Ken could not find any other spirits in the flat, or at least could not communicate with anything else. Lana and I thought it rather strange, because there was definitely something other than an old lady there that night when Lana started crying for no reason and said the spirit was asking for help to move on. Lana said it was a young man that talked to her that night and was not trying to get us out of the flat at all, so when we told Ken about this he said that he would have to visit the flat at night or early morning because it was a prime time for spiritual activity and there was more chance of picking up other entities in the building.

Things quietened down after the medium had been in the flat and the nights in the bakery were better; for a while anyway. We had the odd thump on the ceiling and the flour bucket swinging occasionally, but none of the headaches or nasty cold oven room activity that had plagued us before.

The farm yard consisted of an old derelict farmhouse, four barns and a mobile home on the driveway. Roy decided to convert a smaller barn into a living quarters and I'm sure it was a place for him to escape to at weekends. The other large barn was split into two and he had converted one part into a workshop for renting out, which was leased to a carpenter.

I had split with the band at that time because I had missed so many practice sessions and was getting hassle from a bloody guitarist. So I left with my old pal Tim, who I had known a long time. The band was gutted and I did feel sorry for the drummer Terry and the guitarist Nigel, because they were nice blokes and brilliant musicians too.

Tim and I joined up with one Izzy and Pondy and began practicing out at Roy's farm in the barn that became the carpentry workshop. It was so bloody cold though and I could not play the keyboards at times because my fingers just refused to operate due to being frozen solid. We needed a new drummer because Izzy who was a good drummer, wanted to sing instead. We had this posh bloke come out from Bembridge to have a trial run and see what happened. He was bloody useless and was always stoned out of his brain. I just thought he had all the gear but no idea. He brought cases and cases of equipment out but didn't appear to know what to do with it. We got rid of that idiot as soon as we could and also got out of that barn and moved to a loft space above Beavis's shop in Newport. The weirdo from Bembridge had left a suitcase of music equipment in the barn and even after telling him to come and get it, he did not and we went through it and kept quite a few electronic bits for a drum kit.

Tim and I acquired a radio microphone, which transmitted to a standard FM radio.

There was a weekend when my friends little Wol, big Wol and their mate Andy planned to go off to the New Forest in this Andy's parent's little camper van. All we needed to take was money, alcohol and a tent or two as there wasn't much room in the little van. So off we went to Lymington and then made our way to Brockenhurst and booked into Holland park campsite for the night but for some reason, we didn't put our tents up at the time of booking.

We drove to this pub which I am sure was the Monkey Puzzle or something like that and spent the night there getting very drunk. After we had relocated the campsite because the driver couldn't remember where it was, we arrived and found a pitch near a fallen tree and put our tents up. We chatted for a few hours and drank even more alcohol and by the time it was bedtime, I didn't even know which end of the tent was which. I woke up with my head banging away and a mouth like the bottom of a birdcage and was desperate for a drink. Luckily two of the other dudes had been to the shop and bought some fresh orange juice.

We didn't bother cooking breakfast and just packed up the gear and made for another site near the A31. En route, we stopped for breakfast at a café and stocked up on juice etc.

That night was fine because we didn't drink anything and just spent the evening chatting and laughing. The next day we went all the way to Bournemouth and then to Cheddar Gorge and went into the caves. We drove back down that evening to the second campsite and cooked dinner and then went to this kind of biker's pub nearby, which I have never been able to find since. Not one of my favourite trips to the mainland by a long shot. I was glad to be back home.

It was funny how certain people suddenly became super dirty bikers all of a sudden, especially when a group of bikers who used to visit a campsite in Totland every summer arrived in the village pub. I met them in the Broadway Inn and they were a nice bunch of decent chaps really and just because they rode mostly big Japanese bikes and the occasional Harley Davidson, didn't automatically mean they were evil or nasty people. It was one morning when I was visiting little Wol at his house.

This Harley stops outside the house, along with a group of these bikers and they were asking if we had seen big Wol? We hadn't seen him for ages and I asked one of the blokes why they were looking for him? He said "something had gone missing from a tent last night". So we

assumed big Wol had been up to no good and
obviously with the wrong crowd this time. They
soon left and were off to the pub to find this
friend of ours. I was laughing so much because it
just went to show how people try and be
something they are not and big Wol had tried to
be the big biker boy and got caught out.
On my way to Freshwater that afternoon, I met
up with another of the biker gang and he rode a
Kawasaki Z1000 Custom, the most wanted
machine on my list of have to own bikes. He
was saying that they found big Wol in the pub
and sorted him out. I never had a problem at all
with those dudes; they were always friendly to
me. Some people….

Neptune Icecap pictured in the band room in 1985.
L/R-Me, Simon Pond, Illya Simpson and Tim Haddock.

Chapter 15

Neptune Icecap and a fantasy

The young couple who lived in the mobile home on the farm that Dad's friend Roy had purchased, seemed quite nice people. I often saw the girl in the caravan as I went past on a tractor or on my bike. After a month or so, we became much good friends, sharing smokes outside her caravan etc.

Eventually, she would walk down to the farm when I was working at clearing all the junk and have a fag with me, by the haystack. I don't know how it happened, but we were very soon kissing in the hay barn. After a few days of just kissing, we were making love in the barn amongst the straw bales, right at the back so no one could see us. I wasn't seeing Lana at this point because she was in love with some other biker chap from Newport. Our secret affair carried on for a few weeks until she suddenly moved out of the mobile home and went to Freshwater to live.

One afternoon she waked down to the farm yard in a long coat and walked over to me and kissed me and then undid the buttons on the front of her coat, which revealed white underwear, stockings and suspenders.

I was shocked at what I was seeing. That moment just filled my mind with the song *Fantasy*, which we played in *Neptune Icecap*. I had never experienced anything like this before and to be honest, I was actually stunned and unable to comprehend the situation fully, at first. Love making didn't last long that afternoon but it was a very special moment for both of us. We nearly got caught by the carpenter chap too. We had to hide for ages until he drove off down the long track. We were both giggling at the time and just enjoying each others company.

It was definitely a rebound situation on my part and whatever reasons she had to cheat on her boyfriend were her own. She never talked about her home life or boyfriend, ever. I never saw again after she moved out and it was a shame really because I liked her a lot. Yes I was a bad boy for seeing her. I often thought I would be beat up or something for what had happened between us. I really didn't even think about it at the time. I was young and carefree, so I had no regrets whatsoever.

Coming back to the song Fantasy; Izzy and Tim wrote the song and the lyrics were the product of a Guinness calendar which was on the wall of the pub that Izzy's parents owned. There were scenes of fantasy between men and women and it was while Izzy was looking at the pictures, that he wrote the words for the song.

It was not long after the time I was working for Roy on his smallholding, that things began to re ignite themselves in the flat. I came up with a brilliant plan to record the noises in the flat by placing the radio microphone in the top, back bedroom. I did this with my mate Tim and we tested different rooms by banging on the wall in the bakery and finding the most receptive place. The back bedroom was best and I could lightly tap the wall in the oven room and hear it absolutely perfectly on the radio. That radio mic was so powerful and sensitive.

I finished helping Roy on his farm because Dad had fell out with him yet again, this time over the store cattle that they had supposedly taken on together. To be totally fair, it was only Dad that looked after them and chased them when they escaped. Roy never did a bloody thing so that friendship was on hold for a while.

It was several weeks after the radio mic was placed up in the bedroom and nothing much happened. Things had gone mysteriously quiet in the flat and no one had really gone up there for a month or so. Ken had not been back for his night visit as yet and Lana and I had parted amicably, but still sadly. She had been seeing this chap in Newport and who did bike training at the local high school. It was probably karma for seeing a girl with a boyfriend, as I was not seeing anyone at that time.

I remember the last nights that we worked in that bakery. It was the scariest and weird situation anyone could experience. It all started when our immersion heater packed up in the back of the bakery. Warm water is essential for accelerating the yeast to react in the bread dough's. This was a real problem and unfortunately, there was only one solution. So with great reservations; we had to use the immersion tank in the flat for the hot water supply. We had some big buckets ready and we a fad asked a few friends to come up there with us. There was no way just Dad and I were venturing up those stairs alone, at night.

It was eerie opening the front door to the flat and listening for anything out of the ordinary. It was difficult to hear over the sounds of mixers and fans in the bakery, they resonated through the false wall at the end of the hallway on the ground floor. There were five of us that went in that night, Dad, Liam, Mack, Barry and I. As we walked in and towards the bottom of the stairs there was the problem of who was going first. I think it was Dad that led and Liam's mate brought up the rear. As we all walked as quiet as we could up the first flight of stairs, it was deadly silent as Dad turned the stair light on. The temperature was very cold as we got close to the top of the first flight of stairs. My body was very tense and in anticipation of something coming along the hall or down the second flight of stairs. As we turned towards the left and the corridor towards the kitchen, we turned on the lights that lit up the stairs that led to the top floor, but they did not work. Dad turned on the corridor lights, they were worked fine. Thank God.

As we got into the kitchen and the fluorescent light clicked and flashed a few times before it illuminated properly. We started to relax a little because the temperature was normal in this room and we began to chat amongst ourselves. The more noises we made ourselves, the less we heard from the rest of the building and whatever was residing in it.

We started to fill the big buckets with hot water and I went back down the hall with Liam and his mate and we turned the lounge lights on. Out of the corner of my eye, I saw a light bulb sitting on the next small landing past the lounge door. I said to Liam and his mate "look at that, the landing light bulb was on the floor!" We all walked up to the bulb and just gingerly, peered around the banisters to see two more light bulbs sitting on the floor.

We quickly went back to the kitchen and told Dad, who was just finishing filling the last bucket with hot water. We took the buckets and went down the stairs and shut the front door with a sigh of relief to be out of the building. How all three bulbs had come out of their fittings and landed on the stair carpet without breaking is a complete mystery. The height of the stair wells were almost twenty five feet above the stairs. A bulb dropped from that height would have smashed without a doubt. The bulbs looked as if they were placed there and not fallen or rolled at all. That was really weird and one more oddity to go with the rest of the strange occurrences in that flat.

The worse thing was, we had to go up again in the early hours for more water and this time there was only three of us, as Liam's mate and Mack had gone home. So it was another spooky trip up the stairs and this time I think we all felt more nervous than the first time, knowing about the bulbs and our imaginations running all over the place. I led the group this time and there were no strange things happening until we got into the kitchen, that is. We were filling the bucket up and there was a thump on the ceiling, which was coming from the back bedroom. It was a solitary loud sound and as soon as we had finished, we were out of the flat in seconds.

I put the radio on when I got back in the oven room and made sure it was tuned to the radio mic by thumping the back wall and I could hear it clearly. I was standing there listening on my own as Liam and Dad were getting dough out of the mixer. I was checking the prover, which sat in the back corner of the middle room.

Suddenly there were banging sounds coming from the radio and I quickly pressed record on the tape deck and turned the volume up. I called Dad and my brother into the room and said "listen to this!" They both came running to the radio to hear the noise that was coming from the back bedroom. It lasted for around three minutes and got louder and louder as it went on. It seemed to be moving around the room because of the way it went loud and soft. We could not hear it through the walls or ceiling at all, so it cannot have been too loud.
I left the tape recording just in case it recorded something we missed or could not hear from the bakery. After the first side of the C90 tape ran out, I turned the tape over but I left it off this

time as we had not heard any noises for nearly an hour.

There were no more sounds that night and we managed to get all the baking finished without any further interruptions. The strangest thing was when I took the tape up to our house and played through the music centre. We could here the banging sounds very clearly indeed but in the background there were whispers or very feint voices. That scared the hell out of myself and everyone else while we listened to it We played it to Ken the medium too and he could not believe that we had actually captured it all on tape.

I had recently met up with my old school friend Matt and he was always hanging around in a music shop called *Teagues,* in Newport. He was good friends with Phil the salesman in the instrument section of the shop. Phil was an absolute dictionary of info on electronic stuff and would always let us have a play on the latest synth.

I had saved up enough money to buy a brand new Korg Poly 61 synth and had gone in with Mum to collect it. That's when I had re found Matt and we spent a lot of time hanging around with the rest of my band that day onwards. Matt was into his photography and had just saved up for a new electronic, Canon film camera.

Everywhere he went, the Canon went too and he always embarrassed us by running ahead of us in the high Street and taking loads of photos. Bloody idiot, looked like some press reporter walking backwards down the pavement, so everyone would look round at us. The new Korg was amazing and after having mono synths since playing in my first band, this poly synth was a whole new kettle of fish. It had memory banks, digital controlled oscillators and envelope generators with a tape back up feature to save your sound banks.

I was lost for months on this machine but soon got used to its ways. It had rich sounds that only a poly could produce and having an arppegiator gave me so much more scope for some weird and wonderful sounds which annoyed the hell out of our bass player.

We eventually moved out to a garden shed, situated in the beer garden of The New Inn in Shalfleet. The winter months were absolutely freezing, with only this old fan heater to keep us from freezing. There was a chest freezer in the shed too and space was quite a challenge. We had a full size drum kit in one corner, bass and guitar amps on the floor; plus a PA system and keyboards and amp. There was also a small shelf with an effects unit perched on it for the vocals. Not forgetting the various mic stands and other paraphernalia strewn across the wooden floor. In the summer months, we cooked! Wooden sheds and summer don't mix and I must have lost a few pounds during those months. The amazing thing was no one ever complained about the noise from the shed. If they did, I never heard of any complaints. We had written a vast set list and were starting to think about gigging.

Neptune Icecap playing at Medina Theatre in April 1985. L/R-Me, Simon Pond and Tim Haddock.

Izzy worked in the pub for his parents and so did Tim for a while. That was very handy because Tim was notorious for disappearing for days on end. Pondy the bass player had to travel by bus to the shed. I went there on my bike and sometimes gave Tim a lift, if he was in Totland at the time. Another advantageous event, was Izzy passed his car test and acquired a car very early on in the band's life. This meant we were able to visit prospective venues for gigs and other such tasks.

His little Morris Minor was purple and made a wicked sound when going down through the gearbox. A sort of burping sound came from the exhaust pipe, which Izzy always induced by going down steep hills and dropping a gear or two in the process.

We ended up moving the band practice to our small self contained bedroom, at our house in Totland. I think that the noise, although not annoying at first, became annoying to the neighbours near the pub. The bedroom was no longer used, so the logical step was to turn it into a band room. It was a lot warmer and cooler in there and had its own toilet facilities.

Prior to final night of ghosts and spirits in the bakery and flat, Ken had visited the place with Mum and her friend. He had chosen daylight hours to reduce the risk of causing any harm to them selves. This would have been quite possible if they had gone in at night time, believe me.

Dad had got someone to put the bulbs back in the landing lights up on the third floor and made sure they all worked. Incidentally, all the bulbs were undamaged and didn't need replacing. Ken had picked up some very strong activity in the back bedroom and a lot more spirits appeared to have come in to the flat, since the last time he visited the place. That explained the banging sounds coming from the top room and down the stairs and along the hall that runs directly above the length of the bakery.

He thought that perhaps the resident ghosts had attracted more of the same into the building to warn off anyone wanting to live there. He thought the old spinster had reached the end of her tether and wanted the flat to remain empty for some reason. He still needed to visit at night time but that could only happen on a Saturday evening when no one was working in the bakery. We all wanted to go with him to make up the numbers and to experience what was going on up there.

It was a Friday night and it was getting on for ten o'clock, time to don our white boiler suits and aprons for the long night ahead. Friday nights were always the busiest and most hectic in the bake house. It was just the three of us again but later on we had my brother's mate Abdul to help us with the water problem.

We needed more hot water for these extra orders so we took two buckets up with us and started filling them up. As we all stood in the kitchen, it sounded like someone was walking down the stairs from the upper floor. As we listened with anticipation and fear, there was a loud crash as if glass was smashed and then another bang on the floor. We were very frightened by this time and wanted nothing more than to go outside. We just filled the second bucket half full and slowly walked out of the kitchen, looking all around us all the time.

Dad was saying a prayer that Ken had told him would give us protection against whatever was there. I walked up to the lounge doorway and turned on the landing lights and nothing worked again. Then we saw all the bulbs on the floor but this time one had smashed against the banisters. That was enough for us and we shot out of the front door as fast as possible and trying not to spill too much hot water in the process.

Back in the bakery, we all talked about the light bulbs and the walking sounds on the stairs and I turned the radio back on and pressed record on the tape deck. It must have been no more than fifteen minutes after Abdul had gone home when there was a massive banging noise on the radio and it was so loud that we could hear it from the mixer room. Without the radio mic! Then we heard the sound of something running down the stairs again and right down the hallway above us.

The tape deck had recorded it all on tape so we could prove to the non believers that the sounds were coming from the flat. Luckily it didn't come down to our floor and give us a nice headache for a week or so. The scales started swinging again for about ten minutes after the banging stopped.

Liam went back up to the house after the bulk of the dough's were done and in the prover. It was just Dad and I, left to finish off the baking and get some of the confectionery ready for the shop. We always went outside the bakery shop door for a smoke. It was after midnight and there were not many people around that night, just a police van and *Chizzy* on his police bike going round the roundabout and back through the village.

We started on the oven loading as the first batches of tins and bloomers that were ready to go in the ovens. We had all three deck ovens going and they could chuck some heat out when they were working at their best. It was getting nice and warm in the middle room now and not a freezing cold chill anywhere. I went into the flour room and started to weigh up the bun dough, while Dad did the last of the bread dough. He was putting the pieces through the moulder when suddenly there was a hell of a banging noise above us and it started to move down the hall upstairs. Right above us and seemed to be like something running along the hall. When it reached the end of the hall it seemed to drop down to our floor and whoosh, it went through both Dad and I.

The feeling was strange and it made my back freeze and my head feel like it was very heavy. My energy had gone completely and I just yawned and felt too cold to stay in the flour room, so I went and stood close to the ovens, thinking that it would be warm there, as it usually was. It was even colder in the oven room and I could not believe that there was no heat coming out from the ovens. Another strange thing that happened when whatever it was, ran through us.

The over temp switches on all three decks were turned right down to one hundred and twenty degrees. They were previously set at over two hundred degrees when I put them on. Something had turned the temperature switches down too. How could that happen? The three electric ovens, were producing over two hundred degrees of heat a piece. But as I stood in front of them, it was freezing cold.

I thought that maybe that was the end of it and perhaps the ghost had left. How wrong I was and soon the banging started again and this time on the radio mic. I had to put a new tape in the machine, as it was running out and I wanted to capture this lot on tape before either we left or the ghosts did. The noises coming from the speaker on the radio were very strange indeed, quite different from the ones we had heard before.

There were footsteps across the floor of the bedroom but in the background, lots of voices and very similar to a crowd of people walking down a busy stairway. I could not discriminate between each voice and what they were saying. After a while the voices got louder, as did the footsteps across the floor. Then a running sound came down the stairs to the first floor and once again, along the hallway and to the end bedroom. It did not come down to our floor this time but seemed to turn around and run back along the hallway. Then there was an almighty bang from the bedroom and so many bangs coming down the stairs. It sounded like so many people running and the noise was incredibly loud because we could hear it across the ceiling this time.

It was at this point that we were really worried and wondering what the hell was going to happen next? Dad came into the oven room to listen closely to the radio and then the banging moved across the hall and past the kitchen upstairs, then straight through the middle room of the bakery.

We were stunned as the weighing bucket flew across the room and crashed into the table near the only window in that room. Then the banging moved towards us and went straight through us. My god it was a horrible feeling, as all your energy drained away and the coldest darkest headache you could wish to imagine, crept from your neck to the front of your head. The whole room froze instantly and my body felt so ill and so weak, Dad felt the same and we just ran out of the back door and up the hill to our house. We had to wake Mum up and tell her what happened.

All the bread was in the ovens and probably burning by this time but it didn't matter, there was no way we were going back into that bakery until something was done about those ghosts. Mum was on the phone to Ken in minutes and he very soon appeared at the door. Mum was going into the bakery with Ken to turn off the ovens for now and anything else that needed to be switched off or taken off.

They did all the ovens and Ken had picked up some serious evil presence in that middle room and said "you have thirteen poltergeists in there and they are determined to cause trouble for you. They have been brought in by the old spinster to keep anyone out of that flat!" She certainly achieved her goal and we were not going near the place for quite some time now. We finally arranged with Ken the medium, to go into the haunted flat and bakery one Saturday night.

Nothing ever appeared to happen during the daytime hours, so it was best to visit at night. Well, I say hardly, in loosest of terms because one of our shop staff saw an entity standing near the doorway in the oven room. It appeared to be standing below the floorboards and on the ground. This is apparently what happens to some ghosts as they are standing on the earth where they came from and not on the buildings that are above ground level. This apparition was described to Dad as a perfect description of my brother Tony who had died in nineteen seventy seven. It was not the first time that we had felt his presence in the building but never before had he appeared before any of us. Why this happened, I have no idea and at this time of so much paranormal activity, perhaps he was trying to stop the poltergeists from harming us.

The days after that evil night were not nice at all. We spent most days recovering from the attacks by the spirits. My headache lasted for days and my energy levels were so low that I hardly had any enthusiasm to do anything other than sleep and just rest. I had yet again cancelled band practice because riding ten miles on my bike was beyond my capabilities at that time.

I had got back with Lana and we spent as much time together as possible, as she was working quite a few more hours now and had taken on a new job at the Sentry Mead Hotel, near the Turf Walk in Totland. I had also sold her my CX custom because it was leaking oil badly and did not run very well. I didn't have the time to repair it so I took it off the road and put it in the workshop. I had changed the cam chain and tensioners on it as they were faulty and if I remember correctly, I missed or did not put a gasket in correctly and that's why it leaked oil. Lana knew it was not in good condition when I sold it to her and I think her Father and his mate were going to rebuild it so she could use it.

Lana and I went over to Bembridge motorcycles and I had looked at a Kawasaki KDX250, which was a Canadian import and had a plastic fuel tank, which was not legal in the UK. I test rode it along the embankment and bought it there and then. The power this bike had was amazing and it was basically a motocross bike on the road with lights. The lights were useless and were just for show but everything else about this machine was fantastic. I loved every minute on that bike and it gave me so much bloody fun.

When my Father had left the family home and gone off to live in Guildford, it had a devastating effect on the family. He had opened a butcher's shop in the old part of the town, close to the old castle remains. Things seemed to be falling apart when he left us. My sister was about six years old and my brother was only fourteen at the time. I was nearly twenty one but it still upset me because of what my Mum was going through.

She had so much to sort out on her own and it was so unfair of Dad to just disappear and leave her alone. There were lots of problems with the house that were never fixed properly. Mum had to let out the house at one point and we used the band room and a caravan for our bedrooms.

Suddenly one day, we had no water in the house and when it did work, the pressure was so low that we could not even run the hot water boiler. We had Southern Water in to see if they could detect where the problem was in the pipeline, but they could not find it. Then we got a quote from the builders up near church hill, and that was in the region of £450.00. Because the pipe was not on the main road, it was our responsibility to repair the pipe.

There was no way Mum could afford that sort of money at the drop of a hat. She had three jobs and was working all the hours god sent just to keep her head above water and keep us in food etc. Obviously I was working and bringing in plenty of money to help out but a major bill like that was too much for us.

Dad did not seem very interested in helping out with it all and I do not remember him sending Mum any extra money to cover the costs of the repairs. So we had to make a decision and quickly.

My mate Dilly's girlfriend worked for the only hire shop in Newport at the time and she could get a very good discount on tool hire. So we decided to hire this walking digger thing and a road drill to start with. Dilly drilled most of the channel and pilot holes to find the damn pipe and I did the digging of the trench. It took at least a week to get right down to the main road from the house. We only had evenings to carry out the work, as we were all working full time. When we finally got the trench under the archway, we found the leak. It was at the end of the archway on the left side of the drive, which Southern Water couldn't locate.

Dilly was digging a section of the trench out, half way up the drive and this was in front of the small bungalow half way up the drive way. Unfortunately the old lady that lived there was taken ill and her family were there visiting her at the time. An ambulance was called to take the lady to hospital, but had to park on the main road and the paramedics had to walk up the drive. I will never forget this as long as I live, as Dilly was swinging the digger arm around and nearly knocked the old lady on her stretcher and the two paramedics into the trench with the bucket.

My God, that was a close one and Dilly was banned from digging anymore of the trench. We apologised to the old lady and her family for the near miss and luckily, they also saw the funny side of the incident. The second slight mishap we had was when we reached the bottom of the drive and found where the plastic water pipe joined the mains pipe on the pavement.

We decided that as we had the pilot hole dug out and the trench was only about two feet from it, we would carry on with the digger, after checking for any other pipes in the way. That was fine; no other pipes hindered the digger as I dug through the stinky yellow clay and pulled up this curious looking pipe thing with thousands of wires coming out of it. Oh yes, the telephone cable was there, minus a few wires after my digger chewed through a few of them. So we hastily poked the wires back into its casing and connected the new water pipe up and buried the bloody thing as quickly as possible. Amazingly, there were no reports of telephone problems afterwards.

My sister's friend managed to break her arm by falling into the trench one day and even though we had sheets of metal covering some of the trench, she still managed to fall in.

So the pipe was in and connected and we had full pressure at last and probably for the first time since we moved in the house back in nineteen eighty. The pipe must have been leaking for years and no one had bothered to investigate the low pressure. The only other problem we encountered was when this knob from the council came round looking at the tarmac we had laid on the small section that went into the pavement. He kept going on about the tarmac had to be a finer grade stuff and after just walking off and leaving him to it, we never heard a thing from him again. Turned out he was my old mate from the farm's father.

We bought a ton of tarmac and had it tipped on the bank of the car park, adjacent to our garden. We hired a compactor and managed to lay the whole stretch of tarmac over the trench by hand. There were a few areas that had sunk a little but nothing too bad. The total cost for the whole job was in the region of one hundred and eighty pounds back then. A huge difference, from the four hundred and fifty pounds quote from the builders.

Saturday night was upon us and Ken had come up to the house in readiness for the visit to the flat. We were all very nervous about just walking in the front door, let alone going to the top bedroom and facing up to whatever was haunting the place. There was absolutely no nervousness in Ken as we prepared to walk down to the flat. He was ready to confront these spirits and rid the flat and bakery of them as soon as he could.

There were five of us that were taking part in this venture and in my view, the more the better because these were not friendly spirits and they would harm you if they got the chance. Mum, Dad, Ken, Lana and I were the group who were going up those stairs that night and it was probably the scariest thing I have ever experienced.

It was after eleven at night and it was the best time to go to the flat because activity always started after that time. As we walked down the drive and under the archway, Ken gave us instructions regarding things to say to these spirits if they attacked us. Prayers worked well and even for disbelievers as my Father and I were.

We used these words many times on the nights that those ghosts tried to go through us and it seemed to stop them most of the time. Ken told us to stay together because the power generated from our group could overpower that of the ghosts and they are less likely to start trouble against a number of mortals. Mum was carrying a crucifix and that was going to be placed in the bedroom, when we were ready to let Ken start his prayers and words that would hopefully move these spirits on.

Opening the front door, Dad went in first followed by Ken and then Mum and Lana. I was last to go into the short hallway before going up the stairs. The first stair lights were working and we all walked up the stairs to the first landing and then Ken suggested we go into the kitchen first, so we congregated there and Ken started calling on the spirits in the house to show themselves and let him know they were present. There was silence and we stood there straining our ears to hear something. There was nothing at all. Ken again asked the spirits if they were in the flat and as we waited, I was scared of what would happen and would the running noises come back? Suddenly there was a noise from the room above the kitchen, which was the back bedroom. It was a bang on the floor or the wall, we could not tell where exactly it came from but it seemed as though the whole atmosphere in the flat had changed from a warm feeling to an ice cold feeling.

Ken walked out into the long hallway and started to walk towards the landing and the stairs that led to the top bedrooms. He went into the lounge and we followed closely, but with some apprehension I must admit.

The temperature in the lounge was freezing cold and it seemed like a mist had floated up to about waist height and it gave us a horrible feeling too. It was a little bit like dry ice, but not as visible. It was not just cold; it had a sinister feeling mixed in with it. Ken said more enticing words to bring those spirits out in the open and this time the noises from upstairs were horrendously loud and almost violent in the force and the way they kept getting louder and more powerful.

I grabbed Lana's hand because I could see she was getting scared now and Dad held Mum's hand as we followed Ken slowly out of the lounge door and stood on the bottom of the stair case. More enticing words and then the lampshade from the high light fitting at the very top of the stairway fell down onto the landing.

Now that was frightening and we all knew these evil spirits were capable of moving objects and throwing things about. Knowing this, made us more wary of what was in that bedroom.

Ken told us that he thought that all the spirits were probably in the back room and that is where we had to go to confront them.

He also warned us that there could be things flying around and to watch out for things moving. Luckily we knew that the only moveable objects in that room were light bulbs and the radio microphone that was still against the back wall; well I hoped it was anyway.

Walking up the final few stairs was beyond being scared, because what more could be scarier than confronting real spirits and ghosts and not based on some fictional story or film. This was the real thing and it is nothing like I imagined it to be. It was dark, cold and pure evil that lived up there that night.

Another light bulb was lying on the stairs but not the one from the fallen shade, that bulb was still in place and was lit as we walked up the stairs.

We first went into the front bedroom which was my bedroom about six weeks ago and soon as I went into it, memories of Lana and our long passionate nights came flooding back to me and I looked at her and smiled. She must have been thinking the same naughty thoughts as I was, because she smiled back with a look in those big eyes that turned me to mush every time.

I missed our nights of Captain Morgan's fuelled fun and because we were totally alone in the flat, we could do what we damn well wanted and did.

There were no noises that came from this room and apart from the odd flying object and violin sounds. It was definitely not where these spirits were hiding in the building. The room was not as cold as the stairs coming up to the room. Ken said a prayer in the room; just to be sure that nothing dwelled within the walls of the bedroom.

The last time I had been in the back bedroom was to place the radio microphone in it and I made sure the door was open so any sound could be detected outside the room and on the stairs. No one had been up to that room since that day but the door was now firmly closed! It was obvious to me that whatever was haunting the flat had closed the back bedroom door, for what purpose, I do not know? As Dad opened the door and turned on the light, Ken went in next, followed my Mum and Lana and myself. The temperature was unbelievably cold in there and a mist seemed to float up to about waist height and it was very uncomfortable for all of us.

I looked at the little cupboard door, which opened into a tiny room under the eaves of the roof. This was my first bedroom back in the days when all three of us boys shared this bedroom.

No one really spoke much, apart from Ken of course and he started to ask whoever occupied the room to leave now and go towards the light. The atmosphere was almost crushing on our chests and made my Mother cry, Lana was affected too and she looked quite unwell as the words that ken spoke seemed to be angering whatever shared that room with us.

There were banging sounds from the stairs as we stood there petrified and motionless as the crushing feeling turned into that horrible headache feeling as spirits began to leave the building through Ken's guiding prayers. We all said the words that Ken had told us to use if we had been attacked by a spirit "Please God, give us protection from evil". It worked very well on this occasion. There was little sound from the room we were in but a few sounds still coming from the stairs and upper landing.

Suddenly there was an incredible bang from we thought was the radiator below the window, and it made us all jump; Ken said it was one of the last spirits leaving the building and just as he stopped talking and turned towards the window, another big bang and this was the loudest so far. It came from the bedroom window and we all saw the glass vibrate and saw the frame bend in the middle.

How that window didn't smash and blow itself outwards I will never know. Everyone stood in amazement when it happened and suddenly the cold air vanished and the room began to take on a normal feel to it.

Ken informed us that the window bang was the old spinster finally leaving the place, along with all the other evil spirits she had brought in to do her evil chores.

There was a feeling of peace and subsequent relief in the flat and it didn't appear scary anymore after that night. The bakery returned to its normal self and ovens once again produced heat that was unbearable standing in front of them. I removed the radio mic and all the lights were put back together and worked. It was as nothing had happened at all, a dream like experience but unlike a dream, it was tangible.

Nothing ever bothered us again in that bakery and working nights seemed a doddle compared with the times before Ken had got rid of those dark spirits for us. It is worthy to note that we had let a lay preacher into that flat some months before the real trouble had began, to bless it and hopefully stop things from happening. We may as well have got the mechanic from the garage to come and put his blessing on the place because whatever the so called preacher had done was useless. That fact in mind, if I ever experience anything supernatural again, the only person I will call is a decent spiritual medium to do the job properly.

My parents decided to rent out the flat after the ghosts were gone and that in itself was a bloody nightmare, mainly because of the people who rented it. Not all of them, a couple were not nice people at all. The flat and bakery was sold off and as my parents were splitting up for good. My Father was running off with a young girl who used to work in the bakers shop for us. The trauma of that event took its toll on all of us kids in a great way. We could not understand why he would do such a thing to our Mum in the first place and why throw everything away that had taken so many years to build up?

The butchery, bakery, everything was being dispersed and even our house at the top of the hill *Dreens* was regrettably sold off, because Mum could not afford to keep that big house on her own and Dad had moved back to Guildford where he lived back in the early sixties.

I wanted to stay in that house because it had all we needed and I wish that we could have rented out the spare rooms and maybe some of the workshop buildings to help us to stay there. It was a sad day and I knew it would never be the same family I knew and loved, because now it was all broken and nothing could fix it either. At first, my Dad only went away during the week and used to visit at weekends, but not on a regular basis I hasten to add. He brought us meat and other food but that was about it as far as I was aware. He must have been feeling guilty to keep coming back at weekends or he was trying to con more money out of Mum. I was always at work anyway, so I didn't really see too much of him in that part of his removal from the family. So we had a part-time Father for now and to be totally honest, I do not think it was at all beneficial to my little sister or brother. It upset them both when it came to say goodbye again every Sunday evening, they didn't need this extra emotional pain at this difficult period.

My Dad should have not been allowed to take one penny from my mother for what he did, but alas my Mother is not a hard character and let him have half and more of the accumulated wealth. He had a few endowment policies that they had paid into over the years, plus half the businesses sales and property values and what was Mum left with- a tiny cottage in Freshwater and had to do three jobs to pay the bills while he was opening a butchers shop in Guildford. He was living in a nice flat with his new girlfriend. I have disowned him now, the real truth came to light a long time after this event and I don't forgive that easily. I speak to him occasionally but that's where it stops.

Since the time that our family were rid of that haunted building, many other people have owned it or rented rooms in it. It was not long ago that my sister's friend went to live in the flat and she claimed that very odd things happened to her while she resided there. One day her CD player started to play and it was not even plugged into the socket, it had no batteries in it either. She said she never felt alone in the house and always thought she had eyes watching her every move.

Not too long after she moved out of the place, another couple bought the property and lived there a good number of years. I did not know that this guy had bought the house and I remember kicking about with him when we had mopeds and bikes. Anyway, he moved in with his wife and kids and this must have been around two thousand and ten. It was so out of the blue and for me, out of character but the chap hung himself in a tree in the garden and was the very tree we used to play around and my bike shed was next to it.

I could not believe it when I heard of the tragedy because the man was a rather gentle soul, who never harmed anyone. Amazingly, his wife and children still live in the house to this day. Was it the evil of the house playing its tricks again……………

The eight wheeled Argocat vehicle from 1980.

A view from Wilmingham track to the railway line from Freshwater to Yarmouth. Circa 1985

One evening around four of us on bikes, went out for a ride towards Brook and the Brighstone area. There was myself on my Triumph Thunderbird, little Wol on his Honda Cb550f, big Wol on his Triumph and another bloke on a Triumph US Special. We cruised down the military Road and then turned off and rode through Brook and onto Hulverstone and turned off down Strawberry Lane.

We stopped at the big car park at the top of the lane and had a smoke and a chat, and then we went down the hill from the car park and towards Winkle Street. The other two chaps on Triumphs decided to have a good burn down that road. Little Wol did exactly the same thing and accelerated so quickly that his passenger flew off the back and landed on the road. I saw him fly past me as he came off the back and I was the first to stop and help him up off the road. Little Wol did not realise he had lost his pillion until he put his hand behind his back and felt nothing there. Poor bloke was severely grazed and luckily he had a leather jacket on, which was shredded right down the back.

We picked him up and took him to the Sun Inn at Calbourne and went into the toilets to wash his wounds. The landlady gave us some Dettol and we applied this to his grazes and it must have stung like hell. We all went back to

Totland and dropped the casualty off at his house and then went off to the café for tea.

I had a similar experience with *gravel rash* on my Superdream down at Moa Place car park one night that the fairground was visiting Freshwater. I rode into that car park and saw a couple of lads I was friendly with and as I applied the front brake, the front wheel just slid out from under me and off I went to inspect the gravel. The tarmac had broken down and left a huge pile of loose chippings there. Hence why my wheel just locked up and slid. No cuts or grazes from that mishap but bloody embarrassing though.

The fair always came to Freshwater in the middle of August and set up on the large green near *Acorn Spring Works* and *Greasy Sam's* takeaway. It was invariably *Coles* Fair that came to our area and it was a very good fair, they had every machine that I had ever seen and one of the best Dodgems that I ever saw.

Most of the lads on their mopeds would park up outside Sam's and walk up to the fair, I said most of them as there were a few idiots that took their mopeds right up to the fair perimeter. There was a concrete cricket strip on that green and it was a favourite place for idiots to try and pull wheelies along its length. One night there was this bloke on a Suzuki AP50 moped and he had everything you could bolt on a bike. Top box, extra lights, tassels the lot. He decided he could do the best wheelies on the strip and he rode to one end of it and revved up his smoking can of flies and managed to pull up the front wheel and go right off the back of the bike, dragging his top box along the hard concrete and with him attached to the bars at the same time. So funny, he never ever lived that prank down for a very long time.

Another funny moment at the fair was when one of our group of friends was chasing his mate around on the bumper cars and when he missed the other car; the Dodgem car slammed into the wooden kerb and it fell off and onto the grass, some six feet below. Never ever saw anything like that happen since, it was a classic moment.

A very funny moment, one evening while Marcus and I were standing in the kitchen waiting for the kettle to boil. He was peering out of the large window towards the garden and pointing out the weird red eyes that a moth had, that was on the glass outside. Suddenly this little bug jumped off the inside of the window and went straight down his shirt. It was so funny watching him trying to get his shirt off as quick as he possibly could, the sheer panic on his face was a picture.

So the date was set for a Saturday night for our gig at the *Totland Country Club*. and we were going to share the stage with the owner's new lady, who did discos. It would act as a double attraction to the public and should bring in a few more people than we usually managed to get at our limited number of gigs.

The day arrived and I have to say that there is nothing to beat the excitement that runs through your body when you are setting up all the gear on the stage ready for a performance. It is magical and something I loved very much. We set up the gear and this was to be our debut for the new lighting system that we had made using UV active tubing and two UV strip lights which we fixed to the mic stands facing inwards, towards the drums etc. We attached this tubing all around the drum kit and on my synths and the bass player and guitarist had tassels of the stuff on their guitars.

When the lights were off and the tubes illuminated, the effect was brilliant as everything had an ice blue outline. The only down side of this effect was the UV tubes were horrible to look at after a long period of time and not very good on the eyes.

A good sound check was performed and it was time to go home and sort out our clothes for the gig and have something to eat as we were all starving.

The gig we played before the forthcoming one at the Country Club was at Cowes Youth Club. We arrived at around three in the afternoon to set the gear and then after a sound check, we all went back to my house in Totland for something to eat etc. We drove back to Cowes in Izzy's Morris Minor car and that was a laugh in itself.

So all the gear was switched on and incidentally, we had acquired a pair of speakers that stood over five feet in height and were approximately two feet in depth and breadth. These were bloody loud and required a good PA amp to drive them, which we clubbed together and bought.

First song was going very well and we had a fair amount of people coming into the club to listen, when there was a huge puff of smoke from behind Izzy's drum kit and all the vocals died. Yep, the PA amp had blown up and sadly, that was the end of that gig.

Being a very close bunch of chaps and getting on very well away from the music, we started to have these monthly visits to restaurants. Each member took it in turns to pay for the rather expensive slap up nosh. In the beginning it kind of worked rather well, but unfortunately, not all of us were earning a lot of money and as we progressed to the more popular restaurants, the costs became a burden and we decided to knock it on the head for the good of the band.

We had video evenings at the bass player's house and one particular night, he had hired a film called *Bullshot* from the local video shop. This was the funniest and relevant film to us dudes that was ever made.

We all arrived at the Country Club and went to the bar as the disco was about to start, it was early evening so not many people had started to arrive yet. We made a few adjustments to the gear while the disco was playing and very soon, people started to arrive. That was the most exciting thing about playing in a band, when people were arriving and you are set apart from everyone else because you are what they had come to see. It was not long until the bar area was heaving with people and we had all moved from the bar area to a table close to the stage and were looking around at everyone and spotting people we knew and waving or acknowledging them in other ways. The moment had arrived when the lady DJ announced that Neptune Icecap were about to start playing.

As the lights were switched off and our tubes fired up and we had a smoke machine that gave the ice blue a real boost. It looked excellent from where I was standing, so it must have looked very professional from the other side of the stage. The crowd liked what we had done and we had our first applause of the night and that put a smile on our faces, I can tell you.

After around six songs we had an interval and the disco went straight into playing and we all walked off the stage, chatting and laughing as we made our way to the bar. So many people were saying they loved the lights and what we had played and that alone put me on cloud nine. We got our free drinks and went over to talk to the owner, who was on the left side of the stage. He thought it was good and liked our presentation very much.

As we stood there chatting I saw a few people I knew and chatted to them and then I saw this girl, dressed in black and with a very pretty face, sitting near where I was standing and she said "hello" to me. I replied and chatted to her as she was really enjoying the gig. I said I would come and see her again after the gig.

The rest of the music went down really well and afterwards we had plenty of compliments from other musicians who we recognised as being from other bands around the West Wight. It was all in all, a very good gig and we were all pleased with ourselves. We were allowed to leave all the gear at the Country Club for the night and collect it next morning, so that gave us a break from dismantling it all.

So I went over to see the girl I met in the interval and we got on very well indeed. She came home with me and we had a lovely evening and I think it was about three in the morning when I drove her home in my beetle. We went out together for quite a time and had some good times. She was so into *The Damned* and her bedroom resembled a graveyard but in a gothic style. She lived with her Mother and brother and this odd guy who was her step Dad. He was a lot older than her mother if I remember correctly. She was a very sweet person underneath the dark image that she projected and very homely at heart.

Unfortunately I two timed her and was caught out. I regretted it and wished I had not been tempted by her friend that day. Her friend was a cunning girl and even though I know I should have resisted her, she had planned it, to get one up on her friend.

Some years later I got back in touch with her and she had moved to Australia and was married with two children. She seemed happy with her lot at that time, but fate was turning against her.

She lost her husband so suddenly and it must have almost destroyed the poor girl. I kept in contact with her but she was going through hell on earth and in some ways I can sympathise with her as I lost Tony suddenly and I know what it is like to lose someone you love so dearly.

Some moths later she was talking again and we had quite a lot of chat about her coming back to the Island and we could meet up again. I was not in a good situation myself at the time and could not really do much about it, hence it all faded away and I don't hear from her anymore.

Chapter 16

Twenty One and farming again

On my 21st birthday I had a lovely crystal glass tankard engraved with my name and date. I had it for three days until my Dad dropped it on the kitchen floor while washing up. Oh dear, this is a sign I thought and I had the feeling that this birthday was going to be fraught with disasters and I was right.

I had the Reliant Regal van at the time and myself and my mate little Wol and his mate Moggy were going to visit Barneys Roadhouse nightclub on the Friday evening and using the three wheeler to go out there. First port of call was the *Starks Inn* in Freshwater bay for a drink or two but obviously it was coke for me, even though it was my birthday we were supposedly celebrating. We left there and made our way down the military Road and Moggy was being bounced about all over the place in the back of the little van.

We reached the disco with no problems and had a good night out and little Wol and Moggy were completely drunk as we walked out of the place and chatted to a few people we knew and got into the old regal and drove off towards freshwater. We got as far as Chilton Chine when the engine stopped and we rolled onto the verge and I lifted the bonnet to see if there was anything obviously a miss. Nothing looked out of place and I tried to start it again, but to no avail and my mates were laughing at my van and saying things like "The plastic pig is dead". I suddenly remembered something while I was sitting at the wheel and thought I better not let this lot know or I will never live it down, I had forgot to put petrol in the thing as I planned to do that morning. "It won't go chaps" I announced to the drunkards in the van and suggested we walk or try and hitch a lift as there is a lot of cars at the disco tonight.

Suddenly my mates weren't laughing at the van and the mood changed instantly and they were moaning about walking home and it was that fine rain and mist, the stuff that soaks you in seconds. Off we went and got all the way to Compton and by this time we were bloody soaked and quite cold. What a disastrous birthday that was.

One of the funniest things I ever experienced at Thorley Manor Farm, was when my mate Taylor was washing his hands at the sink and chatting to myself and another chap. As he turned round to grab the towel to dry his hands, this tiny mouse darted across the floor from under a chair and towards the door.

Taylor was standing right in the doorway and the mouse just ran straight up his boiler suit and into his pants. I have never seen someone rip their boiler suit off in such a hurry and I remember being in bloody tears of laughter as Taylor jumped about the place trying to get this mouse out of his trousers. We told him it was after his nuts, which made us all laugh even more. What a classic moment and one that still makes me laugh so much.

When we told Mark about it and how Taylor was dancing about in the Nammet shed, he was in tears within a few minutes too. It was also mentioned the next morning at our usual meeting and made us all laugh and Malcolm told Taylor to get some bicycle clips for his trousers.

We had just finished lunch and were just walking back towards the workshop and Mark cycled in the entrance with blood pouring from his face. He stopped and got off his bike and I asked him "what happened to you Mark?" He started laughing and trying to tell us what had gone on, but he couldn't as he was just laughing and laughing.

Eventually he calmed himself and said "I was coming down the hill and thinking what a nice day with the sun shining and not a breath of wind, when suddenly this bloody Robin flew out of the hedge and flew up to his face, tweeted at him, pecked him on the nose and flew off." "What I said, a Robin" "Yes" he replied "a bloody Robin". That was enough for all of us and our stomachs hurt like hell after the non stop laughing as we staggered into the workshop and Mark was still drying the blood off his nose with his hanky.

The picture that was conjured up in my head of this Robin flying up to him and was almost shouting at him for something that it thought Mark had done wrong and then pecking him for not taking any notice of what he had said was so funny and goes into my funniest things that ever happened on the farm.

We had a young chap who came to work with us during the summer, this dude was quite a character and probably the sleepiest person I ever met. What I mean is that although he was wide awake and at work, he never appeared to be fully awake, if you know what I mean. He was intelligent and very into his music and festivals and had quite long hair and gained the nick name Digby.

Now we all assumed that Digby was staying at Malcolm's cottage and coming to work every morning from his house, because he always came from the direction of the office as he walked to the workshop. I do not know who discovered the truth about where Digby was actually living but we honestly could no believe it when we found out.

He was bloody well camping in the field next to the old chapel graveyard and was using the outside toilet in the manor, near the office. Apparently he was having his meals at Malcolm's house but sleeping in his tent. We could not work it out at all and never really knew if he was supposed to be living at Malcolm's house or just enjoyed camping next to the graveyard.

After a few weeks, his tent was gone and he moved in with his parents near Freshwater. He was a good laugh and did some funny things when he was with us. One day he was sent off in Mark's Ford 5000 which was always used for the McConnell rear mounted digger, to the agricultural engineers in Newport to get it repaired or something. On his way back to the farm, he turned off the main Yarmouth Road towards Thorley and somehow, ended up smashing into a car and ended up very shaken in the process.

Weekend feeding of the cattle was normally a two person task because of the amount of straw that had to be collected from *Wilmingham* barn and brought down to the cow yards for feed and bedding.

If we were particularly organised then we would load two trailers of straw or fit enough on one to last the weekend. Apart from the straw, there was the barley to bag off from the mill hopper and the minerals to mix with it too. Then you had the liquid feeders to fill up with Vituramol or Promax liquid which was very messy old stuff. Filling the old spray cans with liquid and trying to keep them on the trailer in an upright position, or they would fall over and leak all over the straw and barley bags, sticky as hell and not nice to get all over your clothes. The liquid was a molasses based product that smelt a bit like Bovril or Marmite. Filling the liquid feeders was a relatively simple task as long as the feeders were tied or bolted down; else the cows would knock them over and usually damage the cases which held the large plastic balls for the cows to lick. The older feeders were better as they were constructed from steel and were very sturdy in the yards.

Feeding the rolled barley was a completely different ball game, because cattle are very keen on barley and they love the taste of it. When the barley was placed in the troughs in the yard, you had to be very quick and very careful as the cows would stop at nothing to get to their barley and if you were in the way then you would be pushed out of the way the same as other cows would be.

I used to hate doing the barley when I first started working on the farm because it was damn scary doing it and the way those animals charge for their food, just as though they had not been fed for a week. In the yards we had a row of large wooden troughs, which were of a very heavy build but even they were just biffed over by the cows or knocked over by one of them scratching themselves against the troughs. In later years, the troughs were replaced with a set of new metal troughs that acted as gates at the same time, whereby you could lift up one end and open them into the large driveway through the middle of the yards. We had a set of these on both sides of the walkway and they had the diagonal bars on them for the cow's heads and large wire lids that prevented the hay from being thrown out of the troughs.

All these new troughs were built by Mark and Malcolm and were a really good idea and saved so much time and energy at feed time and also kept everything tidy around the yards. Having the opening system gave us more access to the yards at cleaning out time in April. So the McConnell with the dung grab could just drive in anywhere and clear out the dung.

I remember lying and tamping the concrete for the new driveways and putting in the RSJ's for the new feeders to hang on. We had to get these massive steel troughs from the workshop and to the yards. They were too heavy and too long to carry with the loader tractor to handle them so we devised a clever system to move them. We had a large sack truck on each end and the rest of the crew pushing them along, it worked a treat and we managed to get them all in position, ready for hanging on their pins attached to the RSJ's. We had to lift them all by hand onto the locating pins and this was not easy at all.

Everyone who works with gates will know how difficult it is to hang a heavy and long gate, even with two people on the job and these gates weighed roughly three hundred and fifty kilos each and trying to get them up was a learning experience in itself. We tried various things to make it easier to get them up. We settled for a transmatic or walking jack on one end and lifting the other end. Once they were all up and working there were only a few problems with these troughs and mostly due to them dropping on their hinge pins and not opening properly, some of the wire racked lids fell off and had to have locking pins put in the hinges. Otherwise they were excellent and stopped me getting run over at feed time.

We also had a small cattle yard behind the barn at *Wilmingham,* so a trip up there in the tractor was an every day occurrence. Most of the time you could manage to feed the animals at *Wilmingham* on your own and one of us did this while the other did the liquids or minerals. This was our little system and apart from one time, it worked well. The time it didn't work was when the cows had escaped from the main yard and into the manor gardens.

I had chosen to do the liquid and get the minerals and barley into the feeders at the farm while Hayward had gone up the road to deal with the *Wilmingham* cattle. I had finished doing the Atcost yard and was getting the barley bagged for the Tyler yard and I walked around the farm yard, towards the workshop end of the Tyler yard and looked in the little side gate, no cows? They had knocked one of the feeders off the latch and gone for a holiday around the manor grounds. The mess they had made in the garden was horrendous and Andy the gardener, who was Mark the fitter's father, went ballistic over the huge holes in the lawns and the trampled flowers everywhere. It took us quite a while to get them all back into the yard and to lift up the trough that had dropped off its latch. That was probably the longest feeding Sunday that I ever did, thanks to the escaping cattle.

Hayward picked me up from Totland and we went down to Freshwater to collect the Digby character. As we pulled up outside his house we could see that one of the large brick gate pillars had been demolished and there was not a sign of life in the house at all. We knocked on the door several times and in the end banged on the doors to awaken whoever was there.

After ten minutes of trying to get an answer, we decided to give up on him and went to work. We were supposed to be teaching him the feeding Rota for his turn at weekends and give him an insight of the best ways to go about the task. However, he obviously did not want to come out and play that morning so we had to tell Malcolm when he asked "where was Digby?" I think that was the beginning of the end of Digby's farming with us because he was always turning up late or not at all and I think we all got annoyed with it all in the end as you needed people you could rely on, especially at weekends for feeding.

We later found out what at happened to young Digby that Sunday morning and why he had not woke up and why the garden gate pillar was smashed. He had got very drunk in the Albion Hotel on Saturday night and had gone home and decided he was going to drive his land rover out of the drive but unfortunately he did not make it past the gateway and smashed into the brick pillar, demolishing it in the process.

It was apparently his land rover but he did not have a license to drive on the road at the time. Poor chap, felt sorry for Digby because although he was so clumsy and lacked common sense, he was a nice bloke and would do anything to help you. It was arranged by me and Hayward that we would have a leaving drink or two down at the Albion Hotel in Freshwater Bay on a Saturday night.

So we all met there and everyone bar Malcolm arrived and we had a nice evening and drank a little too many rum and cokes but it didn't matter as I was walking and did not have to feed the cows in the morning. Digby was drunk as a lord that night and was slurring his words nicely.

I met Digby again in Yarmouth one day by the ferry terminal and we chatted and shared a smoke or two. He had bought this Matchless combination and the sidecar was more like a mini caravan on one wheel. He convinced me that it was very easy to ride and said I should have a go on it with him in this sidecar.

So I mounted this old beast and slowly rode it from the terminal to the mini roundabout and off towards Thorley. I got around the first bend ok but when I went over the small bridge across the marshes and around the left hand bend, I could not steer the bloody thing at all. I tried to lean it as you would a normal bike but it kept on heading for the hedge, just past the gateway and public footpath sign on the right.

I hit the hedge and the bike spun around and faced towards the railway line and the sidecar flew off and ended up in the lay-by, about two hundred yards up the road on its roof. Digby was laughing and trying to get out of the upturned sidecar at the same time, which was not working at all. I got off the bike and managed to turn the sidecar back over and got Digby out.

It was then that I realised that the sidecar had actually come apart from its base and the frame and wheel were still attached to the bike. Then I saw how the sidecar body was attached to the frame – one inch nails. No wonder it flew off with Digby inside it. Fancy nailing the body down with such tiny nails and hoping it would stay on. It could have fallen off if you stopped suddenly at traffic lights, very dangerous and luckily no one was hurt in the crash; just some blackthorns in my hand and a few scratched knuckles.

It was another load of straw that was destined for a farm in Newchurch and as usual it was done with military precision and in a convoy of tractors and trailers. Most of us made it around the roundabout in Newport except one that is. Yes poor old Graham who had pulled many a load all over the island had the unfortunate luck and his drawbar pin sheared in half and the trailer carried on without him. It turned over and resting 200 odd bales on the side of the road by the IOW College entrance. What a mess that was but did not take many minutes to reload it all and fix the trailer, which did not suffer much damage at all.

It was not long after hay making had finished and we getting prepared for the start of the dreaded barn cleaning It was announced by Mark the fitter in the workshop that morning that Malcolm would be away for the coming week as he was going on his annual holiday. Mark automatically filled in as manager when Malcolm was away for more than a day or more, which was fine as we all knew we could get away with slightly more than we could with the boss. The obvious sense of relief was evident on everyone's faces and some little jokes were made as we walked out of the workshop to begin the days toil.

A barn full of hay trailers were awaiting unloading up at *Wilmingham* barn so we all made our way up there in various tractors and began unloading the hay. Slowly we got through each load and then stopped for our traditional breakfast break at nine thirty as we did every day. In fact I began taking a break at the same time at home too, because it was just the perfect time to have a few sandwiches and some coffee. The fact that we were no longer entitled to the breakfast break didn't really make much difference to us workers but we had to keep it quiet from Malcolm and had to keep a lookout for him or we would be in some serious trouble.

Until the cunning plan of all of us installing CB radios in our tractors, we had no idea where and what the boss was up to and you really needed to know sometimes because it made you feel less on edge all the time, especially at nine thirty am.

When these devices were up and running and communications were set up, we had the upper hand for once. We could inform one another of where he was last seen and which direction he was headed and this gave you time to prepare for his appearance in the field. Grease up the machine you were using or clean the grass from the wheels before he got to you. The best thing was that it had no idea what these radios were for and I think some of the drivers just unplugged them at the end of the day and took them home so they were not stolen.

One of our favourite tricks was to make sure you were at the furthest point in the field from the track or road when he arrived. This gave you a chance not to be visited by him. We often did this at lunch times too and it annoyed him so much that he made a rule about stopping near the gateway/road at lunch times from now on. One of the most annoying things for Malcolm was if you were all working in the same field and you all congregated at the end of the field for lunch time or breakfast.

He hated it so much that he made us stop where we were working at twelve thirty and not drive half way across the field to be with your mate.

We had a young lad start on the farm and it was about the second week that he was there, when Malcolm was on holiday and Mark was left in charge as normal. This lad was very overweight and always sweated heavily whatever task we had to endure. He began to bring these smelly wet wipes with him. The perfume was horrible and smelt like air freshener had been sprayed around the barn or workshop.

There was a particular day when Mark had left the Honda truck outside the workshop doors and it was unlocked too. We borrowed a couple of these smelly wipes from the lad and put them under the seat of the truck. Mark was complaining all day that Malcolm must have installed an air freshener into the cab, but he could not find it anywhere. We did not tell him about the wipes until the end of the week, so we could remove them before his lordship returned from his holidays.

The attraction of heavy dust on surfaces and the urge to write things in the dust or dirt, and we capitalised on it in the drier barns and on Malcolm's Honda truck when he was away. In the drier barns there used to be little cat prints running along the conveyors and other feline related terms (something to do with his nick name). On his truck the remarks were somewhat stronger and the head tractor driver wrote one of the worst things and that is what got us in trouble, when he returned.

He asked all of us, but singularly if we had written on his truck and when it came to me, I admitted that I had added a few words but not swear words as it was the head tractor driver that wrote the swear words. Oops, the bloke was not happy when Malcolm accosted him in the yard for the aforementioned graffiti and he had a go at me too. I told him that I owned up to it and owned up for him too. Oh well I thought, best be honest and tell the truth – so I did.

In the end we all had to wash the truck off and were told never to do it again, we didn't, well not to the truck anyway.

Malcolm always had a black and rusty coloured toolbox in the back of his truck and having never been into the box before I assumed it was just a normal tool box like I had and everyone else carried about in their tractors and cars. Huh, imagine my surprise when he asked me to get an adjustable spanner out of his box and I took the old fert bag off the top and opened it up, because there were just four trays and no bottom tray as it must have rusted away being sat in the back of the truck. At the time I thought my God, that is tight and asked Hayward if he had seen it? He had and laughed as he commented on how it must be time he got a new one.

Next to the workshop building there was a special room that had a locked door. It was never open and always kept shut. We named it Aladdin's Cave because that is where Malcolm hoarded all the things that Mr Solomon had bought from auctions when he bought out complete hire companies and dispersed the contents. The only way into that room was a small hole in the wall in the front of the room and you needed a good ladder for that job. I know of two people who got a ladder at lunch time and went into the secret room. They did not steal anything but were just inquisitive as to what was stored in there. The lads were so fearful that the Honda truck would come in the yard while they were climbing up the ladders and into the room. I was quite tempted to shout out "Here he comes down the Road." but I didn't.

The Kawasaki KDX250 in Lana's garden, The Avenue, Freshwater in 1983.

Next door to that room where we had the grass seed dresser which was an old wooden machine from the USA; it was my job to operate this machine during the winter months to dress or clean all the grass seeds and put it all in Hessian sacks ready for sale. I had an auger that went in to the next section of the building and this was boarded up with chipboard and all the little holes in the stone walls were plugged with Hessian or fert bags and batten.

This room was home to the biggest population of mice I had ever seen and they would be running about all the time while I was operating the dresser. I guess they got used to me being there and they did not seem scared of me. The machine was not at all dusty, unlike the grain dresser I operated during harvest. It was relatively quiet too and I like using it a lot because it was nice and clean and I could even plug my radio into the socket next to it and hear it. I am not sure exactly how many tons of grass seed I put through that machine but when my store was getting low, we would get the big auger in and take a few trailer loads out of the drier barn tanks and put it on the small store for me to carry on cleaning it all.

I listened to operation Dessert Storm When the UK and US invaded Iraq on my little radio whilst using the dresser that year.

I always parked my bike in front of the grass seed storage bin, next to our Massey Ferguson seed drill and the McConnell rear mounted digger. As they did not move very often and there was loads of space there, I thought it was a perfect spot for my Superdream to sit in the dry.

One day while I was out doing some fencing, Malcolm had to move my bike as he wanted to get to something behind it. Hayward and Mark told me he nearly dropped the bike as he didn't realise quite how heavy it was when he went to move it. That was a heavy bike indeed and when I dropped it in the ice that morning, I could not lift it up and it took four blokes to get it on its wheels again. After that episode with moving my bike, I was told to park my bike around by the office with all the cars.

I am sure we had to park them there so he could see us sneaking off home from the office window. I was quick when I had my Yamaha XJ550; I was out of that yard and up the road before anyone could catch me and you needed to be with Malcolm on the prowl.

I wasn't seeing anyone at the time when I met a girl on a bike down at Freshwater Bay. She was on holiday on the island from her home in Muswell Hill, London. Anyway we saw each

other a lot and she used to come round to my
bedroom in the flat and have some wild nights.
One night I was with her in the bedroom and
suddenly someone opened my window and took
a photo with an instant camera and was
laughing as they disappeared onto the flat roof
outside my window. It was a set up by my Dad
and his baker friend and they took a photo of me
lying on the bed with my bike boots still on. It
was the talk of the bakery for weeks and I never
lived that one down for a very long time.
Another example of the somewhat embarrassing
things that I had to endure, and mainly because
of my father.

When it was time for her to go back home to
London, I went back with her and her mate and
it was my first ever visit to a MacDonald's
restaurant, which was in Tottenham Court Road.
Her mate worked in Odeon cinema there and we
all went up to the projection room and watched
a film there. Then we went off to see Harrods, as
she worked there. Then to her home and had
some good fun there too. We went out at night
on the bikes and went to a pub in Epping Forest
and stopped outside White Hart Lane football
ground and then back to her house. We also
went to the Alexandra Palace too and some other
sights that I had never heard of. I was sleeping
in her sister's room and she sneaked in at night

and almost killed me I can tell you. Oh my giddy aunt, I could not keep up with her. It was not long after I came back to the island and really never heard from her for quite a while, well until a bunch of flowers arrived for my Mother with a letter saying that I was the father of her baby?? I was bloody shocked and never heard a bloody word from her from that day onwards-am I a Father or was it a con?

It was a misty morning in late September when the days were growing shorter and the air was starting to become much colder in both the morning and the evening. Harvest was finished and cultivation was well under way on some parts of the farm. I was instructed to put the small Lely fertiliser spinner on my 5000 and to go up to the Ham field and wait for Malcolm to meet me there. So I did the requested tasks and waited on the Ham for him to arrive.

When he arrived I was shown how to mark out the correct distance from my first wheel marks and to put this large stick with an old fertiliser bag attached and wrapped around it, into the ground. After a few attempts at getting it right due to my footsteps being a lot larger than Malcolm's. It was time to get into the tractor and have Malcolm hanging on the side doorway instructing me to pick a landmark on the other side of the field and aim in a straight line towards it. So off I went, very nervously indeed because he was watching every move I made.

We travelled across the field and reached the far headland and the tree I was aiming for. Everything seemed ok at this point and I was pleased that I had done it right for a change. So then I had to turn around and aim for the little stick/flag thing on the other side of the field.

Now this would have been fine if it was not so damn misty, because I could not see the trees on the other headland, let alone this tiny stick thing. I tried to sight the stick but just could not see it in the mist and subsequently missed the flag and ended up about twenty feet away from it.

Malcolm jumped down from the side door and took his hat off, threw it on the soil and jumped on it. I guessed by his reaction that maybe I had got it slightly wrong. So funny looking back, but not at the time I can assure you. I told him I could not see the bloody stick through the mist and he backed off a little and we tried it all again and this time I got it right. I was not actually spinning fertiliser during this test thank god but in later years; I was given the job of doing all the spinning on the farm, which was a kind of promotion.

I remember one day I was in the workshop with Mark and Malcolm asked me to weld up some liquid feeder stands. I had not done very much welding and this was going to be a challenge for me. I did manage to weld one leg back on and was trying to weld the other leg on and it just was not working for me. I ground off the rubbish weld and tried again, but alas I was not very good at welding so I told Mark he could do it because I'm just going to make a mess of it. He laughed and carried on with the job while I did something more accustomed to my abilities instead. I tried over the years to become more competent at welding and tried all types to no avail so I will stick to soldering as it is more "me" and a damn sight easier too.

One of Malcolm's favourite sayings was *never assume anything*. At the time, I didn't really take on board, being a mere teenager with his my in the clouds and thinking of only three things, music, girls and motorbikes. It was highly unlikely for me to comprehend what he had said to me and just blanked it out with all the other advice he gave. In latter days I applied it to every situation that relied on it and especially one occasion concerning young Taylor and a 100 ton bin of barley. Malcolm told me one day to stop walking about in a dream world, I know he was right.

I was running the drier barn from the start of the day at eight o'clock and slowly putting through the final trailer loads of barley from the combine. The grain bin was very near full to its brim. By the time the last of the grain had gone up the elevator, after I had checked the dresser was empty and pushed the weighing machine over to empty it, the bin had to be raked from the edge to the centre so that none would spill into the adjoining bins or catwalk.

This was probably one of the most critical times in the drier barn because cross contamination of the grain would cost the farm a lot of money and probably end up losing your job over it. It was getting near to lunch time and I was just waiting for the barley to finish going through, when young Taylor arrived at the barn door and was relieving me so I could have my half hour break. He knew the barn as well as I did and had spent plenty of time learning the system during the winter months when grain was unloaded from the bins into Lorries.

I was not expecting any problems in the mere thirty minutes for nammet. Malcolm always took over the combine during lunch time because Mark the fitter had to go home and have a proper meal and take his insulin as he was diabetic.

I had my lunch and was chatting to the new grounds man of the manor house, who had been living and working in France designing and building golf courses for a living. Interesting chap, who had plenty of tales to yarn at lunch times and because I had gone round to the manor drive to chat to the gardener and I had not heard the old Thames Trader grain truck drive into the yard.

It had just deposited a load of Avalon wheat into the pit and gone back up to the ninety five acre field, just up the road from the farm. I walked back to the drier barn and saw the pit full of the wheat and the dresser was vibrating away as it was just about to get its first batch of grain. Taylor was standing by the dresser, watching the tail wheat come out of the chutes and into the fert bags and I said "have you changed the cross conveyor direction and opened the right slides?" He just nodded as he carried a bag of chaff out to the trailer next door.

I was checking that the dresser was not chucking out whole wheat grains, which it often did if the flow was too fast for the machine or the incorrect sieves were installed. It was all going nicely on the ground floor so I decided to have a look at the conveyors and make sure Taylor had set the things correctly. I climbed the ladder onto the catwalk and ducked my head as I passed under the cross conveyor, then I looked in horror at the wheat pouring out onto the barley bin I had previously finished loading. I ran over to the edge of the safety rails and shouted to Taylor "Shut the pit slide." He stood there gazing at me for a few seconds and I shouted at him again "shut the fucking pit slide!" He jumped across the lower conveyor and stamped on the slide handle. As he was doing this, I had come down off the catwalk and hit all the stop buttons on the control panel. "You plank" I shouted to Taylor, "You didn't change the slides on the cross conveyor so the wheat has gone on top of the barley bin". He didn't say a thing as he climbed up the ladder to see for himself what he had done. I went up after him and we managed to shovel the majority of the wheat into bags and dump it in the correct bin. When we had finished, there was hardly a grain left on the Barley surface and Taylor's butt was saved.

Now that was a prime example of never assume anything and I should have gone straight up to the bins and checked that Taylor had changed the slides properly in the first place. It did not matter if you had changed the direction of the cross conveyor, if the wrong slides were left open, then the wrong grain would either end up on the catwalk or the wrong bin and cause a lot of trouble.

Marcus with the bikes in a village in Snowdonia in 1981.

Taylor feeding straw on Goldings Marsh in 1987.

One day I was out in one of the Hayles fields up at *Wilmingham* and busy tedding up the straw for baling as there had been heavy dew that morning and the straw needed a good fluffing up to dry it quicker. Moving up and down the rows and suddenly out of the corner of my eye I caught a glimpse of the white pickup turning into the track at the top of the hill. Malcolm drove down to the edge of the field as I was coming along a row close to where he was parked.

He flagged me down and I stopped the Tedder and got out of the tractor and walked over to him. He was picking up the straw in clumps and checking how dry it was as he said "this is drying nicely so I think we can start baling very soon". I said "shall I carry on then and finish the whole field?" he replied "Yes, you carry on and hopefully the baler won't be far behind you, as I do not know if he had finished servicing it yet" I smiled with a devious feeling inside my head and said "He is coming up the road now as he just left the farm about two minutes ago.".

His face was a picture as he looked at me and said "how do you know where the baler is then?" I said "I just talked to him on the CB radio and he said he was on his way up to *Wilmingham* track." "So you can talk to him on that thing?" "Yes I can talk to him and all the others who have them in their cabs." "Oh, well that's good then" he replied, in a somewhat reluctant manner, as he got back into his truck and sped off up the track leaving a cloud of dust in his wake.

Many times I remember being up at the barn at *Wilmingham* and unloading straw into the stacks and the sun was getting higher in the sky over Yarmouth and it was really warming up. Along came our saviour, the Hopkins milk van from Yarmouth, doing his deliveries through *Wilmingham*. We always jumped down off the stack to grab a couple of pints of milk or in latter days, fizzy drinks too. I really enjoyed my morning pint of milk and it seemed to give you that extra bit of energy for the day.

Getting the trailers unloaded before it began to get too warm in August was an essential practice because being up in the roof of the barn was unbearable, especially humping bales about up there. This gave the baler a head start on us "carters" and in turn, the combine needed to await the dew burning off before Mark was unleashed on the crops. Being Mark and knowing his meticulous nature with machines, you could pretty well bet on what time the combine would be starting and then the sorting out of who was running the drier that week. If it was the new barn it was usually myself but the old drier was normally someone else's responsibility, which was fine by me because I was not keen running the old machine as it was a temperamental old beast at the best of times.

I always carried two flasks of either hot water or one coffee and one hot water so I had enough hot drink for the other unofficial break time which was usually at about half six in the evening. This, we referred to as tea time, as I have mentioned earlier. Malcolm stopped at this time every day of the year and would toddle off to his cottage and leave us in the field to have ours. He always said "Have your bit of tea, then carry on" whatever we were doing. If you did not have enough food or drinks then you bloody well cursed yourself because you usually had another five hours of work to do and hunger or thirst does not help you at all doing this amount of physical work.

Now because we could guarantee that Malcolm would be going home at this time, we could use it as our escape time and sneak back to the farm, park up the tractor somewhere where he would not see it straight away, usually behind the Mill House or in the hay barn if there was space.

Then get on your bike and go like hell. How many times did he cotton on to this and caught us and it was always just as you had got on the bike. The excuses that we came up with were pretty poor but usually he would let you go and make up the time the following day.

The working hour's laws had recently changed for the better in many ways, apart from losing our morning break. We now started work half hour later and finished at half four instead of five o'clock.

Overtime began earlier too which helped a lot with extra money. We also lost half hour of our lunch break, but to me it was far too long having an hour lunch break and I was always bored by the time I had eaten my sandwiches and drank my tea.

Although when I first started on the farm I would actually ride home to Totland for my lunch break and it was always handy if you needed fuel or more food and drink for the long days ahead. Fuel was always a problem for me when we worked so many late nights and all the garages had shut by the time I was on my way home. There was always Yarmouth's Mill Road garage, but it was always queued up and when you only had thirty minutes to get there and back plus eat your lunch.

I hardly ever bothered and subsequently always ran out of fuel on the way home. The times I had to borrow some fuel from my mate Taylor on his bike as my bike would first go onto two cylinders and then one cylinder and finally come to a halt along the road past *Wilmingham* barn.

Putting the choke on always got you a few hundred metres but never enough to get home. So siphoning fuel from Taylor's KMX125 was a regular thing and I always gave him a few pounds for his fuel. I do not know why, but I always ran out of fuel near *Wilmingham* Barn? Never anywhere else but always just past it, Strange.

Boredom at lunch time turned into mischievous activities such as removing my exhausts from the Superdream and going up the road and past Malcolm's house sounding like a plane or putting radios in tractors or lights on the back. The other lads had their cars to tinker with and you would always find them fiddling with them at lunch time, around the back of the yard near the office.

One time we were all working in one of the larger fields up near *Wilmingham*, which was on the opposite side of the road to the barn, down a small track amongst some forestry and pheasant rearing areas. The fields were known as big Ham, little Ham and Bushfields; they were connected to the *Barnsfield* fields but farmed separately.

The big ham was a very level area and surrounded on three sides by woodland which made it a very warm place during summer because of the lack of wind that blew there. There was a rather dodgy looking patch of reeds growing at the lower part of the field and it is situated close to the woodland that stretched to the rear of Afton Farm and its adjoining land.

This patch was a peat bog and very deep in places too. I only got stuck in it once and that was enough for me because although I had only skimmed it with my disc harrows, it caught me out nicely and my tractor went down in the bog, right up to the bottom of the sump and cab steps. I had to walk back to the farm and get the head tractor driver to come up with his Ford County and pull me out.

When I arrived in the yard to look for Hayward, I met Malcolm and told him I had got stuck in the bog and his reply was "I hope you tied a flag around the exhaust", laughed and walked off. That made me think and when I had found the driver and we had gone back up to the ham, I was listening to the tales that Hayward was telling me about machines and animals that had disappeared in the bog. To this day, I'm not sure if they were on a wind up mission but seeing the way my tractor sunk so quickly, I thought maybe some of it was true.

It took a few attempts to free the tractor from the bog and even the county was struggling with the pull. I never ever went anywhere near the reeds again after that experience and I don't think anyone else managed to get stuck in it after that.

There was a really smooth track going around the headland of the three fields and it was quite nice not bouncing around the cab for a change. There were at least four of us working the same field and it was quite a rare thing as we were not normally put together in the same place because we may have wasted time talking or such like and that would never do. I remember lunch time and we all moved near the track end of the field and sat on the grass or leaned against the tractor wheels and chatted.

Malcolm's face was a picture when he arrived to give us our wages. All of us chatting and having a good laugh and it did not get a smile of approval from him at all. He just passed out the wage packets, said a few words and drove off for his lunch. One of the only few times he had nothing much to say on the matter.

When he had gone and we had all finished lunch, we decided it would be a good laugh to have a race around the track and see whose tractor was the quickest. I don't know who won the race but it was a bloody good laugh because there was only enough room for one machine on the smooth track so every now and then, you had to go onto the field to overtake and it was a bumpy as hell.

There were tools, nammet bags and drawbar pins flying about in the cab and dust everywhere as it was such a dry area of land. A real escape from the normality of cultivation anyway.

One particular event that always comes back and makes me smile was when Hayward the head tractor driver arranged with his fire brigade associates to stage an exercise in the Old Drier Barn one evening. There was to be a fire in the barn and a dummy stuck under the wheel of the grain lorry and a person inside the cab of the lorry, which the brigade had to rescue wearing breathing apparatus. Yes, I was the dummy in the cab, no jokes please. As the smoke canisters were set off, I was sitting in the lorry looking out into the darkness as the doors closed waiting.

Then I saw the torch beams through the smoke and the firemen open the cab door and carry me out of the smoke filled barn. They jacked up the lorry and removed the dummy from the rear wheels and took that outside. It was damned good fun and something completely different for me at the time too. I was called a dummy for a few weeks after by my colleagues but it was all harmless fun really.

As I may have mentioned occasionally before, Malcolm did not think that having a radio in a tractor was a good idea because it distracted the driver from his work. In some cases he was correct in his thinking because some implements made certain sounds and you tended to tune into the sounds that they made and this gave you the indication that it was working correctly.

When a machine or implement starts to make out of ordinary sounds then you know something is wrong and loud music in the cab does blank out these tell tale noises. This only really applied to the newer tractors back in the eighties, when we started to have *Q cabs*, or quiet cabs

I didn't have a *Q cab* on my Ford 5000 tractor and the noise levels from the engine alone was all you could really hear, regardless of what implements you were using. The only way I could listen to music in that old tractor was to use stereo headphones so some of the background noises were blanked out. There were no places in the cab for a radio, so I had to jam my radio/cassette up in the roof, where there was a small void between the top of the windscreen and the roof, just large enough to ram it in.

When I moved up the ladder so to speak and inherited a Ford 6600 tractor with the new cab, things changed dramatically. I had a purpose made space in the roof for a radio/cassette and it had a heater and a decent tool box. I even had somewhere to put my Nammet bag without it falling down between the rear axle and the gearbox as it did it the 5000. Luxury was entering agriculture at long last and I didn't need my camping stove anymore to keep me warm on cold winter days out in the fields. I had the stove sat on the gearbox at breakfast and lunch breaks in the 5000 because when that cold northerly wind blew across the fields in winter, that cab was bloody useless and was never warm, so the stove worked a treat. Our other 5000's had a back window and this canvas piece that went down from the fixed back window to the rear axle and was a lot warmer. I did not have that on my tractor though I often thought about making some canvas rear cover but never got around to it.

Me about to go off to HMP Camphill Farm with a TW15 and 300 bales in 1987.

Chapter 17

The late 80's

When I was given the John Deere 2130 tractor I was in my element because this machine had a lovely spacious cab with everything I needed for long days out in the fields. I fitted a new radio/cassette deck and CB radio and a few extra halogen Cibie lamps on the back for those late nights on cultivation. I loved that tractor and having a syncro gearbox was an absolute first for me as I was so used to those old crash boxes with the double de clutch element. Fully hydraulic steering and not just assisted steering which made a hell of a difference if you drive a tractor for a living and spend most of your day in one.

That is what people who did not drive these machines never understood about what you had in the cab and thought the added extras were just luxuries that were just there to impress the buyer. As I used to tell people "you spend from eight in the morning until half ten at night in that cab, seven days a week for a month, which I often endured during cultivation and pre cultivation, and tell me what is luxurious about it?

When the Ford TW15's were our main large machines and because of their size and power they were very good for towing the straw trailers about and you knew that the tractor could stop the trailer easily and not have to worry about throwing a parachute out the window as we did with the little 5000's. They were both fitted with radio cassette decks as standard and to us that was a luxury and it meant we didn't have to hide them in the mill house at night and fit the stereos.

Someone used a TW one weekend when there was no one else around on the farm, nothing unusual there; Malcolm would often take the saw bench on the back of a tractor, down to his cottage and spend the weekend logging for the coming winter months. However, this time he was the centre of attention by us workers because Hayward said "someone has tuned my radio into Radio Solent and I left it on a different station on Friday when I went home?" So who was it that did not like radios in tractors but tuned the one in the TW for listening to his preferred station? "Ha Ha" it was one of the best moments amongst us chaps because now we had the ammunition to fire back with if we needed to.

Similarly, with the drier barn when people would say "oh its all automatic, you just sit there and press buttons all day." I really wished it was like that because my job would be wanted by everyone on the farm and the strange thing was – no one else wanted to run the drier barn, I wonder why?

Was it the dust and chaff flying up in the air when our lorry tipped its load from the combine or was it the constant checking and replacing of the dresser bags or was it the noise from the elevators, conveyors, dresser and drier? When I was seventeen, I was put in that barn and learnt everything there was to know about our grain handling systems. I had to learn to set up the blower at the end of the main conveyor which we put outside, next to the silos. So I could clean and dry the corn and send it from my barn right out the back of the barn and eventually, into the silos.

Everything had to be just so or you would have a massive spillage on your hands. The rate that the corn was supplied to the dresser was controlled by an adjustable slide on the pit. If you sent too much from the pit and up the elevator, you would have grain pouring out over the top of the sieves in the dresser and it made a right mess.

In the worst case scenario, you could overload the main elevator and then you were in big trouble because if that jammed up, everything stopped and this was because it was a double sided elevator in which both sides went in unison. One feed came from the pit and up the right side of the elevator and the other was fed from the weigher and this went into the main conveyor and the top of the barn. Then you had the choice of either sending it along the main conveyor to the cross conveyor, which ran ninety degrees to the main conveyor and fed into the one hundred ton bins.

The cross conveyor had slides along its length so you could fill different parts of the bins, it was also reversible, so you could send it to either side of the barn as the bins were on both sides. You could also send it to the end of the main conveyor and outside the back of the barn to a blower. The catwalk ran along the top of the bins and underneath the length of the main conveyor. Underneath the cat walk there was an enclosed tunnel and under the floor of the tunnel was the bottom conveyor. This was fed from the bins via large slides which had to be pulled up to open them. They were a bad design as they would often jam up from grain getting caught in the slide grooves.

Similarly as on a grain trailer with a slide fitted but with a difference, in that you could not get to the internal part of the slide if the bins were full.

The tunnel served two purposes in that it was an air tunnel and access tunnel to the slides and bottom conveyor. At the back of the barn, where a blower would be mounted, was a huge fan which was powered by a Ford diesel engine and it was fed from its own fuel tank mounted on concrete blocks. When the fan was started it would blow air through the tunnel and down through magnetic flaps which had to be opened manually. When the flaps were open to the relevant bin, then the air was directed into ducts in the bottom of the bins. The ducts had slots facing towards the tunnel and should have blown the grain into the open slide ports and finally into the bottom conveyor and then it was taken to the pit. I said should have, because the emptying system was bloody useless and too slow.

It literally took all day to empty one bin by air, so most of the time we had to shovel the bloody grain into the bottom conveyor by hand. It wasn't the shovelling that made you want to get the hell out of there it was the air blowing all the dust and chaff up the side of the tunnel and back into the bins.

Masks were essential and I don't mean paper ones, they had to be rubber masks with filters if you wanted to live longer. It always filled the catwalk with chaff and dust and was a complete waste of time and money in my view. Whoever designed the emptying system was on another planet because it never worked, even with lighter grains such as Linseed or Peas. It was a shame because the rest of the systems worked as they should and made the movement of our crops a lot easier.

Later on we had a big dust extractor fitted in the top of the barn and this made a difference when the lorry tipped its load in the pit. When I first started in that barn, there was no drier and just the dresser. All the drying was done at the back of the farm by the *Allmet* continuous flow drier, or the Old Drier as it was known as.

Now the Allmet was installed circa nineteen sixty nine or early nineteen seventies. Basically, it was a stack of conveyors that moved very slowly along a mesh floor and pushed small metal plates with brushes mounted on the bottom of the conveyors. There were three layers of these conveyors and the grain was fed from the pit, up a double sided elevator and into the top of the drier. It was then pushed along by the conveyor over the mesh floor and then fell down onto the next level down and along the next conveyor and so on.

There were three big extractor fans, one for each level, which blew out into the yard. The diesel powered heater was on the left side of the drier and was like a massive jet engine when it was alight. Loved lighting the burner because of the huge rush of flames and heat it produced, a sense of extreme power. A boy thing I guess. So the heat went into a large metal box on the end of the drier where the heat expanded and was sucked into the conveyor levels by the fans. Thus heating and drying the grain.

There were adjustable Perspex slides on each level, which adjusted the amount of suction on the grain so the chaff would be pulled out of the conveyor and blown out into the yard. At the rear of the drier was a small silo which was fed by a small conveyor mounted above the silo. The feed came from the overflow of the drier and that gave you a good storage space if the grain was very moist. The *holding silo* as we called it was emptied by an auger and went straight back into the pit so you could then send it back through the drier.

So if the combine had slowed down or stopped for some reason, then you could start on the excess grain in the silo until the combine was cutting again.

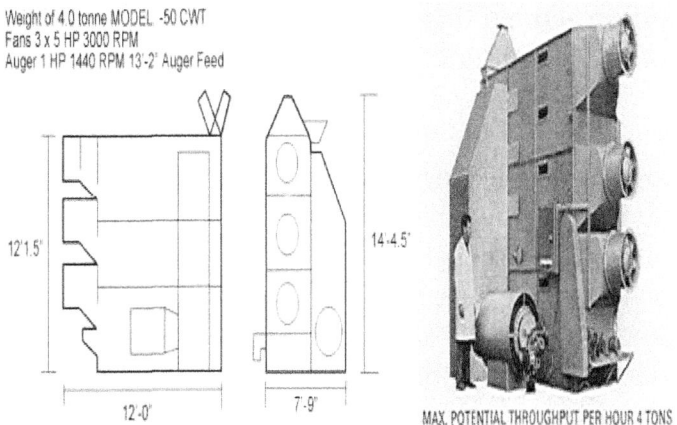

Weight of 4.0 tonne MODEL -50 CWT
Fans 3 x 5 HP 3000 RPM
Auger 1 HP 1440 RPM 13'-2' Auger Feed

12'1.5"

14-4.5'

12'-0'

7'-9"

MAX. POTENTIAL THROUGHPUT PER HOUR 4 TONS

Product information on the Allmet drier.

The output from the drier went into the other side of the elevator and out to either a weighing machine and then into a blower, which blew it all into the back of the barn. If you didn't want to store it in the back of the barn you could direct it into a lorry of trailer for taking around to the dresser and stored in the bins or silos. I remember running the drier one day and the conveyor chain snapped on one side and it was on the top level. The only way you could fix it was to unbolt a panel on the side of the level and climb inside on your belly and drag yourself along the conveyor. Apart from those chains and sometimes the burner refused to fire up, it was very reliable considering how much work it had done through the years. When it was first commissioned there was nothing to collect up the chaff that blew out of the fans.

You can imagine the muddy back yard with huge puddles everywhere and the chaff blowing out into the puddle yard and mixing with the mud and water. It was the biggest mud bath on the farm and the only part that had not been concreted. There were just a couple of dead trees and where the mud went up to the edge of the yard, it was really deep. I used to put fert bags on my feet to walk round to the drier in winter because no matter if you had Wellies on, you would get wet and muddy. So when I left the farm in nineteen eighty, I left all this mess behind me and when I came back in nineteen eighty four it was all concreted and new implement sheds were erected on two sides of the yard. Also someone had the brains to build a cover over the end of the extractor fans with a small door which could allow you to get the loader bucket in there to remove the chaff. What a difference it all made to the working out the back and in the drier barn. We also had a system of pipes that could feed into the silos from the old drier barn, via the blower. This gave us total flexibility in where we wanted to move the grain and made it was less dependant on weather conditions and the use of trailers or lorries.

The annual Agricultural Show in Newport was the place to visit if you worked on a farm in the early eighties, as everyone who worked on farms went to that show to drool over the latest monster tractors etc. We were given the choice of either going in the morning or the afternoon but you had to come back if it was busy. I always went in the afternoons because that way I could go to the town and do some shopping.

Spend an hour or so at the show and then sneak off to town was the only way to get anywhere near decent shops until at least November. There was never any time off from April to around October because harvest then ran into cultivation and then the cattle had to come in and you were then put on a feeding rota. The show itself was quite interesting back in those days and looking around at all the latest machines and labour saving ideas, fascinated me. You always came away with lots of brochures and stickers and things. I enjoyed the show until it became boring and never had much to look at during the nineties.

I don't think I ever went again after that because I just found it a waste of time and I had better things to spend my time doing. I remember Taylor, my workmate was supposedly ill one day and it was a Sunday during harvest and he stupidly went to a fete on Colwell common. You can imagine what happened when the manager's wife saw him there. Silly sod.

One of our four wheelers parked in Wilmingham Barn, awaiting unloading. Circa 1987.

Chapter 18

The last months in Totland Bay

Because we had a large workshop with a garage and a stable block, our house became the meeting point of most adventures and wild evenings back in the early 80's. My friend and I had managed to turn this old workshop into a bike fixing room which had a loft and storage room. We bought the couple of old Honda CB200's and a Yamaha RD200DX to do up and sell. Now this was as well as working full time on the farm so rather a hobby more than a business. We had got some tools together and set up a room with a stereo for stripping down the bikes and cleaning them up.

As I mentioned earlier, there was also a small self contained living area which adjoined the workshop and garage and this was where my brother Liam and I slept. It had its own bathroom with a shower and toilet but was very damp during the winter months, especially when we had our butane gas heater going full blast. My brother had put two fruit machines in the room which he somehow got from the owners of Totland pier amusements. They attracted a lot of attention and there was always a mate of ours putting money in one of them of an evening.

The word soon got round that we could repair bikes very cheaply and we had no end of people turning up wanting a repair doing to their bikes. So that is why the house was so attractive to the hoards of long lost bikers and friends. Now my Father had left us, we had no silly rules to abide by and my Mother would have anyone in the house, well up to a point anyway.

Card games lasting all night and going out on night rides, then returning for coffees later on. It all went on there and looking back, they were good times without a doubt. There was the odd undesirable that would arrive at the house but we put a stop to that by hanging a five bar metal gate across the drive. This gave us time to see who it was and decide if we really wanted them to see our workshop or sheds. There were a number of dodgy thieving people about and they would stop at nothing to steal your tools etc.

We had chickens and one of the best deterrents for dodgy people, a pair of geese. They could hear for miles and we always knew if a bike was coming through the village or up the drive as the geese would kick off. The male goose, George was an evil goose and would chase you around the garden to get his beak on your bum. He must have chased all of us at one time and was better than our dog for keeping people at bay.

One day we started getting problems with foxes coming into the garden and trying to get our chickens. They must have had a couple if I remember correctly and this upset my Mother and sister immensely. So I decided it was time for some action and I had to think of something to keep the buggers away from the chicken house.

Oh I forgot to mention that we didn't have a chicken house at all, but we had converted our greenhouse into a nice home for the chickens and it served them very well. It was aluminium framed which was to work to my advantage in the planning of my anti fox system. I decided to construct an electric fence machine from an old car coil, flasher relay and a car battery. I built it inside an ice cream tub and set it up on the metal gate for testing purposes; what voltage this thing produced, I had no idea but it was very powerful indeed.

One afternoon I was working out how to connect this thing to the chicken greenhouse and came up with putting metal grids all around the base of the house and connecting the earth wire to them all and then putting the HT end from the coil onto the chicken wire which we had going all around the bottom 3 feet of the house. It was lethal to humans, let alone foxes.

I had to test it myself, so I touched the thing while standing bare feet on the grids and bang, it nearly shot me across the garden – no more fox problems after that was installed. Knowing what power this contraption was capable of, I wired up the gate and we all waited for "Magnetron" as he was known as because you couldn't get rid of him. He didn't have a bike and really was the most annoying bloke I ever met. Even if you told him you were out in a minute, he would still hang about. So this time I thought, maybe he would get this bloody message and leave us alone.

We all hid in the garden, behind the chicken greenhouse and kept very quiet as we heard magnetron walking up the drive, the geese making a racket warned us of his arrival. Suddenly there was this scream as he went to put his hand on the gate and the volts must have shot up his arm, he didn't stay and walked off in a hurry.

A party was being held by the drummer, Izzy and it was going to be at his new girlfriend's house in Newport. It was in fact in a block of several rooms in two houses converted into one single residential block. It was on the Parkhurst estate where quite a number of my school friends once lived. It was quite a good night and

I met this nurse and stayed the night as I was slightly drunk and in not fit state to get home, which I couldn't anyway as I had a lift with the drummer. She was a nice girl and we got on well for quite a while but pastures greener came along and it was soon the end of that relationship. It was after all a set-up by the drummer and his girl because this girl didn't have anyone and at the time I was free and single so I treated the whole affair as kind of temporary and almost fake in some respects. The strangest thing about the location of the party was that we moved only one road up from that house in nineteen eighty eight and our house was exactly the same layout as that house.

In nineteen eighty, I met this girl at the Broadway Inn and we started to go out with each other. I was unaware that she had this weird ex boyfriend who would not leave her alone, because she failed to mention him when we first started going out. It was this girl that started me smoking cigarettes and I really wish I had not even met her now for that reason alone. She smoked Rothmans and got me to try it one night; of course I did not do it properly at first and just sucked in the smoke and blew it out again. I thought it was pointless and horrible. From the horrible taste of it and the smell on her breath all the time, I could have been so close to not even trying it again, but unfortunately she taught me to take the smoke inside and keep it there for a few seconds and that was it, I was hooked. Sad really and whenever I see that brand of smokes,

I think of how close I got to not starting smoking. I was engaged to this girl for a very short time, three weeks I think. This was because someone had informed me that a strange bike was parked outside her house on a night I was not going to see her. I figured it out for myself and found out she was seeing her ex again.

Another party and another new girlfriend came along and this time she was very normal and not into weird stuff. We both had a common interest in bikes and rock music. She had a small 125 and it needed some work to get it ready for the road, so I helped her with it and got it roadworthy again. I had just taken off a side panel from the bike and was removing the battery so we could top up the water and charge it up.

I took out the battery and put it on the picnic table in the garden and started to prize off the little plugs so I could top up the cells. I only had a screwdriver so I used it to lever up the caps. The first one was easy but as I lifted the second one, there must have been some pressure in the cells and whoosh the cap shot off and sprayed sulphuric acid into both of my eyes.

I was in agony and could not see a thing and I screamed out to my girlfriend and she came running outside to see what was wrong. She took me into the shower room and sprayed the cold shower on my face and eyes. It took a long time for the pain and burning to die down and my eyes were horrendous for hours. I went straight to the doctor the next day because when I woke up in the morning, I could not see a bloody thing. I had sensitive eyes as it was and this did not help me one bit. I had to have my eyes washed every day and cream and drops put in them for weeks afterwards.

I learnt a painful lesson that day and will never open up a battery like that again. I carried on seeing this girl for a few months but it died out and we went our separate ways.

During the first winter that I did not work on the farm, I had made sure I had accumulated a lot of money for the November to April break and it had to last the duration because I did not want to have to find another job in the winter months. I had bought a few motorcycles in the summer and had them ready in the sheds and stables at *Dreens*. I planned to get them done up and sold and I was hoping that the bikes would give me sufficient extra income to possibly buy a couple more bikes in the winter.

Things were going pretty well and I had finished two bikes before the end of January and one was sold. I was OK for money at the time but could have done with a few more pounds to give me a cushion as it were, just in case one of the bikes did not sell or if I needed a new tyre or parts on my own bike.

Luckily enough for me I had so many mates from all walks of life that I did not need to worry about extra work at all. Back in the eighties, work was never a big problem for me and I never had to sign on as unemployed for more than a month or so at any one time. Being in a band and having a lot of contacts from bikes and the biker fraternity gave me so many job offers that I could not physically do all of them. First of all I was given about 5 wks work doing roofing on a block of flats down in darkest Ryde and it was a first for me as I had never been so bloody high up on scaffold before that one. As I had a Volkswagen beetle at the time and I used to give my mates a lift to the job everyday. They paid me petrol for the lifts so that worked out just fine. There were a few days when it was impossible to get on the roof due to the rain and high winds.

It was getting close to May and I was looking forward to being back on the farm again and earning decent wages again. I went down to see Malcolm and we agreed on a start date which was a week or so from the meeting. So I was back in the earning department and would need to save up for another bike or two, to do up and sell.

The Yamaha RD250DX that I won in a game of cards a year or so ago, was still stored in the old stable where I had parked it. My mate, who got me the job on the dredger, lent me a compressor and spray gun for the task of respraying the frame etc. Also he had so many tins of paint in his shed that he just let me pick a colour for the frame, which was a lot cheaper than buying cans of Dupli-Colour paint from the garage. A lot easier on the fingers because of not having to keep your fingers on the aerosol can nozzle for hours on end too. I went for a metallic green for the frame and white for the tank etc. The bike went through various changes including having Yamaha RD 250LC exhausts and a front nose cone fairing from a Kawasaki GPZ550 including oblong headlamp. Turned out a great looking machine and sold it for a nice profit.

Unfortunately, within a week of selling it, the idiot who bought it crashed it on Colwell bend, due to going too fast. Another classic bike that I bought was a Montesa 247 Cota trials bike. It was not in the best of shape when I got it and although it ran perfectly, the gear lever needed repairing as did the kick start. The clutch lever had to be replaced too as it was so bent that you had no travel on it. It was road registered but like my old Greaves, had no lights and only a bicycle horn on the handlebars.

It was a completely different machine to what I was used to, with its all in one fibreglass tank and seat unit which also formed the rear mudguard too. Not at all comfy for riding on the road but as soon as it was off road it would go almost anywhere. I rode it to work and had some fun riding it across our stubble fields and taking short cuts up across the *Wilmingham* track and down tot the railway line.

New Years Eve in nineteen eighty two was a monumental night in our house. We wanted to have a fancy dress party as we had never had one before. So instead of just providing a loud stereo, we decided to have the band in the lounge.

As the lounge was over twenty five feet long, we were able to set the drum kit up in one corner and had the keyboards and amps in another. The guitarists stood forward of the drums, so he wasn't obscured. We set up a buffet in the kitchen in the afternoon and Mum and Dad prepared all the meats and other nibbles. I came up with a brilliant prank, whilst gazing at all these tubs and bowls of crisps etc. I put a small bowl of Go Cat out amongst the other bowls. Tim was with me when I did it and we were dying to see who would eat them first.

As the evening arrived, we were waiting for Izzy and Pondy to arrive so we could start playing. Tim and I had a bottle or two, so we made sure we had a skinful before playing. Guests were arriving and it was so good to see so many people filling our lounge. The drummer and bass player arrived and we started playing our stuff. The party was absolutely fantastic and I have never enjoyed a new year, like I enjoyed that one! Everyone was dancing and just having fun. Not one complaint from anyone who lived nearby either. Oh, and the Go Cat bowl was empty at the end of the night.

I remember the week I first had the Montesa bike on the road, was the week Malcolm was on holiday and this was about the end of September as all the fields were cut and we had started to burn some of them off. I took the bike down to *Barnsfield* as we were moving some machinery around down there to make some more room. The head tractor driver asked me if he could have a go on the bike in the field just behind the old parlour which was now used as storage for Mr Solomon's vintage tractor collection. He got on the bike and just opened up the throttle and the bike shot out from underneath him and wheelied and almost mounted the bale elevator nearby. It was so funny and we all laughed as he picked himself up off the ground and the bike just stopped as it fell over. It was built so well that falling over did not damage a single part of the bike.

Hayward the head tractor driver obviously had never been on a bike before and I always wondered why he wanted to have a go on that bike as he never bothered with any of my other ones? I kept that bike for the winter and sold it in the spring as I needed something more comfortable on the road.

We had three dogs when we lived at the *Dreens* and one looked almost pure black Labrador and her daughter who was a cross with a Heinz fifty seven, from down the garage. We then got a Jack Russell crossed with a Lakeland terrier as my sister wanted her own little dog. They all got on very well and were always taken out for walks by us kids and usually on the Warren or up on Tennyson Downs and sometimes in the summer, to the beach. Although they got very wet and sandy down there and it made a mess of the dog room so we avoided going to the beach.

The Yamaha RD250DX I customized in 1981. My old beetle in the background.

My sister was about seven years old when we were living in this house and she used to construct all these dog jumps around the garden. She usually made these from buckets and brooms or mops and some garden tools. So if ever you needed one of these items, you could never bloody well find them unless you walked around the garden. The poor dogs were jumped over these contraptions and most of the time I am sure they did not really want to be show jumper animals at all.

They would much rather lie in their beds or have some bones, rather than doing that exercise everyday; yes, everyday as soon as my sister got home from Primary School, the jumps would be up and the poor dogs would be pulled around the garden and jumped over the mop handle a few times.

It was even worse at weekends because my sister would do these things all day long with the dogs. I did not really mind this dog jumping until it was my turn to mow the lawn or strim the garden. I had to move all these things off the grass and then would have to endure my sister telling me off for taking her dog jumps apart.

The worse thing was my sister pretending she was one of the dogs. I can handle most things but when she used to come up to us on all fours and rub her head around your legs and make this so called dog noise, which was very embarrassing indeed. When your mates were around and you were talking bikes or whatever, she would still do this dog thing to you and show you up.

The only plus side of these strange traits is I could use this information against her when we all grew up and it always had the desired effect if I mentioned it at parties or family get togethers. I thought that I was the only one in the family, apart from Mum that remembered all these dog things, until we recently had a family meal at the Fighting Cocks in Arreton. My Brother Liam piped up after I had talked about the dog jumps and mentioned the pretending to be a dog thing and it was so funny and I'm afraid she will never ever live that one down as long her brothers are around.

One night my little Brother was out on one his various nights out; he was hardly ever in the house after school. He and his mates were always up to no good and doing silly things and this particular adventure went very wrong in the end. My brother ended up coming home with his face covered in blood and half scaring Mum to death as he stood by her bed, trying to wake her up. They had gone up to Tennyson downs in his mates Beetle, which was the one I bought for £200, and had managed to get in stuck down this steep slope and into a massive gorse bush.

Apparently it had taken them ages to pull it out and had to get another mate to get his car to tow it out. Then they were messing around down in Freshwater Bay and probably in the car park going through big puddles or something like that. Anyway, my Brother and his mates all stood on the running boards of the beetle as the driver drove the car past The Starks pub. Unfortunately my brother fell off the running board and rolled down the road and cut his face on the gravel.

Another of their adventures was to try a row two rowing boats from Colwell beach to Hurst Castle. Why they wanted to cross over the roughest and strongest current ridden part of the

Solent in rowing boats I will never know. This ended in disaster because one of the boats started to take in water about half way across and the other boat had to tow the holed boat back to Colwell, they were very lucky because by the time they were nearly into Colwell, the boat was sunk completely. They did a similar thing out at Newtown creek and this time it was pitch black and they could not see a thing and could not see the landing stage, hence they got very muddy that night. My Bruvver, as the song goes.

It was late summer when my Granddad, on my mothers side. Fell over on his way up from the Red Funnel ferry to his home, just off Park Road in Cowes. He fell and went into a coma but unfortunately he never regained consciousness and died at Ryde Hospital. It was a sad time because he was not a bad man really, although my Dad never really liked him very much, he was good to us little kids and we spent a vast amount of time at his home.

He was a very good carpenter and handy man and once decorated a flat for Max Bygraves in London, where he originated from. Both my parents were born in the East End and lived through the Second World War as children. Granddad joined the Royal Navy at Woolwich at the age of 15 and stayed in for some years until

he was ready to leave and find a career and
settle down into civilian life.

We always had fun at his house and he was very
into gadgets such as a tape to tape machine and
his pride and joy, a cine projector and camera.
He filmed all of us in various locations around
Cowes in the seventies and loved filming the
power boat races at Cowes Week.

All of us boys would go round to his house in
the evening for a cine film and I will never forget
him showing us some naughty cine films of
naked ladies on trains and a haunted house
where the ghost takes the lady's clothes off. It
was so funny and we didn't think any more of it
apart from it made my trousers a bit tighter than
normal and Mum telling him off for showing us
such films.

When it came to sorting out all the stuff in
Granddad's house in Cowes it was a relatively
simple task because most of the contents had
been taken our relatives and there was hardly
anything of value or use left inside it. Amazing
really, Mum looked after him when our
grandmother had died and we always visited
him, almost every bloody week. We
would all go round to see if he was coping ok
without his wife. Relations only ever came

down about once a year if he was really lucky and they had no involvement in the care of him during the rest of the years. So how is that fair? There is no fairness in it what so ever. Dickens wrote a story that described the whole process perfectly in Martin Chuzzlewit; I have never got over that evening when I went over to his house with Mick Parnell, from the Tulipaan café in his Hilux truck.

I walked in the living room expecting to see the usual sights that I saw only weeks before he died and it was absolutely bare. All the furniture gone and only a settee remained. The massive cine film collection had gone forever and most of it was shot with our family and in Cowes so what they wanted with them is anyone's guess. It was almost spiteful in my eyes because a lot of the belongings I never saw at my uncles house and that included the tools from Granddad's garage, I could go on and on ranting about the whole thing but there is no point in raising my blood pressure over mere scavengers.
How would you feel in this situation?

Jumping back to the evenings when we all sat on the benches by the monument in Totland, just listening to Rainbow on one of the lad's ghetto blasters and watching everyone go about their business. People do strange things. This chap took the biscuit as he rode a very small scooter through Totland every evening without fail. He had a long grey beard and always wore a sowester type yellow coat. OK, so nothing particularly unusual about his appearance really you may be thinking but it was how this chap rode his scooter which was the giveaway. Instead of putting his feet on the pedals, he rested them on the top of the engine casing. I never ever saw him ride that scooter in any other way and he was known as, *the man with no legs*. If you ever mentioned the name amongst us lads, everyone knew who you were talking about and would bring an instant smile to their faces.

My Mother outside Granddad's house with our beloved Daimler in 1979.

Now this little story that I'm about to share, was absolutely hilarious because of the sheer shock on the faces of the victims. We were hedge and verge cutting up on the Bouldnor Block one Saturday morning and there were three of us on this particular job due to the size of the area we had to cover. Two of us went around the headland, one from one direction and the other in the opposite direction as usual. The other chap was on the tractor and trailer picking up the heaps of grass etc. We had reached the corner of the top field; from that corner you could see Hill Place Lane quite clearly through the sparsely planted hedgerow.

We had all met up at that point and were loading up the grass and cuttings on the trailer. We noticed a car pulling up on the verge directly below us, three girls got out and went over to the hedgerow and down came their knickers and they all squatted in the hedge. I could not resist it and shouted "OI" as loud as I possibly could and I have never seen knickers get pulled up so fast and the look of horror on their faces was a picture. They were trying to dress themselves as fast as possible, whilst finishing something that is almost impossible to stop part way.

They were running for the car and eventually sped off down the lane. We were in tears laughing at what we had just seen and I bet those girls must have wet themselves in the panic.

Something similar happened to me up in the North Hills field one day, which runs from *Wilmingham* lane to The Causeway, in Freshwater. I was raking up the straw from the headland and the head tractor driver was ploughing with his Ford County. He had the plough press on the side of the plough, which is a piece of machinery that has large rollers or crumblers, similar to a power harrow would have. The machine is connected or picked up by the plough by a large arm with a hook and dragged along behind the plough. It was lunchtime and I could see him just turning on the headland of South hills, which was the adjacent field to the one I was in; but divided by a bridleway.

I thought I would just wait and see if he stops after the turn and I would walk over and see him. He stopped as I thought he would and off I went to chat to him for a while. He was repairing one of the skims on the plough and checking all the mole boards etc, so we had a chat for about half hour and I sat on the press and had my lunch break.

I liked Hayward the head tractor driver because he was always ready to help out and would do anything for you, if you needed it. Even though he was very fussy about leaving the windows open on his tractor. At the time I didn't understand why he was so particular about the windows, but now I do.. He loved his little jeep and dog; oh and his fire brigade work of course. A good chap all round, in my book.

Anyway, I finished my lunch and watched Hayward go down the field and watched how the press doing its job as it flattened out the plough furrows and left the soil with a perfect tilth for the seed bed. As I walked back along the hedgerow and looking for the gap that I had come through to get to South Hills I decided to take a leak and unzipped my jeans and started. Suddenly there was a giggling and rustling of the hedge as a young girl on a horse went right past the gap and must have seen everything. How bloody embarrassing was that. Worse still, was I often saw her on her horse down that lane and around the other bridleways close to the farm. She always smiled at me and I bet she was secretly laughing at me really.

There was the incident of the lad running across the field at *Wilmingham* thirty acres. This field ran parallel to the old railway line to Yarmouth. On this occasion he was using the Cambridge rolls and unfortunately had a very upset stomach. Something you did not need when you are out in tractor in the middle of nowhere. The next morning in the workshop for a our daily briefing, Malcolm mentioned that he had seen a chap running across the field with a toilet roll in his hand and disappeared into the copse at the bottom of the field. Malcolm said "He hoped he felt better today." That put a smile on our faces that morning.

I remember this chap who lived somewhere in Wellow or Thorley who had a little mini and it had union jacks all over it. He must have loved that little car because it was always immaculately turned out and had every possible accessory bolted to it. I never knew who he was but I must have seen him nearly every day going along Thorley Road and on to Yarmouth. It is strange how you see all these different characters going past and never really know who they are. A lot of people just waved at you in a tractor and God knows who they were or thought you were?

There was a girl that rode her pony past *Wilmingham* barn and who lived in Dairy cottage. She was the talking point in the straw barn on many occasions, because she had long blonde hair and was very pretty indeed. She looked especially lovely sat in the saddle on her pony with her tight jodhpurs. I remember Len was on the trailer, throwing the bales up to us in the barn and *Miss dairy cottage*, as we affectionately called her, went past on her pony. I whistled at her and hid in the bales. Len was left standing there all innocent looking and she was smiling back at him. He nearly thumped me that time because I really showed him up in front of all the lads in the stack. The rest of us were in fits of laughter as they saw how crimson his cheeks had gone.

Len won her heart eventually and went out with her for a long time. I don't know why they split up, but I have a feeling it was because he was showing an interest in yet another girl on a horse. She was from Tattles Lane in Thorley. She was one of three sisters and a very nice girl, although she had the reputation of being a little wild as Len informed me. Len was chasing her and went to a party at her house and that was goodbye to *Miss dairy cottage* forever.

The majority of farms that I knew of used a digger or a hedge cutter to clean out the large amount of ditches on their land. Not on our farm we didn't. A rip hook or slasher, which was similar to a rip hook but with a long handle and which may have a straight blade instead of a curved one. A spade and a sharpening stone was all you needed to complete the job.

Obviously Wellies were essential for ditching and if you had any, a pair of gloves. Now it did not matter if it was sunny or hammering it down with rain, that was your task and you got it done to the best of your ability. I spent days cleaning out all the vegetation from the waterways below the hedges and cleaning out the drainage pipes and culverts. I cleaned out the ditches up at *Wilmingham* and went all the way along those hedgerows and it took me nearly a week in total to finish it. There was of course a huge difference between a machine doing the job and one of us. The finished product was so much neater and there wasn't any damage to the fields, by heavy wheels or tracks etc.

I always remember a day in mid winter when the rain was pouring down and I was slashing my way along this trench full of water. It was when you had the smell of the cut grass and other plants and the rain falling from the leaves in the hedge and onto my head. Such a peaceful time when all you could hear were the sparrows having an argument in the bushes, because I'm sure they do argue? Suddenly they all start cheeping at one another and then all fly off.

The gentle trickle of the water moving down the ditch and you are dry because your waterproofs are doing their job and your Nammet bag is in the back of the tractor. Half a mile away and you really could do with a bite to eat or a cup of coffee. We would make sure that we were near the tractor for breakfast break and both squeeze in the cab and drink our hot tea or coffee and have a few sandwiches.

You dare not start on your lunchtime provisions or you would be starving by twelve thirty. You did not see anyone at all. If you were really lucky and it was a Friday, Malcolm would bring your wages out to you, just before lunchtime.

That small brown paper envelope with the small white pay slip inside made you feel better as you counted all the money in your envelope and checked the wage slip to see how much overtime you earnt that past week. No one ever showed any other co worker their wage slip, it was a kind of code for workers really, it was a personal thing that only your eyes stared at and you either smiled and thought; I can get that bike this weekend, or thought tight bastards.

When you had just done around 80 hours in a week then you were laughing all the way not to the bank. I think Malcolm must have had a small press in his office so he could get all those notes into such a small bloody space. I loved wages day for that reason and the amount of money I earnt at the young age of seventeen was unheard of and certainly treble what all my mates were getting from their factory and building jobs. I can only describe it as another Christmas day because there is nothing that even comes close to the excitement I got from opening those envelopes.

I will say this for Malcolm, he was never late in paying his workers and you always got your money just before lunchtime on Friday. It did not matter if the roads were impassable by normal vehicles because of snow.

Off he would go in a tractor to Freshwater, to the bank without fail. Now that was dedication and reliability beyond the call of duty and that is one of the things that he instilled in me. I am damn proud to have had the chance to learn from him and try to exercise the same traits.

On the subject of snow covered roads and vehicles becoming stuck on the small winding lanes around the farm. There was such an occasion that at first, we thought unbelievable but on reflection, very clever and shrewd in his actions.

All the roads around us were blocked by snow and nothing could get from Yarmouth to Thorley or vice versa. So off goes Malcolm with the Matbro handler out of the back entrance to the farm with the big grain bucket on the front of the machine. We wondered what he was up to with the machine because it was rare to see him using it. We had just got back from *Wilmingham* barn with our loaded trailer of barley and wheat straw for the weekend feeding. It was pretty scary coming back through *Barnsfield* in the snow, but we made it after a couple of attempts at the hill. I remember asking Mark the fitter "where had Malcolm gone with the Matbro". He had as much idea as we did, so it still remained a mystery to all of us.

Its funny how we all become detectives at work and would wonder what so and so are doing with the what's it called, up in that place. It makes conversation I guess and makes the time go quicker; well that is what I put it down to anyway.

It wasn't until just before lunch, when we heard the Matbro come back in rear entrance and saw the boss walking up to the office and disappear for half hour or so. Then he came out with the wages as normal and then disappeared back out in the Matbro again. So we had guessed he might have taken the Yarmouth road to Freshwater and to the bank. It may have been partially cleared by the council ploughs, but not clear enough to drive a normal vehicle. Where has he gone this time, we all wondered?

We never did find out on that day and it was not until Saturday when I was feeding the cattle with Hayward, that we met some chap who lived up the road. He told us the tale of what Malcolm was up to with the Matbro. He was pulling and digging people out of the snow and charging them ten pounds in the process.

Like I said, shrewd was his middle name and brilliant bit of industrious thinking on his part; hats off to the bloke, he could make money out of anything and he did. Staying with that subject in mind, I remember some chap coming into the farm one morning as asking about empty fertiliser bags. So I had to go off and find Malcolm the manager to find out if I could give this chap some bags or not. I found him in the farm office and asked him about the bags. He said "Yes they are 10p each", to anyone who wants them. I was slightly taken aback at his answer and did actually feel slightly embarrassed when I told this customer what the terms were regarding the bags. Only he could get away with it, every other farmer that I knew just gave them away but not Malcolm. He sold loads of them, Brilliant!

My love of fireworks and rockets has stemmed from probably the funniest and most dangerous game that myself and my mates played one Friday night. We had all met up at our house and there were at least six of us all on bikes and one of Liam's mates, Abdul, as he was known as, in his Cortina. It was a misty night and we were finding it hard to decide what we were going to do that evening. We had all been paid and wanted to go and spend it on something more exciting than going to the Highdown Inn for ham, egg and chips. That was our usual Friday night exploits and they were becoming boring. A few of us decided to walk down the hill from my house to the Drug Store, which was just a small convenience store across the road from our butchers shop, in Totland. It sold cigarettes, chocolate, sweets and even fireworks. So there we were, three of us buying smokes and mars bars and other essential Friday evening provisions when someone decided it would be a good idea to buy a load of fireworks too. So we bought almost all the fireworks in the shop and took them up to our workshop to construct some rocket launchers and other crude tools for launching these mini rockets out of plastic gutter pipe and other such materials.

It was not long until we had some perfect shoulder mounted launchers with insulating tape on the end to stop them falling back out. We loaded everything into our friend Abdul's Cortina and then made our way out to the disused Chessell Quarry for some serious fun.

As I had the German tank suit from the farm, I was camouflaged in the darkness and was able to scrabble about up and down the slopes without ripping my knees to shreds and ruining my clothes. I also had a camouflaged jacket which had some seriously deep pockets for loading with fireworks.

We all went our separate ways and found ourselves a good hiding place around the quarry. There were at least seven of us that night, with various lengths of plastic pipe, camo gear and fireworks. It was just some innocent fun with some rather dangerous toys. Alas, that was not the view of the local farmer but that is another story.

I went to the very end of the quarry and up a big slope and hid in the gorse bushes until everyone shouted that they were ready for the battle to commence and then all hell was let loose.

I had my plastic launcher at the ready and could see someone creeping about in the darkness, just below the hill I was on. So I put a mini rocket in the tube and lit the touch paper, suddenly there was this mass of heat and a scream as the rocket shot out of the tube, narrowly missing the figure in the shadows. I was amazed how accurate this thing was and loaded another one up ready. There were mini rockets flying about all over the place and it was such an exciting game that I lost all the tiredness that I was feeling after a days work and was running about all evening firing these things at people. No one was injured or burnt at all and everyone was having a damn good time.

My favourite moment of the night was when I had crept up on my mate who had found a large hollow to lie in and fire his rockets over the small cliff at the people on the lower parts of the quarry. He did not have any idea that I was watching him and I was fumbling about in my pockets for a rocket and realised I had in fact run out of them, but I had one more trick up my sleeve.

A firework known as an Atom Bomb, which when lit, would dispense a small projectile from its tube. After a few seconds, the projectile would explode with that loudest crack I had ever heard. I lit the thing from about twenty feet from this hollow and waited, suddenly there was a whoosh and the missile shot out and landed right next to my friend in the hole. Bang went this thing and I have never seen anyone jump as high as he did when it went off.

The whole thing happened so quickly that he did not have time to realise what was happening. The fact he was letting off rockets, helped to disguise the noise from my firework. One of the most dangerous and funny things that ever happened and I would gladly do it all again because it was so exciting and gave you a pure adrenalin rush. Similar to the laser Quest games nowadays, but much more fun.

After all our fireworks had gone and we were all standing around the entrance to the quarry, near the Cortina and chatting about who hit who and whose rocket went the furthest. When we heard this shouting coming from the top of the quarry fence, where the road went past. We all panicked and thought it was the owner of the place or worse, the police. So we just got in the car and shot out of the entrance and left in a big hurry. Not all of us heard what this person was shouting but a couple of my fiends said it could be the farmer from the end of the road, worried about the rockets hitting his hay barn or something. We decided not to drive off after all and went back up the road to where the farmer was parked and stopped and talked to him. He asked us if we were the lads in the quarry and we said we were and what was the problem? He just said that he was worried that our rockets would hit his barn and set it alight. We explained that we only used these mini rockets and no large ones as they would be too dodgy to fire at one another.

There was no way we could get anywhere close to his buildings with these rockets and it was just some fun we were having. He was OK about it all and laughed when we said "we thought you were the police". So no harm was done to anyone apart from being slightly deaf from the Atom Bomb.

We had now moved from Totland to Freshwater after my Father had left home permanently. As I mentioned earlier, the big house was too expensive for Mum to afford on her own, plus the property was in need of a lot of repairs and refurbishment. I did not like the idea of moving away from the house that formed a lot of my early teenage memories and experiences. I loved the garden and the fact that we had somewhere where we could work on bikes and also a place to band practice too.

The reduction in size and amenities of the smaller house was a bit of a shock to the system. The house was about half way up the High Street in Freshwater, very near to a large nursery and florists and also next door to a jewellers shop. It was quite small but still had an open fire which was a bonus for us as we did not have one at *Dreens*. There was a small shed and a two tiered garden at the back, but no other exciting features to mention really.

A lot of my old junk had to go and that consisted of a lot of bike parts and some large tools. I had all the band gear to find a space for and some of that I had to get rid of in the end. My brother seemed to like the house and so did my sister too, but for me it was just a place to live really and I could have easily stayed where I was, given the choice. On reflection, I really wished I had used all the money I earnt from the farm, more wisely. Perhaps we could have stayed in that house after all, who knows?

Mum had new carpets throughout the new house and the lounge carpet was cream and looked very nice indeed. It was the day Liam bought a brand new drum kit from Teagues of Newport and it was a premier kit in pearl black. It was a lovely looking kit and he was very excited about setting it all up and when it arrived.

He put it up in the lounge while Mum was at work. This was fine until he unfolded the legs of the stool and put it on the floor and sat on it. The base of the telescopic stem was covered in black grease and it put a black circle onto Mum's brand new cream carpet. There was a panic that day I can tell you. My brother was trying everything to get this grease off the pile. I don't think it ever really came out completely though and he was banned from bringing any part of the kit in the lounge again.

Poor old Dilly, who incidentally, could not read or write was sitting in the lounge with a load of us lads. In front of the open fire, we were just chatting and planning what we going to do that day. Mum had just come in from going down the shops and put the shopping in the kitchen and put the kettle on. Then she wandered into the lounge and carrying a newspaper in her hand, passed it to Dilly and said "here, do you want to read the paper Dilly?" Oh my God, the room went silent and Dilly didn't say a thing but took the newspaper and looked at it as if he could read it. We all looked at each other and trying not to burst out laughing, and trying to indicate to Mum that he can't read at the same time. She went back in the kitchen and we heard her laughing out there and obviously, she had clicked to what we were trying to tell her about Dilly.

How bloody embarrassing that was that I wanted the ground to open up and swallow me. Another classic moment in that lounge was when our dog, Anna walked straight over to Dilly and put her tongue straight in his mouth. Ha, his face was a picture and he was spitting and wiping his mouth for ages. We were in tears laughing and it really hurt my stomach muscles that day.

It was when Dilly was on one of his completely, off the cuff, earn some money ventures, the latest scheme was gardening. Now Dilly and his mate knew as much about gardens as I did about nuclear physics. So they went out in Dilly's van with a borrowed lawn mower and knocked on doors for work. Well amazingly, they got a job cutting this large lawned area, somewhere near the Red Lion in Freshwater.

While they were working on this garden, Dilly's mate picked up this chrysalis thing off the grass and was standing in front of Dilly and squeezing it slightly and suddenly whatever was inside this thing, popped out and went straight in Dilly's mouth. You couldn't do that if you tried and Dilly was spitting for ages afterwards trying to get this thing out of his mouth. His mate nearly died of lack of oxygen as he was laughing so much and I would have given anything to have been there that day because if you knew what Dilly was like, you would understand how funny that moment must have been.

In nineteen eighty four, I applied for a job on a farm in Cranleigh, Surrey as it was advertised in the Farmers Weekly. I could not believe it when I got an invitation for an interview through the post. It was for a trainee cowman which included milking and stock management. I knew very little about milking, but I had been working with cattle all my working life, so I did thought I would give it a go.

The interview was in February and I had about three weeks to make arrangements with my Dad who was living in Guildford at that time. I was to go up to Dad's place and stay there the night and he would take me to the interview the following day. So everything was planned and I was getting very excited about the whole thing then suddenly one night it poured with snow on the island and the next day it carried on snowing. It was really deep snow and Dad had rang to say it was absolutely horrendous up there in Surrey. It carried on snowing all week off and on and the date for the interview was one day away. I could not get to the damn interview and I rang up the farm to tell them I could not attend because of the snow.

They said that they couldn't get to the main road, so there was no way I could reach them either. Thank God for that, I thought.

We all planned to go up on Tennyson downs and build an ice slide and we had some fertiliser bags at the ready. So off we went up to the chalk pit at the bottom of the downs. Now it didn't even resemble a chalk pit, as it was covered in snow and all the holes and hills were now completely hidden. We decided to go up the little path on the top of the pit that led right behind the monument on the downs.

On the way up we thought that this path would make the perfect slide. So we built the ice slide right from the top of the path to the chalk pit cliff. It was so damned scary coming down that slide because when you reached the top of the chalk pit, you had to try and stop or you fell forty feet into the snow.

My mate went straight off the edge and disappeared in a massive drift of snow at the bottom. He did not hurt himself one bit so that was the green light for everyone to go off the edge. Oh my life, it was totally amazing coming right from the top of the path and then flying off the small cliff into the loose snow drift. We were up there all day and stayed there until it got dark. We were absolutely starving by this time, so into the Highdown for ham, egg and chips. This was another example of adrenalin giving you so much energy, even if you had not had a bite to eat all day.

After that day, the snow still hung around for over a week or so and I had to wait for it to clear sufficiently, before I could attempt to go for this interview. Anyway, the day arrived and I got on the ferry and then the train to Guildford and met Dad at the station that evening. The next morning we drove out to this estate and we went down this huge driveway. It went for at least three miles and through these big pine trees with snow covering their fanned out branches. It looked like a scene from the Black Forest in Germany that I had seen somewhere. We reached the farm buildings and I met the manager and we walked around the parlour and the cow yards and chatted. What was truly amazing was that the manager told me there and then, that I had the job. I had never been in that situation before and when he said "when can you start?" I was gob smacked and had to think very seriously about when I could get up here and how was I going travel up here?

So I consulted with Dad who was waiting in his van and then confirmed a date when I could start, which was two weeks away. I also asked about accommodation and was told it would be available about two months from the date that I started.

Now I had a logistical problem to overcome. I had no wheels at the time as I sold my Yamaha RD200 and now I needed a bike to get to work from Guildford. Dad lived in a flat with his girlfriend and it was about twenty odd miles away from the farm. Luckily and without even asking, my old mate lent me his Honda CB900F2 bike and I got it insured and some gear together. I moved up to Dad's on the Saturday afternoon, ready to start my new job on the Monday morning.

The work was good fun and I was mostly
working with a chap name Brent from Wiltshire.
He had a cottage on the farm with his girlfriend
and after a while I would go back with him for
breakfast and lunch. He had a massive log fire
in the living room and we used to have hour and
a half for lunch so we would watch this new
programme on BBC called Neighbours. I had to
start learning to milk and I was put with Trent in
the parlour in the afternoons because it was too
early for me to travel from Guildford at three in
the morning. I loved milking and soon had the
parlour running on my own.

By this time, I had rented a room from Brent and
his girlfriend Jilly, and lived with them for a few
months. Jilly was also from Wiltshire and had
such a country accent, that sometimes; I had a
problem understanding some of the words and
phrases she said. Jilly did all the cooking and
Brent and I would wash up and get the wood in,
plus other things to help out. It was bloody cold
in my room at first, so I cleaned out the small
fireplace and made sure the chimney was clear
and got some coal in. My room was bloody
baking hot in the evenings and I never woke up
cold again.

I enjoyed the work and loved living with Brent
and Jilly and we always had a damn good laugh
in the evenings. One weekend I borrowed Jilly's
Fiesta and drove down to the island to get my
synthesisers and keyboard because I missed
playing them very much. I didn't happen to
mention to Jill that I had not taken my car test at
the time and it was not until months later when
we were all comparing driving licenses when I
let it slip that I had no car license. She said "you
little bugger" and laughed in her very
affectionate way as she added "You have got the
cheek of the devil", I agreed.

When Brent and Jilly went off for a week's
holiday then I was left to look after the parlour
and maintain the electric fences around the farm.
Three thousand acres of land and most of it was
arable or forestry with only around three
hundred acres of grassland. The majority of
fencing was temporary electric fences which had
to be moved every other day or so. I had the use
of a land rover to go out and move the fences.
One day I was a long way out from the farm and
very close to some very marshy land. I was busy
walking along the fence line and moving the
posts and ensuring the wire was not tangled.

As I walked along, suddenly there was this
horrendously loud jet noise as a camouflaged
Hawker Harrier came up behind the hedge row

and flew straight over me at about two hundred feet or so. It was so low I felt the heat from the vector jets as it went over me. I did not know that we were so close to Dunsfold Airbase which was a fighter squadron.

Because of the size of the farm and the vastness of the land, we had two of those Volvo BM articulated quarry trucks just for silage. Totally amazing and not what you see very often on a farm. Everything was big and even loading the silage into the auto feeder wagon was done with a tracked bulldozer, with a grab type bucket. I loved driving that beast as nothing was safe when you were trundling about on it.

We had two Muir Hill tractors which are very similar to the Ford County that we had at Thorley. The difference being the cab was more like a JCB digger as you stepped down inside it. Strange machines but they were reliable and did what we needed of them.

All the arable work was done by a team of rough looking dudes who we saw occasionally, when they brought the straw up to the yards. They were responsible for bedding up the yards but not feeding. A very odd setup indeed as I was used to doing all of it. They would sit in the straw barn playing cards at breakfast break and lunchtime, if they were around the dairy.

Their boss was a dodgy looking bloke from Bristol and no one liked him from the dairy side of the business. I did not see him much so I did not form too much of an opinion. They never worked hard at all and bodged everything it seemed. Coming from a farm that was run like an army camp, it was hard to adjust to this totally lax type of working environment.

I left that farm one bank holiday weekend because they promised me accommodation right from the word go, but it never materialised. So I made up my mind to leave. Brent was going to leave in two week's time so I thought it would be best to get out while I could. I asked Dad to come over with his van and get my synths and a few clothes etc on the Friday night and Saturday morning I checked that my wages had been paid into my bank by going to the cash machine down the road. When I knew they had paid me, I was off on the bike and on my way to the ferry in Portsmouth. It had been snowing in Guildford and as I made me way down the A3 through Liphook and Petersfield.

There was a lot of snow on the roads, so I had to be very careful and put my feet down a lot of the way. Luckily I had electric heated inner gloves on and they saved me from stopping constantly and warming my hands on the exhaust down pipes. I was bloody cold by the time I got on the ferry and I couldn't wait to get back to the house in Freshwater. I got in and Mum was pleased to see me and she ran a hot bath for me, because I was frozen. I got all the gear off in seconds and jumped in that bath.

I have never enjoyed a hot bath as I did that day because I was chilled to the bone and needed that heat to defrost my body. So I was back on the Island again and needed to get some work sorted out as soon as I could. Dad brought all my gear over the following weekend and he stayed for the weekend.

Now I'm jumping back a few years to explain the mystery of our friend Dilly's long lost Father It was around nineteen eighty two, when my brother had got friendly with this lad from freshwater. He was probably the most uneducated person I ever met, because as I said earlier, he could not read or write.

I will never forget my brother had to write the numbers and what to fill in, on the inside cover of his cheque book so he knew which one to put in the boxes. He often talked about his long lost Father being from Freshwater, but would never enlighten us any further on the subject. I wondered who his Dad was and tried to picture someone older with the same features, but I never saw anyone who resembled him.

It was Christmas nineteen eighty two, when myself, my brother and Dilly, decided to play all night pontoon on Christmas Eve. It was a great night but Christmas day was so tiring and I think we slept for most of the day. I am not sure who came out with the most money but I basically won a Yamaha RD250 off my brother as he needed the money badly to try and recoup the money he had lost to Dilly. The card games carried on from that early eighties year right up to two thousand and seven. I decided enough was enough and pulled out of the ritual forever.

It became almost a chore and there were always disputes about where we were playing etc. It was during one of these card games that the true identity of this chap's Father was revealed. The Father turned out to be, the one and only Basil the coach driver from way back in my schooldays. When he told us, my thoughts started to flash between basils face and Dilly's; I could now see the resemblance, clearly.

Playing keyboards in a band at the same time as I worked on the farm, was a complete nightmare when I look back on it all. Trying to get time off for practice and even worse, getting away for gigs. The two activities just did not go together at all and caused a lot of problems with the other band members because I could not just finish at four o'clock and just go off and have a band practice at the drop of a hat. It was starting to make me think about giving it all up because of the hassle of it all.

In the end, I decided it was time to give it up and let the others get on with it. It was OK for people who didn't go to work or only worked nine til five with no overtime to do. For me it was nothing like a regular day job because we had a contract to adhere to, so going home early, as I have mentioned before, was not an option and got me into a fair amount of trouble with Malcolm on more than one occasion.

I was not the only one who wanted to be away from work early, we all did sometimes and if you asked and gave plenty of notice, and then it was just about acceptable. You had to remind the boss close to the time or he would forget about it and then that added to the hassle.

The band that was now renamed as *Gone Fishing*, suffered badly from the lack of practices and it really came to head during our first gig at the Riverside in Wootton one Friday night. It started out fine and we got through a couple of songs with some luck and not skill.

During one of our songs the drummer stopped completely, right in the middle of this song. Fatal, there is nothing you could do but hope the ground would open up and swallow us all. Embarrassing as hell, really unbelievable to have it happen to you; that was the end for me so I gave it up and treated it as a bad dream. It was not really the drummer's fault completely because he just didn't know the songs well enough to be able to make a mistake and just let it go and carry on regardless.

One day, It was decided that an oil drilling site would be set up on the land which was known as Little Ham. This was situated on the left as you go down the hill in *Barnsfield*.

A massive road was constructed with limestone, which led from the main Thorley to *Wilmingham* road to the site. I did not ever get close enough to it myself but at night you could see it all lit up with massive floodlights and it looked quite something amongst the darkness of the fields and trees. Correct me if I'm wrong but I am pretty sure it was there for about six months or so before it all disappeared as quickly as it sprouted up.

The road was taken up and dumped up at *Wilmingham*, on the side of the track behind the barn and we used it for various gateways and other things that needed a better surface than mud. I had the task of getting the membrane material out of the limestone with the handler and that was a nightmare job. I think there could still be the remains of it there to this day if you looked hard enough.

Just along the Boadway in Totland, opposite the hairdressers shop, o the corner. There was a very large building that had been converted into flats for unmarried mothers, and I'm thinking it was probably one of the first social housing developments. I used to ride past this building every day and I noticed there was a girl always looking out of her as I went past.

One day she came into the bakers shop and I was very surprised to see it was in fact Malcolm the manager's eldest daughter Celine. She told me that is was her who was always at the window and now living in one of the flats in the large building. We chatted for a while and she invited me up to her flat for a coffee sometime.

So I went up to see her and we got on very well indeed. I ended up going to see her on my afternoons off. We would watch a film or just watch the world of Totland pass by out of her window.

She had a baby from the chap who camped next to the graveyard on the farm, which you can read all about in previous chapters. He had gone off and left her but was still in contact with her occasionally. I don't know exactly what happened between them now but it was a shame really because they seemed a perfect couple and were always together. I was not out to annoy him or come between him and his daughter but somehow he got it into his head that it was my intention to make trouble between them. Totally understandable and I did expect some trouble in that department for sure.

I was round her flat one afternoon and did I have a bloody shock. Who should walk in with some furniture, Malcolm and his wife? Oh my, I was embarrassed and really did not know what to say to them. It made things a lot easier as they were very pleasant towards me and we chatted for a while. I was expecting a rather less friendly reception, considering how different Malcolm was in his working environment. After that initial shock from their visit and the fact that

Celine was in fits of laughter because she had not warned me of their arrival. She loved every minute of my embarrassment and shyness and I was starting to learn her sense of humour rather well.

It became more embarrassing as time went on because one day, I was down at Malcolm's house on my bike, visiting Celine as she was staying there for the weekend. She asked me to go down to the farm on my bike and tell Malcolm his tea was ready. Now I didn't want to do that and complained so much at the time but she persuaded me with a kiss.

She knew it would turn me into butter, I did as she asked. I really did not know what to say as I arrived in the yard and saw Malcolm by the workshop doors. I got off my bike and went over to him and just said "Message from Celine, tea is ready." and ran over to my bike before he had time to reply and rode off back to the cottage as quick as possible.

When I got back, Celine had the cheeky smile thing going on and laughed as she asked if I delivered the message. Bitch, I thought as I went over to her and tickled her, which she hated. I had to get some sort of revenge for her wicked humour. I had to have tea with her and Malcolm and I felt so out of place.

That was the last time I went visiting that cottage because I wasn't comfortable there at all. There are working relationships and there are social ones. I was keeping my relationship with Malcolm as a working type. I believe there is a line that has to be drawn with a boss and it should not be crossed. You can have a friendly working relationship without a doubt, but any kind of social friendship is doomed from the first.

It was not long after the cottage fiasco when I was up at her flat visiting her when she suddenly said "dad wants to see you." with that knowing and cheeky smile on her face. Now I was worried, what the hell did he want to see me about? I thought of millions of possible reasons why he would want to see me and they were all pointing to the negative side. Because I had been having a relationship with his daughter, I thought that he wanted to get us married off or something.

Now Celine was in her element because I was in deep thought about the reason her father wanted to see me and she loved every minute. So I plucked up the courage and rode down to the farm one afternoon and found him in the yard. He greeted me with a smile and then asked if I would come into his office for a chat? I agreed and followed him into the familiar farm office while chatting about the weather etc. Anyway he asked if I was working at the moment, which was a great relief as I soon cottoned on to what was coming next. I said I was only working part time in my family's bakery and I told him it was up for sale, so I would be looking for work soon anyway.

He offered me work from April til November on a full time basis and explained the usual terms and rate of pay etc. He also told me that he had some new employees and asked if I knew them, which I said that I didn't. After all the worrying and nervousness, I was so relieved and to be back at Thorley Manor again was fantastic news. Celine was in fits of laughter, when I went back to see her that evening. I said "you knew what he wanted to see me about, didn't you!" She couldn't stop laughing as eventually owned up to knowing all about it.

We broke up, or rather drifted apart not long after I went back to the farming job. She had a lovely caring nature and a wicked sense of humour as you have no doubt, noticed.

Back in nineteen seventy nine, when I first started work on the farm at Thorley Manor. The old stone workshop was a cold and very dark place in the winter months. We didn't have a nammet room then and had to sit in this workshop, against the racks of machine parts on improvised seats. These seats were made from small wooden boxes that some of the parts came in. A luxury was to have a Hessian sack folded on top of the box.

The wooden racks on one side were homes to all the various implement parts such as plough points and cultivator tines. Most things were in order in the workshop and it was fairly tidy most of the time, unless Mark the fitter was on one of his missions to build some new adaptation to a piece of machinery that was in desperate need of modification.

The welder and compressor always lived just inside the doors on the left, on the right side there was an ancient pillar drill that I never saw working in all the years I was there. At the very back of the room there stood our work bench, the place where all our instructions were received from Malcolm as we lent against that old wooden rest. The bench was always covered in bits and pieces from various machines and usually metal filings and bits of chalk from one of the most menial but important jobs on the farm. Puncture repairs were an art form on Thorley Manor Farm and were always carried out by all members of staff and never by an outside contractor like they are today on many farms. It did not matter how big the tyre or wheel was, if you had a flat than you fixed it. I had a puncture up on the *Wilmingham* thirty acre field on the left of the track. I was in my John Deere 3130 and the wheels weighed a ton as I found out when I jacked the tractor up and undone all the wheel nuts.

I had to get the Matbro telehandler to lift the wheel off the ground and back to the farm for repair. I repaired it and got it back on the tractor on my own that afternoon.

When a puncture repair was carried out and you had cleaned the tube with rubber solvent cleaner and applied the glue and patch. Then usually you would wait until the glue was set and removed the foil or plastic film covering from the patch and apply your French chalk. Now we did not buy in any French chalk but had to grate a lump of chalk on a metal file and into a metal tin. This would take bloody ages to do and I can say that I never filled that bloody tin.

I don't know if it was a money saving exercise or perhaps an old army trick that Malcolm had brought with him from his National Service days.

On the subject of National Service I heard my Dad talking to Malcolm one day when Dad came to get some straw for his horses. I remember they were chatting about the army and Dad was talking about Canvey Island in nineteen fifty three and Malcolm saying that he went to Lynmouth for the flooding disaster in August nineteen fifty two.

On another occasion I was working up on *North Hills* one afternoon and I had a puncture on my Ford 6600 and it was in the rear tyre. I was using the power harrow at the time and I noticed the harrow was going deeper on one side. I was walking across the field, on my way back to the farm so I could grab the Matbro and get the wheel off.

Suddenly, I saw a bus turning into *Wilmingham* Lane and I thought that would be nice and easy if I can jump on that. So I ran over to the gateway and flagged down the bus, which stopped and I got on. It was the open top bus that ran from Alum Bay to Yarmouth and at the time, the bridge at Yarmouth was closed, hence why the bus was using the lane as a diversion. It had a conductor on the bus and I told him what happened and I asked if he could stop at the farm for me. No problem, and it stopped outside the farm entrance and I thanked the driver and conductor and walked across the road and into the farm entrance. If by magic, as I walked in the yard there was Malcolm and Mark standing by the workshop doors chatting away. Malcolm asked what was wrong and I told him about the puncture. Mark thought I had walked all the way until I told them both I just got off that bus. They laughed and I eventually recovered the 6600 and carried on harrowing.

The Lely Acrobat being used on the Wilmingham Left hand side thirty acres in 1985.

It was the late eighties when it was decided to plant a new hedge line a couple of feet, back from the old, original post and rail fence along the Thorley Road. This was the ninety five acre boundary, and by the time the fence had fallen to pieces, there should be a nice cattle proof hedge in place, that was the plan anyway.

Most of the original fence was complete but there were sections that had fallen to pieces or been hit by something. All the time that I was at Thorley, the ninety five acre field was always split in to two, apart from the first year I was there in seventy nine. The field was one giant field and I remember disc harrowing with my Ford 5000 and timing how long it took to get from the Thorley end to the Broad Lane end. It was roughly about ten minutes to get across its length with the discs.

I would hazard a guess and say the road side length of the field, was nearly half a mile and this hedge had to be planted by hand. Each plant was eight inches apart, and it took flipping ages to drop off the plants in bunches along the verge. It took almost five days to plant that lot and it was not the easiest or nicest jobs, due to the constant bending over.

The line we followed was rotavated first and this made Dibbing the plants easier. I was glad when it was completed. We watered the hedge line with our old green water tanker every few days or so, until the plants started to take hold. It was April when we planted the hedge and it was not until the end of September when Mark cycled back from lunch and happened to mention that the council tractor was mowing the verges up the road.

No one took much notice of the trivial news and carried on with their lunch. It was when Malcolm came in the entrance at light speed in his Honda Acty pickup and shot round to the office and disappeared. We knew something was wrong because Malcolm only ever drove that fast into the yard if there was trouble.

After a while, he came walking round to the workshop and spoke to Mark, then got in his truck and drove off for his lunch. We were all in the Nammet room when Mark walked through the door with the biggest grin on his face and said "guess what the council tractor has just done?" "Mown the whole hedge line you planted." We could not believe it, how could this council driver not see the new hedge that we had just finished? Well he didn't see a thing and mowed it completely flat and not one plant survived.

I cannot remember the cost involved in that hedge line but it was a lot of money and that excluded the time to plant and water it. The council had to re plant the whole thing again but to this day it never grew the way it should done, mainly because they did not take the time to water the new plants and it just died out.

As I had made so much money working all those hours on the farm during the summer months, I thought it was time I had a decent motorcycle and not some old cast off. So if I was near the farm out in a tractor or working in the drier. I would shoot down to Yarmouth and grab a County Press and scan the bikes for sale section at lunch time.

I saw this ad for this Triumph Thunderbird bike in Brighstone and soon as I finished work, I rushed home and called the number and then Mum took me out to see it. When I saw it in this bloke's garage, I fell in love with it there and then. It was all black with a chrome rack thing on the tank and massive chrome exhaust pipes. It was in good condition and sounded absolutely awesome when he started it up. I think I paid £800 for it and luckily I had my helmet and gloves with me so I could ride it home.

I remember going up through the village and out towards Brook on the way home. It had so much power, but was quite strange to ride with everything on the wrong side. When I had reached Totland, everyone was at the café so I stopped there and went to see if my mates were around.

I showed off a bit by going around the village a few times and then up the hill and our drive to home. Loved the bike and could not wait to ride it to work as soon as I had insured it, which was not going to be until at least the weekend. My first long ride on the bike was the following Saturday evening and there was a few of us who went to Newport for a spin and a burger of course.

I had got as far as Tapnell and there was this awful rattling coming from somewhere at the rear of the bike. Turns out that all the bolts holding the chain guard in place, had vibrated loose and fallen out. The next thing I knew, the chain guard flew off and landed in the verge, just missing my mate on his Suzuki GS750. There was no way I could fix it on the side of the road, so I stuffed it down my jacket and carried on my way.

Coming down the hill to Carisbrooke, I forgot the brake pedal was in fact the gear lever and tried to stop a bit suddenly as a car braked a rather quickly. When I realised that the machine did not like me stamping on the gear lever, I stamped on the brake pedal and the rear wheel locked instantly and I slid quite a way before the bike came to a stop.

I thought at the time that this bike was nothing like my Yamaha RD200 and handled more like a tank rather than a sporty little motorcycle. We had our burger from *Rumbling Tum* then we all made our way back up through Carisbrooke and headed up towards the Blacksmiths Arms pub, then on to Calbourne. It was when we went up through the tunnel of trees that I noticed how bloody useless the headlight was and could hardly see the road in front of me.

By the time we had got to Calbourne, it appeared that the battery had died completely and all the charge from the generator was diverting its power to charging the battery, instead of the lights. I was not impressed at all and by the time I got to Freshwater my headlight was almost lifeless. I checked all the wiring and charged up the battery but it did not matter what I did, the lights were useless and I had to ditch the bike in our garage and revert back to my trusty little RD200.

I used that Triumph about four times after that experience and then something went bang in the crankcase and on closer inspection; the piston had slammed into the valves. If I had the knowledge of such a machine, I would have probably fixed it or had it repaired. I could not be bothered with it anymore and put it in storage with my other bikes and eventually sold it for a fraction of the price I paid for it. I vowed never to buy another British motorcycle because they were unreliable, old fashioned and clumsy pieces of junk in my view. So that was the very end of my short affair with anything British on two wheels.

I then bought a Reliant Bond Bug very cheaply from a bloke from Kent. That was the strangest machine I ever owned and certainly took a lot of getting used to. I remember the little tape deck and playing Human League at full blast while driving along.

As with most three wheelers, the engine was prone to overheating and even when I stripped it down and put a new head gasket and seals in it, she still ran very hot all the time. Probably had a warped cylinder head but I just wanted to drive it and not spend all my spare time under the bonnet, so I put up with the overheating.

I lent it to my Mum one day as she needed to get to Ventnor for the dentist's. She loved it and took my little sister with her for a ride. She said it was the funniest thing when you lifted up the whole body to get in and out of it and everyone stared at them when they arrived in the car park. It was a head turner without a doubt but as with most used vehicles, had its annoying characteristics.

After a few months the clutch actuator died and I had to get a replacement fitted. I took it for MOT and it passed first time, which I could not believe as I was sure the brakes were not as good as they could have been. Sold it to a mate of mine and never saw it again.

During one of my winter breaks from the farm and at a time when money was running dangerously low, I had to try and find some employment during the months of March and April, until the work resumed at Thorley.

It was my Mother who found me some work through a dude who serviced her car one winter and she had mentioned that I was looking for some work during my regular break from the farm etc. He
was based at the old *Wilmingham* farm and was an ex navy marine engineer who had turned his hand to fixing cars and trucks as well as steel

fabrication and other things. I went down to meet up with him at his workshop one Sunday morning and we had a chat and I was given a job there and then. So on the Monday morning I started work with this guy and it was very enjoyable too.

We did so many varied jobs from repairing peoples wrought iron gates to fixing up lorries and cars. There were two exceptionally funny days that I remember and one was when I decided to make a chopper bike out of a Honda C90 moped and I had asked my new boss if he could extend the length of the front forks in some way, so he cut the bottom of the forks off and welded some steel pipe in the middle.

I replaced the forks and the outcome was bloody odd looking as the forks were now two feet longer and made the bike sit right up. I used it for work for a few months until it decided to die of old age; or was it my mechanical knowledge?

The second occasion was when Malcolm turned up one afternoon to have something repaired. He did not know I was working there and was shocked to see me in the workshop that day. He looked rather worried when he asked me if I was going to be coming back in April. I told him I was coming back next month but I needed some work for the past few months as I was running out of money. He was pleased to hear it I think, and sure enough, when April turned up I was off back to the farm. My new boss did not mind that I was leaving so soon, as his work was drying up and he probably would not be able to employ anyone.

The cattle on Goldings Marsh in 1985.

The most intense and tiring job on the farm had to be carting straw from the field to the barns or in our case, all over the Island. I think we must have travelled to most of the riding stables and various farms to deliver both hay and straw bales. At one point I was given a Ford TW15 to use for deliveries and all I did all day was cart the stuff to customers then come back and drive in the field, hitch up to the next trailer and off I would go to the next customer. This system continued for over 3 weeks and I must have clocked up a fare few miles in that TW15, good job it didn't have an odometer because a prospective buyer of the tractor would have thought more than twice about the high mileage.

On one of my delivery days, I was going to HMP Camphill Farm, near Parkhurst and Albany Prisons. I think I took at least five or six full artic trailer loads of barley and wheat straw there in one week alone. Back in the early eighties, going to the prison farm was an experience that had to be seen to be believed. When you reversed the trailer up to there silage heap or the straw barn and climbed up the side of the stack and took the ropes off, the cons would just jump on the trailer and chuck the whole lot into a heap on the floor and that was it. It took no more than 20 minutes for them to unload 300 bales. The only problem with going there was the amount of things the cons would try and sell you. Gloves, hats and donkey jackets, in fact anything that they could lay their hands on.

We were told by Malcolm not to accept anything or give them anything because we could get into trouble with the prison officers. We stuck to that rule even though it was quite intimidating when one of the cons would ask you for a smoke or some baccy, you just had to say you didn't smoke.

One day I was instructed to go to Haylands Farm in Ryde, which was a charity run venture for disabled people. Malcolm specifically instructed me to go through Havenstreet as it was sometimes easier because of the traffic.

So off I went to Newport with a seven raring load on the trailer of barley straw. I went up Staplers Road and then followed the Road to Havenstreet and just took no notice of the rather low looking railway bridge that I was heading for. Perhaps the bus driver flashing his headlights at me was a warning?

As I passed under the bridge I could feel the trailer move to one side or a pulling feeling as if something was trying to pull me backwards. I carried on through and looked in my mirror as some bales fell off the nearside and onto the verge.

I stopped and put my hazards on, then walked round the back and looked in amazement because the bridge was obviously too bloody low and it had just caught the back end of the stack and took off about 20 bales and the rest remained intact.

So I pulled up the road a bit so I could get to the verge where the bales had landed and I noticed a load of cows in the field had come over to the gateway. They must have known there was a treat coming their way. So I chucked the twenty or so broken bales into their field and they were munching on this fresh barley straw and appeared to be enjoying it. I climbed up the stack and rearranged the ropes and bales, and then I was back on my way to Hayland's, minus twenty or so bales.

That was not the end of the fun though. As I drove down this winding, narrow lane I noticed that there was a very low telephone cable that crossed the road and as I went under it with the tractor, I looked behind me as it caught on the top layer of bales and suddenly disappeared, then looked in the mirror as I saw the two ends of the wire hit the opposite hedges and fall behind the hedgerows. I didn't bother stopping for that one because I didn't know how to fix telephone wires. I finally reached the lane that lead to Haylands farm and went down it slowly because I had no idea where I was going. I had never visited the place before and it was in a residential area and not what I was expecting at all. Found the farm and went in the yard to find someone to take delivery of this straw and this bloke comes out as says "there is no one here now, they have all gone home, you will have to unload it yourself." I thought to myself "I am not unloading this lot and stacking it after the hassle I have had today, so I chucked it all off the trailer in their yard and tidied the rope up and put it back in the cab, then pulled out of their yard and snap!

I had caught their telephone line across their yard with the ladder of the trailer. Flat out all the way home, parked up and went home.

What a bloody nightmare day and I remember saying to Malcolm "You didn't tell me about the low bridge that was slightly too low for seven raring's." "Oh he said, I forgot about that, did you get under it OK?" I said "just a couple of bales fell off, nothing major". Lucky cows must have been stuffed that night.

Our farm rented a field along Bouldnor Road which was used as an airfield by a chap who lived near one of our hay fields, adjacent to Hill Place Lane.

There was a very narrow entrance into the field and it had no visibility when exiting the field at all. I hated leaving that field because there was a slight bend just before the gateway and the speed limit was 60 mph on that particular stretch. Very often, a car or bike would jump on the brakes when they saw the front of my Ford 6600 merging into their path. Just in the gateway there was a rutted track that went off to the right and lead to a small hanger where the plane was stored.

The landing strip was right in the centre of the grass field and it was quite a steep climb up to the top of the field, this was because the plane landed from the bottom of the field and came over the road as it approached the strip. This obviously helped the aircraft to reduce considerable speed when it hit the grass hill. The whole field was surrounded by Bouldnor Forestry and I suppose made the landing quite hairy at times.

We would cut all the grass around the strip and sometimes the actual strip too, depending on how long the grass was at the time of haymaking. Enduring the dodgy entrance was one thing but raking or turning the grass on the strip was equally scary because I half expected the bloody plane trying to land whilst I was going up and down its landing strip at the same time. Constant watch on the air above the power lines, looking over towards Thorley just in case I could see a light or some wheels coming my way. Luckily, I never experienced it but did see the plane take off when I was raking the headland one day.

1985   2017

Neptune Icecap in 1985 and 2017.

Chapter 19

Medina Theatre and Carisbrooke High

April the thirteenth, nineteen eighty seven and this was to be the pinnacle of our series of gigs for the band, *Neptune Icecap*. We decided to hire Medina Theatre and try and get another act to play with us so we had at least two attractions to sell tickets for.

The easy bit was booking the place and arranging what we needed for the gig but the most difficult part was finding another act to put on for the show. It took us ages to find someone who already had some sort of reputation or following. Finally, we managed to hire a chap from Southampton called Mike Osman, a comedian and impersonator who had recently been on a TV talent show. He was not cheap but not beyond our means so we hired him for the night. Setting up the gear was not too bad in the morning but trying to persuade the lighting technicians to do what we wanted was far more challenging.

We were very inexperienced with this size of venue; we were not used to the terminology and systems used in a big theatre and therefore, the lighting was not as we originally wanted.

After all the problems of the lighting were sorted out to a reasonably satisfactory outcome, but far from what was originally planned. We had our sound check and we were reasonably satisfied with the audio after a few tweaks here and there. So we all went home to change into our new hand made short sleeved, black and very shiny tops and white jeans. Not the kind of clothing I really wanted to wear but we had to look reasonably smart to sell it to the customers. That's what we were told anyway. Total load of old rowlocks!

Neptune Icecap playing Medina Thratre on the 13th of Aptil 1985. Simon Pond, Tim Haddock and me.

We arrived at the theatre quite early and had to wait for my Dad to arrive as he went to the ferry to collect our comedian chap. Once he arrived, we felt less on edge and more confident that the gig would be ok after all. We met Mike Osman and he was a really lovely bloke and had our photos taken with him before the gig began. Our make up ladies were friends of ours and they chucked it on like there was no tomorrow. Finally we were all sorted and we sneaked a look at the people in the crowd, just to see how full the seats were. I was shocked at how many people had arrived and it was really quite early in the evening. That got the butterflies bouncing around in my stomach and I was very nervous about the whole thing now. Luckily for me, someone had sneaked a bottle of Captain Morgan's into the dressing rooms. A few swigs of that made me feel less nervous.

Mike Osman went on and he had the crowd almost wetting their selves with laughter and he really was very good at what he did. He had some of the audience chasing him down the steps at the front, in one of his jokes. I can't remember exactly who he impersonated but it went down very well with the crowd. As soon as his act finished there was a short interval and he came in to see us and wish us good luck, which was nice of him I thought. Then Dad had to whisk him away and back to the ferry terminal in Cowes. He then had to rush back to the theatre before we went on.

I should add that my father had started to visit us more frequently in the late eighties. Also he seemed more interested in looking after Neptune Icecap's interests too. Obviously, when he left in eighty two, my mind set was naturally resistant to his character and I wasn't interested in seeing him back then. Time heals the wounds slowly and that's exactly what happened here. It was nice that he took an interest in what I was doing with the band for sure, as previously, he had shown little interest.

We needed guidance without a doubt and it seemed at last we were getting it in one form or another. Izzy's dad was another person who supported our cause and I had total respect for him for that. Similarly, Pondy's mum and dad helped out when they could and gave us that boost that you sometimes needed.

It was fantastic being on that big stage and having professional lighting and sound for a change. We played very well that night and had some people dancing in the aisles too. It was a success and we didn't lose money, but didn't make a huge amount either. The gig was great and a shame we did not do more of them in that calibre. Oh and the gig was on my birthday too, so I had a very happy birthday indeed.

Medina Theatre again.

Medina yet again. L/R Makeup girls, me, Simon, Tim, Mike Osman and Illya.

Another gig was planned after Medina and it was arranged through the music department of Carisbrooke High School and it was in conjunction with two school bands too. We sold lots of tickets for this gig and more than we sold for Medina too. The planning was more difficult for this gig because it was in a School and it was not in a holiday period either. We went back and forwards to the music teacher so many times to finalise all the arrangements and the gig was set at last.

We hired a PA and lights from *Happy Daze* in Newport and had to borrow a van for the gig too. It was the afternoon of the gig when we arrived at the school and set up all the gear on the stage and had just done the final sound check. When the music teacher came up to one of us and said the gig was cancelled. "What" was the reaction from all of us and we could not believe they would do that just five hours before the gig. Unreal and the explanations were total bollocks too. They said they could not get any teachers to supervise the concert for that evening, even though there were two school bands playing with us.

We had enough of all the rubbish they fed us so we went straight to the small claims courts and paid the court fees and issued a summons against the Education Authority.

Of course they settled out of court and we got our money back but that was not the point was it. We lost out and the school bands lost out on a valuable gig and a chance to be heard. We vowed never to deal with any schools in the future after that fiasco.

DECISION TO CANCEL BAND CONCERT: HEAD IS CRITICISED

THE DECISION of a high school headmaster to cancel a young Island band's first big concert hours before it was due to take place has been criticised by the father of one of the group's four members.

Recently-formed Neptune Ice-cap were to have played at Carisbrooke High School on Wednesday evening but Mr. Michael Outlaw, headmaster, decided to cancel the concert because of "inadequate preparation" and the lack of available staffing.

Mr. Robert Green, father of keyboards player Gary, said the concert had been arranged through the proper channels weeks in advance and he personally had returned from the mainland to hire a van to transport the equipment to the school.

He also said the band had been left with the "impossible task" of tracing all the youngsters who had bought tickets to tell them the concert was off.

"It is a real kick in the teeth for the lads, they have been looking forward to the concert for ages," said Mr. Green.

"It has also cost a lot of money in publicity, hiring the van out and loss of earnings for those who had to take time off work to prepare for the concert. I personally am about £150 out of pocket.

The school knew about the concert about a month ago and if the headmaster was unhappy with the arrangements he should not have left the decision to the last minute.

"The lads had even agreed to donate one third of the takings to the school's Parent-Teacher Association.

"I am absolutely disgusted with the way it has been dealt with." he added.

'INADEQUATE'

Mr. Outlaw said, "I was not prepared to let the concert go ahead as I was unhappy with the inadequate supervision which would have been available."

He said sufficient care had not been taken to make sure the concert was properly supervised.

"It is a case of six of one and half a dozen of the other. It was with regret that I had to take the decision but I felt I was left with no other option." he said.

Mr. Outlaw said he was prepared to let the concert go ahead at a later date provided suitable

uffering

Three-year ban

County Press cutting regarding the cancelled gig at Carisbrooke High School in 1985.

In the early nineties, the farm had moved on a bit with technology and with the upgraded tractors from Ford 6600's to TW15's and one of the 5000's was replaced with a Deutz Fahr. We also got a Ford 6610 column shift which was a horrible thing to drive, slow on the road and not easy to get into gear either. The small Deutz was probably the most cumbersome and slowest tractor ever built. It was completely alien to what we had been used to, weird controls and even weirder symbols and not a favourite amongst us workers at all.

The only person who really liked the thing was young Taylor and he seemed to have the tractor for most jobs around the farm. Then there was the Matbro Bray Telestar, telehandler, which arrived on the scene in 1989-90 and was such an improvement on the front end loader attached to an old pre Q cab Ford 6600. The Matbro came with all the attachments that you would ever need, which included a large front bucket that could be used for both grain and other materials. A large forked grab for dung and straw/silage use and a set of pallet forks which were so handy for fertiliser and the milling pallets.

The best piece of equipment was the flat ten bale grab. The old flat eight grab was getting tired and the extra two bales made a big difference when loading the trailers.

I spent a lot of time on this loader and really enjoyed learning to use it too. I was sent out to the Bouldnor block one day with the Matbro and I had not even had a drive in it. Taking her up the road for the first time was quite unnerving, because of the rear wheel steering and the hydrostatic power train.

It was fairly easy to use but not something you could just take for granted and especially the forward and reverse controls. I had a nasty experience a few months into harvest when I was going down a hill collecting bales and stacking them up in thirties or forty's so it was quicker to just grab them off the little stacks and drop them on the trailers. The hill was quite steep and the machine was in high gear and as I went down the gradient I accidentally hit the controls from forward into reverse and not neutral as I intended to do. I nearly shot through the windscreen because of the speed the machine going forward and the momentum was suddenly reversed. I banged my head on the window and that hurt.

I was so careful after that and always took my time when changing direction in the field. The machine made such easy work of things that used to take us hours to achieve and it was so useful for so many tasks around the farm.

Cleaning out the cow yards with the old McConnell digger took days to do and when the new loader took on the task, we could almost clear all the yards in two days and it left a much neater job too.

A stock photo of a very similar Matbro Bray Telestar.

Having a large amount of cattle meant we needed a large amount of feed for them and I guess the most logical thing if your land was mostly arable, was to mill your own produce instead of wasting money on bought in foodstuffs. Mineral supplements were bought in as were liquid supplements but the staple feed was milled by the farm for the cattle.

The mill in the late seventies only had a small roller mill and one hopper on a precarious looking stand. There were a couple of old scales and a heap of old fert bags for filling with barley or oats. The barley was taken from a small silo which was between the mill house and the large hay barn in the main yard. The hopper was old as the hills and had a nasty habit of caking up when you wanted to bag off some barley. Hitting it with a grain shovel usually fixed the problem but left huge dents in the old hopper sides, then your bag would fall off the pins on the back of the slide and a ton of barley would come out all over the place.

After a time, nothing that was stored in the mill house was ever seen again, because the dust just hid everything inside it. However, it was the perfect place to hide your tractor if you wanted to fit a new stereo in, which we did on several occasions as I may have mentioned earlier.

Taylor was the bloke who was designated the miller and adopted the mill house as his own domain and was always to be found in there milling away all day long. He was given a new air mask that blew air across your face to prevent dust reaching your nose or mouth. He appeared to love it in there and had the place running just fine. I particularly like this, as it meant I wasn't put in there because it wasn't my favourite job. We sold a lot of milled produce and had customers coming in all the time for a bag of barley or some tail wheat, a by product of dressing wheat. Most of the customers were either horse owners or gamekeepers of some description. We eventually gained a large contract to supply Leigh Thomas with milled feed and a very large pig farm in Ryde that had a mixed milled grain. So the mill house became a centre of activity when a large order came in. We had new paper bags and a bag stitcher to seal up the bags. I think it was good for the farm and added another string to its bow, and made our jobs more secure because little did we know it, but big changes were coming in latter years of both farming in general and at Thorley Manor Farm.

The new flat ten bale sledge in 1987.

Thorley had acquired a small Dumper for some project or other and it sat in the hay barn for a long time collecting dust and hay. Then Mark and Malcolm got hold of it and converted it into a perfect little vehicle for carrying straw and bags of barley. They removed the front hopper/barrow thing and replaced it with a flat bed framework with a nice wooden planked floor and a low metal frame at the back of it to stop things falling off. We could easily get ten bales on the front and/or bags of barley to take out into the fields for feeding the cattle. This was when the cattle had been moved closer to the farm during the early winter months, before they were eventually brought inside.

A tractor would make such a mess, churning up the grass and gateways during winter and this little machine did none of that, even when it was very wet. The large wooden troughs were set out on *Goldings* Marsh, just down the back of the manor, past the office and over the little bridge. It got pretty muddy out in that field in winter and the cows did their best to churn up the soil near the troughs. So something small and light to carry the feed was essential.

Many an afternoon, we could be seen chugging across the front fields on the dumper with a load of feed and usually one of us holding on for dear life as we blasted around the fields. When there was no one around that was. One afternoon, Taylor was sitting on the front and not holding on so I decided to do a sharp turn in the mud and laughed as he shot off one side and landed in a nice squashy load of mud. He got me back though and instead of going forward as I was expecting him to, he shoved it in reverse and almost left me sitting in mid air as I hit the mud on my bum.

That little dumper was used for loads of jobs and it was very good at towing the old Lister Bale Elevator around the yard and also the Lister Fan for drying the seed hay at haymaking time. Great days we had and not just the job but the people I shared those days with and although it was very hard work, I miss it all terribly.

We were combining and carting all the straw for a small farm at the top of Broad Lane and most of the fields were close to Chessell Quarry. There were a fair few bales to cart and most of them went to the tiny stone barn that belonged to the small farm. I was using the Matbro to load up the trailers and move some of the bales closer together, while trailers were taken to be unloaded. There were two fields that lay behind a very tall and very long hedge and the gateway was at one end of the field and not in the middle as most gateways seem to be. We had loaded up this artic trailer and Taylor wanted a lift up to the top of the field to get his Deutz tractor and trailer to bring it down to the stack of bales.

Now we often just stood or sat on the bars for the flat ten grab and held on as the Matbro slowly bounced across the old tramlines. Admittedly, not the safest way to travel but it was a damn sight easier than walking miles up the fields. So I told Taylor to get on the grab and started off down the field, towards the stack of bales and this large hedge.

Instead of going up to his tractor, where he thought I was heading. I got to the hedge and lifted him right over the top and then lowered him down to about a foot off the ground. He was laughing and putting two fingers up at me at the same time, so I shook the grab and he jumped off the other side and had to walk about half a mile to reach the gateway to get back in the field again. Just one of those crazy moments and funny things we got up to when the boss was not there.

On the same subject, there was the time when Malcolm was on the Matbro and loading a trailer of straw up on one of the Hayles fields, which were originally separate from the *Wilmingham* group of fields and previously owned by the small farm directly opposite *Wilmingham* barn.

He had loaded about four raring's on to the trailer and was just about to dump another ten bales on the stack when the main ram failed and the whole arm and grab slammed into the stack, just missing whoever was on the trailer. The actual ram seals had blown out and the sudden loss of pressure resulted in all the oil being leaked onto the field and an even bigger problem of getting the arm back off the trailer.

I was not in the field when it all happened as I was in my drier barn that day but I remember we had to disconnect the telescopic arm from its ram and manually pull and lift it out in front of the workshop. That was a feat of engineering to man handle that thing off the machine and repair the machine without the use of any crane or hoist. Thanks to that wizard of a mechanic Mark, we had that telehandler back in action in a few days.

I was not very keen on heights at all and avoided anything that required me to be above ten feet off the ground, such as ladders and front buckets. Sometimes I had to climb the silo ladders to shut the top or adjust a pipe and I really wasn't happy going up those bloody things at all. "Great view of Yarmouth from the top" I remember one of my workmates telling me as I climbed up slowly, leaning against the metal frame surrounding the ladder. I didn't care if you could see Lymington from the top of it I thought; I just wanted to get down as soon as I could and go and do something less scary instead.

There was a time when a pipe that filled the main silo had come apart at the joint and it had to be repaired as soon as possible. I was about to start blowing wheat through this pipe from the new drier. It was a Sunday morning and everyone was at *Wilmingham* unloading the previous day's straw and Malcolm decided I had to go up and repair this pipe. Looking up at it was making me feel dizzy and it was at least 25 feet up and attached to an old telegraph pole.

The joints we used between the galvanised pipes were just sections of inner tubes which fitted very tightly to the pipe and gave it flexibility cheaper and very effective. It was far better than the original self-tapping screw affair. I thought

Malcolm was going to put the front bucket on the Matbro for the job but, no. He put the pallet tines on the front with a standard wooden pallet. Well I was pretty scared of going up that high in the bucket let alone a damn wobbly pallet. I went up there and changed the inner tube section and came back down safely, shaking a bit, but fine. I still don't know how I did that job, but I did and that was good for my fear of heights - I think.

We had a new member of staff at Thorley when I returned there after my winter break and he was very young in his ways and hadn't grown up, even if he was built like a giant. Staff seemed to come and go quite often back in the eighties but not compared with some of the other businesses that my friends had experience of. You either loved Thorley Manor or hated it.

A lot of the younger people, including myself, hated it with a passion. They could not handle the long hours in the summer, the hard physical work and detested the manager's working practices so much that they often just packed up and just left. I think you have to be of a certain character to be able to fit in to the way a farm like Thorley worked. You had to be prepared to give up all social activities and put up with being totally whacked and the end of each day. There were no holidays from May until September and hardly any room for a day off during the harvest or cultivation periods as I have already mentioned.

A young lad started work and was just totally out of place on the farm. He burnt the candle at both ends by going out every night after work and god knows what else, always late and the first one out of the gate at half four too. He was given the job of cleaning out one of the one hundred ton grain bins with a broom and shovel.

It was a Friday and Malcolm was on the wages delivery round and he climbed up the ladder to the catwalk and peered down into the grain bin where this lad was supposed to be working. The lad was in the very corner and leaning against the wall sound asleep. He woke up with a start as Malcolm threw his wage packet at him, which was half full of coins and it sailed through the air beautifully and hit this sleeping worker nicely. He very soon left the farm.

Another new chap called Dave was sent to the back of the farm near to the old chapel to clear up and burn the felled trees and bushes. We had some sheep that had this small paddock adjoining the chapel and graveyard and their paddock had become overgrown and needed to be cleared out as it had not been done for many years.

So this guy had built a large bonfire and was dragging all the foliage and burning it, but the fire was too damp to start with just a wedge of straw. So he had used some waste oil to give it some combustion. I guess the fire must have died down too much during his lunch break and he had the brilliant idea of climbing onto the front loader and pouring waste oil onto the fire. The sight of him coming round to the workshop with this blackened face and no eyebrows were a picture to be seen. He was lucky not to have suffered serious injury from that stunt.

Another thing that sticks in my mind was the time we were stacking straw in *Wilmingham* barn. We had started to fill a bay of the barn and had reached about eight layers up from the floor and I was in second place in the chain, passing back the bales to the stacker. This bloke was at the front of the stack and taking the bales from the guy on the trailer, but instead of throwing them to me, he thought it was funny to keep hitting my side with a bale as I was facing the other way.

After about the third time these bales had hit me, I had reached the end of my tether and picked up the next bale and returned the gesture but with so much force that I knocked the bloke clean off the stack and he landed flat on his back on the trailer boards. Luckily the trailer was covered in loose straw so his landing wasn't completely solid. Slowly he picked himself up and recovered from his fall. I said that I didn't mean to make him fall off the stack, but if he threw bales at me like that, he had to take the consequences. He agreed and apologised later and we became good mates after that.

This chap Dave smoked, as I did and one of the manager's pet hates was of course smoking. He was sent out to do some power harrowing up at *Wilmingham* and was just stopping for his lunch break when into the field, came the dreaded Honda pickup. Dave calmly sat in the cab and lit up the fattest cigar as Malcolm walked over to him. He remarked on the complete lack of words that were exchanged on that occasion.

We had a young student chap start on the bale cart job during harvest, he lived close to the farm, in Wellow. Taylor and I were just finishing off loading one of the four wheeler trailers up on the left hand side of *Wilmingham* track, Taylor and this lad were stacking and I was loading with the Matbro. Taylor had come down from the stack on the bale grab and threw the rope up to this chap so he could start uncoiling the rope and lowering one end down to Taylor. Expecting to see the end of the rope coming down the stack, the chap threw the whole coil over. Taylor stood there stunned with disbelief.

Those moments when you are lifting something heavy and someone cracks a joke and all your strength fades away. There were four of us trying to lift the bale sledge up at *Wilmingham* one afternoon, one of the wheels had broken away from the frame and we had to get the frame off the ground. So we all braced ourselves and lifted this very heavy piece of framework. As we got it about six inches off the stubble, Mark says "If you had a length of steel up ya ass, you would be making penny washers with this weight." That was enough for everyone to burst out laughing and put the sledge down rapidly. Even Malcolm was grinning after hearing Mark's words of wisdom.

Mark always came out with some classic sayings and it was always when we were doing something critical and with Malcolm there too. You couldn't help yourself; you would just be in fits of laughter whatever the situation.

We were all in the workshop one morning, waiting for our usual meeting with the manager. Malcolm walks in and is just about to start his plan for the day, when a car drives in the yard and parks outside the workshop doors.

Malcolm turned to see who had driven in and said "I wonder who that is?" Mark pipes up and says oh it's "Ticker Morris." and someone replied "Who?" Mark replies with a grin on his face "Ticker Morris, the man with the clockwork asshole." That was the end of that meeting.

What the hell was a *Wing Wong off a Goose's Bridle,* anyway? That was Mark's reply to any question that we didn't understand!

Chapter 20

End of an era

I don't think anyone knew of the impending changes that were going to take place on the farm and some of them were disastrous in the eyes of those who worked there and knew the lay of the land. The new owners were from Southampton and we were all even more surprised when they also purchased Dunsbury Farm over at Brook, not long after they bought Thorley Manor Farm.

We had even more land to look after and some of it was very hilly indeed and was in dire need of new fences and generally a damn good tidy up. There were ancient machines and tools in the old sheds and these old cattle sheds that was very impractical for what we needed and had to be refurbished completely. We inherited a few tractors a Manitou forklift and various machines such as power harrows and other cultivators. Most of these were poorly maintained and required many new parts or repairing before they could be used in the field. Two John Deere's came from there and ended up at Thorley most of the time and that is when I appeared to have been assigned the 3130 model. After driving Ford's all my farming life, this change of machine took some getting used to.

The hills were very steep in places and the soil was very sandy and almost red in some places, easy to work on but contained some massive rocks and stones as we all found out. Working on the fields there was interesting to say the least and the views were in places, spectacular. I enjoyed working over at Dunsbury when it was fine and dry. When it was wet, it was wet, as the weather came straight in from the sea and it seemed much worse than it was on the other farm.

A bonus was we were left alone to get on with jobs and didn't have to keep a look out for Malcolm so often. He wasn't that bad really it was just he had this amazing skill of appearing out of thin air and it was always when something broke or would not do as it was supposed to.

Another big job was to refurbish the farmhouse and gardens so it could be rented out. A new lawn was sown and various other jobs were done to improve the house. A similar task we had at Thorley was to take out the old AGA from the manor house and put a new one in. Heavy as hell and so awkward to manoeuvre into place too.

We also inherited a shepherd complete with flocks of sheep. He kept them mostly over at Dunsbury but on some occasions, he grazed them on some of the fields at Thorley. We did not have much to do with the sheep thank God, but occasionally helped to move them from field to field. One of the new chaps that worked with me was very into sheep in a big way as his parents were sheep farmers over Calbourne way. He used to help out with lambing and other such jobs and was a nice bloke all round. I think he moved off the island some years ago to manage a farm somewhere.

One special occasion that I have fond memories of, was my workmate Taylor had a birthday party at his house in Freshwater but we went out to some pubs around Ningwood and Calbourne and most of my workmates were there. We got very drunk indeed and had a damn good time. I can't remember exactly what happened, but I fell in love with Taylor's next door neighbour and got I got a very passionate kiss that night. OK, I was absolutely legless and to me, she was very good looking, although a lot older than me and very pretty. I got more than my fair share of stick from that night. When I went round to see Taylor a few days after that night, his sexy neighbour was in the kitchen, talking to his mum. Red, huh, I was absolutely crimson as she said "hello again". She smiled at me as she went out of the kitchen and Taylor's mum was giggling too. A treasured moment, although embarrassing!

It was in the April of 1989 when we started to put up fences right across the hillside at Dunsbury and it was dry and warm when we started to job. We had put a complete new fence that ran from the military Road and across the lower part of the hill and were nearly at the end of the line of stakes in the middle of the afternoon. Our workmate Taylor was driving around the field with all the equipment for the fence line in the new John Deere tractor. He was pulling one of our small wooden sided trailers, full of stakes, wire and various tools. He had dropped off a selection of stakes and was about to come down the hillside with the rolls of barbed wire, ready for us to start going up the hill. We had made our way towards the brow of the hill, but could not see the fence line from where we stood.

Suddenly there was the sound of thunder coming from the end of the field and we knew it was something serious, we ran over the brow and just got there as the John Deere had come to rest back on its wheels after a complete summersault. Taylor was badly shaken and was so lucky not to have fallen out of the open roof.

He had locked his hands onto the steering wheel and it prevented him from being thrown around the cab as the tractor went over. We all helped to get him out of the cab and the only injury he suffered was a large gash on his side and a few scratches to his arms. The tractor was less fortunate and was probably a write off as the front wheels were bent out of line and the cab was a wreck too. The trailer was repairable and survived the roll pretty well. One of the other lads rushed off to find Malcolm to tell him of the accident.

It was not long after that incident that I was given the task of topping the hillside in a TW15. That was a scary job because of the steep hill and the fact that there was a fence half way down the hill, which meant I had to disengage the four wheel drive every time I had to make a turn or the damn thing would refuse to turn properly. I had a few moments when the wheels began to slip as I descended the slopes but most of the time it was fine.

A lot of hills and a lot of sheep was Dunsbury Farm and all it ever reminds me of is fencing and dangerous conditions on a tractor.
As I mentioned before, there was the power harrow that we inherited from the purchase of Dunsbury and it also came with its own transporting trailer, which was very handy as

the two farms were over seven miles apart.
Another thing that the trailer was good for was
to transport my Yamaha XJ550 to and fro from
Thorley to Dunsbury. This saved a lot of hassle
and meant I could leave the tractor and harrow
in the field and leave when I wanted to, instead
of waiting for someone to come and pick me up.
I remember going up the road past Tapnell farm
and all the tractor drivers staring in disbelief as I
past them on my John Deere with harrow and
motorbike in tow, it was a funny moment.

We had some very wide verges on the roads
around the farm and although they were not the
farm's responsibility, we occasionally mowed or
trimmed them with the hedge cutter. It was late
April and we were cutting and turning the hay
up on Bouldnor Road and at the same time, the
council had decided to cut all the verges from
Yarmouth and all the way through to
Wilmingham Lane.

There was a lot of grass on some of the verges
and by the time we had baled and carted all our
fields, the verges had dried out nicely. I could
not believe the sheer cheek of our manager
Malcolm, as he instructed the head tractor driver
to bale all the large verges. I have no idea how
many bales he got from the verges but it was
quite a few and all added to his profit margins I

guess. No one ever believed me when I told them that we baled the grass verges until I had a second witness to it all in my old pal Len.

I had no pigging idea where Malcolm wanted me to go with the rotavator and tilth up the ground, as he explained it so quickly and in his Derbyshire accent. It was not always easy to understand what he meant exactly. So I thought he said the small strip of land between the ditch and the road which was opposite the rear gates to the farm. I was bloody miles off and rotavated the council verge anyway and made a lovely job of it too.

Malcolm came along and stopped me, laughing as he explained it was the strip of land inside the gateway to the marshes and not the verge. I felt a right spanner that day I can tell you. Damn funny though and everyone took great pleasure in asking me "what verges I was cultivating today?"

The original LOGO from a ticket for the Medina Theatre gig.

The farm owned two bungalows at the very end of Tattles Lane in Thorley and one was occupied by the head tractor driver for a short time and the other was let out privately. In the field directly behind these houses was an old sewage bed which still had the old rotary spreader system attached to it. The time had come to remove this old system and put in new sewage tanks.

Working at Thorley was never just a straightforward farming job and many times we had to be builders, plumbers or whatever tradesmen were required at the time. Such as when we had to put brand new drains in for the two bungalows and lay them ready for the new tanks to be installed. Mark and I always seemed to get the job of digging the trenches with our ever-faithful McConnell digger.

So off we went to dig out the trenches and use a theodolite for levels and eventually start to lay all the pipes. It was while we were doing this job that I had to borrow Mark's bicycle and sneak up to the little post office in Wellow. I had ran out of smokes and was so desperate for a puff that I had to try and find a way to get some fags before I went completely mad. It was a Friday morning and Malcolm had just been round with our wages so I knew he would not be visiting us again until at least after lunchtime. Luckily Mark had his bicycle with him to travel back home for lunch. So I asked Mark if I could borrow his bike and ride up to Wellow, although we didn't know if the little shop actually sold fags, I decided to take the risk anyway.

I pedalled off like a bat out of hell and reached the post office in record time, especially as Mark's bike was this ancient three geared thing. Luckily the shop had some Red Band fags so I was saved and went like hell to get back to the bottom of the lane without Malcolm seeing me because who knows what he would have said if he had seen me sneaking off to the shop during work time. Anyway I got away with it, really was satisfied with a smoke at long last and Mark was laughing at my relief at the desperate and considerably sad situation I was in. He went off for his lunch on the bike and I walked back across *Goldings marsh* to the farm for my lunch. We finished the drains a few days later and did an excellent job.

Sunday afternoon, I was on my way to feed the cattle on my bike after spending a lazy afternoon doing very little. As I approached the barn at *Wilmingham* I was shocked to see a fire engine parked on the chalk in front of the building, lights flashing and firemen all over the place. I was going quite fast on my bike as I usually did on that road. It was a good job I slowed down as another fire engine was coming up to the narrow part of the road, just past the barn towards *Barnsfield*. As I went past that engine and then I saw another coming up the road, smoke coming from the side of the barn that backed onto the Hayles field.

I carried on to the farm and fed the cattle as normal and then the manager appeared with Hayward the head tractor driver and we went off to move the cattle that were kept at the rear of the barn to the marshes to safety. None of the cows seemed affected by the fire, which was bloody lucky really as asbestos was exploding all over the yard and adjacent field. The head tractor driver later took our Matbro handler to pull out the burning bales so it was easier to dampen them down, which he later explained to us.

I stopped at the barn on the way home from feeding and saw the extent and felt the heat of the fire from the roadside. The steel RSJ's of the barn were bending like they were made of rubber, incredible to see but on the other hand very sad to see our whole summer's work of carting and stacking gone up in flames. We lost almost every thing in that fire and it was our main supply of wheat and barley straw for the winter ahead. We were now in a bad situation as having over three hundred head of cattle and nothing to feed them or bed them with. Donations were given of straw and silage from farms all over the island and I remember carting silage bales from the Blackgang side of Chale to Dunsbury farm and collecting some old straw bales from the old brickworks on long lane in Newport. It did not matter how old the straw or silage was, we needed it badly. I am not sure on the exact figure of bales we lost but it was close to twelve thousand.

Mr Buddling's Farm was located at the Chessell end of Broad Lane and opposite the entrance to the disused quarry. We cut and baled his crops every year and this particular occasion, I was carting the grain to his old silage pits and auguring it to the back of the buildings.

He had put black plastic up on the walls all around the pits as a temporary silo. It worked to a point but some of the plastic sheeting moved under the weight and gave him a lot less area for which to store the grain and to stop the weather getting at it. It was late afternoon and I was unloading my fifth load. The auger was working well and all I had to do was stand there and occasionally check it. I wandered around the yard just looking about the place and then I noticed Mr Buddling coming across the lane with some orange squash and followed closely by this giant Great Dane. He came over and asked how it was all going and gave me a glass of squash and put the jug of iced drink down on the ground. I thanked him and informed him that we would have to move the auger over a bit soon as the grain was reaching the top of the sheet on one side. He said that he would move it while I was collecting another load from the combine.

So I drank my squash, which was very welcome as the day was a very warm one and dusty too. I filled my glass again and drank another glass of the squash, then I put my glass down on the ground and watched Mr Buddling walk back to the farmhouse but the dog was not following him. The bloody thing came straight over to me and sniffed around the glass and jug on the floor then decided I was tastier and bit me on the bum. It was only a nip but made me jump and I grabbed a stone off the floor and hit the damn thing on the butt as it ran off towards the house.

Our farm had the task of combining and carting the grain to Newclose Farm and auguring it into their grain store for their mill. I was put on this job near the end of the barley and wheat cutting of our own crops. I had to collect it from the combine, which was cutting their crops up the top of Broad Lane on the right side, adjacent to our ninety five acre field.

 It was quite a job to reverse the grain trailer around the yard at the back of the farm to the sheds near the milking parlour. The chap that looked after to farm was a really happy chap and always had time for a chat and a laugh. I don't think I ever saw him without a smile on his face in all the time I worked at Thorley Manor Farm. The original stockman there was the father of our head tractor driver and he had retired from the farm not long after I had started on the farm.

I always liked that particular job because we knew what had to be done and left alone to do it. Plus it was a change to see different views from fields that otherwise you would not go in. In particularly the fields that backed onto our *Barnsfield* land, because it was strange to see the fields from a completely different angle if you know what I mean. There was a really long grassy lane that went down the side of a solitary cottage up at Broad Lane and it was quite an incline too.

Some thirty years after I worked at that job I was given one of the original Pyrex holding containers from the milking parlour, which I still have as a personal memorial to that farm. In the mid nineties, the farm was sold off and basically demolished and the parlour was eventually converted into a cottage and the builder who was none other than my Dad's DJ mate, Roy.

He gave the jar to the step father of my long time girlfriend whom I met in France. Now there are coincidences and there are coincidences and this was so damn coincidental that you may call it almost weird. I could not believe it when my girlfriend's step Father was clearing out his shed In Okehampton, Devon and asked me if I wanted this huge glass jar thing? I recognised what it was, but had no idea it even came from the Island, let alone Newclose Farm.
Amazing....

I remember there was a very strange character that frequented the footpath from the manor garden to the manager's cottage and he was always on his bicycle and usually carried a metal detector or it was strapped to the frame of the bike. Very often he would be chased out of the manor gardens by the gardener because he would wander from the path to collect apples and other fruits from the trees.

Chapter 21

Change

Visiting the places that played the biggest part of my childhood and teenage years is something that brings all those memories flooding back and in recent years I have gone back to quite a few of them. My last visit to Totland Bay in two thousand and seventeen was an eye opener to say the least and a complete shock to see how desolate the village is now.

All those thriving little shops and businesses that were part of my upbringing and that made the village such a busy place to visit are no more. Especially during those long hot summer months that we enjoyed back then in the late seventies and eighties. The little petrol station with old Frank on the pumps and fixing punctured tyres and Digger the mechanic with his colourful language, but always had a smile for everyone. My favourite sweet shop which had everything you ever needed to fulfil a sweet toothed teenager and the supplier of all those packs of No 6 for the lodger and Dad.

The lovely Mary, who was always there for a chat, Kev and Andy who were mad heavy metal sons but who were very good friends of mine and the first people I ever met when I moved there.

Gone is the VG shop with all its vegetables on crates outside. The impeccable Stationers shop with its immaculately polished floors and beautiful displays of pens and pencils and other writing implements. I loved that shop because it was classy and sold lots of interesting things that other shops did not have. There was the Alum Bay Glass Shop which was next to the Broadway Inn and even the pub itself is now boarded up and long gone. *Since you been gone* or *747 Strangers in the night* emanated from the juke box or the fire that always burned in the bar has been silenced and extinguished forever.

The tiny bank across the road from our house disappeared and it transformed into a bookshop for a while if I remember correctly; now it's a flat. Charlie Browns the first takeaway shop we ever had in the village which replaced the famous Braemar café where a vast amount of my personal history was made. The police house, is now just a normal everyday house and no police bike parks in the drive, ready to chase us lads around the villages on our bikes.

The doctor's surgery at the Freshwater end of the village has gone and due to centralisation, all the doctors have moved to Freshwater which gives people further to travel to fix their ailments. The Tulipaan café has transformed into flats or a house and so have many other shops both in Totland and other surrounding villages.

How or why do builders keep building houses in a place where there is a complete lack of employment I will never know? Surely industrial units should have been built to attract business back into the area so all the people in the new houses would have something to do. In my view, the whole area has been over developed with housing and no thought of the future impacts have been given to any of the construction or conversions.

The first time I heard *Ghost Town* by *The Specials* was the Tulipan cafe on their juke box. Now it should to be blasted out around the village to remind the last remaining residents that they live in a ghost town now. Although I suspect they already realise it. It is with sadness that I look back to what my life consisted of and how all these elements model you, as you grow up. It has all been changed or destroyed to make way for a who knows what,. The short sighted developers have taken the spark from the village and surrounding areas and killed the true meaning of business with bricks and mortar for their short lived profits and greed.

Visiting my Brother Tony's gravestone at the Christchurch up at Church Hill is probably one of the experiences that gives me little or no confidence in any kind of religion. Looking around the state of the graveyard, seeing how disgusting the so called church, that owns more property than the royal family, looks after the graveyard. They cannot even bother to cut the grass or tidy up the place for the relatives to visit their loved ones. People have paid vast amounts of money for these plots for their relatives, so why can they not look after these sacred places and keep them tidy anymore? In other countries such as France or even Australia, they maintain their graveyards immaculately and it is their pride in respecting the people who have passed away.

Go and see the graveyard in France for all those that perished on Omaha Beach, Normandy during the Second World War. You won't see one tree out of place or one stone that is not clean. It is basic respect for those people who fought and died for our freedom and it is exactly the same for the people in our graveyards. Yes, they are war graves and do attract a lot of money to maintain but these are the people who saved us. They deserve the best.

Seeing the old pier in such a state of decay, the building on the end of the pier, now gone completely and all the planking has become dangerous. It was a fantastic place to go with a pocketful of pennies when we were kids, the Crompton Cakewalk machine, pushing those coppers all day long and the pinball machines with their flippers and loud sounds. Fishing off that pier was incredible, the crabs were massive and we sold so many to the local people. Now you cannot even get on the damned pier, let alone fish off it.

I remember the Totland Bay Chalet Hotel, towering over the bay, with its tended lawns and bridge across the road to the turf walk. It must have been a lovely place to go and stay because its views had to have been spectacular to say the least. Flattened and replaced with the ugliest block of so called luxury flats for the wealthy retired to enjoy and nothing for the people that made the village what it was.

I have to pay tribute to my fellow workers and friends at Thorley Manor Farm; Hayward, Mark, Taylor, Dave, Kev and Len.

To Malcolm, the best boss I have ever worked for and who instilled in me so much knowledge and know how. For the fantastic experiences and most comical times that anyone could wish to have.

To the friends that have come and gone through the years and to my family who were always there for support and love.
Long live you all.

Dedicated to the memory of my dearest brother
Tony Green
07-08-65 – 19-04-77
Tragically taken from us so suddenly and still
missed to this day.

Printed in Great Britain
by Amazon

21845480R00411